PENGUIN BOOKS

FORCING THE SPRING

Jo Becker is a Pulitzer Prize–winning investigative reporter for *The New York Times*, where she has broken stories on everything from the United States' lethal program to kill suspected terrorists to the British phone-hacking affair and the Penn State child sexual abuse scandal. She has taught investigative journalism as a visiting professor at Princeton University, and her work has earned her numerous awards. A *Washington Post* series she coauthored on Vice President Dick Cheney won the Pulitzer Prize for National Reporting.

Praise for Jo Becker's *Forcing the Spring*

A *New York Times* Notable Book of the Year

A *Washington Post* Best Book of the Year (Nonfiction)

A *Kirkus Reviews* Best Book of the Year

One of The Fix's Best Political Books of the Year

A *Frontiers* Best LGBT Book of the Year

A Bilerico Project Best LGBT Book of the Year

"*Forcing the Spring* is a riveting legal drama, a snapshot in time, when the gay rights movement altered course and public opinion shifted with the speed of a bullet train. . . . Becker's most remarkable accomplishment is to weave a spellbinder of a tale that, despite a finale reported around the world, manages to keep readers gripped until the very end." —*The Washington Post*

"A stunningly intimate story . . . Maybe because she's such a versatile reporter, Becker saw the big picture. The fight for marriage equality did not end in a total victory on the Supreme Court steps but triumphed in a higher court, the court of public opinion. It may not be the story she set out to tell, but it's a great one nonetheless." —*The New York Times Book Review*

"Becker's account of the hearings, and her analysis of the complicated legal theories involved in the long appeals process, are excellent. Her writing about the four plaintiffs in the case—the true emotional heroes of this book—is particularly affecting. . . . If you are interested in the story of how a Hollywood political consultant and a conservative lawyer joined forces in 2009, in the belief that they could really make a difference, and, no doubt, gain some notoriety for themselves and their cause, helping to dramatically change the way Americans thought of gay people and the way gay people thought of themselves—this book is for you. The real story it tells is how seemingly small moments, occurring by happenstance, when combined with boldness and imagination, can help to change the course of history." —Richard Socarides, *The New Yorker*

"A stunning account of the legal battles stemming from Prop 8 . . . Drawing on five years of unlimited access to Olson and Boies's team, [Becker] has crafted an engrossing narrative filled with details gleaned from fraught backroom conversations and private e-mails. Though some critics allege that Becker highlights certain key figures at the expense of others, the history she re-creates using material as dry as court records and judges' written opinions is as taut and suspenseful as a novel. She also zeroes in on human moments. *Forcing the Spring* stands as not just the definitive account of the battle for same-sex marriage rights but a thrilling and compassionate one too. Grade: A" —*Entertainment Weekly*

"A gripping narrative . . . [Becker's] momentum is resolutely forward, her writing so brisk and urgent that even though we know the outcome, the tension in the courtroom scenes and the intervals of waiting for decisions remains taut, even nerve-racking. Becker's access gives us insights into other aspects of the story, as well—the deliberations within the Obama administration, the pro-gay marriage statements of Vice President Biden that seemed to animate the president, and the thinking in the Justice Department. She gives a gripping account of the trial in the U.S. District Court (with some fine analysis of the role of Judge Vaughn Walker, gay himself), some of which she reproduces directly from court records. Becker follows the case from there to the U.S. Court of Appeals and then the Supreme Court, where we listen to the oral arguments and follow the sometimes-twisted thinking of the justices. First-rate reporting informs this thrilling narrative of hope." —*Kirkus Reviews* (starred review)

"Channeling the extended legal battle over California's Proposition 8 ban on same-sex marriage into an engaging narrative, Pulitzer Prize–winning journalist Becker presents a thorough, perceptive read. Beginning with private conversations among friends and moving all the way to the Supreme Court, Becker constructs the legal story with the privilege of generous access to the plaintiffs and legal team that fought for marriage equality. Along the way, everyone from President Obama to director/actor Rob Reiner and current Human Rights Campaign president Chad Griffin find their way into the action. Becker navigates the vast amount of legal history, backroom conversations, media wrangling, and personal stories with an ease that makes what could otherwise be a demanding or partisan story into learned political journalism. . . . Becker's insights into the legal process are evenhanded. In the end, the book stands testament to good political writing and a wealth of information made alive through prose." —*Publishers Weekly* (starred review)

"Becker takes the reader on an extraordinary journey inside a single piece of test case litigation, a riveting tale with a full cast of colorful characters, the very best of which are the four authentic and down-to-earth plaintiffs. . . . Rarely has an episode of one piece of LGBT work been captured in such sharp relief and detail. The story unfolds like a journal, revealing an unlikely cast of characters that literally orchestrate the death of a very painful episode of California's history. . . . No one should miss reading this book!"

—*Elizabeth Birch,* former executive director of the Human Rights Campaign

"A riveting account of how California's Proposition 8, which outlawed same-sex marriage there, went from voter passage in 2008 to Supreme Court invalidation in 2013. The incredible access the *New York Times* investigative reporter had with the principals involved and others will satisfy that political-junky thirst for the backstory swirling around historical events. . . . Becker gives readers an insider's view of what they watched in real time over four and a half years. Her interviews and observations are presented in a riveting fashion that reminded me of Taylor Branch's *Parting the Waters,* the first of three books on Martin Luther King and the civil rights movement."

—Jonathan Capehart, MSNBC contributor and
Washington Post columnist

"Jo Becker's *Forcing the Spring* is a superb behind-the-scenes account of the legal battle to bring marriage equality to the nation. Drawing on extraordinary access to the internal deliberations of the plaintiffs' team, Becker shows how law, politics, and personality combined to create a landmark in the history of the Supreme Court—and of the United States."

—Jeffrey Toobin, author of *The Nine* and *The Oath*

"*Forcing the Spring* is a thrilling book. We know the ending and we still want to read every word . . . . We *feel* what the plaintiffs feel as their lives are splayed open by Supreme Court justices. We see the parade of witnesses (experts in sociology, history, psychology, economics, and more) bearing and baring our collective truth, making the case our humanity from very conceivable point of view. . . . Movements are not made by single historic court cases, even those that generate big historical decisions. But a great writer can portray a brilliant strategist, a few amazing legal minds, some brave plaintiffs and a cast of characters committed to big change at the right time in history, and craft these portraits into a story that is magnificent and unforgettable, and that stands as a permanent tribute to all who have gone before. That's what Jo Becker has done."

—Torie Osborn, former executive director of
the National Gay and Lesbian Task Force

"Jo Becker's *Forcing the Spring* provides the definitive insider account of one of the great civil rights struggles of our times. It is an important and moving historical account that reads like a page-turning legal thriller. This is a must-read for anyone who wants to move our nation forward."
—Benjamin Todd Jealous, former president and CEO of the National Association for the Advancement of Colored People

"The movement for marriage equality has been an extraordinary example of historic change at hyper speed. Jo Becker, a gifted journalist, had unparalleled access to the legal drama as well as the human stories of love and courage, and she weaves her witness into a fast-paced narrative of lasting importance."
—David Von Drehle, author of *Rise to Greatness: Abraham Lincoln and America's Most Perilous Year* and *Triangle: The Fire That Changed America*

"Jo Becker is one of America's very best journalists, and this book showcases her at her finest. Meticulously reported and passionately written, *Forcing the Spring* not only illuminates the fight in America for marriage equality, it's also a thrilling and exhilarating page-turner."
—David Finkel, author of *Thank You for Your Service* and *The Good Soldiers*

Forcing the Spring

INSIDE THE FIGHT FOR
MARRIAGE EQUALITY

JO BECKER

PENGUIN BOOKS

PENGUIN BOOKS
Published by the Penguin Group
Penguin Group (USA) LLC
375 Hudson Street
New York, New York 10014

USA | Canada | UK | Ireland | Australia | New Zealand | India | South Africa | China
penguin.com
A Penguin Random House Company

First published in the United States of America by The Penguin Press,
a member of Penguin Group (USA) LLC, 2014
Published in Penguin Books 2015

Photograph credits appear on page 457.

THE LIBRARY OF CONGRESS HAS CATALOGED THE HARDCOVER EDITION AS FOLLOWS:
Becker, Jo, author.
Forcing the spring : inside the fight for marriage equality / Jo Becker.
pages cm
Includes bibliographical references and index.
ISBN 978-1-59420-444-9 (hc.)
ISBN 978-0-14-312723-9 (pbk.)
1. Hollingsworth, Dennis, 1967—Trials, litigation, etc.   2. Perry, Kristin–Trials, litigation, etc.
3. Locus standi–United States–Cases.   4. Same-sex marriage–Law and legislation–United States–
Cases.   5. California. Proposition 8 (2008)   6. United States. Defense of Marriage Act.   I. Title.
KF228.H645B43   2014
346.79401'68–dc23   2014005342

Printed in the United States of America
1   3   5   7   9   10   8   6   4   2

DESIGNED BY AMANDA DEWEY

For Serge

The nature of injustice is that you can't see it in your own times.

—*Supreme Court Justice Anthony Kennedy*

CONTENTS

Forcing the Spring

Section I

ONE

THE "PACT"

This is how a revolution begins.

It begins when someone grows tired of standing idly by, waiting for history's arc to bend toward justice, and instead decides to give it a swift shove. It begins when a black seamstress named Rosa Parks refuses to give up her seat on a bus to a white man in the segregated South. And in this story, it begins with a handsome, bespectacled thirty-five-year-old political consultant named Chad Griffin, in a spacious suite at the Westin St. Francis hotel in San Francisco on election night 2008.

It was hours before the final votes were counted, but already Chad knew he was about to experience the most bittersweet election of his life. On the suite's large television screen he watched as Barack Obama stepped onto the stage in Grant Park, Chicago, and into his place in history as the first African American elected president of the United States.

"If there is anyone out there who still doubts that America is a place where all things are possible," the president-elect boomed to the electrified crowd, "who still wonders if the dream of our founders is alive in our time, who still questions the power of our democracy, tonight is your answer."

Outside the hotel on the street, a crowd chanted the Obama mantra: "Yes we can!"

Chad wanted to celebrate too. He had been working in Democratic politics since he was nineteen years old. Inspired by then Arkansas governor Bill Clinton, he had worked on the governor's presidential campaign, then left Ouachita Baptist University in Arkadelphia to follow him to Washington, becoming the youngest staffer in the Clinton White House. He was six feet tall, on the slender side, and with his ubiquitous sports jackets and ties he still looked very much like the Washington staffer he once was.

Obama's election meant more to him than just a repudiation of eight years of Republican control of the White House. It was not just a turning point in the nation's fraught racial history, though it was certainly that. It was a signal that, as the president-elect told the Grant Park crowd, "change has come to America."

But Chad's eyes kept flickering away from the television and back to his computer screen, where early returns from another race suggested change had not come for everybody, and especially not for people like him.

In a campaign known as Proposition 8, California voters had gone to the polls to decide whether to strip gays and lesbians of the ability to marry by amending the state's constitution. The referendum had been placed on the ballot after the California Supreme Court found that denying same-sex couples marriage licenses violated their rights—a decision that had briefly allowed same-sex couples to wed in the most populous state in the nation.

Looking on with concern was Chad's closest friend and business partner, Kristina Schake. With her wavy red hair, curvaceous figure, and wide, engaging smile, she looked like the kind of girl who might have once graced a 1950s pin-up calendar. But at age thirty-eight, she had political instincts every bit as sharp as Chad's. They had been in business together for close to a decade, and their Los Angeles–based communications firm, Griffin Schake, counted everyone from actor Brad Pitt to California's first lady, Maria Shriver, as clients. They were known for their ability to raise big-time Hollywood money for national Democratic candidates, and for their expertise in running California's never-ending ballot initiative campaigns.

The two friends believed that the "No on Prop 8" campaign had been marred by a failure to reach out to California's African American, Asian and Latino populations and messaging that, while pleasing to the gay community, did little to move voters on the fence. But despite their expertise, they had not been brought in to help turn the polls around until late in the game. They had cut some last-minute ads that nudged the numbers up, but Kristina could see by the way Chad was tensely raking his hand though his closely cropped brown hair that he didn't think it was going to be enough.

Part of what made Chad such an effective political operative was his tendency to envision and plan for worst-case scenarios that never materialized. It meant he lived in a perpetually stressed-out world. Kristina had a sunnier disposition, and saw it as her role to provide Chad with some balance. But as more precincts came in, she could see that this time he was right to worry.

Kristina thought back to how hard it had been for Chad to come out eight years earlier. She had known he was gay long before he worked up the nerve to tell her, and he had done so only after she gently nudged him one night as they sipped cocktails on the rooftop of the Standard Hotel in downtown Los Angeles.

"Look around the room," she had asked. "What's your type?"

The two were like brother and sister, completing one another's sentences, there to prop the other up when relationships foundered or other life crises struck. Now she ached for her friend. How could Chad not feel singled out and rejected? Not only had Californians passed Proposition 8 by a margin of 52 percent to 48 percent, but voters in Florida and Chad's home state of Arkansas had also passed antigay initiatives.

"It feels," he told Kristina, "like a triple gut punch."

"That night, we made a pact," Kristina recalled. "We were going to look for a way to move this cause forward. And if we found it, we would take it."

———

Ten days later, Chad and Kristina found themselves sitting in the sun at the Beverly Hills Hotel's Polo Lounge, where celebrities, agents, and studio deal makers mingle under trellises laden with pink bougainvillea. Joining them at their outdoor patio table were movie director Rob Reiner and his wife, Michele. The Reiners were clients of Chad and Kristina's firm, but they were much more than that, almost surrogate parents. They had invited the two young consultants to lunch to rally around Chad and commiserate about the election results.

Chad had first met the movie director when Rob was doing research for his film *The American President.* As one of President Clinton's press aides, Chad

had been tapped to show the director around the White House. Rob loved the movie business, but he was almost as famous for supporting progressive political causes and candidates as he was for movie classics like *When Harry Met Sally . . .* and *Stand by Me.*

Rob was impressed with Chad. He had vision and a confidence that belied his youth, and he seemed completely unfazed by Hollywood celebrity. The two had kept in touch, and eventually Rob had convinced Chad to move out to California to run his charitable Los Angeles–based Reiner Foundation and help direct his political giving. Together they had saved three thousand acres of wilderness space in the Santa Monica Mountains from development, and, with others, had battled oil companies in an attempt to pass a tax on extraction in order to pay for clean energy initiatives.

It was Rob who had introduced Chad to Kristina, when he and his wife hired her to help with their "I Am Your Child" campaign. The goal was to convince voters to levy a tax on tobacco products that would pay for an ambitious statewide early childhood development program. Kristina had gone into the communications business after working for the Los Angeles mayor, and with the tobacco companies pouring money into the race, Rob figured he could use all the help he could get. Outspent and against the odds, they managed to actually win the thing.

The Reiners were fighters, whose worldview had been shaped by their own upbringing. Rob, a balding, bearded bear of a man whose booming voice announced his New York roots, had marched with his parents in the 1960s for civil rights and against the Vietnam War, while Michele, a raven-haired former news photographer, was the daughter of a Holocaust survivor. Her mother had spent two harrowing years at Auschwitz, and, growing up, the number the Nazis had tattooed on her arm was a daily reminder to Michele of the very worst that can happen when a group of people is singled out for persecution.

But what, the four friends wondered aloud as they lunched at the Polo Lounge, could be done now about the passage of Proposition 8, and the larger issue of gay rights? Most Americans did not realize that in more than half the states a person could legally be fired, denied a room at an inn or even an apartment just for being gay; no federal law prohibits such discrimination. Gays and lesbians could not openly serve in the military, and there were places in America where they were effectively banned from adopting children and could not as a matter of course make medical decisions on behalf of lifelong partners.

All of those battles were important, but Chad still felt that marriage was the right fight to choose. It steered the conversation toward principles of love and commitment, rather than rights and demands, and it showed that gay and lesbian couples wanted the same things in life as their straight counterparts.

But enduring endless more rounds at the ballot box did not seem a particularly good strategy. Thirty states, including California, had now amended their constitutions to ensure that their bans on same-sex marriage were enshrined in a way that state courts could never undo. A staggering $44.1 million had been spent trying to defeat Proposition 8, and donors were exhausted.

"Every single time the rights of gays and lesbians are put up to a popular vote, big surprise, we lose," Chad said. "If we can't win in California, where can we win?"

Just then, an acquaintance of the Reiners named Kate Moulene stopped by their table. They chatted about their kids, who attended the same school, and Michele Reiner promised to call Moulene soon to catch up.

It was a brief conversation, easily forgettable in the bustle of daily chores. Lunch finished up without any real resolution as to the way forward. With time on her hands as she inched her way home through Los Angeles traffic in her black hybrid SUV, Michele dialed Moulene's number and, almost as an afterthought, filled her in on what the group had been talking about at lunch. Among the possibilities the four friends had discussed was filing a federal civil rights challenge to bans like Proposition 8.

"My ex-brother-in-law is a constitutional lawyer," Moulene exclaimed. "His name is Ted Olson. And knowing him as I do, I bet he'd be on your side of this."

"Ted Olson?!" Michele exclaimed. "Why on earth would I want to talk to him?"

Olson, after all, had represented George W. Bush in the disputed 2000 presidential election. On the night the Supreme Court issued the *Bush v. Gore* opinion that ended the Florida recount and handed Olson his greatest victory, Rob and Chad had endured defeat at the Naval Observatory with Vice President Gore and his family.

The two had left and driven to the Supreme Court, where they watched a lone man holding up a sign that said BULLSHIT, while Olson celebrated over a dinner of steak and caviar with guests that included Kenneth Starr, the special counsel best known for his impeachment prosecution of President Clinton.

And the *Bush v. Gore* case was just the highlight of Olson's lifelong service to conservative causes. As a senior Justice Department official during the Reagan administration, he was a leading architect of the president's legal revolution to ease government regulation, promote school prayer, and end race- and gender-based affirmative action programs. He had successfully defended President Reagan in the Iran-Contra scandal, and aggressively gone after President Clinton during the Monica Lewinsky affair. After helping elect President Bush, he served as his solicitor general. There, he had defended the administration's controversial war on terror before the Supreme Court.

Olson was also a leader in the Federalist Society, a group that promoted conservative legal theory. In that venue, he had delivered numerous speeches decrying "activist" judges for circumventing the political process by finding rights within the Constitution that were not explicitly spelled out—the very legal thesis espoused by those who argued that the issue of same-sex marriage should be left to voters and state legislatures. He was, in short, a man liberals loved to hate.

But Moulene felt that conservative caricature didn't capture the nuance of his thinking. Even though he and her sister had divorced, they had all remained close. Just call him, she urged Michele.

"I've watched for twenty years how he treats people," she would later explain. "His warmth, his acceptance and genuine respect for people—he's one of the most interesting, intelligent, and decent human beings I've ever known."

Arriving home, Michele filled her husband in on the conversation. Chad and Kristina were driving back to their office when the Reiners reached them on Chad's car phone. They both burst out laughing when they heard Moulene's suggestion.

"This sounds crazy," Chad said.

But Rob was intrigued. Olson was known as one of the best Supreme Court advocates of his generation. Almost despite himself, Rob had a grudging admiration for the man who had, in his words, "kicked our asses" in the deadlocked 2000 election. The tactician in him saw the wisdom in bringing on a lawyer who had won forty-four of the fifty-five cases he had argued before the nation's high court, while the director immediately grasped the attention-grabbling potential of such a casting call.

It would be an incredibly bold stroke. The gay rights movement was made up of a constellation of established groups that had been fighting for years for equal rights for the "LGBT" community, made up of lesbians, gay men, bisexuals, and transgender individuals. A federal lawsuit would completely upend the cautious, state-by-state strategy that those groups had been pursuing. They wanted to see gays and lesbians work state legislatures and state courts to win marriage, civil union, or some other form of relationship recognition in thirty states before taking the risk of asking the federal courts to weigh in with a nationwide marriage decision.

At the moment, same-sex couples could marry in only two states, Massachusetts and Connecticut. But Chad and Rob shared a willingness to challenge conventional wisdom, especially if they believed the reward great enough. The passage of Proposition 8 had illuminated, in stark relief, a fundamental problem with the state-by-state strategy, which was that hard-fought victories won in state courts or legislatures could be easily undone by popular vote. In three hundred cities across the country, tens of thousands had marched in protest, a grassroots uprising that seemed to reflect not just a community's collective anguish, but a hunger for bold new ideas. After talking it through, they decided it was worth gauging Olson's interest in filing a first-of-its-kind, federal constitutional challenge to California's same-sex marriage ban. If nothing else, perhaps it could be used as a way to change the political dynamic.

Ever since a 2003 ruling by the Massachusetts Supreme Judicial Court had made that state the first in the nation to allow gays and lesbians to marry, the issue of same-sex marriage had been used as a potent political wedge issue. Republicans put bans on the ballot in presidential swing states to try to drive their base of evangelical conservatives to the polls.

Democrats weren't much better. Politicians like Senator Dianne Feinstein publicly blamed the push to legalize same-sex marriage for helping to reelect George W. Bush president in 2004, though there was little evidence to support that claim. "The whole issue has been too much, too fast, too soon," she had complained at the time. "People aren't ready for it."

And it was President Clinton, Chad's political hero, who had signed into law the Defense of Marriage Act, which defined marriage as a union between a man and a woman for the purpose of denying legally married same-sex couples federal benefits available to married heterosexuals.

It was not, as Clinton claimed when he signed the bill into law, that he truly "opposed governmental recognition of same-gender marriages." It was that he knew he would be politically clobbered if he vetoed the measure, according to Richard Socarides, his top adviser on gay rights issues. Clinton had already taken a beating for trying to end a policy that allowed the military to discharge a service member for being gay; he wound up forced to settle on a compromise policy called "Don't Ask, Don't Tell" that allowed gays and lesbians to serve only if they kept their sexual orientation hidden.

"He was never against gay marriage," Socarides recalled. "But you have to remember the context. There were only fourteen votes in the entire Senate against this. It was the last thing he wanted to do. He kept asking, 'Was there any way around it?'"

Every Democratic presidential candidate since had adopted the same position as Clinton, including his wife, Hillary Rodham Clinton, and Obama: Marriage should be between a man and a woman.

"If someone as conservative as Ted Olson were to get involved in this issue," Chad said to Rob, "it would go a long way in terms of recasting same-sex marriage as a civil rights fight, rather than a partisan one."

"It could be a game-changer," Rob agreed.

TWO

A CONSERVATIVE ICON
JOINS THE CAUSE

A week later, shortly before noon on November 21, 2008, Chad was ushered through the white marble lobby of Gibson Dunn's Washington, D.C., office, where Olson was a senior partner in charge of the firm's Supreme Court practice.

Chad had talked with Olson by phone beforehand to ensure his interest. Still, on the trip out, Chad hadn't been able to shake a sense of the surreal. "I'm going to Washington to meet *this* guy?" he kept thinking.

Olson's office décor did little to dispel his preconceptions. A framed photograph of President Reagan was inscribed with "heartfelt thanks." Another, from the second President Bush, was signed with "respect and admiration." Displayed on the bookshelf was a medal bestowed upon Olson by former defense secretary Donald Rumsfeld, while on the coffee table sat a compilation of the dissents of Justice Antonin Scalia, an anchor of the Court's conservative wing whom Olson counted as a good friend.

Olson was a tall man with a mop of strawberry blond hair, a bit of a paunch well disguised by beautifully tailored pinstriped suits, and sloping blue eyes that radiated genuine warmth. He could be deeply combative, but what struck Chad on first impression was an earnest boyishness that immediately put him at ease.

Setting aside any lingering misgivings, Chad began.

"Too often in the debate over same-sex marriage, the real-life consequences of the government treating gays and lesbians differently are lost."

From Chad's perspective, the problem with bans on gay marriage were that they sent the message that the government believed there was something wrong, and unworthy, about gay and lesbian relationships. And that kind of state-sponsored discrimination, he told Olson, not only provided cover for routine schoolyard bullying, it also, in his view, fueled the type of extreme hatred that had led to the 2008 headline-grabbing murder of Lawrence King, an eighth grader who was killed for wearing women's clothing and identifying as gay.

One-third of gay, lesbian, bisexual, and transgender teens acknowledge contemplating suicide, a rate nearly four times that of their straight peers, Chad told Olson. A quarter of gay, lesbian, bisexual, and transgender teens are kicked out of their homes when they come out.

That, he argued forcefully, was the story they had to tell. "This is not about me, Chad Griffin, getting married," he told the lawyer.

"God, it's hard enough being a teenager," Olson said, as he digested the numbers for the first time and thought through how the powerful narrative Chad had just laid out could be channeled for legal purpose.

———

Unbeknownst to Chad, Olson had already been asked to become involved in California's gay marriage fight; the backers of Proposition 8 had wanted him to defend the ban. He had declined, telling them that their position was at odds with both his personal and legal views.

Olson was no RINO—a pejorative term conservatives used to denote moderates they see as "Republican in Name Only." But he had become active in the Republican Party before the advent of the religious right, with its focus on inserting the government into morality debates.

As a college and law school student in California, he gravitated toward a particularly western brand of small government, maximum individual liberty, becoming one of a lonely few students at the University of California's Berkeley Law and Boalt Hall to support Arizona senator Barry Goldwater's 1964 bid for president.

At that time, segregation was still in full throttle in the South, and during a trip to Texas with his college debate team, Olson got his first close-up view of blatant discrimination, when a black teammate was refused service at a restaurant. Olson tore into the owner, as the team insisted it would not eat unless everyone was served. During a similar incident at another restaurant, Olson went into the kitchen, pushed the cooks aside, and made his teammate breakfast.

When that owner threatened to call the police, "Ted said, 'Go ahead and do it,'" Paul Winters, the debate team's coach, recalled. "That's just the way he is. If he sees something that is wrong in his mind, he goes after it." Gays and lesbians, Olson told Chad, had long been the victims of similarly "hideous discrimination."

During the Reagan administration, Olson had joined the Justice Department as head of the Office of Legal Counsel, a post from which he rendered legal opinions about what federal agencies could and could not do. When a federal prosecutor was fired for being gay, Olson wrote a blunt legal opinion concluding that it was "improper to deny employment or to terminate anyone on the basis of sexual conduct."

When Olson left the Justice Department to return to private practice in 1984, it was views like those that led some to say that "what was seen as a certain libertarian squishiness at the Office of Legal Counsel under Ted" had been eliminated, recalled Steven Calabresi, a law professor at Northwestern University who cofounded the Federalist Society.

After winning *Bush v. Gore,* Olson was named President George W. Bush's solicitor general. The Office of the Solicitor General argues on behalf of the government before the Supreme Court, deciding when the federal government should weigh in on a case and what position it should take. When Olson was asked for his views on a proposal to amend the U.S. Constitution to define marriage as a union between a man and a woman, he was characteristically blunt, despite the fact that it had the president's support. Not only was it bad policy, he told the White House, but "what were we thinking putting something like that in the Constitution?"

State legislatures around the country were debating alternatives to same-sex marriage such as civil unions and domestic partnership arrangements, but

Olson felt those were crass political half measures that continued to treat gays and lesbians as separate and unequal.

One night early in Bush's first term over dinner at the Caucus Room, a Capitol Hill hangout, Olson launched into an argument that marriage was an essential component of human happiness that same-sex couples should be able to enjoy, recalled his friend, conservative author and former Bush speechwriter David Frum. Most everyone else at the dinner table was opposed, but Olson wouldn't be moved. Frum was struck by how passionately Olson seemed to feel.

"You have to make peace with this because it is sure to happen," Olson told the other dinner attendees, "and you will see it in your lifetime."

So when Chad had asked for an appointment to discuss making that prediction a reality, Olson readily agreed. To him, it was an axiom that good lawyers didn't take on only popular cases. And if his reading of the law led him in a different direction than most of his conservative peers, he had never given much of a damn what others might think.

A case in point: his behind-the-scenes willingness to stand up to then vice president Dick Cheney when it came to the Bush administration's controversial interpretation of its wartime powers in the wake of 9/11. Olson was the only senior administration official to lose a family member in the 9/11 attacks; his third wife, Barbara, a conservative commentator, died aboard one of the hijacked planes. Yet even as he publicly defended the administration's prerogatives, those involved in the debate said he privately and correctly warned that failure to give terror suspects basic legal rights like access to a lawyer would lead to Supreme Court setbacks.

Besides, in Olson's view, fighting to overturn gay marriage bans was entirely consistent with his devotion to more traditionally conservative causes, such as his efforts to overturn affirmative action programs aimed at redressing past discrimination. Both were informed by an antipathy toward government-sponsored discrimination, whatever the goal, and a belief that the Constitution's promise of equal protection under the law means just that.

"Why shouldn't I take this case?" he thought as he listened to Chad. "Because someone at the Federalist Society thinks I'd be making bad law? I wouldn't be making bad law."

Then, leaning forward in his chair, he laid out his theory of the case for Chad.

Courts are historically reluctant to arrive at novel interpretations of the Constitution, so one key to the same-sex marriage battle would be to stress that they weren't asking for a new right.

The Supreme Court had on fourteen separate occasions recognized marriage as a fundamental right. It had struck down laws banning prisoners and deadbeat dads from marrying. And, most notably, in a 1967 case called *Loving v. Virginia* it had found bans on interracial marriages unconstitutional. "The freedom to marry," Chief Justice Earl Warren had written on behalf of a unanimous Court, "has long been recognized as one of the vital personal rights essential to the orderly pursuit of happiness by free men."

The question was whether the state could deny that fundamental right to same-sex couples by defining marriage as a union between a man and a woman. A big part of the answer, Olson believed, lay in two more recent Supreme Court decisions.

The first was a 1996 case called *Romer v. Evans,* in which six of the nine justices struck down a voter-enacted amendment to the Colorado constitution that, like Proposition 8, stripped gays and lesbians of legal protections they had previously enjoyed under the law—in Colorado's case, civil rights protections enacted by certain municipalities that prohibited discrimination based on sexual orientation.

The Court found that the Colorado initiative violated the Constitution's equal protection clause, which declares that no state may "deny to any person within its jurisdiction the equal protection of the laws." The initiative, the Court's majority held, disadvantaged gays and lesbians for no good purpose beyond a "bare . . . desire to harm a politically unpopular group."

The second case was *Lawrence v. Texas,* a 6–3 decision that struck down laws criminalizing sodomy in 2003. The majority found that Texas had no legitimate reason to intrude into private sexual behavior protected by the Constitution's due process clause, which states that the government may not "deprive any person of life, liberty or property, without due process of law."

"Liberty presumes an autonomy of self that includes freedom of thought, belief, expression, and certain intimate conduct," the majority found.

The state may, under certain circumstances, single out and disadvantage a class of citizens if doing so advances a legitimate state interest, but the majority in *Lawrence* found that mere moral condemnation wasn't enough to meet that test.

The landmark decision spoke to the stigmatizing effect of Texas's antisodomy law, and declared that gays should be free to enter into relationships in their homes and "still retain their dignity as free persons."

"The State cannot demean their existence or control their destiny by making their private sexual conduct a crime."

Olson noted that no less a conservative than Justice Scalia had argued in a blistering dissent that the majority in *Lawrence* had opened the door to same-sex marriage.

Generally, the Court defers to the political process by presuming that duly enacted laws are constitutional. But laws may not arbitrarily treat similarly situated citizens differently. At the very least, Proposition 8 had to pass what is known as a "rational basis" test, meaning that the decision to strip gays and lesbians of the ability to marry must be rationally related to some legitimate state purpose. Finding one, Olson believed, was going to be difficult.

Justifying the ballot initiative would be harder still if he could persuade the Supreme Court to set the bar higher. Laws that infringe upon fundamental rights or that target certain vulnerable minority groups that have been historic targets of discrimination receive additional scrutiny from the Court. If Olson could convince the justices that the fundamental right to marry was the right to marry the person one loves, rather than a person of the opposite sex, or show that gays and lesbians constitute what is known as a "suspect" or "quasi-suspect" class, the Supreme Court would apply a much less deferential balancing test in weighing the constitutionality of Proposition 8.

In determining whether a group is a class in need of extra judicial protection, the Court considers whether the group has been subject to a history of discrimination; whether it lacks the political power to protect itself in the majoritarian political process; and whether its members exhibit an obvious or immutable trait that makes them readily distinguishable as a class but does not prevent them from contributing to society.

Racial minorities, for instance, are considered a suspect class. Therefore laws that discriminate against them—as well as those that infringe upon a fundamental right—must meet a strict scrutiny test, meaning that they must serve a "compelling" governmental interest, be narrowly tailored, and represent the least restrictive means of achieving the government's objective. Women constitute a quasi-suspect class, and laws that discriminate against them are subject to intermediate scrutiny, meaning they must serve an "important governmental objective" and be "substantially" related to achieving that objective.

Sexual orientation, Olson believed, was no more a choice than skin color or sex. "The Court should treat it similarly," he told Chad.

Chad listened, mesmerized. Olson was talking about some of the murkiest areas of the Supreme Court's jurisprudence, and divining the true meaning and extent of the justices' opinions was akin to what an archaeologist faces when trying to decipher recently unearthed ancient cave drawings. The marking were there, but what did they really mean?

But the lawyer was incredibly charismatic, able to take a highly divisive issue and, in his forceful but always pleasant voice, boil it down into a plainspoken legal argument that seemed so reasonable that it was hard to believe there was any other side.

Olson could be, Chad thought, one of the most eloquent spokespeople the gay rights movement had ever seen. Stepping outside onto Connecticut Avenue after the meeting, he phoned Kristina.

"You will not believe this, but he will take the case," Chad told her.

"I was just shocked," she recalled. "We thought, 'Game on.'"

⸺

Walking up the circular brick driveway of the Reiners' home in Brentwood the following month, Olson wondered what type of reception awaited him. He knew he was seen as something of the devil incarnate in liberal circles like the Reiners'. But the movie director could not have been more welcoming when he greeted him at the door. Rob trusted Chad's instincts—he simply wanted to hear for himself what journey had brought Olson to his home, and this cause.

Walking Olson through his home, he explained its storied history. The actor Henry Fonda, an ardent Democrat, had planted its rose bushes when he owned it. The liberal producer Norman Lear, who gave Rob his first big break when he cast him as Archie Bunker's son-in-law "Meathead" in the 1970s television show *All in the Family*, had lived in it next. All told, the director told Olson, more money had been raised for Democratic candidates here than perhaps any other home in Hollywood.

"I certainly never thought you would be in my living room," the director joked as they entered the comfortable, tastefully decorated space.

Chad and Kristina were already there. Bruce Cohen, an Academy Award–winning producer of box office hits like *American Beauty*, soon joined the group. Chad and Cohen had gotten to know one another when the two put together a high-dollar fund-raiser to fight Proposition 8, and Cohen had been with Chad and Kristina on election night at the Westin St. Francis. Cohen was a gay Yale graduate whose political activism dated back to childhood door knocking on behalf of Democratic candidates in Virginia.

He was a strategic thinker, and, as important, he had credibility with the gay rights community that Chad knew they would need to mollify if they were to move forward with a lawsuit; Cohen's latest film was a biopic about the first openly gay elected official in San Francisco, city supervisor and activist Harvey Milk.

The night before, Chad had called him to explain what the group was contemplating and invite him to meet Olson. "What do you think the lesson of Obama's election was?" Chad had asked.

"The time for playing it safe, the time for waiting, is over," Cohen answered.

Every major gay rights legal group in the country had adopted the slogan "Make Change, Not Lawsuits," issuing press releases that stated that the fastest way to win the freedom to marry was through state courts and state legislatures. "One thing couples shouldn't do is just sue the federal government," read one. "Pushing the federal government before we have a critical mass of states recognizing same sex relationships, or suing in states where the courts aren't ready is likely to get us bad rulings."

But Cohen did not feel time was necessarily on the side of the gay community. The chances that the Supreme Court was going to become more liberal over time seemed slim to him: The conservative justices were among the youngest on the Court, and who knew whether Obama would be reelected? Maybe it was that he could still remember watching his dad, a well-known labor lawyer, argue a case before the Supreme Court on behalf of workers, but he had faith in the justices.

"I'm in," he had told Chad.

Now, walking across the room, he introduced himself to the lawyer. Olson chatted about Cohen's film *Milk*, which he had recently seen. Then the group moved into the dining room for a simple lunch of fish and salad.

Rob Reiner typically dominated conversations. But he was uncharacteristically silent as Olson, seated at the head of the table normally reserved for his host, made his pitch.

Basically, there were two ways to go, Olson said. One path involved challenging the constitutionality of the Clinton-era Defense of Marriage Act. DOMA, as it was known, created real financial hardships for gay and lesbian couples that had legally married in states like Massachusetts by denying them more than eleven hundred federal benefits. They were not entitled to the federal income tax break straight married couples enjoyed when they filed jointly. Federal employees could not cover their same-sex husbands or wives under their insurance policies. In death, married same-sex couples also were penalized. Unlike their straight counterparts, surviving spouses had to pay estate taxes on the assets left to them, and had no right to their partners' Social Security death benefits.

But challenging DOMA would potentially pit the group against the Obama administration's Justice Department, forcing a president who had said during the campaign that he believed marriage was between a man and a woman to choose a side. Besides, Olson said, he wanted to keep it simple.

"Don't bring DOMA into this," Olson advised. "I don't want to talk about taxation or health insurance. I want to talk about equal protection under the law."

The second, and better option, he said, was a lawsuit specifically targeting California's ban on same-sex marriage. In Olson's analysis, the passage of Proposition 8 was tragic, but it presented a unique and sympathetic set of facts for bringing an equal protection and due process case.

In 2004, San Francisco mayor Gavin Newsom had unilaterally begun issuing marriage licenses to same-sex couples in violation of a state law that defined marriage as a union between a man and a woman. The California Supreme Court had voided those unions, but in 2008 it found that the law itself violated the state constitution. The ruling legalized same-sex marriage in the state for four and a half months. Proposition 8 was a response to that court decision; it amended the state constitution in order to reinstate the same-sex couple marriage ban.

Its passage created what Olson would later refer to as a "crazy quilt" of marriage regulations. California now had three classes of citizens: opposite-sex couples who could marry, and remarry if divorced or widowed; eighteen thousand gay and lesbian couples married in the months after the California Supreme Court ruling made it legal but before the passage of Proposition 8, who could not remarry if divorced or widowed; and unmarried same-sex couples who now wanted to wed but were prohibited from doing so by Proposition 8. Given that set of facts, even if the Supreme Court weren't ready to find a nationwide right of same-sex couples to marry, Olson believed that at the very least it might still declare California's ban unconstitutional, paving the way for future gains elsewhere with a helpful precedent.

Another benefit of challenging Proposition 8 was that the defendants would be the governor, Arnold Schwarzenegger, and attorney general, Jerry Brown. Both had come out against the passage of Proposition 8 and thus would be unlikely to vigorously defend it. And the governor's wife, California's first lady, Maria Shriver, was a friend and client of Kristina's who passionately believed in the gay rights cause.

In addition, a Proposition 8 challenge would play out on friendly legal terrain. The case would first be heard in the U.S. district court in San Francisco, which meant that the appeals court that would review the verdict, since win or lose it was sure to be appealed, would be the Ninth Circuit Court of Appeals, considered the most liberal in the nation.

Winning in the Ninth Circuit would represent a huge victory, potentially legalizing same-sex marriage not just in California, but also in Washington, Oregon, Idaho, Arizona, Hawaii, Nevada, Montana, and Alaska. Ultimately, though, Olson expected that a deeply divided Supreme Court would have the final say.

There, Justice Anthony Kennedy would likely be the swing vote. He had authored the majority opinions in both the *Romer v. Evans* and *Lawrence v. Texas* cases.

But Olson said it was important not to take any votes for granted. He knew all nine justices both professionally and socially. Justice Kennedy had attended his wedding. Justice Scalia, whose eldest son worked for Olson's firm, and the more liberal Justice Ruth Bader Ginsburg had a tradition of spending New Year's Eve at the Olsons' home, with Justice Ginsburg's husband cooking up game that Justice Scalia had shot on a hunting trip.

Olson believed that a majority would find bans like Proposition 8 unconstitutional, but each would have issues that would need to be addressed, he said. Justice Ginsburg, for instance, had stated publicly that she believed the Court moved too far too fast in finding a constitutional right to abortion in its 1973 *Roe v. Wade* decision. Despite her support for abortion rights and her place as an anchor of the Court's liberal wing, she felt that the Court had short-circuited the democratic process and might have avoided backlash had it allowed more states to take the lead in legalizing abortion before issuing such a sweeping decision.

She could have similar concerns about same-sex marriage. Abortion was legal under some circumstances in twenty states when *Roe* was handed down, eighteen more than currently allowed same-sex marriage. And although public attitudes on same-sex marriage were shifting, particularly among young people, the majority of Americans remained opposed.

"This isn't about winning five to four—this is about winning as many of the nine as you can," Olson told the group. "So you need to run nine separate cases at once."

Rob Reiner was struck by how similarly Olson and he viewed the case: Both saw the battle for marriage equality as one of the last pieces in the American civil rights puzzle, the only arena left in which the government openly discriminated against its citizens. Still, he asked, "Won't this cause issues for you both professionally and personally within your circle in D.C.?"

"No," Olson replied. "I've been in the eye of the storm before, and if I believe in something, I do it." Pausing, he looked around the table. "I will not just be some hired gun," he said. "I would be honored to be the voice for this cause."

It was a turning point. Until then, the group had been feeling Olson out. Now the discussion turned to the way forward.

Olson was willing to take the case for a discounted, flat-rate fee: $2.9 million plus expenses to take the case to the Supreme Court. The Reiners and Chad said they would begin looking for potential donors, while quietly sounding out activists in the gay rights community.

But Olson's involvement was deemed by the group to be so potentially explosive among conservatives and gay activists alike that everyone was sworn to secrecy on that front. Olson, for his part, promised to take the lead in finding a Democratic co-counsel with sterling credentials, to help alleviate the suspicion his involvement was sure to engender on the left.

In the meantime, he said, the first order of business was to find sympathetic plaintiffs who wanted to get married but could not because of the passage of Proposition 8. The couples should be in long-term, committed relationships, Olson advised, and they should be regular folks whom people could identify with, not activists or celebrities.

"I want a teacher, a police officer, and someone who owns a bookstore," he said.

Hugging Olson as he walked him to the door, Rob Reiner couldn't contain himself. "We are going to the Supreme Court!" he declared. "And we are going to win!"

THREE

"JUST WAIT"

On March 9, 2009, Chad strode through the modern lobby of the Creative Artists Agency in Century City, California, home to some of Hollywood's biggest stars. A friend, a top talent agent there, had suggested he meet with one of Creative Artists' most promising young screenwriters.

His name was Dustin Lance Black, and he had just won the Academy Award for Best Original Screenplay for *Milk,* the movie starring actor Sean Penn as the gay rights activist Harvey Milk that Cohen had produced.

Chad had heard about Black through Cohen, and he had come to the meeting hoping to enlist his help in convincing the gay community that a federal lawsuit was the way forward. When Milk was assassinated in 1978 by a former city supervisor who had clashed with him over gay rights, he was organizing a federal march on Washington in an effort to nationalize the struggle—a bolder course of action than the current state-by-state strategy of "Make Change, Not Lawsuits," and one that Black had seemed to advocate during his Academy Award acceptance speech.

"If Harvey had not been taken from us thirty years ago," Black had told a televised audience of tens of millions, "I think he'd want me to say to all the gay and lesbian kids out there tonight who have been told that they are 'less than' by their churches or by the government or by their families, that you are beautiful, wonderful creatures of value and that no matter what anyone tells you,

God does love you and that very soon, I promise you, you will have equal rights, federally, across this great nation of ours."

With his sculpted cheekbones, stylishly cut blond hair, and laid-back uniform of Chuck Taylors and black jeans, Black looked every bit as at home in California as Chad did in D.C. But within minutes of sitting down in one of the agency's conference rooms, the two men recognized themselves in one another. Both had grown up in conservative parts of the South, unaware that they even knew another gay person, with all the baggage that entailed.

Chad hailed from Hope, Arkansas, where he had worked at a local Walmart as a teenager. Before Bill Clinton walked into his life, he had thought he might make a pretty good store manager someday.

But one day a friend had phoned him, asking, "What the fuck are you doing? The next president of the United States has a campaign headquarters an hour from your house." He volunteered, and soon found himself working for top Clinton aide Dee Dee Myers and walking into the West Wing as a nineteen-year-old press staffer on inauguration day, part of a skeleton crew that had been welcomed at the gate by a Secret Service agent with the words, "Welcome. This is your White House now."

While Chad was settling into his desk in the White House press office, outside, under a crystalline January sky, the new president was delivering a speech that spoke to the promise of America. For nearly a hundred years, in a country founded upon the immortal declaration that "all men are created equal," slavery was legal in parts of the United States. Until the 1920s, women were denied the right to vote. During World War II, Japanese Americans were rounded up and imprisoned in internment camps. Jim Crow laws relegated African Americans to second-class citizenship into the 1960s. But America is also a country that corrects course, edging, in fits and starts, but inexorably, toward inclusion.

"This ceremony is held in the depth of winter, but by the words we speak and the faces we show the world, we force the spring," the new president, the first baby boomer to hold the office, declared.

"When our founders boldly declared America's independence to the world and our purposes to the Almighty, they knew that America, to endure, would have to change. Not change for change's sake but change to preserve America's ideals: life, liberty, the pursuit of happiness. Though we marched to the music of our own time, our mission is timeless. Each generation of Americans must define what it means to be an American."

It was a wildly improbable journey, one that had led Chad to believe that "anything was possible, if you just worked hard enough," said one of his best friends, President Obama's senior adviser Daniel Pfeiffer. "His whole experience tells him that. Here's a kid from a small town in Arkansas who was going to a tiny Baptist college. And all of a sudden he is flying the world aboard Air Force One with the president of the United States. He is not intimidated by the prospect of failure."

Still, for all of his outward confidence, throughout his years in Washington, Chad had been haunted by the fear that if he told anyone he was gay, his friends and everything he dreamed for his future would evaporate. He had left the White House in 1994 to finish his college degree at Georgetown University. One day he wanted to return home and, like his mentor, run for office.

"I can't come out," he thought. "I can't go back to Arkansas and run for governor as a gay man."

And so he had found other ways to fill his life, dating girls sporadically and working nonstop, first for Bill Clinton and later for the Reiners in California. There, he had finally felt comfortable enough to begin dating men, but it wasn't until a friend was killed in the 9/11 terror attacks that he decided to stop keeping it a secret. He was twenty-eight years old.

"Life is too short," he told himself. "Being governor isn't everything."

Black, at thirty-four, was a year younger than Chad. Born in Texas, he grew up in a military community attending the Mormon Church, which taught that homosexuality was a sin that must never be acted upon. (The church would later flood California with money and get-out-the-vote volunteers critical to the passage of Proposition 8.)

He spent portions of kindergarten in the principal's office, so shy and frightened of his schoolmates that he suffered panic attacks. His first crush, at age six, brought an overwhelming sense of shame. Adolescence, with its first stirrings of real desire, brought thoughts of suicide. He did not dare act on his feelings until he was twenty-one.

"What's so messed up," he told Chad at that first meeting, "is that the movies celebrate first love, first kisses. But gay kids are robbed of that ability to have a celebrated adolescence," and even with a lot of therapy grow up with poor self-esteem as a result.

"I think that sometimes we think we don't deserve full equality," he said. "We are all a little bit broken."

Black was in the midst of writing his next screenplay, about J. Edgar Hoover, and researching the relationship between the famed and feared former FBI director and Martin Luther King Jr. "King," he told Chad, "wasn't afraid to name the dream. We shouldn't be either."

Black and Cleve Jones, an aide of Milk's who had gone on to become one of the country's best-known AIDS activists, had been working on a plan to put together a grassroots political organization to press for full federal equality for gays and lesbians in all 435 congressional districts. But when Chad floated the idea of a lawsuit instead, he was immediately intrigued. That promised much faster action.

The two men wrapped up the meeting with a promise to reconvene soon. Chad would bring Cohen, and Black would bring Jones. If Jones, who had conceived of the AIDS quilt to memorialize the disease's victims, could be persuaded to sign on to the plan to file a federal challenge to California's ban, it would send a powerful signal that this wasn't just some scheme by a group of Hollywood know-nothings.

———

Jones, at age fifty-four, was not predisposed to like Chad. He had seen many a glib whiz-kid operative come and go, promising the world and delivering failure. So when the four men sat down for breakfast at Palihouse, a boutique hotel in West Hollywood, a few days later, he was skeptical.

Chad began the meeting by talking about his experience as a political operative, and how litigation could be used to move public opinion. He made it all seem eminently doable—here are the steps, we need to raise this much, we need to file by this date so we can get a decision by that one.

Jones had agreed to the meeting because he too was frustrated with a movement that seemed to have no sense of urgency about it. Its leadership ranks had been decimated by the plague of HIV/AIDS. The demonstrations of groups like

ACT UP, which in the 1980s staged protests to demand access to better and lower-cost drugs to treat the disease, had given way to a sort of entrenched "Gay Inc." health care delivery bureaucracy. The result, Jones believed, was a generation of leaders unwilling to rock the boat for fear of losing corporate donors, and willing to settle for just a fraction of equality.

But Chad seemed different, he thought as he listened to him spell out his vision for a federal lawsuit. He was aggressive, a control freak in a good way, and, most important, he wanted to win.

Midway through breakfast, Chad excused himself and walked away to make a phone call. He had saved the best for last, but needed permission to share the information with Black and Jones. When he came back, he said, "I have something to tell you. We can get Ted Olson to represent us."

Jones drew in a sharp breath; this actually might work. Black lit a cigarette. Imagine, he thought, going home and telling his Texas friends and Mormon family that someone like Olson was on their side.

"What can we do?" Black asked.

Twice a year, some of the richest gay donors in the country gather at an event called OutGiving. It is a place where donors learn about the work being done on both a political and charitable level to help improve the lot of the gay community. It was, Chad thought, the perfect venue to test the waters on the new direction the group was contemplating. The event was to be held later that month at the Ritz-Carlton Lake Las Vegas. Black had been invited, but had yet to accept.

Come with me, Chad urged. Give a speech that builds upon your Oscar acceptance and let's see how it flies.

———

Standing before the audience of donors in Nevada on March 21, Black knew before uttering a word that he was in for trouble. Hours earlier, he had been confronted in the hotel's courtyard by Evan Wolfson, the fifty-two-year-old founder of a group called Freedom to Marry and the primary author of the cautious state-by-state marriage strategy that the gay rights movement had been pursuing.

Wolfson had berated the younger man over his Oscar speech, explaining as though to a willful but ignorant child his ongoing, twenty-five-year plan to build support for marriage equality nationwide. Twenty-five years? Black had practically gasped. But he had said little; it was intimidating, to say the least, to be dressed down by a pioneer of the marriage equality movement.

Wolfson had devoted his life to the cause, writing his third-year thesis at Harvard Law School in 1983 on the right of gays and lesbians to marry, an idea considered so radical at the time that he had trouble finding an academic adviser. He had served as co-counsel in the first state court case challenging a same-sex marriage ban, filing a lawsuit in the early 1990s in Hawaii. He had won the case but lost the battle when voters there enacted a Prop 8–like constitutional amendment. His book on the subject had been called "perhaps the most important gay-marriage primer ever written."

Following the encounter, a shaken Black had called Chad in his room for reassurance.

There was, both felt, a generation gap at work. Younger activists like Chad and Black had grown up in a relatively safer world, where gays and lesbians were not forced to congregate in bars with no windows for fear of being raided and attacked, where courts did not routinely strip custody from gay parents in divorce proceedings, and where they saw themselves reflected positively in television shows like *Will & Grace*. It was easier for them to envision success now.

"This just means we are doing the right thing," Chad had said.

Still, it was with some trepidation that Black launched into his speech. Following the passage of Proposition 8, he told the crowd, he was shocked when a leader of one of the largest gay rights organizations in the country offered this advice: "He said, 'If we just quiet down, they'—whoever they are—'will let us do whatever we want.'

"Those are the words of one of the leaders of our current organizations, and as a student of Harvey Milk, I will tell you they are not just the same 'kind' of people who told Milk it was too soon for a gay elected official back in 1977—some of them are the very same people."

The movement was at a critical juncture, he continued, and "as Martin Luther King said on the steps of the Lincoln Memorial in 1963, 'This is no time to engage in the luxury of cooling off or to take the tranquilizing drug of gradualism.'" Full equality, he said, could only happen at the federal level.

"The strategy of the past decade has failed," he declared, a direct rebuke to many in the audience. "We have lost state and local fights time and again.

"It has been thirty years since Harvey Milk gave his life in our struggle for equality, and we will not wait thirty years more. It is time for us to stop asking for crumbs and demand the real thing."

If there was applause, Black didn't remember any. Instead, he recalled an ocean of pursed lips and crossed arms, and that he was literally trembling as he walked off the stage. Wolfson was silently seething. The idea that this new-comer thought his strategy timid and incremental infuriated him; no one wanted full federal equality more than him, but national change required more than wishful thinking.

"Harvey Milk didn't start by running for president," he later grumbled. "He ran for city supervisor, and he ran and lost twice before he won."

Tim Gill, whose foundation was the largest funder of gay rights causes in the country, denounced Black outright, telling the crowd he was naïve and mis-guided. Chad, who was standing in the wings with Bruce Cohen, was shocked at the level of open hostility. After all, Black hadn't even specifically mentioned marriage or a federal lawsuit.

"Chad was saying, 'Oh my God, we are going to be loathed and hated. How are we going to sell this?'" Black recalled.

And things were about to get worse.

———

On May 14, 2009, Chad, Kristina, and Cohen once again assembled for lunch at the Reiners'. It was time to talk to the lawyers who had been fighting this battle for years—and ask for their support.

Jenny Pizer, the law and policy director of Lambda Legal, was there, as was Jon Davidson, the group's legal director. Lambda was the oldest and largest legal organization devoted to fighting for the rights of gays and lesbians. Ra-mona Ripston, executive director of the American Civil Liberties Union's Southern California office, had also come with her chief counsel, Mark Rosen-baum. Both Lambda and the ACLU had been deeply involved in the effort to win the freedom to marry at the California State Supreme Court.

Since Olson's involvement in a potential lawsuit was sure to be the subject of controversy, it would not do to have him present the group's still confidential plans. Instead, he sent an emissary: Ted Boutrous, a liberal forty-eight-year-old managing partner in the firm's Los Angeles office with thick silver hair and a perpetual California tan.

Rob Reiner gave a quick synopsis of their discussions to date. Then he turned it over to Boutrous.

Boutrous and Olson had worked on numerous high-profile Supreme Court cases together, across a broad swath of the legal landscape. They had won limits on excessive punitive damages on behalf of corporate clients, worked with John Roberts before he became a Supreme Court justice on a case involving complex securities law, and litigated a major federal separation-of-powers case that constrained Congress's ability to pass laws aimed at undermining Supreme Court decisions.

"Someone is going to bring a federal marriage lawsuit," Boutrous said. "And you won't find a better advocate than Ted Olson."

But he hadn't gotten far before the invited lawyers all seemed to pile on at once, a cacophony of criticism that grew increasingly heated. How dare they entrust something so important to someone who wasn't one of them? They were upstarts who didn't know what they were doing. They couldn't get to five votes on the Supreme Court. This was going to have a terrible ending.

"It just felt like there was a lot of disrespect for the fact that a lot of people who had been working on these issues for a very long time had a different viewpoint," Davidson would later recall. "I was like 'who are you?'"

It was not that the movement lawyers disagreed with the goal. But they were old enough to remember the terrible setback that had occurred when the Supreme Court, in a 1986 case called *Bowers v. Hardwick* brought by the ACLU, upheld the constitutionality of laws criminalizing sodomy. Chief Justice Warren E. Burger, citing the "ancient roots" of prohibitions against sodomy, had gone out of his way in a concurring opinion to quote Sir William Blackstone's description of homosexual sex as an "infamous crime against nature."

The consensus was that the case had been brought too soon, at a time when nearly half the states still had criminal sodomy laws on their books. Supreme Court justices tend to abide by a legal principle called stare decisis, which means, in Latin, "to stand by decisions and not disturb the undisturbed." What it means in practice is that the justices are generally reluctant to overturn previous decisions. It had taken seventeen years, and the repeal of antisodomy laws in all but fourteen states, for the Court to reverse itself and declare laws criminalizing gay sex unconstitutional in the *Lawrence* case. In the interim, the precedent that the Court set with its biting *Bowers* opinion had been relied upon by lower courts to uphold the military's policy of discharging gay and lesbian service members, to find laws prohibiting gays and lesbians from becoming foster or adoptive parents constitutional, and to justify denying a lesbian mother custody of her children and a requirement that a gay father's visit with his daughter be supervised.

How long would it take for a reversal on marriage, and what other precedents might be set, if Olson was to lose?

"Just wait," Rosenbaum pleaded.

"Really?" said Boutrous, by now angry. "Should we wait until the Mitt Romney administration?" he asked, referring to the likely 2012 Republican presidential nominee.

Davidson threw a multipage dossier on the dining room table, outlining all the conservative causes Olson had championed over the years. This, and more, would be released to the media if they went ahead with their ill-fated plan, he threatened.

"Wonderful," Kristina retorted. "Do it. That only helps us."

"We hired him because he is a conservative," Chad added. "Someone who represented all these people"—he gestured at the dossier—"is going to be able to move public opinion."

The meeting abruptly ended on that angry note. "Well, that," Michele Reiner declared in her typically blunt but indefatigable fashion, "was a disaster!"

They were now on notice. If they proceeded, they would do so in the face of the full-throated opposition of the gay rights community. It was not the best of outcomes, but neither was it a real deterrent. They did not need the gay establishment. They had already put in place an organization with the wherewithal to go it alone. Their detractors just did not realize it yet.

———

The first fund-raiser for the American Foundation for Equal Rights had taken place the previous month in a private upstairs room at Mr. Chow, a Chinese restaurant in Beverly Hills as famous for its celebrity clientele as its Peking duck.

Chad and Kristina spent an entire night coming up with the name for the nonprofit they had formed to raise money for the lawsuit. "It has to have the word 'American' in it," Chad had said. "And it shouldn't sound like a gay rights group."

All told, he and Kristina estimated they would need about $3.5 million to pay Olson's bills and build a first-class media war room to publicize their effort. The Reiners had kicked in $100,000, and invited a select group of Hollywood friends to Mr. Chow on April 21 to begin raising the rest. Together with Chad, they had worked the room, explaining the needs of the new nonprofit— AFER for short—while Olson briefed the potential donors on the legal plan of attack.

Hundreds of thousands of dollars had been raised from people in the entertainment industry like John August, a lanky screenwriter with a shaved head whose credits included movies like *Charlie's Angels*. Norman Lear was visibly moved by the enthusiasm in the room. "You know," he mused, "we're going to look back and remember this as the beginning."

Then Lear, whose progressive activism included founding a group called People for the American Way to advocate keeping religion out of the public square, had made a suggestion that surprised Olson.

"I think we should all join hands and pray," Lear said.

And they did.

Success had bred success. Other industry people soon came forward; J. J. Abrams, a film director and creator of television hits such as *Lost* and *Alias*, had written a check with his wife, Katie, for $100,000. So had Ron Burkle, a billionaire supermarket magnet and a close friend of Bill Clinton whom Chad knew well from Democratic fund-raising circles. During one meeting with potential donors, Cohen had run in with a copy of a decision by the Iowa Supreme Court that made that state the third where gays and lesbians could legally marry, proof, he declared, that momentum was on their side.

But the biggest breakthrough had come when Rob Reiner reached out to David Geffen, an entertainment mogul who had made billions in the music and movie business, a huge Democratic donor, and a philanthropist who had been one of the largest contributors to the fight against HIV/AIDS. Geffen not only had kicked in $1.5 million of his own money, but he convinced Steve Bing, another billionaire Clinton friend with whom Chad had worked on environmental causes, to match that gift.

"Whatever you need, I'm there," Bing told Rob.

The fund-raising piece had all been so easy. Within a matter of weeks, the lawsuit had been "green-lighted," in movie parlance. They had the money to go forward. But should they? Following the meeting with Lambda Legal and the ACLU, Chad was beginning to wonder. Plenty of perfectly decent-sounding screenplays turned into box-office disasters, and here there were real lives at stake.

Chad had built a career in politics by effectively controlling the narrative and the circumstances that informed it. But with a legal case, so much would be out of his hands, starting with the judges who would be randomly chosen to hear the case as it made its way up to the Supreme Court. One unlucky draw and they could wind up hurting the very community they were trying to help.

"Are we making the wrong choice?" Chad asked Kristina one night.

Suggesting they take a walk, she gave him the advice she always did when he went into his dark, Clinton war room mode, anticipating lines of attack and finding his own responses wanting: "Keep your focus." She reminded Chad that he had asked Olson and Boutrous to consider all the arguments that had been raised by Lambda and the ACLU. Olson had taken the assignment seriously, rereading Martin Luther King Jr.'s famous "Letter from Birmingham Jail."

"Freedom is never voluntarily given by the oppressor; it must be demanded by the oppressed," the civil rights leader had written in 1963. "For years now, I have heard the word 'Wait!' It rings in the ear of every Negro with a piercing familiarity. This 'Wait' has almost always meant 'Never.'"

The lawyers then produced a memo for Chad entitled "The Time Is Now."

When it came to ending pernicious race-based laws, the Supreme Court "did not wait for the South to change; it changed the South," the memo read. When the Court struck down interracial marriage bans more than thirty years before, only 20 percent of the country approved of allowing people of different color to marry.

One need look no farther than California, the memo continued, to see why a state-by-state strategy of putting the fundamental rights of minorities up for a vote was not a fast track to achieving the ultimate goal of equal rights.

The world had changed since the Court upheld laws criminalizing gay sex in its 1986 *Bowers* decision, the lawyers wrote, and it was highly unlikely that the Supreme Court would go out of its way to denigrate gays and lesbians in the way that decision did.

"Moreover, a loss in the Supreme Court would at worst result in a decision that the right to marry is a question for the states to decide which would require us to focus on obtaining change on a State-by-State basis—exactly where we are today."

Kristina had read the memo and been comforted, as had Chad. During the Proposition 8 campaign, she had been appalled at what she saw as the political ineptitude and dysfunction of the gay rights community. It was filled with impassioned activists, but what it needed, she believed, was skilled political operators like Chad. She was sure it was his calling to become a movement leader, even if he wasn't.

"Take the emotion out of it," she said. "We have to forget about everything else and focus on one question: Do we believe in our strategy?"

Chad allowed that he still did.

"Then if our reasons are sound," she said, "and we didn't buy any of their arguments, we shouldn't let it affect what we do."

Now all they needed were some plaintiffs.

FOUR

A MAD DASH

For months, Kristina had been searching for plaintiffs who met Olson's criteria. To be safe, Olson wanted six couples. That way, if one couple split, or someone died, or their opponents dug up something about the background of another that could surprise them at trial, they had a fallback.

She and Chad had launched what they jokingly referred to as a "major casting call" at the beginning of the year. But it had proven far harder than they thought, both because they had been forced to operate in secrecy to prevent their plans from leaking and because all the couples they knew in the kind of committed relationships Olson wanted had married during the window before Proposition 8 was passed.

So the two political consultants set up an elaborate ruse, putting out the word that they were looking for couples to take part in a public education campaign on same-sex marriage. Kristina then funneled applicants' names to an opposition researcher she had hired to dig into their pasts. Some fell out in that process. Those who survived were invited to the firm's office and grilled by Kristina or, if she was tied up, Chad: Are there any embarrassing photos or YouTube videos we need to know about? What is your health status? Do you have a monogamous relationship, and have you ever cheated?

Only if couples made it through that round of vetting would Kristina disclose the real purpose behind the interview and have them meet the lawyers.

But of the few who did, several decided that they did not want to put them-selves through the publicity that a lawsuit would engender.

By the end of April, she was running out of time. Any day now, the Cali-fornia Supreme Court was expected to rule on a lawsuit that argued that tech-nically, Proposition 8 had revised, rather than amended, the California constitution, and as such was invalid; a quirk in California law gives voters the right to amend the state constitution, but requires a vote of the legislature to revise it. Few had any hope that the challenge would succeed.

Assuming it did not, same-sex marriage supporters would have no further means of redress in the state's courts. At that point, Olson worried, someone was bound to challenge the initiative in federal court; however much the estab-lished gay legal groups protested, there was simply no way to stop it.

He wanted their lawsuit to be *the* challenge to Proposition 8. "The worst-case scenario is that the first case to reach the Supreme Court is an ill-conceived suit brought by inexperienced lawyers," he had written in the "Time Is Now" memo for Chad. "It is imperative that the Supreme Court view the issue through the lens of the *right* case."

The only way to ensure that was to be the first to file. Yet Kristina had yet to identify a single couple willing to stand as plaintiffs, much less the six that Olson wanted.

Both she and Chad felt it was important to find some couples of color. They intended to use the lawsuit, and the attention it would draw, as a vehicle to mount a national public education campaign on same-sex marriage. Proposi-tion 8 had passed in part because the campaign against it had done little to try to reach out to California's large African American, Asian, and Latino mi-nority groups, and they did not want to repeat that mistake.

They could talk all they wanted about the similarities between the civil rights battles of the 1960s and the fight gays and lesbians were waging for equality today, but the truth was that exit polls showed that 70 percent of black voters, who turned out in record numbers to vote for President Obama, had supported Proposition 8, and more than half of Latino and Asian voters had too.

So on the afternoon that she learned that her dream couple—a Latina les-bian and her white partner who had been together forever—had decided to back out, she walked down the hall to Chad's office, plunked down in one of his chrome-and-black-leather chairs, and just shook her head.

"What are we going to do?" she said.

As it happened, Chad had just gotten off the phone with Kris Perry, the head of the statewide early education office funded by the cigarette tax increase they had passed for the Reiners. She and her partner, Sandy, both in their forties, had been together for ten years.

"What about Kris?" he asked.

"I think she's married," Kristina said.

"I don't know about that."

Kristina perked up. "Call her!"

Chad picked up the phone. It turned out that Kris had indeed tried to marry Sandy, when San Francisco first began issuing marriage licenses, but theirs was among the licenses invalidated when the California Supreme Court ruled that the mayor had no right to disobey a state law whose constitutionality the courts had yet to consider.

Chad knew that the couple wasn't perfect. Sandy, an IT director for Alameda County, had been married before, to a man, a complicating though not insurmountable factor in a case that rested in part on convincing the court that sexual orientation was not a choice. Plus, the two women had four teenage boys, two conceived by Sandy and her ex-husband, and two Kris had conceived in vitro with her former partner.

Olson had wanted to avoid couples with children. Opponents of same-sex marriage used children as a hot-button issue, maintaining that they do better when raised by a mother and father, and he worried it could introduce a whole complicated set of parenting issues into the mix that were best avoided.

On the other hand, Chad and Kristina really knew the women; there would be no surprises with these two. They were warm and quick-witted, and as the head of a state agency, Kris knew how to weather a political storm, an experience that Chad felt would serve them well in the high-pressure months to come.

At this late date, they would do, Chad decided, and he filled Kris in on the plan. Warning her that it would be a huge commitment, he said, "Maybe you should sleep on it."

But Kris was so excited that she immediately phoned Sandy at work. "Come home right now," she said. "I want to tell you about a conversation I just had."

═══════

A few weeks later, a similar discussion took place at Theresa's Family Restaurant in Burbank, where Jeff Zarrillo lived with his partner, Paul Katami, and their two French bulldogs in a small but tasteful California bungalow. The two had met eight years earlier in an online dating success story.

Paul, thirty-seven, was an intense former actor turned personal trainer who grew up in San Francisco. Jeff, a year younger, was a stocky self-described Jersey boy and Dallas Cowboys fan who hadn't quite managed to lose the accent in his years out west. He had worked his way up from a ticket taker at a Los Angeles movie theater to its general manager.

Friends had urged them to get married when the window in California opened. A few years earlier, Jeff had gotten down on his knee and proposed, and the two had even exchanged rings. But with opponents of gay marriage already gearing up to put Proposition 8 on the ballot, they were reluctant to put themselves and their family through the emotion of a wedding that could later be invalidated at the polls. Instead, they had decided to wait to see what California's voters did.

During the Proposition 8 campaign, they had stayed on the sidelines while their neighbors put up YES ON PROP 8 lawn signs; one had even quoted the Bible to them and declared their relationship sinful. But a television ad urging voters to pass the initiative so infuriated the couple that they decided they had to do something. Over images of dark, ominous skies, the ad suggested that gay marriage was a threat to freedom, faith, and children. "There's a storm gathering," one person featured in the ad states. "The clouds are dark and the winds are strong," says another. "And I am afraid," says a third.

"This is literally making me nauseous," Paul told Jeff.

Drawing on Paul's skill at making exercise videos, they gathered some friends and shot a homemade public service announcement. "We will weather this storm," the video said, but opponents of same-sex marriage were "using fear to cloud the truth."

One of the people in the video happened to be Chad and Kristina's realtor. Knowing only that they were interested in finding couples for a public service campaign, he made the introduction. Kristina and Chad met with the couple multiple times. Paul and Jeff were shocked by how much the two consultants knew about them; Chad even asked about Paul's previous roles in a few small art-house movies. After reassuring themselves that the films contained no nudity or other potentially embarrassing scenes, they finally filled the couple in on their plan to file a lawsuit.

Afterward, at the diner, the couple talked it over with Jeff's parents, who were visiting from New Jersey. They had been married for forty-one years, and they knew what it would mean to their son. "Just as long as you are safe," Jeff's mother said, grabbing their hands.

The consensus of the legal team was that the case would likely be decided fairly quickly; while no federal case like this one had ever been filed, all but one of the cases that had come before state courts had been decided based on legal motions alone, with no need for a trial. Chad and Kristina told the plaintiffs they would likely never have to testify.

By lunch's end, the two men had made up their minds. They weren't cops or bookstore owners. And they, like Sandy and Kris, were white. But they were willing.

The movie version of the story of how Olson decided upon his choice of Democratic co-counsel goes like this: Early on, in a flash of genius, he tells Rob Reiner he has the perfect candidate in mind—David Boies, a genial but ruthless trial lawyer and, in the *Bush v. Gore* election dispute, the man who represented Gore.

And indeed, that is the way the two men tell it. But in fact, Boies wasn't Olson's first, or even second, choice. Initially, Olson had wanted a Supreme Court specialist like himself, preferably someone the gay community knew and trusted.

The first person Olson approached was Paul Smith, an openly gay, savvy Supreme Court advocate, and the man who won *Lawrence v. Texas*. He was at his desk when Olson phoned, saying he wanted to talk to him in strict confidence. Smith, who had recently been asked to join the board of Lambda Legal, had to promise not to share what Olson was about to say with anyone in the movement.

Before filing the *Lawrence* case, Smith had analyzed what he thought was possible at the Supreme Court. Both Justice Kennedy and then-justice Sandra Day O'Connor had voted the right way in the *Romer* case. That gave him the courage to go forward.

But he hadn't argued that gays and lesbians ought to be considered a "suspect" or "quasi-suspect" class deserving of heightened scrutiny, as Olson was doing. It was, Smith had felt, too big an ask. The Supreme Court was clearly reluctant to create new suspect classes—it had last done so in the 1970s. And, perhaps more important, the justices liked to move incrementally. If heightened scrutiny applied, not only would the sodomy laws at issue in *Lawrence* likely fail to meet constitutional muster, but so too would policies such as Don't Ask, Don't Tell, banning gays and lesbians from openly serving in the military.

In the end the Court had wound up striking down sodomy laws in *Lawrence* without reaching the question of what standard of scrutiny should be applied to gays and lesbians. In the wake of that victory, Smith had entertained the idea of bringing a federal challenge to same-sex marriage bans. But, he told Olson, he ultimately decided against it after talking to a number of former Supreme Court clerks. There was a big difference in Kennedy's mind, they had told him, between telling a state it had no right to criminalize private sexual relationships and telling all fifty that there was no rational reason to refuse to legally sanction those relationships.

Olson disagreed, telling Smith he believed he could get Kennedy's vote. But the time to act was now, while Justice Stevens was still on the Court. Stevens, the leading member of the Court's liberal wing, was known to stop by Kennedy's chamber and chew over cases, a judicial courtship that Olson believed had given him a fair amount of influence with the Court's most unpredictable swing voter.

"We've got the right district in the right circuit with the right opponents at the right time," Olson would later say. "You gotta be willing to take chances. You can't be afraid to swing for the fences."

Smith hoped Olson was right. But he wasn't sure enough to sign on. It's just too risky, he told Olson, wishing him luck.

Another potential co-counsel whom Olson considered was Kathleen Sullivan, a constitutional law professor and litigator named by the *National Law Journal* as one of the most influential lawyers in the nation. She was a lesbian, and she had served as co-counsel on the losing side of the first, unsuccessful challenge to laws criminalizing sodomy, *Bowers v. Hardwick*.

Bringing her on board could help with the gay community in the short term, but Olson had to consider the long game. Justice David Souter was planning to retire at the end of the Court's term, and Sullivan was thought to be on President Obama's short list to replace him. If she joined the team and then was nominated and confirmed, she would have to recuse herself in the event the case reached the Supreme Court, which would make the odds of winning much steeper. So after an initial outreach, Olson reluctantly concluded he had to resume his search.

By May, he too was running out of time. Kristina and Chad had the plaintiffs, but he had yet to find co-counsel.

It was then that he hit on the idea to call Boies. In addition to representing Gore in the recount, Boies had successfully taken on goliaths such as Microsoft, was the go-to legal shark for some of Wall Street's most powerful players, and had represented everyone from Yankees owner George Steinbrenner to radio talk show host Don Imus.

Since the deadlocked election, the two men had formed a surprising friendship. As Boies put it, in all-consuming cases like that one, "there are only a few people you can really talk to—a few reporters, maybe your spouse, and the lawyers on the other side. They are the only ones who are as obsessed as you are."

They made for an odd pair, and not just because of their politics. Boies, lanky and balding, with a beaked nose that stopped just short of looking predatory, eschewed the type of bespoke suits and Prada shoes Olson favored, instead religiously wearing to court rumpled blue Lands' End suits, black Merrell sneakers, and a twenty-dollar Casio watch he strapped over his shirtsleeve. It was a cultivated everyman image that belied a lifestyle that afforded him private jets, a Manhattan pied-à-terre, and homes in places like the Turks and Caicos.

But the two lawyers soon found they had much in common, starting with a love of very expensive wine; Boies owned a vineyard in Lake County, California, while Olson's cellar was considered among the finest in the D.C. area. Both men were in their late sixties but had the energy of much younger men and, despite their wealth, showed no sign of slowing down.

Together with their wives and friends like former NBC anchor Tom Brokaw, they had begun taking annual bicycling trips through Europe. And while they generally avoided talking politics, their discussion of the legal issues of the day had convinced each that neither was the partisan they were made out to be. So when Democrats had held up Olson's appointment to become President Bush's solicitor general because of his role in the 2000 recount, Boies had called several senators he knew to personally vouch for his friend and lobby for his confirmation.

Boies had long admired Olson's ability to anticipate the questions that the justices were going to throw his way and strip the vulnerable points out of his argument before they pointed to them. Olson, for his part, was impressed with Boies's quick-footedness in a courtroom. His ability to rapidly digest complex subject matter was remarkable, especially given that he suffered from dyslexia. And, unlike Olson, he was a virtuoso at deposing and cross-examining hostile witnesses, a skill that could prove helpful in what Olson considered the unlikely event of a full-blown trial.

After securing Chad's and the Reiners' enthusiastic go-ahead—"Katie, bar the door!" Rob Reiner recalled saying of the marquee idea of having "both the winner and the loser of *Bush v. Gore* on my team"—Olson called Boies's firm on May 10, and the two connected a few days later.

The Democratic lawyer hadn't given much thought to the issue of gay marriage until he saw the long lines of same-sex couples waiting for hours to get married after San Francisco's mayor directed the city clerk to issue marriage licenses in 2004. He recalled gazing at the televised images and thinking, "Why shouldn't they get married?"

The case was perfect for Boies. Not only was it challenging legally, but its history-making potential and odd-couple story line was sure to garner a huge amount of press interest, and Boies "liked his column inches," as one person at his firm put it, almost as much as he liked to win.

"Let's do it," he told Olson, even agreeing to a deeply discounted fee that, at $250,000 plus expenses, represented a fraction of what Olson would be paid.

FIVE

GOING PUBLIC

Enrique Monagas, an associate at Olson's firm, could barely swallow as he nervously glanced over every few seconds at the clerk's window in San Francisco's federal courthouse, a stack of papers clutched in his hand.

It was May 22, 2009, the Friday before Memorial Day weekend. The team of lawyers that Olson had begun assembling to work on the Proposition 8 case had just gotten word that the California Supreme Court was going to issue its ruling on the last-ditch challenge to Proposition 8 following the long weekend.

Timing is everything, and Olson and Chad had put a lot of thought into when they should file their lawsuit. Olson, still worried about the prospect of other federal challenges to Proposition 8 jumping out ahead of theirs, did not want to wait to file until after the California Supreme Court had ruled. But Chad, the expert on messaging and news cycles, knew it would not look good to announce a federal lawsuit on behalf of same-sex couples before the state's high court had even ruled against them. The plan was to announce it with maximum fanfare directly after the ruling; it would be ruined if it dribbled out.

So they had sent Monagas, the youngest and least-known lawyer on the team, to the courthouse that day. He was under orders to slip the paperwork in just under the court's 3:30 P.M. filing deadline, with the hope that the court would close before the lawsuit could attract any media attention.

As he sat on a bench biding his time, Monagas thought about all that had brought him to this point. Born in Puerto Rico, he had pursued a career in theater design before deciding to study law. As a thirty-three-year-old fourth-year associate, he had never imagined he would be involved in a case of this import, much less one so personal.

That morning, in the San Francisco apartment he shared with his husband, Jason, Monagas had looked in on their eighteen-month-old daughter, Elisa, as she slept in her crib, blond curly hair damp and tousled. The two men had wed before Proposition 8 had passed and had been blessed to be able to quickly adopt. But they worried that Elisa would grow up in a world where their family was not universally accepted. If gays and lesbians were able to marry, Monagas thought, it would go a long way toward dispelling their concern.

As the 3:30 P.M. deadline for filing complaints drew closer, he grew increasingly antsy. The clerk seemed puzzled by his presence in the empty room, asking him several times if he needed help. "No, no, just waiting on an edit," he said, by way of an excuse. But when a few people sauntered into the room, threatening to form a line ahead of him just as the court was about to close, he leaped up and, scurrying around them, thrust the paperwork at the clerk.

"This must be an important filing," she said, bemused at his apparent agitation.

"I don't know—I haven't even read it," he quickly dissembled.

The clerk entered the case into her computer system, which randomly assigns cases to judges with the aim of ensuring equal caseloads. As she began stamping the paperwork, Monagas noticed the initials VRW and, grabbing his BlackBerry, e-mailed the rest of the team.

The case, he wrote, had been assigned to the chief judge of the U.S. district court, Vaughn R. Walker. The team had worried that it would go to someone whom critics could easily label a San Francisco liberal, which would diminish a victory at the trial level. But Judge Walker was a Republican appointee, first nominated to the bench by President Ronald Reagan.

Walker's nomination had been fiercely opposed by gay groups because of his representation of the U.S. Olympic Committee in a trademark suit that prevented a Bay Area group from calling its athletic competition the Gay Olympic Games. Walker, then in private practice, had managed to slap a lien on the home of the group's founder, who was at the time dying of AIDS, sparking outrage in the community. The groups had held up his nomination for so long that George H. W. Bush had become president by the time he won confirmation.

The Olympics case did not trouble Olson. Intellectual property was a complex area of the law, one that had nothing to do with where the judge might come down in a civil rights case. And on the bench, Walker had compiled a record as a bit of a maverick. While in some ways a law-and-order man, he had allowed reporters to watch all stages of the state's lethal injection executions. His record suggested that he did not think voters should always have the final say: He had overturned a San Francisco voter-approved limit on ATM fees.

He was tough and blunt, suggesting to one struggling lawyer in open court that acting lessons might help her performance, and in another case calling the city's attorney, chief of police, and district attorney on the carpet for failing to do enough to stop drug dealing and panhandling around his courthouse. He also had a libertarian streak that Olson particularly liked, having publicly called for the legalization of drugs.

"Very good draw—an independent thinker but widely respected," Matt McGill, a thirty-five-year-old new partner at Gibson Dunn, wrote back.

The team's stealth strategy worked: Word of the high-profile lawsuit did not leak before the California Supreme Court issued its decision on May 26. As expected, the court ruled that voters had properly amended the constitution to prohibit same-sex marriage. While the court let stand the eighteen thousand same-sex marriages that had already occurred, the window was now officially slammed shut to others. Protesters once again took to the streets, and within the gay community there was a sense of anguish that the end of the line had been reached.

But on the following day, there came a reed of hope.

═══

On May 27, standing in front of an array of American flags at the Biltmore Hotel in Los Angeles, Olson and Boies went public with their effort, announcing at a press conference that they had filed a federal lawsuit challenging the constitutionality of Proposition 8 on behalf of two same-sex couples. Flanking the lawyers were Chad and the freshly minted plaintiffs, Paul and Jeff and Kris and Sandy.

The week before the press conference, Monagas and another Gibson Dunn lawyer had escorted both couples to their local courthouses to file for a license. As expected, they were denied, giving them standing to sue. "Unfortunately, gentlemen, at this time I can't do that," the clerk at the teller window in Beverly Hills told Paul and Jeff. "But should circumstances change, come back to us."

Both had seized on her words, looking at one another. That's just what they were there to do: Change the circumstances. "We are going to plan your wedding in a couple of years—this is going to happen," Olson promised them just before the start of the press conference.

Now, introducing the two couples, Olson declared that California voters, in amending the state constitution, had discriminated against gay men and lesbians simply because they had "the temerity to wish to express their love and commitment to one another by getting married."

Boies, whom Olson had introduced to the plaintiffs just before the start of the press conference, had nearly missed the event altogether. Chad had gotten word from his office the day before that he would not be there but might be able to appear via satellite. Chad was furious. The whole point, he had argued, was for the two lawyers to stand side by side, the very picture of bipartisanship.

Somehow Boies had managed to get himself to California, and now he played up the odd-couple story line that had, as predicted, packed the room with reporters and would land the press conference on the front page of the *New York Times* the following day. "Mr. Olson and I are from different ends of the political spectrum, but we are fighting this case together because Proposition 8 clearly and fundamentally violates the freedoms guaranteed to all of us by the Constitution," he said.

But it was Olson whose raw emotion stole the show. "These are our neighbors, coworkers, teachers, friends, and family," he thundered. "Whatever discrimination California law now might permit, I can assure you, the United States Constitution does not."

Watching the press conference from his computer at home in Brentwood, Rob Reiner turned to his wife. "I started crying," he recalled. "We were saying, 'Can you believe we've done this?'"

That afternoon, the clerk in San Francisco federal court, as was her habit, dropped the pile of complaints that had been assigned to Judge Walker over the last week on his desk. As he leisurely leafed through them, the name *Perry v. Schwarzenegger* jumped out.

The judge had not seen the press conference with Kris Perry and the other plaintiffs. Who was suing the governor of California? he wondered, plucking the case out of the pile.

It didn't take more that a few paragraphs for him to grasp the significance. "Oh shit," he thought.

The legal team's initial quick scrub of Judge Walker's record had, the lawyers believed, given them a pretty good handle on Walker's judicial philosophy. But by now they knew it had overlooked a salient fact about his private life: The judge who was to preside over their case was himself gay.

But that was not what was giving the judge pause. He had hoped to retire by the end of the year, after the resolution of a slew of complicated national security cases involving the government's counterterrorism surveillance policies currently pending before him. Unless he could find a way to get rid of *Perry v. Schwarzenegger,* that plan was about to blow up. The only legitimate way he could duck the case was to tell the court he had a conflict of interest, and that, Judge Walker quickly determined, wasn't warranted in this case.

The sixty-five-year-old judge had long struggled with the question of when and how to come out. He had grown up in a rock-ribbed Republican town in rural Illinois, and graduated at the top of his class at Stanford Law School. He did not believe he could reach the pinnacle of his career if it were widely known that he was gay.

"You think that you can't be yourself and live the life you want to live," he said.

So, much like Chad, he had for years sublimated his sexuality to the rest of his life. He was handsome in a patrician way, with luminous green eyes, a dry wit, and a gentleman's manners. Women liked him, and over the years he had some faux romances. He was not unhappy, but the pretending took a toll; not only was his own existence bound up in a lie, but he was stringing along decent women, whom he liked.

"When you are not able to be yourself and have the kind of relationship you consider fulfilling," he said, "there's this element of dishonesty and deception."

It wasn't until he was in his late thirties that he had his first relationship with a man. It had felt so different, so right, that he began considering coming out, to hell with the consequences. But then, in 1982, along came the Gay Olympics case. If he had said he was gay at that point, he felt he would have been vouching for his client, something he believed good lawyers should not do.

Soon after that came his nomination to the bench. Some of his friends told him that the FBI had asked them about his sexuality as part of his background check, but no one at the Reagan Justice Department ever confronted him directly. Given that there wasn't a single "out" federal judge at the time, who knew how such a disclosure might complicate his nomination?

And so he had stayed mum, even having one more faux romance with a woman. They had fun, rode horses together. But when she broke things off after he kept putting off the question of marriage, he knew that she would be his last girlfriend. By his own, somewhat rueful admission, "I was no gay rights pioneer."

Over the years, though, as he grew more comfortable on the bench, he began to live a little more openly. He stopped worrying about waking up to a newspaper article outing him. He could occasionally be found at the Lone Star Saloon, a gay bar. Then he fell in love. While he never made any big public announcement about his sexual orientation, he and his partner of many years, a physician, were often spotted together at social events and even court conferences.

Judges are required to disqualify themselves in cases where they have a nonfinancial but "substantial" interest in the outcome, or in cases where their "impartiality might reasonably be questioned." Walker did not think he met that test for several reasons.

He would later tell friends that he had never even discussed marriage with his partner. And when the window briefly opened in California, he had not given the idea of marrying him any real consideration. Given DOMA, it made no financial or estate planning sense, and he was quite happy with things as they were.

Besides, he figured, even if he did want to marry someday, the courts had held that a judge is not disqualified from hearing a case just because he or she shares a fundamental characteristic with a litigant and stands to benefit from the outcome in the same way as general members of the public. African American judges hear race discrimination cases all the time, while female judges hear cases charging gender bias, he thought. Why shouldn't a gay man hear the challenge to Proposition 8?

———

Arriving back at his office in Washington from the press conference, Olson found his in-box flooded with accusatory and at times hateful e-mail: "A disgraceful betrayal of the legal principles you purported to stand for," read one message. "Homo," read another.

Colleagues were kinder, but many remained bewildered. Up until this point, the highest-profile supporter of gay marriage was former vice president Dick Cheney, whose daughter was a lesbian, and even he said it should be left up to the states. Was someone in Olson's family gay? The answer to that question—no—led some to whisper disparagingly that it must be the influence of Olson's new wife, Lady, a beautiful blond Kentucky-born tax lawyer and self-confessed liberal whom he had married in 2006.

Longtime law firm partner Doug Cox, a fellow conservative, was dismayed that he had been kept in the dark about the plans to place the firm in the middle of a battle he did not support. Former judge Robert Bork, a dear friend of Olson's who had written that "radical" court-ordered gay marriages constitute a "judicial sin," couldn't bear to talk to him about the case.

"I don't want to get into an argument," he said. "But I'd like to know why."

At the annual Federalist Society lunch, Olson kept his tradition of delivering a conservative red-meat roundup of the just-concluded Supreme Court term. But there was a palpable sense of discomfort in the room about the just-filed Proposition 8 case. Olson may have wanted to keep one foot planted in the conservative circles that had long been his ideological home, but it was clear as he made his rounds that his decision to step so far outside its doctrinal orthodoxy was going to come at some personal and professional cost.

When it comes to interpreting the Constitution, there are two distinct schools of thought. One school sees it as a living, breathing document, in which rights that are not explicitly enumerated may be found. The Federalist Society is an incubator for the other school. The substantive due process right to privacy that led the Court to strike down first laws prohibiting contraception and abortion and later the antisodomy law at issue in the *Lawrence* case that Olson was relying upon? Made up out of whole cloth. Judges should stick to the Constitution's actual text, and to what the framers intended.

To many adherents of this school, it bordered on the absurd to believe that the authors of the Fourteenth Amendment to the Constitution, which added the equal protection clause and was passed in the wake of the Civil War in order to confer citizenship on freed slaves, would someday intend for it to be used to force states to marry same-sex couples. Justices had a hard enough time using it to invalidate race-based school segregation in the *Brown v. Board of Education* decision, given that it was ratified by the same Congress that had segregated schools in the District of Columbia; Justice Robert H. Jackson, in a draft opinion, summed up that Court's struggle when he wrote that however abhorrent he found segregation, "layman as well as lawyer must query how it is that the Constitution this morning forbids what for three-quarters of a century it has tolerated or approved."

What was so perplexing and, for many conservative lawyers at the Federalist Society luncheon, controversial about Olson's involvement in the same-sex marriage fight was that, as conservative law professor Orin Kerr charged on his blog, Olson was now making the "same kinds of constitutional arguments that he has specialized in ridiculing for so long," relying on case law and legal theories he had critiqued in that very forum.

"Those who have watched Olson's annual Supreme Court Roundups for the Federalist Society know how harsh Olson tends to be about judges who Olson thinks are constitutionalizing their policy views, especially when that means constitutionalizing social policies popular among elites," Kerr wrote. "Olson hasn't just been critical of those who take a broad view of constitutional meaning in this setting: he has been dismissive and sometimes even brutal."

But not a single person at the lunch even mentioned the Proposition 8 case to him, save for an oblique ribbing by David Bossie. In the bifurcated world he now inhabited, Olson was representing Bossie, the president of a conservative advocacy group called Citizens United, in a case involving a scathing documentary about Hillary Rodham Clinton that challenged campaign finance limits put in place by Congress. After pecking Lady on the cheek, Bossie looked over at her husband and drily said, "I'm not going to kiss you, even though apparently you wouldn't mind."

Seated at Olson's table to his right was Robert McConnell, one of his oldest friends. The two men had worked together in the Reagan Justice Department, and shortly before filing the lawsuit Olson had taken McConnell aside at a dinner party to give him a heads-up and solicit his views. McConnell, a practicing Catholic, told Olson that as a religious matter he believed marriage ought to be reserved for two people who can procreate.

Olson, who was not a regular churchgoer, replied that while he respected McConnell's conviction, he saw it as a civil rights issue. He then began to elaborate on his view that religious beliefs were insufficient legal justification for the government to refuse to recognize same-sex marriage, but soon paused. "You don't agree with me, do you?" Olson asked. The conversation was never resumed.

The litigation was not going over any better in the gay rights community. Another lawsuit, challenging the provision in DOMA that denied legally married same-sex couples federal benefits had been filed two months earlier. Its author, Mary Bonauto of the Gay & Lesbian Advocates & Defenders, was enormously respected within the gay rights legal community—her victories included the landmark state court case that in 2004 made Massachusetts the first state in the country to recognize same-sex marriage—and she had spent years convincing movement colleagues that a DOMA challenge was a winnable first step toward nationwide marriage equality. But even she had encountered skepticism about bringing a case in federal court. As she would later put it, "when we filed, there were some who were still opposed, still uncomfortable and holding their breath, though there were many more who had come around to the idea that this was not just bold, but doable."

As bold as the DOMA challenge was, the case challenging Proposition 8, with its demand that the courts immediately recognize the far broader right of same-sex couples to marry in states that currently banned such unions, was bolder still, and its authors had none of Bonauto's cred. All the leading groups issued a joint press release calling the Proposition 8 lawsuit ill timed and ill advised. Conspiracy theories abounded that Olson had taken the case to sabotage it. Nan Hunter, founder of the ACLU's LGBT Project, told reporters that a very careful, collaborative strategy had been tossed out the window by "a small number of people who are wealthy enough to pay for a major litigation effort."

Chad and Bruce Cohen redoubled their efforts to bring the groups around. Olson did his part too, with limited success. He phoned in from a bicycling trip in Provence to listen to the concerns of leaders like Kate Kendall, the executive director of the National Center for Lesbian Rights. Olson told her that he hadn't gotten as far as he had by taking on losing causes, and he added an emotional personal note: "This may well be the most important fight I have ever been a part of in my life."

Kendall was convinced of his commitment, even though she remained concerned about the timing. "By the power vested in me, I am anointing you an honorary lesbian," she joked at the end of the conversation.

"It is a badge I will wear with pride and honor," he replied.

SIX

"PROVE IT"

David Boies was sitting at the bar of the Millennium Hilton hotel in New York City, having just finished preparing for the next day's testimony in a complicated trial involving the insurance giant AIG, when an aide handed him Judge Walker's first order in the case. It was June 30, 2009, a little over a month after the lawsuit had been filed.

Olson and Boies had asked the court to issue a preliminary injunction prohibiting the state from enforcing Proposition 8, which would have the effect of allowing same-sex couples to begin marrying again while the court considered the legal issues at hand.

Injunctive relief of the type the plaintiffs were requesting is given in cases where it can be established that their constitutional claim has merit and that continued enforcement of the law under challenge would cause real harm. Judge Walker tabled the request, on the grounds that he did not want to inject more confusion into California's already confusing marital landscape by allowing weddings to resume before the legal questions were definitively resolved.

Whichever way he ruled, his word would likely not be the final one. The losing party would appeal his decision to the Ninth Circuit Court of Appeals, charged with reviewing the judgments of federal district and bankruptcy courts in nine states and two U.S. territories. Depending on that outcome, it seemed likely that the Supreme Court would be the ultimate arbiter, assuming it decided to hear the case. If Walker or some subsequent court were to rule against the plaintiffs and uphold Proposition 8, marriages performed while the case made its way through the federal court system could be rendered invalid. California had already been down that road before, when San Francisco mayor Gavin Newsom had unilaterally decided to hand out licenses to same-sex couples, and the state did not need a repeat.

But in a passage Boies found quite heartening, Judge Walker said that the legal filings in the case so far "may well suffice to establish a serious question" as to the constitutionality of Proposition 8. The judge particularly singled out the fact that the state had refused to defend the initiative. It was not an outcome that the team had left entirely to chance. The two named defendants in the lawsuit were Republican governor Schwarzenegger and Democratic attorney general Jerry Brown, the state officials charged with enforcing Prop 8.

Kristina had back-channeled a request to the governor using connections she had made through her client, California's first lady, Maria Shriver. If he couldn't support the lawsuit, would he at least say nothing? "Just play dead," she had begged. But the governor did her one better, suggesting in a court filing declining to defend it that Proposition 8 raised serious constitutional questions. Brown for his part unambiguously declared that it was unconstitutional.

Over his years in office, Schwarzenegger's position on same-sex marriage had evolved. Following his veto of a bill that would have legislatively legalized the practice, he had begun talking to gay staff members, friends, and, most important, his wife. Unbeknownst to the public, he had presided over the marriage of two of his closest gay staffers, and had offered to marry a third, Daniel Zingale, a senior adviser to the governor and chief of staff to the first lady, during the window in which it was legal. Zingale had kept the marriages confidential, but confided to Chad and Kristina that the governor was better on the issue than they knew.

Paging through the judge's order over a tall screwdriver—during trials he limited himself to a maximum of three and kept track by placing the straws in his shirt pocket—Boies picked up his cell and called Olson, who was in California for a July 2 hearing in the case.

In advance of that hearing, supporters of Proposition 8 had filed briefs arguing that allowing gays and lesbians to marry could destabilize the institution of marriage, and that a married mother and father provided the optimal child-rearing environment. Olson, for his part, had asserted that there was no reason to believe that allowing gays and lesbians to marry would harm traditional marriage. Prop 8, he argued, had been motivated by nothing more than animus—unconstitutional prejudice—toward gay people.

But Walker decided that neither side had provided sufficient evidence for their claims. "Prove it," he would later recall thinking. In his order, the judge signaled his intention to hold a full-blown trial, and he listed questions that the parties should be prepared to answer.

The team had always known that this was a possibility, and Walker's order was not unprecedented. The landmark *Romer* case had begun with a trial. Citing the evidence that had been presented, the district court rejected arguments that the Colorado initiative was justified because including gays and lesbians in antidiscrimination laws could lead married individuals to "choose" to become homosexual.

But up to now, the state courts that had considered same-sex marriage had come to their conclusions based largely on legal arguments alone, so the order came as something of a surprise. If Walker held to his plan, the public would hear evidence and actual testimony on issues such as the intent and effect of Proposition 8, the history of discrimination against gays and lesbians, the history and purpose of marriage, the science of sexuality, and whether excluding gays and lesbians from marriage promotes the well-being of children.

"I don't know what your view is," Boies told Olson as he signaled a hotel waiter for another round, "but I rather like this opinion."

―――――

Terry Stewart was worried. As San Francisco's chief deputy city attorney, she had been one of the lead lawyers in the California Supreme Court case that briefly legalized same-sex marriage.

She would have killed for the type of trial that Walker was proposing. The judge was offering Olson a golden opportunity to put prejudice on trial, by calling expert witnesses and cross-examining opponents of same-sex marriage. Even more important, he was giving Olson a chance to bulletproof his case before it got to the Supreme Court. Appeals courts, which review the decisions of lower courts, do not hear from witnesses or relitigate evidence. They are supposed to defer to a trial judge's factual findings and limit their review to whether the law was correctly applied, meaning that later courts would be forced to contend with whatever Judge Walker decided the evidence showed when it came to issues like whether sexuality is changeable or what motivated Proposition 8.

But Olson, unlike Boies, was not initially keen on the idea of a trial. Olson wanted to reach the nation's high court as quickly as possible, and a trial would slow them down. "Every day that Proposition 8 is enforced perpetuates a tragic injustice on tens of thousands of Californians, including, specifically, the plaintiffs who are here, today, before you," he protested at the July 2 hearing.

In Olson's view, the case could be decided on an expedited basis simply by looking to the Constitution and applying Supreme Court precedent. Walker, however, had other ideas.

There were questions not just of law, but of fact that needed to be resolved, the judge said.

"This is a trial court, this is not the Supreme Court of the United States where we deal with these boxcar philosophical issues," the judge said. "We deal with facts; we deal with evidence; we deal with the testimony of witnesses."

"I'm reasonably sure, given the issues involved and given the personnel that are in the courtroom, that this case is only touching down in this court, that it will have a life after this court, and what happens here, in many ways, is only a prelude to what is going to happen later," Walker continued. "Our job, in this case, at this point, is to make a record."

Olson then made a suggestion for streamlining the trial proceedings, one that made Stewart particularly uneasy.

When the governor and the state had refused to defend Proposition 8, Judge Walker had allowed the proponents of Proposition 8, who had gathered the signatures to put the initiative on the ballot on behalf of a campaign called "ProtectMarriage.com," to do so as intervenors in the case. Their lawyer was Chuck Cooper. He was an old friend of Olson's from back in their days in the Reagan Justice Department and had succeeded him as head of the Office of Legal Counsel.

Olson had pulled Cooper aside just before the start of the hearing to privately suggest that they jointly oppose Walker's trial plan. "We don't want to have some Scopes monkey trial here, do we?" Cooper recalled Olson saying, a reference to the famous 1925 case in which the then controversial theory of evolution was debated by two famed lawyers of the day. When it became clear the judge would not be deterred, Olson had suggested in more diplomatic language that perhaps he and Cooper could stipulate to some of the facts at issue in order to move things along. "That might help to narrow the issues upon which there then might have to be expert testimony," Olson told the judge.

Stewart was appalled by Olson's suggestion. Cooper had defended Hawaii's right to ban same-sex marriage in state courts there. And he had written a brief in the *Romer* case defending the constitutionality of the Colorado initiative that prohibited municipalities from including gays and lesbians in their antidiscrimination laws. Any offer of cooperation by Cooper, Stewart thought, could not possibly be good for the case.

Gibson Dunn, Olson's firm, had already asked the city of San Francisco to file an amicus brief, a legal argument filed by a party not directly involved but with an interest in a case. Stewart had readily agreed. Whatever the establishment gay rights groups thought about Olson's lawsuit, what was done was done. It was imperative that he succeeded.

Now, worried about the direction the case was taking, she wanted to advocate for a larger role. Following the hearing where Olson and Cooper had suggested limiting the facts in dispute, she went to see her boss, City Attorney Dennis Herrera. He looked up as she came in, a five-foot-three whirlwind in a dark pantsuit, with short white-blond hair and preppy glasses. Stewart tended to convey urgency in breathlessly fast sentences, one tumbling over the next. Forget the amicus brief, she said. We need to file a motion now, asking that the city of San Francisco be made a party to the case. That would give her and Herrera a far greater say in charting the course of the trial.

"They need our help," she said, "even if they don't know it."

Herrera, a jovial politician well liked by both the city's gay community and its more conservative Catholic population, agreed to reach out to Chad, whom he knew well. He had been the one who hired Chad and Kristina to help fight Proposition 8 in the waning days of the campaign, paying them out of his own political coffers because he felt that the people in charge of the official "No on 8" campaign were running it into the ground. The city, he told Chad when he reached him, wanted to intervene in the case, and allowing that to happen could help Chad with a problem of his own.

After publicly questioning the wisdom of AFER's legal strategy, the American Civil Liberties Union, Lambda Legal, and the National Center for Lesbian Rights now wanted to be made parties to the case as well. "We think it will be very helpful to Judge Walker and the ultimate resolution of the questions in the case for the litigation to have the benefit of the community in all of its diversity," Lambda's Jenny Pizer, explaining the motion they had filed with the court, told reporters.

Kristina had never seen Chad so furious. By this time, a real us-versus-them mentality had taken hold. After everything that Lambda Legal and the other groups had done to trash their case, now they wanted in? When Chad got angry, his southern accent became more pronounced, and he was in a full-on drawl as he shouted from his office, "We're screwed."

It was also the last thing Olson wanted. The team was going to have a hard enough time winning. A united front was needed, not infighting and second guessing. But what could they do? Chad had already shifted gears to try to deal with this unpleasant new reality when Kristina slowed him down. These groups already hate us, she reminded him. What do we have to lose by going to war to try to shut their motion down?

She was right, Chad thought. Together, they crafted a tough response.

"You have unrelentingly and unequivocally acted to undermine this case, even before it was filed," Chad charged in a letter to the three groups he released to the press. "In light of this, it is inconceivable that you would zealously and effectively litigate this case if you were successful in intervening."

But it was anyone's guess what Walker might do. Judges often like to hear from a number of parties. Why not back San Francisco's bid, Herrera asked Chad, as a way to look reasonable? Stewart, his deputy, had the expertise. She already had a list of experts in the fields of sociology, sexuality, and history whose testimony could help convince the court that gays and lesbians suffered real harm from being deprived of the ability to marry. Plus, she was a lesbian who enjoyed a good working relationship with the established gay rights legal community; having her join a team that at the moment consisted of two straight men might ease the groups' concerns.

"I can help give you cover," Herrera recalled saying. "You can say that we oppose all interveners, but if you are going to let someone in, let San Francisco in."

The strategy worked. On August 19, Judge Walker granted the city's motion to join the case but denied everyone else's. Stewart immediately began funneling the team the names of expert witnesses whom she had cited in her California Supreme Court case, as well as experts used in the other state court cases challenging marriage bans. The Gibson Dunn team seemed appreciative of the help. But Stewart found the unflagging confidence of some of her new cohorts off-putting.

During the California Supreme Court proceedings, she had devoted every spare moment to the case. It was as though she carried in her briefcase the pain of the entire gay community. She was so worried about letting people down that it wasn't until after she had won that she even considered what it might mean for her personally.

A reporter from the *San Jose Mercury News* had called for comment, asking whether she would now marry her longtime partner, Carole Scagnetti. She had burst into tears. "I realized I had been holding it all at bay because I didn't want to dare to hope for the unattainable."

Watching that victory be snatched back by the voters had sapped some of her belief in the system. On election night, she and Carole had spoken to their daughter, Tasha, who was attending college at Mount Holyoke. As an African American, Tasha had been thrilled by Obama's historic election. They had taken Tasha in when she was in eighth grade, becoming her legal guardians the following year, and they were proud of the poised young woman she had become. They tried to share in her celebratory mood, but it was difficult. Black voters had flocked to the polls in record numbers to elect the first black president, but a majority had also supported Proposition 8. Both women cried before drifting off to sleep that night.

In a contemplative moment shortly after the case was filed, Stewart pulled aside one of the Gibson Dunn lawyers assigned to it, Chris Dusseault.

"What if we lose?" she recalled asking.

"That's why they hire us, to take the tough cases," he replied.

Stewart held her tongue, because Dusseault seemed nice enough, and as a straight white guy, she figured he had never faced any real prejudice.

"But I thought, 'This isn't some big antitrust case, asshole. These are real people.'"

Cooper had begged Judge Walker to throw out Olson's lawsuit, arguing that the Supreme Court had already had the final say on same-sex marriage when in 1972 it declined to review a lower court's finding that Minnesota could rightfully deny gay couples marriage licenses in a case called *Baker v. Nelson*. Instead, Walker set a fast-track schedule that had Cooper scrambling to find experts willing to testify at a three-week trial set to begin on January 11, 2010, only months away.

A courtly man with blue eyes, elfin ears, and the smooth flushed cheeks of a child just in from the cold, Cooper spoke in what *Washington Post* columnist Mary McGrory once described as a "kind of Victorian copybook prose, ever seeking the elegant variation for the blunt." Over breakfast in Dupont Circle one day in September, he wondered aloud how he could possibly juggle a major constitutional case like *Perry v. Schwarzenegger* with all his other obligations.

Cooper had a twelve-member firm with a single office in Washington, D.C. Between Olson's and Boies's firms there were nearly three times that number working on the case, in offices in Washington, New York, Los Angeles, and San Francisco. And besides the *Perry* case, Cooper was suing Duke University and the city of Durham on behalf of thirty-eight university lacrosse players who had been falsely accused of rape, representing former attorney general John Ashcroft against torture allegations connected to Bush administration counterterror interrogation techniques, Boeing in a multibillion-dollar dispute over the awarding of a government contract, and defending a Michigan law barring race-conscious admissions policies at state universities.

"We've been on a Bataan death march," he complained, running a hand through white hair that looked Brylcreemed into its precise 1930s-style part. "It's unbelievable to be trying this case in less than five months—I've never seen anything like it. It's a grueling schedule for both sides really, but I think for my side in particular."

In Cooper's mind, same-sex marriage simply was not a federal issue, but rather one that should be left to the people and their representatives. That summer, legislatures in New Hampshire, Maine, and Vermont had passed same-sex marriage, bringing the total number of states allowing gays and lesbians to marry to six.

"If the state of Vermont's decision to legalize gay marriage were challenged, I'd defend it too," he said. "I don't understand why extremes on both sides insist on seeing this issue in terms of good and evil."

But even some members of his own family did not agree with his position in the Proposition 8 case—"With six kids, there's a variety of opinions on this issue," he said—and he felt he was getting killed in the media.

Gay marriage opponents weren't making his job any easier. Cooper's strategy hinged on convincing one person—Justice Kennedy—that the bulk of the people who had voted for Prop 8 bore no animus toward gay people. But a group called the Campaign for California Families had attempted to intervene in the case, making arguments that Justice Kennedy could well find offensive. The group claimed that Cooper was conceding too much by acknowledging, for instance, that gays and lesbians could form "lasting, committed relationships" and that "same-sex sexual orientation doesn't result in any impairment of judgment."

Judge Walker, at Cooper's request, had denied the group's motion to intervene. He then called the remaining parties—Cooper, Olson, and the city of San Francisco—together for a case management hearing. It was scheduled to take place in four weeks, on October 14 in San Francisco.

In advance of the hearing, Cooper had managed to file a voluminous 117-page brief. He reckoned he and Olson would remain friends even after the lawsuit had reached its conclusion. But he charged that Olson was calling for a "radical redefinition of the ancient institution of marriage" completely unconnected to rights spelled out in the Constitution. The due process clause, he said, "specially protects those fundamental rights and liberties *which are objectively deeply rooted in the nation's history and tradition.*" That could hardly be said of same-sex marriage, he argued.

Next he turned to *Lawrence v. Texas.* That case dealt with the criminalization of private sexual behavior, not the state's affirmative duty to recognize a marriage, he argued. And while gays and lesbians may once have been the victims of persecution, he wrote, today they formed a powerful political constituency.

The court, as a result, should not apply heightened scrutiny, and should only determine whether there was any rational reason for California voters to have done what they did. That interest, he concluded, was clear: The state was in the marriage business to "channel naturally procreative sexual activity between men and women into stable, enduring unions," thereby reducing the number of children born out of wedlock. With that goal in mind, the state was not unconstitutionally treating similarly situated people differently, he said, because same-sex couples were not similarly situated in that they cannot accidentally impregnate one another.

But as the hearing got under way, Cooper quickly found himself in Judge Walker's crosshairs.

"Well, the last marriage that I performed, Mr. Cooper, involved a groom who was ninety-five, and the bride was eighty-three," said the judge, the smile under his neat gray goatee serving to emphasize his amusement. "I did not demand that they prove that they intended to engage in procreative activity. Now, was I missing something?"

"No, Your Honor, you weren't. Of course you didn't," Cooper replied.

"And I might say it was a very happy relationship," Judge Walker said in his deep baritone.

"I rejoice to hear that," Cooper responded, before trying to move on.

Olson, who had watched the exchange with delight, wasn't quite ready to let him. "My mother was married three years ago," he volunteered when given the chance. "And she, at the time, was eighty-seven and married someone who was the same age."

Judge Walker moved on to another point. If the state's interest was to try to ensure that biological mothers and fathers marry and raise their children together, it wasn't working very well, he said. "I don't want to base any decisions on what I hear on the radio coming to court in the morning, but there was some statistic that 40 percent—can this be right?—40 percent of female pregnancies in the United States are to unwed females."

Cooper, figuring he had been given a lifeline, argued that statistics like that show why the state needs to nurture the institution of marriage.

"Well, let's assume I agree with you that's an unfortunate phenomenon," Judge Walker countered. "How does that convert to a constitutional standard?"

The judge put Olson on the spot as well, drilling him on whether he had brought the case too soon. What about the point that "Mr. Cooper made repeatedly and very ably," Walker asked. Why not let the political process play out, given that states are starting to recognize same-sex marriage? "Aren't you just getting ahead of yourself?"

"Well, that would be exactly the same argument that was made and was rejected in *Loving versus Virginia*," Olson replied, referring to the 1967 Supreme Court case striking down interracial marriage bans. "We don't say to people in this country, 'Wait until the population agrees that your constitutional rights can be recognized.'"

Olson had a point; when the landmark *Loving* decision was handed down, Gallup polling showed that nearly 75 percent of voters disapproved of interracial marriage. But this was tricky ground, because in 1967 interracial marriage was permitted in the majority of states, something that could not be said of same-sex marriage today.

"Let's talk about rational basis," the judge said. "Mr. Cooper argues very effectively that if Proposition 8 is assessed under the rational basis standard, then there is a rational basis in the tradition and history of opposite-sex marriage. Why isn't he absolutely correct?"

"Because he's asking the wrong question," Olson said. "He's saying, 'Is there a rational basis for [encouraging] opposite-sex couples to get married?' Of course there's a rational basis for that." The correct question, Olson said, was what state purpose was rationally served by the decision to *exclude* same-sex couples from the institution of marriage.

"Assume I agree with you that the state's interest in marriage is essentially procreative, as you've put it," Walker asked Cooper. "What is the harm to the procreative purpose or function of marriage that you outline of permitting same-sex marriage?"

Cooper tried a number of answers, including that the question wasn't legally relevant, before the judge cut him off.

"I'm asking you to tell me how it would harm opposite-sex couples."

"All right," Cooper replied.

"All right," Walker repeated. "Let's play on the same playing field for once. Okay?"

"Your Honor, my answer is, I don't know. I don't know."

Walker was stunned. How could Cooper not have anticipated the question? States had to have a reason when they discriminate. "I don't know" didn't seem much of a rationale to him.

Judges are not supposed to be strategists. But old habits die hard, and as an old trial attorney himself, Walker's instinct was to leave well enough alone when a party made a damaging admission like that one. "I'm going to let that answer sit," he recalled thinking. "But I was flabbergasted."

What Cooper actually meant to say, and tried to clarify a few moments later, was that because same-sex marriage was still a relatively new phenomenon in the United States, it was rational for Californians to want to wait and see what, if any, effect it might have on traditional marriage.

But as soon as the words "I don't know" left his mouth, the damage was done. The Associated Press reporter jumped out of his seat and ran out of the room to update his story.

Sitting in the first row, Chad couldn't believe his luck. If he had anything to do with it—and he did—Cooper was going to relive this moment repeatedly in the coming months as the case headed to trial and beyond.

"I'm going to hang him," he vowed to himself, "with those words."

SEVEN

WHERE'S DAVID?

T he team began to assemble for the trial two and a half months later in San Francisco, in the gleaming modern office tower overlooking the Bay Bridge that housed Gibson Dunn's San Francisco office. More than forty people, many of whom had never met one another, were now working furiously on the case, prepping witnesses, reading and rereading relevant Supreme Court cases, rushing back and forth to court on last-minute pretrial motions, and preparing for a media onslaught.

In a makeshift war room on the thirtieth floor on January 8, 2010, Chad and Kristina briefed the political operatives they had hired to staff the public education end of the operation. The omens in recent weeks had not been heartening. Voters in Maine had overruled their legislature, repealing the law legalizing same-sex marriage in that state before it had even had a chance to go into effect, while New York and New Jersey state lawmakers had rejected legislation to allow gays and lesbians to marry in those states. Nationally, polls put public support for same-sex marriage at only between 37 to 40 percent.

Which made their goal all the more audacious: to flip public opinion on same-sex marriage from majority opposed to majority support by the time the case reached the U.S. Supreme Court, in the hope that a more hospitable political climate would make the justices feel more comfortable ruling their way. Everything they did, Kristina instructed, needed to be coordinated with the lawyers, with that single guiding principle in mind.

"Ultimately, we know that we have an audience of nine," she explained. "Ted told us from the beginning that as much as people think that Supreme Court justices live in this rarefied world, they read the papers and they have conversations about the news with their friends, and all of that affects their thinking."

Television images from the trial would shape the way both the court and the public viewed their cause, and to that end boxes filled with two thousand American flags were stacked around the perimeter of the conference room, to be handed out at a vigil gay rights groups had planned for opening day. The colors of the rainbow may have been embraced as a symbol by the movement, but Chad wanted something that evoked more traditional values.

On the long rectangular table around which they had all gathered, empty soda cans, stale coffee, junk food, and laptops fought for space, giving the room the disheveled air of a campaign headquarters on election eve. On a whiteboard, Kristina had outlined everyone's duties.

Adam Umhoefer, as senior project director, was charged with overseeing the nuts and bolts of the operation, responsible for everything from donor outreach to the plaintiffs' security and the ambitious social media effort planned for Twitter and Facebook. With pale blue eyes, windswept brown hair, and the barest hint of scruff on a face Botticelli might have painted, he was often mistaken for a model. But at twenty-eight, he had built an impressive political résumé, coordinating political and philanthropic giving for movie moguls Steven Spielberg and Jeffrey Katzenberg, and joining AFER as a senior project director fresh off a stint as an Obama campaign organizer in Montana.

Amanda Crumley, a blond thirty-year-old national Democratic consultant from Arkansas who had worked with Chad in the Clinton White House, and Yusef Robb, a California campaign veteran who worked for him now as communications director for Griffin Schake, rounded out the core group.

Crumley would focus on building a national progressive mailing list for the group—the one Hillary Clinton used in her 2008 presidential campaign "is going to fall off the truck and into my e-mail box any minute," she reported. Her other task was to cultivate national editorial boards and columnists, with the goal of moving the nation's elite opinion makers firmly into their camp.

Robb, who reveled in his reputation as an operative willing to go for the jugular in political bouts, would serve as the team's rapid response man, the perfect role for someone whose first response to an opponent's spin was often to say something like, "We need to shoot that shit down!"

So far the coverage had been overwhelmingly positive. An essay written by Olson, "The Conservative Case for Gay Marriage," had made the cover of *Newsweek*. "Prepare the tweet," Adam joked as it went live. The team was also about to announce additions to the AFER board that would bolster its bipartisan civil rights credentials: The chairman of the conservative Cato Institute, the chairman of the liberal Center for American Progress, and the immediate past chairman of the National Association for the Advancement of Colored People (NAACP) had all agreed to serve as advisory members and would soon be deployed to write op-eds and act as surrogates on television.

But working in the besieged Clinton White House had taught Chad several political maxims: Never let a challenge go unanswered, and if you want to fight for something and win, you need to go on the offensive.

"Two things should be given to every reporter," he instructed the group. The first: "Cooper's foolish statement that he doesn't know the harm," or as Chad had taken to calling it, "the Cooper Blooper." The second: a press release issued that very morning by the National Organization for Marriage, the driving force behind Proposition 8, that "we do not expect to win at trial level."

"Cooper should have to answer those two questions every time they are in an interview."

"That goes to another thing," Crumley said. When it came to hitting the other side, how negative did Chad want to go? "Do we want to be up here?" She raised her hand above her head.

"Yes," Chad replied.

"So leave others to do the punch back?"

"Yes."

———

Shortly before noon, Ted Boutrous burst into the war room with news from the courthouse: Dr. Hak-Shing William Tam, one of the five official Proposition 8 proponents who had been granted status to defend the initiative in lieu of the state, had just filed an emergency motion asking to withdraw from the case.

By now, the Gibson Dunn offices were a frenzy of activity. Stories previewing the trial were beginning to post online, lawyers were frenetically scurrying about, and the whole place hummed with anticipation as the hours ticked down to trial.

"Breaking news!" Boutrous exclaimed. "Tam is on the lam!"

Tam was claiming that he feared for his safety if he remained a party to the lawsuit, a position Boutrous said he found ironic, given that Tam and other Prop 8 proponents "were trying to strip the rights away from people who have been subject to years of being discriminated against and harassed."

Matt McGill joined the discussion. The thirty-five-year-old Gibson Dunn lawyer had shaggy blond hair and dressed, Chad joked, like the "Young Republican he was." He had clerked for Justice John Roberts when Roberts served on the D.C. Circuit Court of Appeals. Prior to that he had worked for Cooper's firm, and he knew the way their opponents thought.

"My strong suspicion is that this has all been orchestrated by Cooper's team," he said.

Tam's vitriolic writings about gays and lesbians had already played a key role in an ongoing dispute over what documents the proponents had to turn over to the plaintiffs. If Tam was allowed to withdraw, the only way to force him to testify would be to serve him with a subpoena—but first they would have to find him. There was also some concern that Cooper might take the position that if Tam was no longer a party to the case, his writings—which the plaintiffs planned to offer as evidence of animus—weren't admissible.

In civil lawsuits, either party can seek to compel the other to turn over material likely to "lead to admissible evidence," through a process known as discovery. Stewart, of the San Francisco Attorney's Office, had pressed the team from the outset to go after the internal campaign documents of ProtectMarriage.com as a way to prove that Proposition 8, just like the Colorado voter initiative that Justice Kennedy had found unconstitutional in *Romer*, was motivated by animus toward gays and lesbians.

The question of motivation was an important one, because it had the potential to make their path to victory easier; the Supreme Court had ruled in a number of cases that laws motivated solely by animus cannot survive even the rational basis test, regardless of whether or not they targeted a suspect class. When citizens, such as Tam, undertake to pass an initiative, they are acting as legislators, Stewart argued, meaning that their communications no longer fall within the sphere of protected private political speech.

Olson, however, was initially reluctant. Portraying the proponents of Proposition 8 as bigots might backfire, he felt, given that more than half the country opposed same-sex marriage. Besides, even if they could prove animus on the part of campaign leaders, who knew what was in the minds of the 7,001,084 Californians who had voted yes on Prop 8? And making an argument that was fact-specific as to what motivated the California initiative could result in a California-only decision; he believed that gays and lesbians had a fundamental right to marry regardless of the tone of any given campaign.

It might not even be necessary. Justice Kennedy had made clear that a finding of animus does not require proof of outright hostility.

"Prejudice, we are beginning to understand, rises not from malice or hostile animus alone," he had written in a 2001 case involving the Americans with Disabilities Act. "It may result as well from insensitivity caused by simple want of careful, rational reflection or from some instinctive mechanism to guard against people who appear to be different in some respects from ourselves."

But Olson had come around after McGill, who worked closely with him on some of his most important Supreme Court cases, sided with Stewart. It was true that in and of itself, evidence of animus on the part of campaign operatives was not dispositive. But Cooper was arguing the Prop 8 campaign was all about encouraging responsible procreation, McGill argued, so if they could show that the arguments made to voters had nothing to do with that, it could seriously undermine his contention that the ban on same-sex marriage had been passed with a rational purpose in mind. Let's get everything we can get our hands on, he pressed, and sort out what we want to use later.

The discovery fight had bounced back and forth for the better part of a month between Judge Walker and the Ninth Circuit Court of Appeals. Judge Walker had sided with the plaintiffs, ordering that internal campaign communications relating to advertising and strategy be turned over. A three-judge panel of the Ninth Circuit had reversed, agreeing with Cooper that such internal political communications were privileged and that their release would set a precedent that could have a chilling effect on political association. "The freedom to associate with others for the common advancement of political beliefs and ideas lies at the heart of the First Amendment," the panel wrote.

That was when the Olson team went back to the Ninth Circuit for a second time with campaign material they had found buried online written by Tam, a Chinese American evangelical Christian minister and a leader in the campaign to pass Prop 8. Entitled "What If We Lose," it had been sent out to church members and promised that if same-sex marriage became the law of the land in California, "one by one, other states would fall into Satan's hand. What will be next?" Tam wrote. "On their agenda list is: legalize having sex with children."

Surely, the Olson team argued, communications like these weren't covered by privilege. On January 4, the Ninth Circuit panel amended its opinion, stating in a footnote that communications like Tam's, circulated outside the core group of Prop 8 campaign proponents and operatives, were "plainly not a private, internal formulation of strategy" and were indeed fair game.

Cooper would now have to sort through tens of thousands of pages of documents and turn over whatever fell under the newly amended order. When a lawyer from his firm complained that they simply did not have the resources to do that at this late date, he was tartly told that by attempting to shield the documents for as long as they had, the proponents of Prop 8 had created a "problem of their own making." (Olson would later scoff, "This is like a child killing his parents, and then claiming, poor me, I'm an orphan.")

The court had ordered Cooper to deliver the documents in batches, beginning on Sunday, January 10—the eve of the trial—and finishing the following Sunday. It would be a huge undertaking to sort through it all while the trial was ongoing, but McGill was hopeful it would yield evidentiary gold. "I think there's bad, radioactive stuff," he told Chad.

"What these people are afraid of is being shown as the hateful bigots that they are under cross-examination," Chad replied. "There's a good story line developing here. Transparency is their enemy."

———

Melding what amounted to three different law firms, each with distinct cultures, into a smoothly running machine was no easy task, as Olson was finding out. For the most part, the Gibson Dunn lawyers, who now numbered twenty, the ten lawyers that Boies had assigned from his firm, and a team of ten from the San Francisco Attorney's Office were working well together.

But there was a key component missing: Boies himself. By midday Friday, with just three days to go until trial, he had yet to make an appearance at the office. "Where's David?" had become a constant refrain.

"I did see him last night, sipping screwdrivers while reviewing documents," McGill told Chad.

Chad rolled his eyes. "So we know he's in town."

The clerk of the Supreme Court once quipped that there were three secrets to Olson's success: "Prepare, prepare, prepare." For the better part of a week, he had been in San Francisco, writing and rewriting his opening statement, whittling the team's witness list, and overseeing a massive organizational effort that so far had produced some forty three-inch-thick binders filled with two thousand exhibits that would need to be introduced at trial.

Olson knew that Boies had to take a deposition in a complex bankruptcy case that week, while at the same time preparing for a number of other upcoming trials. He knew too that Boies's style was far more seat-of-the-pants than his own. If Olson approached his cases the way a classical pianist tackles a particularly difficult concerto, playing it over and over in his head with metronomic precision, Boies was more of a jazz player, always in search of the unexpected riff and best when improvising on the fly. The day before he took Bill Gates's deposition in the Microsoft trial, he had watched the movie *Tombstone* on television to clear his mind.

"Not everyone is a genius like David is," Olson said. "Seriously. His wife told me that he'd drive me crazy but that he always comes through." Still, at a case management meeting, Olson decided to reassign a number of potential witnesses to other lawyers.

During the disputed 2000 election, the Bush legal team had run a highly compartmentalized operation. One team specialized in hanging chads and oversaw the counting of ballots in South Florida, another monitored overseas military ballots, and still another handled the Florida Supreme Court arguments. Olson focused solely on the U.S. Supreme Court. Boies, meanwhile, raced from one end of the state to the other, before going head-to-head with Olson in the nation's highest court. He was brilliant, but he was just one man playing far too many roles to effectively counterbalance the Republican legal Leviathan.

Olson didn't want anyone spread too thin in this case. As it was, Boies was going to have his hands full. He was responsible for taking two of the plaintiffs, Paul and Jeff, and at least one expert witness through their direct testimony. He would be responsible for questioning the Prop 8 proponents, if the team decided to call them, and for the cross-examination of all the witnesses that Cooper planned to call. Olson had assigned himself only two witnesses, Kris and Sandy, planning to spend the rest of the trial listening for nuggets he could use or that would need to be addressed during closing arguments and beyond.

"He's great on cross when he's had a chance to listen to the direct examination," Olson told Chris Dusseault, who was acting as a liaison between the Gibson Dunn team and the other lawyers. "That's different from doing the direct examination, where you need to know what we need to elicit, which David may or may not have time to do."

"The sensitivity was, what if Cooper doesn't put on much of a case, and then David wouldn't have much of a role," Dusseault said.

Olson understood, but ensuring that Boies had a prominent enough role in the trial was not as important as ensuring that they deployed everyone in a manner that gave them the best shot at winning. "So we'll say, 'This is not about that. This is about the case,'" he replied.

EIGHT

AN UNEXPECTED
DEVELOPMENT

Trials, by their nature, can be unpredictable, but even by that standard the news the team awoke to on Saturday, January 9, was surprising: *Perry v. Schwarzenegger* was headed to the Supreme Court, before a single witness had even testified, on a sideshow issue that had nothing to do with the constitutionality of California's same-sex marriage ban.

At a hearing three days earlier, Judge Walker had announced his intention to broadcast the trial on a delayed basis via YouTube, as part of an experimental program in the Ninth Circuit to bring cameras into the courtroom. A lawyer for Cooper's firm had objected, arguing that it would subject his witnesses to intimidation. Walker wasn't buying that, noting that Cooper's clients had assumed a public face when they "put together a political campaign to change the constitution of California." As for the rest of the witnesses Cooper planned to call, they were academics, Walker said, "people who stand up before classrooms all the time and express their views and opinions and so forth."

Much of the rest of the hearing had been taken up on a technical issue: whether allowing cameras in the court required public comment because it constituted a change in the court's rules. Walker did not think so, but he said he was willing to seek public input as though it did.

The legal team had relayed that news to Chad, who swung into action. People who know gay couples are far more likely to support same-sex marriage than those who don't. Envisioning saturation cable and nightly network news coverage of the trial that would introduce their plaintiffs to viewers across America, he called Rick Jacobs, the head of a grassroots gay rights organization called the Courage Campaign, asking him to activate his members. "You need to move fast," Chad said.

Within forty-eight hours, Jacobs had delivered nearly forty thousand neatly boxed letters to Walker's chambers. Cooper couldn't begin to match the effort; there were only thirty-eight comments opposing the move.

Cooper had appealed first to the Ninth Circuit, which backed Walker's broadcast plan, and then, that morning, to the Supreme Court. Now the matter rested with Justice Kennedy, who as the justice overseeing the Ninth Circuit would decide whether to grant the emergency stay Cooper was requesting, so that the Supreme Court could decide whether to consider the underlying legal issues Cooper had raised.

"Same message," McGill told Chad after briefing him: The other side is afraid of transparency.

Kennedy had given the team until 9 A.M. the following morning to respond.

Supreme Court briefs typically take weeks to write; this was lawyering on steroids. McGill, along with two of Gibson Dunn's brightest young appellate associates, would be up all night. Still, Olson liked the idea that Kennedy, likely to be the swing vote in the event of a 5–4 decision, was, as he put it, "going to get an advance peek at this case."

"We should drop a note to Justice Kennedy," joked Dusseault, who had dropped by the war room to talk to Chad. "'By the way, how do you feel about our case?' Like a P.S."

Chad laughed. "Yeah—'Are you down with being one of the five? Much love, Ted.'"

———

"What do you think of the Supreme Court?" Jeff asked.

He and Paul were sitting in a conference room with Boies, who had finally shown up the previous afternoon. With opening arguments less than forty-eight hours away, both sets of plaintiffs were already nervous, and this latest videotaping development was not helping matters.

Dressed casually in a dark blue V-neck sweater and sneakers, Boies smiled reassuringly. Just because Cooper had appealed the decision to broadcast the trial did not mean the justices would hear it; four of the nine must first decide that the issue was worthy of their attention, and thousands of petitions are turned away each year. "I don't think the Supreme Court is going to touch it, myself," he said.

At their best, trials are like morality plays, transcending the awkward question-and-answer format to tell a coherent, compelling story. Each of the seventeen witnesses the team planned to call were there to illustrate one of three main points: that Proposition 8 was but the latest chapter in a long and odious history of discrimination against gays and lesbians; that denying gays and lesbians the right to marry caused them and the children they were raising great harm; and that permitting them to marry would not harm heterosexual marriages whatsoever.

For all the concern about ensuring Boies a prominent enough role, he was fine with the way the witnesses had been divvied up. As he put it, "Both Ted and I recognize that if we win this case, it's not going to matter who did what, and if we lose this case, it's not going to matter who did what." The trial worried him a lot less than a factor over which he had no control: the average age of the judges and justices who would ultimately decide the case as it made its way up on appeal.

"They, like myself, grew up at a time when homosexuals were considered criminals, despised sexual deviants," he said, out of earshot of the plaintiffs. "If anything kills us, that is going to be what kills us."

But in the meantime there was a case to put on, and there was no question that much would rest on the testimony of Jeff, Paul, Kris, and Sandy. They were the leadoff witnesses, and a big part of the weekend was devoted to ensuring that they knew what to expect.

A cadre of lawyers from Boies's firm had been working with Paul and Jeff in his absence, eliciting details about their lives together and the discrimination they had faced. The couple had talked of the humiliation of having hotel desk clerks, upon seeing that they had booked a king-sized bed, say there must be some sort of mistake. Whatever answer they gave—yes, we do want to sleep together—inevitably and uncomfortably made an exchange with a perfect stranger about sex. They were shut out from using vocabulary that would at least make people understand, if not agree with, the true nature of their relationship.

"Calling him my husband makes everything easier," Jeff said. "Meeting people, greeting people—there's a certain reverence that comes with the word 'marriage.'"

The couple had been studying a long outline of points the lawyers wanted them to make. Still, over several more sessions on Saturday and Sunday, Boies walked them through it again. During the direct examination, the idea was to relax and have a conversation with the judge, he counseled. When Cooper cross-examined them, however, he would try to trick them into giving answers that would hurt the case. Then, it was important to be on guard and answer in a way that could not be taken out of context.

"Be careful with the concessions," Boies advised. "If they say, 'Isn't domestic partnership the same thing?' you say, 'No, it is not. It's not to me and it's not to you.'"

He asked Jeff, "Is it possible that you would marry a woman if you couldn't marry Paul?"

"No."

"Why not?"

"Because I have no attraction to women."

Given the discrimination gays and lesbians face, Jeff added, who would voluntarily choose such a lifestyle?

After about ten more minutes, Boies cut the session short. He did not want them sounding overrehearsed. "Excellent. It's natural. It all flowed very smoothly except that one question. I would not use the word 'lifestyle.'"

———

In a conference room just down the hall, Olson and lawyers in his firm were similarly trying to steel Kris and Sandy for what lay ahead.

Chad had insisted that the team include a number of gay lawyers, both because they would bring a sensitivity born of personal experience to the legal argument and because he felt it would be a comfort to the plaintiffs.

Sarah Piepmeier, a thirty-five-year-old Gibson Dunn associate and the only lesbian besides Terry Stewart on the team, had conducted the mock cross-examination. She had thrown herself into the role, peppering them with the sorts of questions that the other side might be expected to ask. How many men had Sandy slept with? How many women for Kris? After each one she had apologized. "I just hope it was easier that it came from me," she said afterward.

Now, Enrique Monagas, the young gay lawyer who had filed the original complaint in the case, tried to keep the two women upbeat during a lunch break on Sunday. But they were clearly unsettled by the prospect of having to take the stand, given that they had been assured at the outset that a trial of the sort that was now about to take place was unlikely.

"I think cross will be an interesting experience for you," Monagas said.

"Yeah, in a bad way," Kris said with a laugh. She made quote marks with her fingers. "Interesting."

Earlier, Olson had listened as the couple fielded questions from a partner in his firm. Even on the defensive, Kris was powerful and emotive. "You don't come out because it's a choice, you know," she said. "You will be ostracized, you will be mistreated. That's how powerful it is. You can't not do it. You can't not feel it. You *have* to tolerate all this negativity in the world about who you are."

But Sandy had been more hesitant, particularly when asked about her ex-husband, Matt. It was something Olson knew he had to address, no matter how uncomfortable.

"Let me interrupt," Olson said. "To what degree have you gone over the overlapping of your relationship and your marriage?"

The best answer, and the truth, was simple: Sandy's marriage was all but over when she and Kris fell in love in January 1999. But it was complicated by Walker's decision to broadcast the trial, and her own desire to protect her two boys, now aged nineteen and twenty-one. Sandy did not want to testify to the real reason that her marriage had fallen apart: Her husband was an alcoholic.

Before she and Kris had agreed to become plaintiffs in the case, they had talked it over with their kids. Kris's twin boys, Spencer and Elliott, were all for it. Spencer was studying the judicial system in his eighth-grade social studies class, and when she started to explain how the case might travel from one court to the next, he interrupted. "Like to the Supreme Court?" he said, excited.

"Yes," she replied.

"Like *Dred Scott?*" he asked, mistakenly referring to the infamous 1857 Supreme Court case that had declared that blacks, slaves as well as free, could never be citizens of the United States.

"Not exactly," she said with a smile. "Hopefully more like *Brown v. Board of Education*," the landmark case that had ended segregation.

But the blending of their families had been tougher on Tom and Frank, Sandy's boys. After Sandy left and moved them in with Kris, their father's alcoholism had worsened. He had died of the disease just a week before Kris and Sandy's wedding ceremony, the one they held to mark the San Francisco City Hall marriage that had subsequently been deemed invalid.

The boys had told her that if she wanted to go ahead with the lawsuit, it was fine with them, but they did not want to play a role. They certainly did not need to hear their father's name dragged through the mud, Sandy worried, in testimony broadcast to the nation.

"I don't want this to be about speaking ill of Matt," she said, especially "with this YouTube crap and his family watching."

Olson understood, but he worried that Cooper could try to use her affair against them in a panoply of ways. Her ex-husband's alcoholism, he said gently, was important to address, because "it sounds to me that your relationship with Kris was not a precipitating factor in the dissolution of your marriage."

The two women had met in a computer class Sandy taught for government employees. Kris, who was working as a county child welfare worker at the time, was immediately drawn to Sandy. She was hyper and funny, with dishwater blond hair that fell below her shoulders and a long hooked nose that made her look a bit like the actress Meryl Streep. Sandy noticed Kris right way too. A masculine woman with short brown hair and an expressive face, she wore stylishly bold black-framed glasses and had an adventurous spirit. She had been raised in Bakersfield, California, a deeply conservative part of the state, but had been brave enough to embrace her sexuality in college.

Growing up in a Catholic family on a farm in Iowa, for Sandy life's options had seemed narrower. You rode horses and cheered for the high school team. You dated boys, and eventually you married one of them. If at times she wondered why she did not seem as caught up in the romance of it all as her friends, she had her mother to advise her: "Don't look for fireworks. Look for stability."

Matt Stier was handsome and, at least initially, solid. "He was the kind of man I'd always thought I'd marry," Sandy told Olson.

But her husband drank, more and more, and by the time she met Kris he was spiraling out of control. At first, Kris was someone she could talk to about the stress, a confidante with whom she wanted to spend more and more time, until one day it was something far more. Suddenly, Sandy understood what her friends had been talking about.

"I'd had a number of relationships with different men," she told Olson, "but it was never anything close to what I experienced with Kris."

By midafternoon Sunday, Olson was satisfied. "Fantastic," he said, coming around the table to hug Sandy. "We can write all the legal briefs in the world, but what you do is explain with passion and from your heart," he said. "If it goes like this in court, and I think it will, and maybe even better, it will be wonderful."

Later that afternoon, he did a practice run of the fourteen-minute opening statement he had written out in longhand on a yellow legal pad. Tears welled in Chad's eyes as Olson spoke of the painful treatment that gays and lesbians had endured over the years, "targeted by the police, harassed in the workplace, censored, demonized, fired from government jobs, excluded from the armed forces, arrested for their private sexual conduct and repeatedly stripped of their fundamental rights by popular vote."

All Proposition 8 had done, he declared, was to inflict upon gays and lesbians "badges of inferiority that forever stigmatize their loving relationships as different, separate, unequal, and less worthy."

Walking out the door that night, Olson seemed confident that would all soon end. "I'm as ready as I can be," he said.

Section II

NINE

"ALL RISE!"

P recisely at 7:37 A.M. on the opening day of the trial, the plaintiffs emerged from the rented Victorian home that Chad, Kristina, and Adam were sharing with Jeff and Paul. The camera crews huddled outside in the chill of a typically overcast San Francisco morning snapped to attention.

Jeff had been chosen to give the brief statement that would come to dominate the early morning news cycle. Rehearsing earlier with Kristina, he had been overcome, tears spilling uncontrollably down his cheeks. "Smile," Chad whispered as they walked out the door, and, gripping Paul's hand, Jeff did his best to keep it together.

"We're all Americans who simply want to get married, just like everyone else," he said, his voice steady. "We believe in our Constitution, and that the courts will lead the way to equality like they have so many times in the past."

Sixty seconds later, they were back in the sanctuary of the Victorian's renovated kitchen, where coffee and pastries awaited. "Everything else will be easier from here," Chad promised, but of course they all knew that wasn't true.

For all the minute-by-minute planning that had gone into the day, it had already been a rocky morning. The *Today* show had abruptly yanked what was supposed to have been an exclusive with Olson, Boies, and the two couples that it had planned to air that morning to its nearly six million viewers. The show had been pretaped over the weekend. Kristina, shaking her head in disbelief, wondered aloud whether the cancellation was tied to the fact that Boies, without consulting AFER, had agreed to appear on a competitor's Sunday show that, as she put it, "hardly anybody watches." But there was no time to dwell on lost opportunities.

Tam, the Proposition 8 proponent who had tried to withdraw from the case, had been located and served with a subpoena the night before. "YES!" Chad had e-mailed the lawyers. "You can run but you can't hide." But there was still no word from the Supreme Court about whether the cameras would be rolling for Olson's opening statement and the plaintiffs' testimony.

From the courthouse came reports that a man in a wedding dress had shown up at the vigil, catnip to the camera crews stationed outside but exactly the kind of visuals Chad wanted to avoid. For too long, he felt, the gay rights movement had been defined by flamboyant, off-putting imagery. Men wearing leather chaps and bare-chested women on motorcycles at gay pride parades made the news, but did not reflect the reality of modern gay life, a reality in which people dressed for work and came home to families just like their straight counterparts. Kristina could only hope that the team's plan to use the allure of Hollywood to divert the cameras' attention—Lance Black had been dispatched to the vigil to give a speech—would work. Because right now, she had her hands full.

Adam Umhoefer, the AFER staffer who had formed the closest bond with the plaintiffs, had already left for the courthouse. It was as personal for him as it was to them; he had yet to find the right person, but when he did, he wanted to be able to marry him. On his way out the door, he had tucked a talisman in his pocket: a wedding ring, his dad's, who had been killed by a drunk driver when Adam was fourteen.

That left Kristina to keep everyone on an even keel.

Sandy kept tugging uncomfortably at the coral pink jacket the team had chosen over her favored black. Paul, who couldn't seem to keep his left leg from buckling slightly as he paced the kitchen, declared that he was a "wreck." He and Jeff had stayed up late the night before, reminding each other of why they had decided to take part in the case. "I love you," Jeff had told Paul before they finally fell asleep, and really it was as simple as that.

But it was one thing to agree in principle to be the faces of the litigation. It was another thing altogether to have their most intimate thoughts exposed in a trial they had never thought would happen in the first place. What would Paul and Jeff's neighbors, the ones who had put signs supporting Prop 8 in their yards, think? And what about Sandy's mom in Iowa? One of the first questions she had asked after Sandy told her about Kris was, "Is she at least Catholic?" She had tried to be supportive, but their relationship still confused her. She frequently questioned her daughter's happiness, unable to understand why she did not just pursue a relationship with a man. And she worried about her church friends finding out that her daughter was a lesbian.

There was just no knowing how the spotlight of this trial might disrupt their lives, and so they did what people often do when faced with uncertainty: They distracted themselves with minutiae in order to avoid thinking about boarding the minibus that was waiting outside to take them to the courthouse and a future from which there would be no turning back.

Ties were knotted and double-knotted, straightened and then discarded. Paul's was too narrow, Kristina decided. Chad fretted about the proper camera-friendly color of his before Kristina came down firmly on the side of red. "Love it—I'm ready to vote for you, Governor!"

Facebook pages and e-mails were checked. A blow dryer was fetched to remedy a water spot on Kris's shirt. No sooner was it dry than she grabbed a sponge and began wiping crumbs and coffee stains off the kitchen counter. "This I can control," she announced. "This will look good when I'm done, when everything else is just"—she paused, searching for the right word—"nebulous."

And then, too soon, it was time to go. As they headed across town, a manic humor took hold, the way it does when people are trying to keep dread from swallowing them. "What if we just didn't show up?" Chad joked. Quoting from Tam's motion to withdraw, he added, "I am tired! I want peace!"

"Yeah!" Sandy yelped. "Road trip to Vegas!"

But as the bus passed City Hall, where Harvey Milk had been shot thirty-one years earlier, everyone grew silent. The police presence grew heavier as they turned toward the federal courthouse. Gazing out the window, Chad could see by the national cable and network satellites lining the sidewalk what a friend from the Obama White House had meant when he e-mailed earlier that "you own the news cycle this morning."

"Wow, look at all the camera trucks," he said, clasping his hands together, fingers digging into knuckles.

Then they were out and moving fast, past the crowd waving AFER-supplied American flags and signs emblazoned with lines from past Supreme Court rulings like SEPARATE IS UNEQUAL and MARRIAGE IS A BASIC CIVIL RIGHT. One minute they were shedding their shoes and walking through a metal detector, and the next they were hustled onto a freight elevator off-limits to the public, down a corridor, and into an empty courtroom just down the hall from Judge Walker's.

Minutes earlier, at 8:02 A.M., the Supreme Court had issued an order on Judge Walker's plan to broadcast the trial on YouTube. Notwithstanding Boies's prediction to the contrary, the justices had decided that Cooper's argument merited their attention. By a vote of 5–4, with Justice Kennedy casting his with the conservatives, the broadcast was temporarily halted until Wednesday, when the Court was expected to rule on the merits of Cooper's argument.

Chad, learning the news, hurriedly excused himself. He and Kristina had hatched a contingency plan to have Olson give a dramatic reading of his opening statement so that the networks would still be able to carry it on the nightly news, but it needed to be put into action.

That left just the two couples in the quiet of the empty holding area. They laughed about some of the questions that reporters had shouted at them—"'Is it an emotional experience?'" Paul mimicked. "Um, yeah"—until a representative from the U.S. Marshals Service came in to talk about the thing they had been trying hardest all morning to shove to the edge of their consciousness.

"As plaintiffs, you are now under our protection," the marshal said. "If you get anything—it doesn't have to be, 'I'm going to kill you,' but anything worrisome—let us know."

It was meant to be reassuring, but it had the opposite effect. One didn't have to go far back in history to find people who had manned the civil rights barricades only to meet a violent end.

"Trying to keep my mind off of it," Jeff whispered to Paul, who sighed.

"Very hard to do," he said.

Sandy and Kris just looked stricken. They didn't exchange a word, but they both thought about their boys.

———

"All rise!"

Everyone rose as Judge Walker, a burnt orange tie peeking out from underneath his black robe, took his seat in front of the expanse of cream-colored marble that rose from floor to ceiling behind him. He peered over his spectacles at the army of lawyers arrayed before him.

"Now, I trust that you all have had a quiet and restful few days," Walker cracked, with the droll sense of humor that would become his trademark as the trial got under way. "I can assure you, I have."

The packed courtroom erupted in laughter. Cooper, wearing a dark suit and a deep green tie, sat to the judge's right with his core team. It was an impressive group of lawyers that included a former clerk of Justice Kennedy's, an experienced trial attorney who had won verdicts totaling hundreds of millions of dollars on behalf of clients, and a former deputy attorney general and associate White House counsel from President George W. Bush's administration. Several of the campaign's official proponents were in court, as were Cooper's co-counsels, the conservative Alliance Defense Fund, and Andy Pugno, the Prop 8 campaign's chief lawyer.

To the judge's left, in the first row on the plaintiffs' side of the courtroom, were Paul and Jeff; Sandy and Kris; Chad and Kristina; Olson's wife, Lady; Bruce Cohen and his husband, Gabe Catone; and Adam. Behind them were Lance Black, Cleve Jones, Rob and Michele Reiner, and two of their kids—or, as Jones put it, "the motley crew that started all this."

The Reiners had flown in the night before. "I can't wait, I can't wait to see these guys go at it," Rob had exclaimed to Chad as he toured the Gibson Dunn offices. Now, looking over at her husband, Michele Reiner widened her eyes, as if to say, "Here we go," while in front of them, Kristina gave Chad's shoulder a quick squeeze.

"Now, you probably know, we received this morning an order from the Supreme Court, which has stayed the transmission of any audio or visual images of this case until at least 4 P.M. eastern time on Wednesday," Judge Walker said.

He reiterated, somewhat defensively, his position that broadcasting the trial via YouTube did not require public input. "Nonetheless, we have received a very substantial number of comments in response to that change. As of—as of Friday, 5 P.M. Friday, we had received 138,574 responses or comments."

Chad, whose instigating role in that paper onslaught remained hidden, kept a poker face as the judge continued, speaking to the court but also, it seemed, to the justices: "And if the results are any indication of where sentiment lies on this issue, it's overwhelmingly in favor of the rule change."

Ted Boutrous jumped up, asking that the cameras continue to record the proceedings while they awaited the Supreme Court's guidance on whether the video could ultimately be broadcast. Walker granted the motion over Cooper's objection. With that piece of housekeeping out of the way, it was time to delve into the real legal issue at hand.

"Mr. Olson, you are going to make the opening statement for the plaintiffs."

"Thank you, Your Honor," Olson said, then plunged in.

———

"This case is about marriage and equality. Plaintiffs are being denied both the right to marry and the right to equality under the law. The Supreme Court of the United States has repeatedly described the right to marriage as one of the most vital personal rights essential to the orderly pursuit of happiness, a basic civil right, a component of the constitutional rights to liberty, privacy, association, an intimate choice, an expression of emotional support and public commitment, the exercise of spiritual unity, and the fulfillment of one's self—"

Olson was just hitting his stride when, less than a minute into his prepared statement, Judge Walker did something unexpected. He interrupted him, hammering him with one skeptical question after the next. It was, thought Matt McGill, the type of barrage one might expect from the justices of the Supreme Court. But it was unusual for a trial judge, and not something they had prepared for in the practice sessions over the weekend.

"Now, does the right to marry, as secured by the Constitution, mean the right to have a marriage license issued by the state?" Walker asked.

Olson said he believed it did, leading Walker to another question.

"Could the state get out of the marriage license business?"

"If California allowed people to marry without a license," Olson conceded after some back-and-forth, "which is what I think is part of the import of your suggestion, and said that the only thing we're regulating is something called domestic partnership, and everybody can do that, yes, that might mean that California is treating people equally." But, he said, "that will never happen."

"Why?" the judge wanted to know. "That would solve this problem, wouldn't it?"

Olson said that while he did not hold himself out as a political prognosticator, he suspected that the people of California would not be willing to abandon an institution that means a great deal to people, one that indeed is so important that the defenders of Proposition 8 maintain it must "be preserved for opposite-sex couples and withheld from same-sex couples."

"Well, but the proponents argue that marriage has never been extended to same-sex couples in the past, and so we're simply preserving a tradition that is long established and that is, indeed, implicit in the very concept of marriage," Walker countered.

Olson cited the California Supreme Court decision that found that same-sex couples had the right to marry under the state's constitution, but Walker was unimpressed. This was a federal court, and he wanted to know what had changed so that now the U.S. Constitution's due process and equal protection guarantees must be understood to protect what many states had always forbidden.

"What changed was Proposition 8, which isolated gay men and lesbian individuals and said: You're different," Olson replied. "It put them in a different category. That's discrimination."

Would the evidence show that Proposition 8 was motivated by an intent to discriminate against gays and lesbians? Walker demanded. "The evidence, what's the evidence?"

"The evidence will show that each of the rationalizations for Proposition 8, invented, invented by its proponents, is without merit," Olson said. "They mention procreation. Procreation cannot be a justification, inasmuch as Proposition 8 permits marriage by persons who are unable or who have no intention or no ability whatsoever to have children or produce children.

"Proposition 8 also has no rational relationship to the parenting of children," he continued, "because same-sex couples and opposite-sex couples are equally, in California, permitted to have and raise children in this state. The evidence in this case, from the experts, will demonstrate that gay and lesbian individuals are every bit as capable of being loving, caring, and effective parents as heterosexuals. The quality of the parent is not measured by gender, but by the content of the heart."

"If same-sex couples are permitted to enter this institution, this esteemed institution of marriage, doesn't that change the institution?" Walker asked.

"No," Olson answered. "It will fulfill the institution."

Prior to the *Loving* decision, President Obama's biracial parents would not have been able to marry in Virginia, Olson noted. "The history, a point I was just about to make, of marriage has evolved. It has changed to shed irrational, unwarranted, and discriminatory restrictions and limitations that reflected the biases, and prejudices, and stereotypes of the past."

It went on like that, until Walker finally let Olson alone long enough to make the points he had come to make. Convicted criminals, substance abusers, and sex offenders are all legally permitted to marry in California, he declared, just as long as they aren't gay.

Olson's own mother, when he first told her he was taking the case, had questioned him as to why the voters of California shouldn't have the final say in the matter. He had convinced her of the merits of his argument by explaining that while marriage is traditionally regulated by the states, the state's power is subject to constitutional limitations, and it was a point he knew he needed to hit hard now.

"We wouldn't need a Constitution if we left everything to the political process, but if we left everything to the political process, the majority would always prevail, which is the great thing about democracy, but it's not so good if you are a minority or if you're a disfavored minority or you're new or you're different," Olson declared, his voice growing at once softer and more emphatic.

"We have courts to declare enactments like Proposition 8 that take our citizens, our worthy, loving upstanding citizens who are being treated differently and being hurt every single day, we have courts to declare those measures unconstitutional. And that is why we are here today."

"Very well," the judge said.

"Good morning again, Chief Judge Walker, and may it please the court," Cooper began, when it was his turn to give an opening statement. "On November 4, 2008, fourteen million Californians went to the polls to cast their ballots on an issue of overriding social and cultural importance: whether the institution of marriage should be redefined to include couples of the same sex. Over 52 percent of the—those—Californians voted to restore and preserve the traditional definition of marriage as a union of a man and a woman. A definition that has prevailed in virtually every society in recorded history."

Cooper's theory of the case was pretty straightforward. No court in the country had held that laws targeting gays and lesbians should be subject to heightened scrutiny. Assuming that he could keep the court from reaching that conclusion in this case, it would be up to Olson to prove that Proposition 8 served no conceivable state purpose and had instead been motivated by animus.

Californians, Cooper argued, had been very generous in extending rights and benefits to gay and lesbian couples, enacting antidiscrimination protections and recognizing same-sex relationships through domestic partnerships.

"Gays and lesbians have secured these and many other legislative victories by mobilizing a strong and growing coalition of supporters," he said, ticking off a number of allies. When he got to "Hollywood," Michele Reiner compressed her lips and looked to the ceiling. One of the great ironies about Hollywood is that with studio executives afraid to cast openly gay actors in romantic leads, it was still one of the most closeted places in America.

Those victories, Cooper argued, demonstrated not only that gays and lesbians wielded substantial political power and therefore should not be considered a suspect class, but also that Californians bore no ill will toward gays and lesbians, but simply had a "special regard for this venerable institution."

"There are millions of Americans who believe in equality for gays and lesbians, but draw the line at marriage," he said, quoting a prominent rabbi before turning, as Olson had, to Obama.

Cooper intended to turn the president into a star, uncalled witness in his case, a man who exemplified the notion that thoughtful people of goodwill can differ on the subject of same-sex marriage without being bigots.

Obama had carved out a tortured position on same-sex marriage. During the presidential campaign, he promised to support the repeal of the Clinton-era Defense of Marriage Act, because he said the definition of marriage should be left to the states. But he also said he personally did not support allowing gays and lesbians to wed, and that arrangements like civil unions that offered all the benefits of marriage were the best way to "secure equal treatment" for gays and lesbians.

Why? Cooper quoted the president's own words: "Marriage has religious and social connotations and I consider marriage to be between a man and a woman."

Walker, who had allowed Cooper to make his case without interruption up to this point, finally felt compelled to jump in. "Mr. Olson made the point if the president's parents had been in Virginia at the time of his birth, their marriage would have been unlawful. That indicates that there is quite a change in the understanding of people's entitlement to enter into the institution of marriage."

If the specter of *Roe v. Wade* hung over Olson as he tried to convince the court that the time to act was now, given Ginsburg's statements that the decision had moved "too fast," the historic *Loving v. Virginia* case that had overturned interracial marriage bans was one of Cooper's biggest hurdles.

In finding that the Virginia statute both violated the Constitution's promise of equal protection under law and deprived the Lovings of a fundamental freedom without due process of law, the Court had declared that "the freedom to marry has long been recognized as one of the vital personal rights essential to the orderly pursuit of happiness by free men."

Shortly before her death in 2008, Mildred Loving, whose marriage to a white man sparked that historic litigation, had issued a statement endorsing same-sex marriage. "My generation was bitterly divided over something that should have been so clear and right," she wrote. "I support the freedom to marry for all. That's what *Loving,* and loving, are all about."

"*Loving* is by far [Olson's] best case," Cooper later said.

Cooper's only recourse was to circle back to his main argument: that marriage, as he put it, is "fundamentally a pro-child social institution anchored in socially-approved sexual intercourse between a man and a woman," a view that caused not a few people in the courtroom to giggle.

"The racial restriction in *Loving* was at war with the central purpose of marriage," Cooper continued. "You had a situation where two individuals whose sexual relations would [naturally] lead to procreation, and yet the state forbade those individuals from forming a marital union."

"Is that the only purpose of marriage?" Walker asked. "Where do the other values associated with marriage come in, companionship, support?"

"The question is, Your Honor, is this institution designed for these pro-child reasons, or is it to produce companionship and personal fulfillment and expression of love? Are those purposes themselves important enough to run the risks to the accomplishment of the pro-child purposes?"

"What are those risks?" interjected Walker, back in his what-is-the-evidence mode.

"The risks are, Your Honor, that the nature of the institution will be altered, that it will be deinstitutionalized," Cooper responded. "Now, the plaintiffs dispute. They dispute the likelihood that these harms will result from same-sex marriage. And our point, Your Honor, is that they cannot prove that they will not flow from legalizing same-sex marriage."

"Excuse me," Walker interjected. "Is there any evidence from the countries and states that have permitted same-sex couples to marry that marriage has been deinstitutionalized, or has led to lower marriage rates or higher rates of divorce or greater incidents of nonmarital cohabitation, these other matters you've described?"

Cooper said there was and he believed the evidence would show that it had.

"Which witness will speak to this?" Walker asked.

"The plaintiffs actually will have witnesses who speak to this," Cooper answered. Olson looked puzzled; the witnesses he had lined up had made no such concessions.

"But my point also, Your Honor," Cooper hurried along, "is that with respect even to the foreign countries, where there is a greater body of experience, or at least a longer period of experience, confident and reliable judgments simply cannot be made."

Walker turned to Cooper's assertion that allowing same-sex couples to marry would increase the likelihood that bisexuals would be allowed to enter into polygamous relationships. "What's the evidence?"

Cooper dodged, saying such a conclusion flowed from logic.

"This is ridiculous," Michele Reiner whispered to her husband. Cooper, meanwhile, was winding up his argument.

"The reality is, Your Honor, you will hear nothing but predictions in this trial about what this—about what the long-term effects of adopting same-sex marriage will be on the institution of marriage itself, and on the social purposes that it serves."

Attitudes about same-sex marriage might be changing, Cooper said, but that "is not a reason that the constitution has somehow changed to ordain the results" that Olson was seeking. "It's a reason, and he has spoken eloquently to many reasons, why the people of California, perhaps the people of other states in this country, should consider his arguments the next time the issue is before them in the political process."

"Thank you, Mr. Cooper," Walker said. "I believe those are the opening statements and we will take a break until ten minutes after the hour."

_____

"News of the day!" Matt McGill exclaimed, wandering back from his seat at the counsel table with Olson to where the Reiners and the plaintiffs were conferring about the morning's events.

Earlier that morning, while Olson had been digesting the news from the Supreme Court, Cooper had filed a remarkable two-page document there in the district court. Time-stamped at 8:30 A.M., it effectively gutted Cooper's case.

"They dropped four of their witnesses!" McGill explained, grinning broadly.

It had been difficult for Cooper to find experts willing to testify on his side of the case; at least ten that he approached had turned him down. Though he believed that the burden should be on the plaintiffs in this case, he knew that it would shift to him if he could not knock down both Olson's argument that gays and lesbians ought to be considered a suspect class and that the fundamental right to marry was the right to marry a person of one's choice.

And assuming he succeeded on those fronts, he still had to get past the hurdle the Supreme Court had erected in the *Romer* decision. In that case, the majority held that if a law serves no rational purpose, it can be inferred that it was passed out of prejudice. Cooper needed to advance some nonbigoted rationale for Prop 8, and now he was down to just two experts. He did not panic; as he later put it, "We always thought the most important things would come out of the mouths of the plaintiffs' witnesses." Still, putting on an affirmative case using hostile experts called by your opponent is difficult in the best of circumstances.

In the coming days, Cooper and his team would tell the court that the witnesses had backed out at the last minute because of the plan to broadcast the trial, a stance he maintained years later when he said they were worried that the ban handed down that very morning was only temporary. "The media focus on this case, if fed by videotape of the proceedings—it was fraught with risk for the side the media did not favor," he said. "That was very much in the minds of these witnesses."

But there were other, strategic reasons for Cooper to pull the four experts. Prior to the start of a trial, lawyers are given the opportunity to interview, or in legal lingo, "depose," the other side's witnesses. All four had made damaging admissions during those depositions. An Oxford University philosophy professor who was to have testified that people have the moral power to overcome being gay, for instance, was forced to acknowledge that he had never done a study of human sexuality or interviewed gay or lesbian subjects before reaching that conclusion. And at least two of the withdrawn witnesses would later say that their decision not to testify stemmed at least in part from not wanting to go another round with the plaintiffs' attorneys in open court.

Loren Marks, a professor at Louisiana State University, had been slated to testify that the ideal family structure for children is one in which they are raised by their biological parents—a possible rationale for Prop 8, since that is not possible for gay and lesbian parents. But McGill had forced him to admit that he did not realize that the studies he relied upon to conclude that children do best when raised by a mother and father defined "biological" parents in a way that included adoptive parents. Nor had he studied how the children of gays and lesbians fared. The publicity that could result from cameras was of some concern, but the deposition had—he remembered this later very clearly— at times made him seem "foolish and naïve."

"I wouldn't have wished fifteen minutes of it on my worst enemy."

And Boies, in his depositions of two religious studies scholars from McGill University in Canada, had demonstrated just what his wife had meant when she told Olson that putting up with his occasionally eccentric ways would be worth it.

"It was like watching someone pull the foundation out from underneath their house," Terry Stewart, who accompanied him to the depositions, recalled. "It's hard to describe what happened."

Katherine Young was to have testified that the historical purpose of marriage was to bind men and women together, for the good of society, in order to foster an ideal climate to raise children. But Boies had forced her to admit that the primary purpose of marriage today is to express love and commitment. And though Cooper had said in his opening statement that marriage had always and "across cultures" been defined as a union between a man and a woman, Young had acknowledged that at varying times same-sex marriage rituals had been practiced in parts of India, China, and West Africa, as well as among certain North American Indian tribes. Even the Roman emperors were sometimes known to marry other men, she had added.

Her colleague Paul Nathanson had expected to be questioned about the expert report he had prepared on the varying positions that religious denominations took in the Prop 8 fight. Instead he found himself defending views he had expressed in books he had coauthored with Young on the role fathers play in families.

As a gay man who opposed gay marriage, he held complicated views. He believed that the modern concept of marriage as an expression of love, as opposed to duty, gave parents permission to split when their emotional bond ended. Allowing same-sex couples to wed, he feared, would only lend further currency to that adult-centric view. But Boies's deposition left little room for nuance.

"He spent all of the entire day asking me had I ever heard of the American Psychological Society, all these hundreds of academic societies all of which are in the social studies field," Nathanson recounted. "I am not in the social sciences, but in each case he asked, 'Have you read this or that?' I appeared like an idiot."

Forced to acknowledge that many prominent national organizations, including the American Academy of Pediatrics, disagreed with his view that allowing same-sex couples to marry could hurt children, by the end Nathanson was agreeing with Boies that allowing gays and lesbians to marry would increase the stability of their relationships and enhance their ability to be good parents.

It was, Nathanson would later say, an "extremely negative experience," and both he and Young decided shortly thereafter not to testify. Cameras, he said, had little to do with his decision.

Explaining the import of the move to the Reiners and the plaintiffs, McGill had no way of knowing what was in the minds of Cooper's witnesses. What he knew was that both the legal and media team would have a field day with this information. And it was a buoying piece of news to deliver to the plaintiffs right before they had to testify.

Straightening Jeff's tie, Paul asked if he was ready.

Listening to Cooper's opening argument, Jeff said, "emboldens me more to want to respond."

"Kill 'em," Paul said. "I mean in a good way. Kill 'em with kindness. Just tell the truth, because the truth negates all these points."

TEN

"A HIGHER ARC"

M r. Boies, your first witness."

"Thank you, Your Honor. We call Jeffrey Zarrillo."

Boies wore his usual off-the-rack suit and sneakers, but for this case he had decided that an additional sartorial statement was appropriate: Prominently affixed to his lapel was an American flag pin. Jeff kept his eyes on the lawyer as he took the stand and began telling the court about growing up in Brick, New Jersey, and the fear that had gripped him once he realized he was gay.

He recalled watching an *Afterschool Special* about a child who was thrown out of his home after coming out to his parents. He had badly wanted to play football in high school, but had been afraid to be alone in a locker room with other boys for fear that they would somehow know what he was. He was twenty-five years old by the time he confided his secret to friends, and almost thirty before he told his parents.

"Coming out is a very personal and internal process," Jeff said, then choked up. "Excuse me."

Walker, who had jotted notes during the opening statements, was now watching intently.

"Today you are in a committed relationship with another gay man, correct?" Boies asked.

"Yes, sir."

"Tell me a little bit about that man."

"He's the love of my life. I love him probably more than I love myself," Jeff said, the words spilling out, unrehearsed and raw. "I would do anything for him. I would put his needs ahead of my own. I would be with him in sickness and in health, for richer, for poorer, death do us part, just like vows. I would do anything for him. And I want nothing more than to marry him."

Boies was moving quickly now, hoping to get Jeff off the stand well before lunch so Cooper would have no time to prepare for cross-examination. He needed to knock down the idea that domestic partnerships represented the generous compromise Cooper had painted them out to be in his opening, and one way to do that was to ask Jeff why he and Paul had decided against registering.

"It's giving me part of the pie, but not the whole thing," Jeff explained. "We would be saying that we are satisfied with domestic partnership as a way to live our lives, but it doesn't give due respect to the relationship we have had for almost nine years. Only marriage could do that."

"Do you believe that if you were married, that would affect the way other people who don't know you deal with you?" Boies asked.

"Sure."

"Why?"

"It says to them, these individuals are serious; these individuals are committed to one another; they have taken that step to be involved in a relationship that one hopes lasts the rest of their life."

"Now, assume that the state of California continues to tell you that you can't get married to someone of the same sex. Might that lead you to desire to get married and marry somebody of the opposite sex?"

"No," Jeff answered.

"Do you think if somehow you were able to be forced into a marriage with somebody of the opposite sex, that would lead to a stable, loving relationship?"

"Again, no."

"Your Honor, I have no further questions."

Walker turned to Cooper and the team defending Prop 8.

"No questions, Your Honor."

Walker could hear the murmuring in the audience, and even he seemed surprised. "Cross-examination?"

"No questions."

———

"Raise your right hand," the clerk instructed Paul.

There had been no time to talk about the way Paul had felt listening to Jeff's testimony, only to lightly kiss him on the cheek as he passed him on the way to the witness stand.

Where Boies had sought to elicit from Jeff a heartfelt testament to the importance of marriage, with Paul he focused more on the next prong of the argument; that Prop 8, in denying gays and lesbians the ability to marry, caused them tangible harm.

"What are your views about having children?" Boies asked.

"I would love to have a family."

"Why haven't you so far?"

"I think the time line for us has always been marriage first, before family," Paul answered. "For many reasons. But for us, marriage is so important because it solidifies the relationship."

Boies moved on to his next point. "Have you experienced discrimination as a result of being gay?" he asked.

Paul hesitated. He might have talked about how his own brother had told him that his decision to become a plaintiff in this very case would be seen by his father's side of the family—conservative Catholic immigrants from Jordan—as bringing shame to the Katami name, or about why only his sister was attending the trial. But that cut too deep, was too private.

So instead he talked about having rocks and eggs thrown at him the first time he went to a gay bar in college, and how later, during the Prop 8 campaign, he pulled up beside a woman with a YES ON 8 bumper sticker on her car. Her window was open. He looked at her, and she shot him a "very distinctive, 'What?' look back," he testified.

"And I said, 'I just disagree with your bumper sticker.'"

"She said, 'Well, marriage is not for you people, anyway.'"

"I couldn't even respond," he continued, crying now. "It rocks you to the core."

"What was the image on the bumper sticker?" Boies asked.

It was not an idle question. The team had collected reams of evidence that it wanted to introduce at trial, but the rules required that each exhibit be authenticated and introduced through a witness, after a foundation had been laid for relevance. Boies wanted to use Paul to introduce Prop 8 campaign material as a way to counter Cooper's claims that homophobia was not the driving force behind Prop 8.

The bumper sticker featured two stick-figure children holding hands with their parents, a visual representation of one of the campaign's main slogans, that voters should pass Prop 8 to "Protect Our Children." "It's so damning, it's so angering, because I love kids," Paul said.

Boies then moved to play a number of campaign ads for the court. In one, threatening music played over the image of a freight train barreling down the tracks. The ad featured the ProtectMarriage.com campaign's executive director, Ron Prentice, warning that "if California loses on the subject of marriage, then this goes nationwide." Others talked of the "homosexual agenda," "Christians walking in fear," and how "the devil wants to blur the lines between right and wrong when it comes to family structure." The video ended with the tag line, "Stand up for righteousness. Vote Yes on Proposition 8."

"When you saw this video," Boies asked Paul, "were you affected?"

"My heart was racing and I was angry watching it. I mean, again, 'Stand up for righteousness'? Okay. So we're a class of citizens that need to be stood up against, for some reason. And not to mention, what I find most disturbing is the reference to 'the devil blurring lines,' and 'don't deny Jesus like Peter did,' and this oncoming freight train. Well, what happens when a freight train hits you? You're going to be either majorly harmed or killed by that, right?"

Paul was wound up now, couldn't help it. "I love Jeff Zarrillo. I want to get married to Jeff. I want to start a family. I'm not going to start some movement that's going to harm any institution or any person or any child. I'm not."

At 12:27 P.M., Boies wrapped up. A lawyer on Cooper's team jumped to his feet, asking that the judge call a recess for lunch. "Good idea," Walker said. Court would resume just after 1:30.

Everyone waited until the doors shut on the freight elevator that would take them down to the court cafeteria before breaking into applause. Kris's mother had brought the twins, Spencer and Elliott, to hear her testimony later that afternoon.

How did the morning go? Spencer wanted to know. "Oh, it was so good!" Kris exclaimed, as Jeff and Paul beamed.

The team commandeered a long table in the lunchroom, where a quote from Eleanor Roosevelt was memorialized on one wall. "Where, after all, do universal human rights begin?" the wife of the thirty-second president had asked. "In small places, close to home—so close and so small that they cannot be seen on any maps of the world. Yet they are the world of the individual person, the neighborhood he lives in; the school or college he attends; the factory, farm or office where he works. Such are the places where every man, woman and child seeks equal justice, equal opportunity, equal dignity without discrimination. Unless those rights have meaning there, they have little meaning anywhere."

Kris pointed it out to Sandy, and then, after everyone had grabbed a sandwich, she introduced her two boys to Cleve Jones and Bruce Cohen.

"These have been the happiest months of my life," Jones told them. "It's so cool."

Pulling up to the courthouse, the thirteen-year-old twins had been unnerved by the number of people gathered outside. "Whoa," Elliott had thought as they passed protesters waving antigay signs and who were clustered around a van plastered with biblical references.

But Jones's optimism was catching. It was cool, now that they were safely away from the crowd, to think that Kris, their mom, might actually bring about the change she was seeking.

"What are you doing?" Kris asked Elliott, whose sandy head was bent in concentration.

He held up his phone. "Returning texts from a friend."

"About?"

"This," he answered, the universal monosyllabic response of teens everywhere when parents fuss or pry.

Kris tensed. This was one reason why she had been so reluctant in the weeks leading up to the trial to do any interviews. Her boys hadn't signed up for this; she had. And while Jeff had escaped cross-examination, who knew what Cooper had planned for the rest of them?

"About what is happening? Or why this is happening?"

Elliott seemed surprised. Unlike Sandy's boys, he'd grown up with two moms. Apart from those moments when someone would say something like, "That's so gay," and then quickly apologize—"Dude, I wasn't thinking!"—it was no big deal. All of his friends knew Sandy and Kris, as well as his other mother, and were supportive.

He gave Kris an "oh Mom" look before answering: "Just asking questions."

Kris gave up, deciding to keep things light. "Maybe you should invite all your friends over," she joked. "Gather 'round, kids, I've got a story to tell you."

Spencer laughed. "Yeah, about the birds and the bees!"

=====

While the plaintiffs finished their lunch, Cooper was upstairs grappling with a dilemma.

In the weeks leading up to the trial, he had decided against cross-examining any of the plaintiffs. Litigation is a zero-sum game. Something that might help you, but has the potential to help your opponent more, is something to be avoided.

That Sandy had been married to a man might be relevant as it related to the question of whether sexual orientation was an immutable characteristic, one of the criteria the Supreme Court considers when deciding whether to apply heightened scrutiny, Cooper thought. But Olson was likely to preemptively put that fact into the record himself. Whatever explanation Sandy might give under cross-examination would only serve to undercut the point. And atmospherically, it would do more harm than good to be seen to be beating up on the plaintiffs in a case that centered on proving that Proposition 8 was not driven by animus toward gay people.

No, there was simply no truck in playing in Olson's sandbox, he decided. Unless one of the plaintiffs brought up something that he simply could not allow to go unchallenged, he would stand down.

And that was the problem Cooper was now mulling with his team in a little room down the hall from Judge Walker's courtroom. Cooper's argument that there had been no discriminatory intent behind the initiative was potentially undercut by Paul's testimony about how the Prop 8 campaign slogan, "Protect Our Children," made him feel. That had to be addressed.

―――

"Good afternoon, Mr. Katami," Brian Raum began.

Raum, of the Alliance Defense Fund, had been chosen because he had taken Paul's deposition back in December. His mission on cross was clear: Confront Paul with an alternative interpretation for the slogan "Protect Our Children," no more, no less.

To that end, Raum played a campaign ad of his own, with the same stick-figure rendering of a child and its parents that had been on the bumper sticker Paul had testified about. The ad featured a couple from Massachusetts talking about how, after that state's high court legalized same-sex marriage there, their son's elementary school teacher had read his class a book about a "prince marrying a prince." "If Proposition 8 fails to pass," the ad warned, some of the "most profound consequences are for children."

Spencer, sitting behind his mother and Sandy, felt sick. Listening to that ad, he would later recall, "was absolutely awful. It felt like ignorant people commenting on a life they did not know anything about." But Raum forged ahead, seemingly confident that if he could show that this was one motivation behind the passage of Prop 8, it would offer a rationale that could survive the animus test and pass constitutional muster.

Directing Paul to a Yes on 8 voter guide, he asked him to read a passage out loud. "We should not accept a court decision that may result in public schools teaching our kids that gay marriage is okay," Paul read.

Raum pounced. "In fact, that's what the Yes on 8 on Prop 8 campaign was seeking to protect children from, am I right?" He then circled back to the ad he had just played. "There is nothing in this ad that says that the Yes on Prop 8 campaign wanted to protect children against you because you were bad, right? It didn't say anything like that, did it?"

"This ad doesn't literally state—"

"That's what I'm asking. It does not literally state it, does it?"

"This ad does not literally state that there is a harm. It insinuates one to me—"

"Thank you, Mr. Katami."

On redirect, Boies had only one point to make: Prop 8 had been about one thing, and one thing only—stripping gays and lesbians of the right to marry. "Was there anything in Proposition 8 about what was going to be taught in schools?" he asked Paul.

"No," Paul answered.

"No more questions, Your Honor."

Judge Walker looked at Olson. "Plaintiffs' next witness."

———

Olson took his time with first Kris and then Sandy, his voice soft and steadying, like you might use with a horse known to startle.

Kris described how in 2003 she had proposed to Sandy, "the most sparkliest person I ever met," at Indian Rock, an outcropping near their home in Berkeley that looked out over the entire Bay Area. She had chosen the place, she testified, so that they could always go back there as they grew old together.

"She didn't know I had a ring, and we sat down on the rock and I put my arm around her and I said, 'Will you marry me?' And she looked really happy, and then she looked really confused."

"Yes," Sandy had answered, followed by, "Well, what does that mean? How will we even do that?"

This was before the mayor of San Francisco began marrying gay and lesbian couples at City Hall, Kris said, so "we had to invent it for ourselves." But while they were in the midst of planning a ceremony, the city began issuing marriage licenses.

The day they were issued one of their own, Kris told the court, she was as "amazed and happy as I could ever imagine feeling." As a lesbian, marriage was not something she had allowed herself to want, "because everyone tells you you are never going to get it." Throughout that day, she felt as though she were floating above the ceremony: "Oh, that's me getting married! I never thought that would happen."

What, Olson asked, was her reaction when she learned, via a form letter, that the marriage license had been deemed invalid?

"Well, the part of me that was disbelieving and unsure of it in the first place was confirmed. That, in fact I really—almost when you're gay, you think you don't really deserve things."

"And what feelings did that evoke, that experience?"

"I'm not good enough to be married."

First Spencer, then Kris's mother, and finally Elliott began to cry. Kris was talking now about how, recognizing that her sexual orientation was something that some people would not like, she had gone to great lengths to be funny, likable, to "develop other traits that people do like."

"Oh my God, that's Chad," Kristina said.

Kris's boys had never seen her so vulnerable. She had told them stories about her life, but her manner had been matter-of-fact. "All these years, this has been eating away at her," Elliott thought, "and I never knew."

Even Cooper, leaning back in his chair at the counsel's table, was deeply moved. "They seemed like two of the most decent, likable, friendly, good people that you would ever want to meet," he said, recalling their testimony years later.

In the days and months ahead, there would be times when the plaintiffs would wonder whether Cooper's heart was really in this fight. That wasn't it, not exactly. For him, the question of whether the Constitution mandated same-sex marriage was an easy one. But, he said, "I don't think this is an easy political issue." He would not say whether he would have voted for or against Prop 8 had he lived in California, but it was clear that his views were more nuanced than his clients', the initiative's proponents. Listening to Kris testify, he said, reminded him of "why this is such an agonizingly difficult issue."

"What was going through my head? The best I can do is say that I believe that her position, and the view that many people take in favor of allowing people like her and her partner to get married, is a legitimate position that I respect."

Olson, oblivious to the effect this was having on his opponent, pressed on. He was having a hard enough time not breaking down himself.

As Cooper had expected, Olson preemptively asked Sandy about her first marriage, and whether she was sure that she was gay. "You've lived with a husband. You said you loved him. Some people might say, 'Well, it's this and then it's that and it could be this again.' Answer that."

"Well, I'm convinced because at forty-seven years old I have fallen in love one time," she replied, "and it's with Kris."

Why, then, he wanted to know, did the two women not try to marry again when the California Supreme Court struck down the law that had banned cities like San Francisco from issuing them a license?

"I don't want to be humiliated anymore," Sandy said. "I told Kris, 'I want to marry you in the worst way, but I want it to be permanent and I don't want any possibility of it being taken away.'"

What sorts of awkward or humiliating situations did they face as a result of not being married? Olson asked. "Give the court some examples of things in everyday life."

Sandy described picking up Kris's boys from school. She thought of herself as their stepmother, but she would have to explain that she was "the domestic partner of their mother." At the doctor's office, forms asked if patients were single, married, or divorced. There was no box for them, like they didn't even exist. And how when they went to stores together, someone was always asking if they were sisters, a question that meant they had to decide whether to come out to a perfect stranger or simply buy the microwave they were there to get.

"The decision every day to come out or not come out, at work, at home, at PTA, at music, at soccer, is exhausting," Kris said. "I'm a forty-five-year-old woman. I have been in love with a woman for ten years, and I don't have a word to tell anybody about that. I don't have a word."

"Would a word do it?" Olson asked.

"Well, why would everybody be getting married if it didn't do anything? I think it must do something."

If the courts of the United States were ultimately to decide that same-sex couples did have a constitutional right to marry, "do you think that would have an effect on other acts of discrimination against you?" Olson asked Kris.

"Objection, Your Honor." Raum stood. "Speculation."

"Close, but objection overruled," Walker said. "State of mind. You may answer."

"I believe for me, personally as a lesbian, that if I had grown up in a world where the most important decision I was going to make as an adult was treated the same way as everybody else's decision, that I would not have been treated the way I was," Kris said.

"There's something so humiliating about everybody knowing that you want to make that decision and you don't get to—that, you know, it's hard to face the people at work and the people even here right now. And many of you have this, but I don't. So I have to still find a way to feel okay and not take every bit of discriminatory behavior toward me too personally, because in the end that will only hurt me and my family.

"So if Prop 8 were undone, and kids like me growing up in Bakersfield right now could never know what this felt like, then I assume that their entire lives would be on a higher arc. They would live with a higher sense of themselves that would improve the quality of their entire life."

"Thank you, Your Honor," Olson said. "I have no further questions."

Neither did Cooper's team. At 4:02 P.M., court adjourned for the day. Spencer made a dash for Kris. "Mom, do you know how much I love you, and how proud I am of you?" he asked, enfolding her in a hug. Kris's mother joined in. "The whole darned court was crying," she said.

———

Back at the Gibson Dunn offices that night, the mood was celebratory. Walking into the war room where everybody had gathered, Olson was all smiles, shouting, "A standing ovation for our plaintiffs!"

The day had gone off with very few glitches from a media standpoint. The image from the rally that had moved on the Associated Press wire service had been "theirs," Kristina reported: no men in wedding dresses. Olson's postcourt dramatic reading of his opening statement had made the local news. Yusef Robb, the team's rapid response man, shook his head at it all.

"There are some people in the world who can make crazy shit happen, and Chad's one of them," he said. "Everyone lost hope after Prop 8 won and said, 'What should we do?' But this guy got it done. It's Ted Olson and David Boies and a full trial!"

Legally, Boies crowed about the fact that Cooper hadn't cross-examined three of the plaintiffs and had barely questioned Paul—"a mistake," he called it. Sipping a diet A&W root beer and nibbling on pretzels, he mused about what he would have done had he been in Cooper's shoes. "When you get hit like that, you need to pull the sting out of it. For example, Paul and Jeff did not get married between June and November of 2008. They had an excuse for that, but it wasn't perfect. You go, 'How important was it to you?'"

Olson got closer to the truth. "They're afraid of them," he said. "They think asking more questions would only help our case."

But this was no time to rest on laurels. Before leaving for the day, Olson convened the lawyers for a quick planning conference. There had been some problems with exhibits and technical difficulties playing the campaign ads that morning, the kind that could cause them to lose credibility with the court if repeated, he warned.

"I think we had a very good day," he said, "but the rest of the week has to be flawless."

Walking over to the St. Regis Hotel bar with Kristina for a drink, Matt McGill had much the same take. Cooper might, as Michele Reiner had put it earlier that day, seem "unimpressive" to the unschooled, but McGill knew better. His argument that allowing gays and lesbians to marry could lead to bisexual polygamy was "an intellectually appealing sophistry," he told Kristina, and one "we'll have to grapple with."

Cooper had gone up against Boies and Olson in two other cases, one involving a school desegregation busing policy in Delaware, and another an election recount in Puerto Rico. He had emerged the victor in both. Notwithstanding the Ninth Circuit's narrow discovery carve-out, Cooper so far had managed to keep them from seeing the campaign's most sensitive internal communications, and he had convinced the Supreme Court to hear his arguments on why the proceedings shouldn't be broadcast.

"I don't believe they will just lay down and die," McGill told Kristina. "I know these guys too well."

ELEVEN

HISTORY LESSONS

With the plaintiffs' emotional testimony behind them, Olson and the rest of the team now moved into the next phase of their case, a methodical unspooling of expert testimony by academics in the fields of history, sociology, psychology, economics, and political science. It was going to be "like getting a PhD in all things gay," Chad enthused.

But Cooper, looking over the lineup, dismissed it as largely irrelevant. Olson's case, he would later say, amounted to "one big Brandeis brief," a term that refers to twentieth-century litigator Louis Brandeis, who in 1908 pioneered a style of argument that rejected the conservative notion of the law as a static set of truths etched into stone at the time of the nation's founding. and instead demanded that it respond to changing realities, taking into account not only the framers' original intent and precedent but new facts that could be gleaned from sociological and scientific study.

Cooper and many "originalists" like him viewed social science research as a treacherous and philosophically flawed foundation upon which to build constitutional rulings. The Constitution, they argued, is "dead, dead, dead," as Justice Scalia liked to say, and its interpretation should not change over time as a result of studies that may or may not reflect the biases of those conducting them, or scientific consensus that might later prove wrong.

But the debate was largely academic. The power of social science to move the justices in major civil rights litigation was undeniable. In *Brown v. Board of*

Education, for instance, the high court relied on the testimony of some thirty witnesses and reams of sociological data in concluding that the "separate but equal" doctrine used to justify segregation in the public schools was in fact inherently unequal, generating in black children "a feeling of inferiority as to their status in the community that may affect their hearts and minds in a way unlikely ever to be undone."

Among the evidence the justices considered was a powerful study in which black children who attended segregated schools were given two dolls. Overwhelmingly, they chose the white doll to play with and associated the black doll with being "bad." Chief Justice Earl Warren, writing for the Court, declared that "in approaching this problem we cannot turn the clock back" to 1868, the year that the Fourteenth Amendment, with its promise of equal protection under the law, was adopted, or even to 1896, the year the high court upheld segregation laws. "We must consider public education in the light of its full development and its present place in American life throughout the nation."

Olson hoped the courts would do the same when it came to marriage. The first order of business, then, was to help the court understand the roots of the institution, and to that end, the team called Nancy Cott, a professor of history at Harvard University and the author of the book *Public Vows: A History of Marriage and the Nation.*

Far from being the tradition-bound union that Cooper had portrayed, Cott testified that marriage is a complex and dynamic institution that has evolved over time to reflect society's changing values. It has not always been a union of one man and one woman, she said; the Bible is filled with examples of polygamists. The ancient Jews practiced polygamy, and it is still practiced in many Muslim cultures today. Nor is marriage an institution whose historic central purpose was to encourage responsible procreation, though that certainly is a benefit, she said. In this country, the ability to bear children has never been a prerequisite for marriage.

"In fact, it's a surprise to many people to learn that George Washington, who is often called the father of our country, was sterile."

Rather, she testified, marriage is both a private and public institution. It is "the principal happy ending in all of our romantic tales," with a social meaning that domestic partnership cannot approach. And, she said, as far as the state is concerned, it is primarily a tool of political governance.

Initially, it set up men as heads of households so that they would be economically responsible for their spouses and for all of their dependents, whether biological children, relatives, slaves, or apprentices. The point, she said, was to make it easier for a sovereign to govern a large, varied population by dividing it up into the smaller units now known as households. "The institution of marriage has always been at least as much about supporting adults as it has been about supporting minors."

The ability to marry has also long been equated with liberty in the United States, she testified, becoming more inclusive over time as the discriminatory impulses of the majority fell by the wayside. "This can be seen very strikingly in American history through the fact that slaves during the period, the long period that American states had slavery, slaves could not marry," she said.

"Why were slaves barred from marrying?" asked Ted Boutrous, who was handling her direct examination.

"Because as unfree persons, they could not consent," she answered. "They lacked that very basic liberty of person, control over their own actions that enabled them to say, 'I do,' with the force that 'I do' has to have. Which is to say, 'I am accepting the state's terms for what a valid marriage is.'"

"What happened when the slaves were emancipated?" Boutrous asked, lingering on this point, because it was critical to their due process argument that marriage was a fundamental liberty right.

"They flocked to get married," she answered.

Citing contemporaneous historical accounts, Cott said that an ex-slave and Union soldier called the marriage covenant "'the foundation of all our rights,' meaning that it was the most everyday exhibit of the fact that he was a free person."

"In addition to the restrictions on slaves marrying, do any other restrictions come to mind?" Boutrous asked.

"Yes," Cott answered. In the mid-1800s, a series of laws were passed barring white women from marrying the Asian laborers who had migrated by the tens of thousands to the nation's western states.

So, Boutrous asked, when Cooper, in his opening statement, declared that "racial restrictions were never a definitional feature of the institution of marriage," was that accurate?

"No," she answered.

He pressed the point, asking if she saw any parallels between the race restrictions of the past and the restrictions that Prop 8 had put in place forbidding same-sex couples from marrying.

"I think that the most direct parallel is that racially restrictive laws prevented individuals from having complete choice on whom they married, in a way that designated some groups as less worthy than other groups."

And what about the justifications that were proffered for restricting interracial marriages? Boutrous wanted to know.

"These laws were defended as naturally based and God's plan," she said, adding that efforts to undo them were met with predictions very similar to the predictions now being made about what would happen if gays and lesbians were allowed to marry, that the institution of marriage "would be degraded" and somehow "devalued."

Did that happen? she was asked.

No, she answered, citing statistics that showed that people continued to marry apace.

The team had predicted that the most difficult cross-examination question Cott was likely to face was, as Chris Dusseault had put it, "If marriage is so adaptable, why has it always been between a man and a woman"—or, as Cooper frequently called it, a "gendered institution" by its very nature?

We need a good way for her to say, well, we're at a point in history where that is not relevant, Boutrous had said.

Now he turned to how marriage laws in the United States had changed over time to reflect society's evolving understanding of the role the different sexes play in a union.

Early on in our country's history, Cott said, the state dictated the roles of spouses through a doctrine called "coverture." When a woman married a man, she lost her independent legal and economic identity, "which is really why Jane Doe became Mrs. John Smith." It was a reciprocal bargain in which the husband's duty, enforced by the state, was to provide the wife and his other dependents with basic material goods, while the wife was obligated to lend him all her property and serve and obey him.

"'That asymmetry was seen as absolutely essential," Cott explained, "because assumptions were, at the time, that men were suited to be providers, were suited for certain sorts of work, whereas women, the weaker sex, were suited to be dependent."

But with the move away from an agrarian society and into a more mechanized one, the sexual division of labor became less rigid. As the suffrage movement gained steam and women were given the right to vote, the doctrine of coverture seemed more and more archaic. By the 1970s, the laws had caught up, and today the spousal roles the state assigns are gender neutral, obligating both spouses to support one another.

Because the sexual division of labor is no longer the founding feature of how economic benefit is created in this country, she said, "there is no longer an expectation that the man-woman difference is needed to found [a] household." And given that couples can and do have children outside of the natural procreative process, she added, "it seems to me that by excluding same-sex couples from the ability to marry . . . that society is actually denying itself another resource for stability."

It was a strong point to end on, and Boutrous decided to do so. "Your Honor," he said, "I think I may have covered the waterfront."

———

David Thompson, the trial lawyer on Cooper's team, did not have Boies's flair when it came to tearing into adversarial witnesses. But he was workmanlike and thorough. His habit of ending most of his questions with the word "correct?" was vaguely annoying in its repetitiveness but effective in eliciting the kind of yes-or-no answer that he wanted. Over the course of the trial, Judge Walker would come to admire Thompson as the best on Cooper's team.

Cooper's researchers had compiled dossiers on each of the expert witnesses whom Olson planned to call. Some, perhaps not surprisingly given that gay and lesbian studies had long been considered an academic backwater, were themselves gay. Cooper, assuming Olson and Boies would "pull those teeth" themselves, had decided not to raise their sexual orientation as an issue. But the plan was to try to paint the experts as impassioned activists whose work should not be considered reliable for the purpose of deciding this case.

Approaching Cott, Thompson set to it. With red hair and a plump face framed by preppy wire-rimmed glasses, he looked younger than his forty-one years, making it easy—and dangerous—to underestimate him. He had not become a managing partner of Cooper's firm by happenstance.

Thompson began by noting that Cott had, without compensation, participated in a number of the cases challenging same-sex marriage bans in state courts, describing herself in one deposition as "somewhat between a neutral party and an advocate."

"You think that gays and lesbians should have the right to marry, correct?" he asked.

Cott, who is straight, refused to budge. "I have come to that view from my research and study of the history of marriage, yes."

For the next two-plus hours, he questioned her about her past writings, years-old syllabi, and even Bill Clinton's dalliance with White House intern Monica Lewinsky, hoping to show that her views were out of the mainstream. "In your opinion, morality has been uncoupled from marriage, correct?"

Cott answered in an impatient tone that a schoolteacher might use with a particularly disappointing student. If you are quoting my work on Clinton, she lectured Thompson, the only point she had been trying to make was that the law no longer saw adultery as a crime. The public's forgiveness of the president showed that people believed that spouses themselves, not the state, were best able to judge what is appropriate within a marriage.

There was little Thompson could do about her most powerful testimony, regarding the history of slavery and marriage, besides to note that interracial marriage bans were not as widespread as today's bans on same-sex unions. Instead, he worked to reframe the debate, from one about liberty to one involving a conflict between religion and tradition on the one hand and modernity on the other.

Cott acknowledged that it was true that civil marriage had never been hermetically sealed off from religion; the church, she acknowledged, played a role. And while polygamy was practiced in some parts of the world, she agreed with Thompson that the American tradition of monogamy reflected its Christian traditions. But when Thompson began a discourse on "Jesus Christ and his apostles," Cott curtly shut him down: "I know very little about Jesus Christ and his apostles."

At times, Cott appeared to be a mere prop for Thompson, who seemed to be speaking right past everyone in this courtroom and directly to the justices of the Supreme Court, like when he asked Cott whether she had ever read the writings of Edmund Burke.

To Cott, the question seemed to come out of left field, but as Cooper watched the exchange, he was animated, happy even, rocking back and forth in his chair and twiddling his thumbs.

Burke, an Anglo-Irishman considered the father of American conservatism, had counseled "infinite caution" when "pulling down" or expanding "an edifice which has answered in any tolerable degree for ages to common purposes," without "having models and patterns of approved utility before his eyes."

The point Thompson was making with his obscure reference, Cooper would later explain, was that it was prudent, not irrational or bigoted, for voters who supported Proposition 8 to be reluctant to break with tradition when it came to an ages-old institution. And Cooper could care less that the reference passed over the heads of many in the courtroom; he was sure the one person at whom it was aimed would understand the reference: Justice Kennedy, who had quoted Burke in one of his own opinions.

Thompson, pressing that point, confronted Cott with her own words. As adaptable as marriage in this country has been, during a 2004 NPR interview Cott had acknowledged that allowing same-sex couples to wed would represent a "distinctive watershed" moment.

"The consequences of same-sex marriage is an impossible question to answer—yes or no?" Thompson asked.

"You're asking me to say yes or no?"

"I am."

"Right. I believe no one predicts the future that accurately."

"That was, if not the most important concession made by one of the other side's witnesses at trial, in the top five, because it went to the heart of our Burkean argument," Cooper later said.

The testimony was hardly the "disaster" that Prop 8's defenders claimed it to be during their midday news conference, and the consensus of Olson and the team was that Cott had held up well under pressure. But Thompson had scored some points.

"A little different than yesterday," Kris's mom said to Sandy.

The next witness called was George Chauncey, a history professor at Yale University. He had authored several books on the history of discrimination against gays and lesbians, and his testimony on that subject was critical to convincing the court that it ought to subject Proposition 8 to heightened scrutiny.

Olson was worried about tasking Terry Stewart, the chief deputy city attorney, with the direct examination of such an important witness. At one level, his trepidation was a little patronizing. It was Stewart, after all, who had won the right for gays and lesbians to marry at the California Supreme Court long before Olson had gotten involved in the cause. And it was Stewart who had been integral to finding Chauncey and ten of the other witnesses who would testify on behalf of the plaintiffs. But the team was still gelling, and Olson had never seen Stewart in court. The night before, he had wondered out loud whether Boies ought to handle the direct.

"My question is, how good is she going to be?" Olson asked. "Not the witness. Her."

Boies, who had been helping Stewart prepare, assured Olson that she was ready. Besides, he said, Chauncey was not the most flexible of witnesses. It would be jarring for him, this late in the game, to change horses.

Now, as Stewart guided Chauncey back through time, the court was riveted. That at times the audience had to strain to hear the soft-spoken professor did nothing to diminish the ugliness of his narrative.

Throughout much of modern American history, gays and lesbians were demonized as criminals and perverts. They were prohibited by decency standards from being depicted in Hollywood movies, lumped in with Communists and barred from government service, hunted down in the bars where they congregated, and thrown in jail or summarily fired for their private sexual conduct. Proposition 8, Chauncey testified, was just the latest manifestation of a sustained campaign of prejudice, and its messaging echoed past efforts to portray gays and lesbians as enemies of children.

Beginning in the late nineteenth century, with the emergence of gay and lesbian subcultures in large American cities, police began looking for innovative new ways to combat what they deemed "degenerate" homosexual conduct. Sodomy laws, which would not be struck down as unconstitutional until 2003, had been on the books in one form or another since colonial-era prohibitions against nonprocreative sex, but they required catching someone in the act.

And so disorderly conduct statutes became the go-to tool for stepped-up enforcement, resulting in tens of thousands of arrests in the mid-twentieth century, especially after the New York Legislature specified that one form of disorderly conduct involved standing about in public for the purpose of soliciting a man for unnatural sex acts. Chauncey testified that the law was even used to arrest people for attending parties at private homes.

Liquor licensing offered another tool, Chauncey said. In 1933, New York became the first of many states to prohibit any establishment from serving gays and lesbians, or allowing them to congregate on their premises. To be sure that bartenders who suspected customers of being gay would "86" them, publicly asking them to leave, the police sent plainclothes officers to loiter in establishments. They looked for women sporting short hair or men whose dress was unconventional or effeminate. In one case that Chauncey stumbled across, they even used the fact that two men were talking about opera as evidence that they were gay, since that was "something that no real man would do in the 1950s," Chauncey said.

The result was that gay culture was driven further underground, to establishments willing to pay off police, often run by criminal syndicates. Gay life was thus enmeshed in a "web of criminality," Chauncey explained, and the fear of being arrested kept many people from coming out at all.

"Of course, this also meant that fewer heterosexuals, or relatively few heterosexuals, thought that they knew gay people," he told the court, which made it "easier for demonic stereotypes to develop, given that real living gay people had to be so careful to hide themselves."

The most dangerous of those stereotypes developed between the 1930s and 1950s, Chauncey said, with a series of police and press campaigns that identified homosexuals as child molesters. In the fall of 1950, *Coronet* magazine published an article entitled "New Moral Menace to Our Youth." Chauncey read an excerpt for the court:

"Once a man assumes the role of homosexual he often throws off all moral restraints," the article charged. "Some male sex deviants do not stop with infecting their often innocent partners: they descend through perversions to other forms of depravity, such as drug addiction, burglary, sadism, and even murder."

Soon, Senator Joe McCarthy would be trying to root out homosexuals from government in addition to Communists, and in 1953 one of President Dwight Eisenhower's first acts in office was to ban homosexuals from serving in the federal government in any capacity.

It would take more than a decade and a half, and a sea change in the popular culture, for the gay community to become angry enough to revolt. By 1969, protesters had taken to the streets on a variety of fronts—to end the Vietnam War, to protest the treatment of blacks in the South, to demand equal rights for women. That year, on a hot summer night, when the police raided a gay bar in Greenwich Village called the Stonewall Inn, the customers took a stand. As word of the demonstration spread, more than five hundred demonstrators showed up, shouting "gay power" and clashing with police in a days-long riot. Stonewall marked a turning point, spawning a movement that saw gay rights groups spring up in nearly every major city in the United States.

A mentor had once told Stewart that the art of being a good lawyer was "to make the other side look like shit and then give the judge the tools—the law— to flush them down the toilet." From her point of view, the history that Chauncey had just recounted went a ways toward both goals. But in the event that the court was reluctant to apply heightened scrutiny to a new class of people and instead wanted to decide the Prop 8 case based solely on a *Romer*-like analysis that it was motivated by animus, she needed to link the past to the present.

She began with the backlash that had occurred when municipalities, responding to the newly organized gay community, began including gays and lesbians in antidiscrimination measures. Most, Chauncey told the court, ended up getting stripped from the books as the result of campaigns like the one Anita Bryant, a famous Baptist singer, organized in Florida in 1977.

Bryant's "Save Our Children" campaign was overt in its animus, with ads that played into the stereotype of gays as child molesters. One that Stewart introduced into the record claimed that the "recruitment of our children is absolutely necessary for the survival and growth of homosexuality, for since homosexuals cannot reproduce, they must recruit, must freshen their ranks."

The official Prop 8 campaign material was more coded, but Chauncey said its "Protect Our Children" messaging evoked the same stereotype.

"You have to ask the question, protect against what?" he said, adding an expert's perspective to Paul's earlier testimony about how the ads had made him feel. "It evokes, for me, the language of saving our children, the need to protect children from exposure to homosexuality. Not just from exposure to homosexuals as presumed child molesters, but protecting them from exposure, from the idea of openly gay people."

Kris, listening as Chauncey wrapped up the testimony for the day, looked at Sandy. At family get-togethers, Kris was still referred to as Aunt Sandy's "good friend, Miss Kris." One of Sandy's sisters did not acknowledge their relationship, or the case. Her brother worried that the front-page treatment of the trial would force him to have to explain their relationship and legal battle to his nine-year-old twins, whom he felt were too young to be told. Sandy loved her brother and did not want to be overly confrontational, so she had simply said that if they were old enough to know about marriage, they were old enough to understand.

But the notion that her nieces and nephews needed to be shielded from something about her had hurt. Sandy yearned for the support and validation of her closest family members, but it was elusive.

"It's really hard on Sandy," Kris said. "I think they would all just like to blink their eyes and have me be a man."

TWELVE

A DAY OF SURPRISES

Your Honor, we would object!" said David Thompson, jumping to his feet.

It was the afternoon of the third day of trial, and the AFER legal team had just sprung what was referred to internally as "the Tam Surprise." Lawyers for the plaintiffs had stayed up most of the night putting together a mini-movie. It featured clips from the videotaped deposition of Hak-Shing William Tam, the proponent of Prop 8 who had attempted to withdraw from the case. So far, Judge Walker had refused to allow him to do so, and the idea was to use Tam's own words to punctuate Chauncey's academic testimony that prejudice had fueled the Proposition 8 campaign.

Cooper, clearly caught off guard, began pacing. He had fully expected Olson to call Tam at some point, and he had a plan for how to deal with that. But with no Tam on the stand to question, he had no way to try to mitigate the damage.

Moving evidence like the Tam deposition into the record generally requires asking a witness about it. Thompson argued that Chauncey, the witness the plaintiffs were using, was not qualified to comment on Tam's views because he had not covered that ground in his expert report. Terry Stewart interjected, noting that Thompson, cross-examining Chauncey that morning, had suggested that attitudes on gays and lesbians had become far less hostile over time.

"He opened the door to it," Stewart said. "This goes directly to that topic."

"Well," Judge Walker agreed, "I think he did open the door to that subject."

Cooper had never disputed that gays and lesbians suffered a history of discrimination; he had been willing to stipulate to that when he and Olson had discussed how they might streamline the trial. And so Thompson had instead spent much of the morning just trying to show that the discrimination described by Chauncey was a thing of the past. Wasn't it true that Hollywood's censorship of gay characters had given way to box-office hits like *Brokeback Mountain* and *Philadelphia*? he had asked. Didn't the federal government, with the exception of the military, now ban discrimination based on sexual orientation? Hadn't attitudes, particularly among young people, undergone a sea change?

And while Thompson's attempt to portray House Speaker Nancy Pelosi as a powerful ally of gays and lesbians—she had not attended a gay pride parade in her hometown of San Francisco since 2001—had prompted Cleve Jones to waggle his hand and whisper, "Not so much," to Kristina, Kristina was worried that Thompson's cross-examination had been more effective when he turned to President Obama.

"Do President Obama's views on same-sex marriage reflect a moral disapproval of gays and lesbians?" Thompson had asked.

"I believe they reflect a sense that gay relationships are not equal to heterosexual relationships," Chauncey parried.

"Is it possible for someone to have that position and not morally disapprove of gays and lesbians?" Thompson pressed.

"It would be possible," Chauncey finally conceded.

Kristina knew that the president's views presented both a legal and a media problem. Boies had even taken to publicly calling Obama out, with statements like, "I hope my Democratic president will catch up to my conservative Republican co-counsel."

The night before, Kristina had contemplated putting out a press release clarifying that President Obama had actually opposed the passage of Prop 8 as a candidate because he did not believe in writing discrimination into the law. In other words, while he personally believed marriage should be for hetero-

sexual couples, he opposed the passage of same-sex marriage bans that re-
stricted marriage to heterosexual couples. She had dropped the idea, though,
after others in the war room argued that it would be hard to present that
cognitively dissonant position to the public in a way that would actually help
their case.

But as Tam's deposition began to play, Kristina's fear that Thompson's use
of the president might have succeeded in muddying the waters dissipated as
Tam described in graphic terms what had motivated him. He confirmed that
he had sent out campaign literature declaring that the city of San Francisco was
"under the rule of homosexuals," who wanted to legalize "having sex with children," and that he believed that if same-sex marriage were legalized, children
would find homosexuality irresistible.

"My daughter told me her classmates chose to become lesbians and experiment with it after they noticed that same-sex marriage, they think it is a cool
thing," Tam said. "They have some problem getting dates from boys, so same-
sex marriage, since it is in the air, they think, 'Oh, then why not try girls?'"

Listening to it was one of the low points of the trial for Cooper. When he
had been brought on board to argue the case, he did not have a choice of clients:
The Alliance Defense Fund had already filed a motion to intervene on behalf
of the official proponents of Proposition 8. He was hired to represent the Pro-
tectMarriage.com campaign and five California citizens who had collected
voter signatures and petitioned to place Proposition 8 on the ballot: Besides
Tam, they included Republican state senator Dennis Hollingsworth, Mark
Jansson, the Mormon Church's representative on the campaign's executive
committee, and two others.

The first Cooper heard of Tam's views was at the December 1, 2009, argument before the Ninth Circuit, when Olson's team had flagged Tam's writings
during the Ninth Circuit discovery fight. Matt McGill had guessed correctly
that Cooper was behind Tam's subsequent attempt to withdraw. Cooper had
refused to continue to represent Tam, leading Tam's new lawyer, a man who
had served jail time for blocking an abortion clinic, to file the motion. In it, he
told the court that Tam no longer wished to participate in the case because he
did not like "the burden of discovery and the privacy invasion associated with
being a defendant."

Cooper would later say that he had always known that some people had voted for Prop 8 out of ignorance or hostility toward gays and lesbians. But "I believed from the beginning until this day that animus was not the truth of the Prop 8 campaign." His job, as he saw it, was to keep the other side from making it appear as though a "fringe" element was what drove the campaign.

Having Tam continue to represent the proponents in court was not helpful in terms of making that case. Lunch could not come soon enough.

"Trial is a young man's game," an exhausted Olson had told his wife, Lady, before heading to court that day, and throughout much of the morning and early afternoon he had struggled to stay alert.

But the news that arrived on his smartphone at 1:57 P.M. Pacific time jolted him awake. The Supreme Court, after considering Cooper's arguments against broadcasting the trial, had made its temporary prohibition on broadcasting the trial permanent.

Olson read the opinion as Chris Dusseault examined the team's next witness, Letitia Peplau, a professor of social psychology at UCLA. Peplau had prepared an expert report showing that married couples do better than their nonmarried counterparts on a host of fronts: They are likely on average to be healthier and wealthier. And because marriage creates an "exit barrier" that makes it more difficult to separate, they and their children enjoy greater stability.

Most gays and lesbians—74 percent according to one Kaiser Family Foundation study—would like to marry someday, she said, and while she acknowledged that there were no definitive studies on the topic, she saw no reason why they would not enjoy the same benefits that married heterosexual couples did if allowed to do so. As for the impact on straight married couples, she had this to say: "It is very hard for me to imagine that you would have a happily married couple who would say, 'Gertrude, we've been married for thirty years, but I think we have to throw in the towel because Adam and Stuart down the block got married.'"

It was important testimony, but from a news cycle vantage point, both it and Cooper's bad morning had just been eclipsed. On a vote of five to four, with Justice Kennedy once again siding with the conservatives, the Supreme Court declared that Judge Walker had improperly "attempted to change its rules at the eleventh hour to treat this case differently than other trials in the district," and it bought Cooper's argument that witnesses might be subject to harassment if the proceedings were televised.

The four liberal justices vehemently disagreed. Citing the nearly 140,000 comments that had been delivered to Judge Walker's chambers, Justice Stephen Breyer asked, "How much more 'opportunity for comment' does the Court believe necessary?" The majority, he concluded in his dissent, "identifies no real harm" to justify its "extraordinary intervention" on an arcane matter that ought to have been left to Judge Walker and the Ninth Circuit, which had after all signed off on the plan.

Olson put the best face on the decision, both internally and when questioned by the press. The Court's decision meant only that five justices did not like the notion of cameras in the courtroom, which was not a big surprise given that the Supreme Court had for years resisted pressure to televise its own proceedings. It had, he insisted, nothing to do with the merits of their case.

Still, other members of the team could not help but think the decision, with its personal asides, was a bad omen. "This was a smackdown of Judge Walker," McGill told the young gay lawyer Enrique Monagas—"the Big E," McGill had nicknamed him—who had filed the case.

Amir Tayrani, a precisely spoken Gibson Dunn associate who had worked closely with McGill on Olson's Supreme Court cases, noted that it wasn't just Walker the Supreme Court had singled out. The majority had buttressed its finding that witnesses could be subject to intimidation by footnoting Olson's own words in his pending challenge of the nation's campaign finance laws. In a brief filed months before he first met with the Reiners, Olson had pointed to "widespread economic reprisals against financial supporters of California's Proposition 8" to argue that organizations like his client, Citizens United, should not be forced to disclose political donors.

"Troubling," was how Tayrani put it.

When Olson had first asked Tayrani to work on the case, the thirty-two-year-old associate had been skeptical that the Constitution contained a right for gays and lesbians to marry. He had once clerked for one of the most conservative judges on the Ninth Circuit, and he generally took a like-minded view of the law.

But as Tayrani had immersed himself in the case law, he had come to believe that bans like Prop 8 were indefensible and ought to be struck down. Now he had a personal stake as well in not seeing the plaintiffs lose. "I haven't had many gay and lesbian friends," he said. "Just talking to our clients and realizing how much they want to marry and that we've been keeping them from being happy—it has been eye-opening."

———

It had been a draining few days for everyone on the team, and not just because of the Supreme Court ruling. Listening to the cross-examinations had at times been maddening, as when Thompson repeatedly noted that the gay rights movement had historically never made marriage a priority.

"That's a bit like suggesting that because slaves never demanded the right to run for governor, they did not want their freedom," Cleve Jones said after court adjourned for the day. Growing up, he had prayed every night, "Please, God, fix me." When someone at school beat him up and called him a homosexual, he had looked the word up in a book his father, a psychologist, kept in the study. It was in the same chapter as genital deformities and pedophilia.

It was true that the burgeoning gay rights movement he had joined when he moved to San Francisco in 1973 was informed by women's liberation and the sense of sexual freedom sweeping the nation in the late 1960s and early 1970s. But to Jones, its early priorities, so modest as to be sad, had more to do with the reality of the times: Just to be able to cease being invisible and live out in the open seemed a lot. And later, during the height of the HIV/AIDS crisis, the goal was simply to stay alive when so many friends were being buried, which Jones had managed to do despite being stricken.

To calm his nerves, he decided to walk over to City Hall and pay his respects to his mentor, Harvey Milk. He would have loved the audacity of the trial, and especially the sense of self-worth that infused it.

Walking into the building, Jones headed for a grand marble staircase. At the top sits a bust of the gay rights leader, near the office where Jones had found him sprawled on the carpet, shot dead with his stocking feet sticking out into the hallway. He gently patted the bust's bronze cheek.

"Oh, Harvey," he said. "If only you could see what's going on down the street."

THIRTEEN

STIGMA

On the fourth day of trial, the plaintiffs called Dr. Ilan Meyer, a psychiatric epidemiologist, to the stand. His job was to tell the court about the consequences of the discrimination that Chauncey had described. It felt, Chad would tell Kristina afterward, like "you're in therapy, in court, in front of your closest friends—and your enemies."

Meyer, an associate professor of sociomedical sciences at Columbia University's Mailman School of Public Health, had developed a groundbreaking theory called "minority stress syndrome" about how the small and large slights faced by gays and lesbians have a cumulative adverse impact on their psychological well-being, making them twice as likely as their straight counterparts to suffer from disorders ranging from depression and anxiety to substance abuse.

The team had other witnesses who could speak to the harm caused by discrimination, and for that reason, several of the senior members of the team were initially hesitant about calling Meyer. Why give Cooper two bites at that apple?

But the lawyer who had helped find and prep him, Sarah Piepmeier, felt strongly that his study of minority stress syndrome provided uniquely compelling connective tissue that would ultimately help the justices understand how difficult it was to be gay and excluded, just as the doll test had once aided the Warren Court in understanding what it meant to be black and segregated.

Since she was one of only a few gay lawyers on the Gibson team, her view was given weight.

Now, listening to Meyer talk about how society stigmatizes gays and lesbians, Boutrous leaned over and whispered to her that she had been right: "What he's saying is perfect!"

People in general experience different kinds of stress. There is the acute stress of a life event, such as a death in the family; the chronic stress of an ongoing condition such as unemployment; or daily life stressors, such as traffic or a long line at the bank. But when a person has an attribute that society perceives to be a negative one, Meyer testified, that attribute becomes inseparable from the person, who is then devalued, made into a pariah of sorts. That, Meyer said, is the source of an additional stress, called minority stress.

Meyer had studied this effect in hundreds of gays and lesbians, and his work had been given the stamp of approval of the National Academy of Sciences' Institute of Medicine.

Minority stress, he explained, can be caused by outright prejudice, such as being called a name, or worse, being the victim of a hate crime. But it can also be caused by events that in isolation seem innocuous, like the fact that the form Sandy's doctor used did not have a box for her to check.

"One of the things we hear over and over is forms, filling out forms. And it's kind of bewildering, because on one hand you might say, 'What's the big deal about filling out a form?'" he testified. "And the only way I can explain it is that it is really not anything about the form. It is that the form evokes something much larger for the person. It evokes a social disapproval, a rejection."

Same thing when Paul and Jeff checked into a hotel and a desk clerk became confused about the type of room they wanted. A straight couple would probably never be asked, and if they were, they would simply sort it out. But for a gay person, Meyer said, "it's an area of great sensitivity because it really talks to their rejection."

Another source of minority stress comes from the expectation of discrimination and rejection, he said, whether it happens or not. "This is a very—well, to me, interesting process that occurs in populations that are—that are used to prejudice. By 'used' I mean that they know about the prejudice that exists in society. And what happens is that a person who knows that they might be rejected or discriminated against needs to maintain a certain vigilance about their interactions in society that would, first of all, guarantee their safety. So an example that I often use when I talk about this is a gay couple walking down the street. In my experience, very often, regardless of how friendly their street is, they would have to monitor the kind of affection that they display with each other, because perhaps somebody will come and throw stones and eggs, and so forth."

A third source of minority stress for gays and lesbians comes from the effort of concealing something so fundamental to their identity. Even people who are "out" do it occasionally, and members of the U.S. military must, thanks to the Don't Ask, Don't Tell policy. Maintaining a lie takes a very strong cognitive effort, and researchers who have studied concealment in other contexts have called it a "private hell."

Finally, Meyer told the court, gays and lesbians experience the stress of internalized homophobia, "basically internalizing or taking in negative attitudes" and thus living with a diminished expectation about what is possible in their lives.

Take, for instance, one pervasive societal stigma: that gays and lesbians are "incapable of relationships, of intimate relationships, they may be undesiring, even, of intimate relationships," Meyer said. That stereotype can be found in an excerpt of a book, popular in the 1960s and 1970s, called *Everything You Always Wanted to Know About Sex (but Were Afraid to Ask)*.

The book was written in a Q&A format, and one question posed was, "What about all the homosexuals who live together happily for years?" The answer: "They are mighty rare birds among the homosexual flock. Moreover, the 'happy' part remains to be seen. The bitterest argument between husband and wife is a passionate love sonnet by comparison with a dialogue between a butch and his queen. Live together? Yes. Happily? Hardly."

The portrayal, Meyer said, was filled with "ridicule and contempt," and if a young gay man read it he might internalize that stigma. Meyer told the court that shutting gays and lesbians out of marriage as Prop 8 did was to shut them out of an institution with social meaning that people aspire to, telling them, "If you are gay or lesbian, you cannot achieve this particular goal."

Cross-examining Meyer, a lawyer on Cooper's team questioned the professor's analytics, noting that he had not studied whether gays and lesbians fared better in places where marriage was legal, and made a point of telling the court that Meyer had given money to defeat Proposition 8. But Meyer held firm to his conclusions.

Kristina, watching Judge Walker scribbling down notes, wondered what he was thinking—and whether he realized what might soon be headed his way.

―――――

The first sign of trouble had come a day earlier in the form of a headline in the *Wall Street Journal:* QUIRKY JUDGE PRESIDES IN GAY MARRIAGE CASE.

"So it begins," Kristina said with a sigh.

"Can't spell 'quirky' without 'queer,'" the opposition researcher she and Chad had just brought on board agreed.

No one knew for sure whether Cooper and his team were aware of Judge Walker's sexuality, and the *Journal* piece did not mention it. But by day four of the trial, it was clear that there was a concerted effort to attack the judge as biased.

Former attorney general Edwin Meese III, who had led the Justice Department when Walker was nominated, had penned an op-ed in the *New York Times* accusing Walker of "stacking the deck" in favor of the plaintiffs with his pretrial rulings. "Kangaroo-court procedures," declared Edward Whelan III, a former Justice Scalia clerk and a contributor to the *National Review Online*'s Bench Memos, an influential outlet in the conservative legal echo chamber.

That day, the war room fielded its first call from a reporter asking whether Walker was gay. "Unconfirmable," was the response.

Olson's legal team and Chad's media war room were now working in near-perfect synchrony, helping one another address both the court and the court of public opinion. The lawyers had compiled a list of phrases, drawn from Justice Kennedy's opinions, that they felt would resonate with the Court's swing voter. Chad and the plaintiffs wove them into their daily public statements and press releases, framing the right to marry as a matter of "human dignity," "individual liberty," and "freedom" whenever possible. Meanwhile, Chad conferred with the legal team about when to call key witnesses for maximum news cycle advantage, while the researcher that AFER had hired dug into the background of Cooper's star witness, David Blankenhorn.

Blankenhorn held himself out to be a liberal Democrat opposed to same-sex marriage, but his foundation work on marriage and fatherhood was funded by right-wing warriors like billionaire Richard Scaife. And it turned out that the highest degree he had earned was a master's, in a field that had nothing to do with the subject of his testimony: His thesis was on labor union disputes among cabinetmakers in Victorian England.

"Oh, that's too good!" Kristina exclaimed when she heard it. "Let's push that out on the day he goes on the stand."

"Interesting," McGill agreed, and then, because he was, in his words, "the most right-wing nut job on our legal team besides Ted O.," he had to jokingly add, "You elites! Thinking you need a PhD to be an expert."

But the attacks on the judge, amplified by the Supreme Court's reversal of his decision to broadcast the trial, were worrisome. Something needed to be done.

"They've got surrogates to paint the picture of a judge gone wild, and trial run amok," McGill said. "The volume on that is going to get turned up and up and up."

The judge could not defend himself. And the plaintiffs could not be seen to be defending him. So Yusef Robb had been dispatched to line up California Bar Association types to, as he put it, "talk about how careful and boring he is."

Margaret Hoover, a Republican political commentator who had worked in several capacities for President George W. Bush and was the great-granddaughter of the thirty-first president, was also helpful. She had recently agreed to join AFER's advisory board, and in a post on FoxNews.com, she defended the proceedings in California. "You may think, 'San Francisco liberals are at it again! Hijacking the courts, inventing new constitutional rights! Stop there," she wrote. Olson, the lead counsel in the case, was "one of the most respected conservatives in America."

Chad and Kristina, meanwhile, focused on attacking the Supreme Court's decision prohibiting the broadcasting of the trial, which their opponents were now citing as the latest evidence of Walker's wrongheadedness. The team did not want to criticize the justices directly.

But surrogates like Los Angeles mayor Antonio Villaraigosa, writing in the *Huffington Post,* said the "unjust" ruling was keeping the public from seeing "the true face of intolerance and prejudice behind Proposition 8," while behind the scenes Chad and his team worked newspaper editorial boards. Olson, after seeing that the *New York Times* had called proponents' claims of intimidation "hazy and unsubstantiated," e-mailed Chad: "For once I agree with a NYT editorial."

They had done what they could do. That night in the war room, Chad turned to a tangential issue. Appellate courts such as the Ninth Circuit and the Supreme Court do not hear from witnesses directly; they simply review the written record to determine whether the law was correctly applied. Now that there was no chance that the justices of the Supreme Court would see the plaintiffs' emotional testimony on television, Olson was urging Chad to try to find other ways to circulate their stories.

That morning, Cooper had asked that Judge Walker turn off the cameras and destroy the footage filmed to date. Walker had refused, saying he wanted to be able to review the footage in chambers, and the back-and-forth had given Chad an idea.

The war room should turn the fact that "the other side is trying to have the plaintiffs' testimony destroyed" into an opportunity, he said. It could make the plaintiffs more attractive to daytime talk shows, for instance. Never mind that it was impossible at the moment to break through the wall-to-wall coverage of a catastrophic earthquake that had just hit Haiti. Chad was not one to listen to excuses.

"Free the plaintiffs," he said, urging them to be creative. "It's a great message."

FOURTEEN

ON PARENTS AND FAMILIES

The e-mail was buried in the thirty thousand pages of documents that ProtectMarriage.com had been forced to deliver to Gibson Dunn. And as soon as Matt McGill saw it, he knew that the fight to win an exception to the Ninth Circuit's order protecting internal campaign documents from discovery had been worth it.

Attached was an inflammatory article entitled "21 Reasons Why Gender Matters" that portrayed gays and lesbians as sick "sex addicts" and same-gender parents as a danger to children. Ron Prentice, the executive director of Protect-Marriage.com, had e-mailed it to an undisclosed list of Proposition 8 supporters, instructing them to make use of it in the campaign.

"All—the following is self-explanatory," he wrote. "It should be very helpful in many ways, such as sermons, etc. Ron."

The team had spotted the article well before trial, but until now had no way to tie the views it expressed to the proponents of Prop 8. It was, McGill thought, the perfect framing device for the testimony of the expert witness whom he called on the fifth day of trial, Michael Lamb, a psychologist affiliated with the Department of Social and Developmental Psychology at Cambridge University. The article was filled with claims unsupported by science, and it offered an opportunity to rebut the oft-stated claim, repeated in the article that Prentice had sent around, that bans like Prop 8 were justified because they promoted the optimal child-rearing environment.

For a law to pass the rational basis test, the Supreme Court has held that its justification must have "some footing" in reality. As McGill liked to say, "You could not pass a law based on the idea that the earth is flat, when the evidence is conclusive that it is not." McGill hoped to use Lamb, a renowned child development expert who had written or edited some forty books on developmental psychology, to portray the proponents of Proposition 8 as the flat-earthers of today.

McGill had never before examined a witness during a trial. As an appellate guy, he spent his days buried in Supreme Court precedent and drafting briefs. *Perry Mason* it was not. But McGill had swagger and, it soon became clear, a natural feel for what makes for good courtroom drama.

"So, Dr. Lamb," he began, "what makes a good parent?"

"A good parent," Lamb answered, "is one who is effective at reading the signals of that child, understanding what that child needs, and providing appropriate stimulation, guidance, and setting appropriate limits for their children."

The "21 Reasons Why Gender Matters" article contained a quote from a Rutgers University sociologist: "We should disavow the notion that mummies could make good daddies, just as we should disavow the notion of radical feminists that daddies can make good mummies," he argued. "The two sexes are different to the core and each is necessary."

But Lamb told the court that the "overwhelming consensus" in his field, since at least the early 1990s, was that having parents of different genders is not necessarily determinative of whether a child will be well adjusted. Nor is a biological connection; studies showed that adopted children and children conceived with the help of an egg or sperm donor are just as likely to achieve good outcomes.

Rather, the optimal environment for children is one in which they are raised by loving, caring parents who live in harmony with each other and are able to provide adequate economic resources. Gender and blood connections are irrelevant, Lamb told the court.

What about a point that Cooper had raised during his opening argument, when he quoted President Obama on the importance of fathers? McGill asked. He showed Obama's quote on an overhead: "Children who grow up without a father are five times more likely to live in poverty and commit crime; nine times more likely to drop out of schools and twenty times more likely to end up in prison."

First, Lamb said, those studies compared children being raised by two heterosexual parents to children being raised by a single, heterosexual mom. And "actually, the research, now quite voluminous, shows that the absence of a father in and of itself isn't the crucial factor." Rather, what accounted for the differences cited by the president, he said, was that children are more likely to have problems when deprived of a parent's involvement in their life and forced to cope with the economic deprivation that often accompanies divorce or separation.

McGill moved now to the heart of the matter. "Dr. Lamb, have researchers within your field conducted any studies of the adjustment of children raised by gay or lesbian parents?"

Lamb said that there had been more than one hundred peer-reviewed studies on the subject, "documenting very conclusively that children who are raised by gays and lesbians are just as likely to be well adjusted as children raised by heterosexual parents."

McGill, lest the court miss the significance of that statement, entered a number of those studies into the record and had Lamb read aloud the conclusion of the American Psychological Association's policy statement:

"There is no scientific basis for concluding that lesbian mothers and gay fathers are unfit parents on the basis of their sexual orientation," Lamb read. "On the contrary, results of research suggest that lesbian and gay parents are as likely as heterosexual parents to provide supportive, healthy environments for their children."

The American Academy of Child and Adolescent Psychiatry, the American Academy of Pediatrics, the American Psychiatric Association, the American Psychoanalytic Association, the Child Welfare League of America, the National Association of Social Workers, and the North American Council on Adoptable Children had all reached similar conclusions, and McGill dumped them into the record as well.

The inference, of course, was that if the rationale offered by proponents of Prop 8 was not fact- or evidence-based, it must be the result of the kind of prejudice that Justice Kennedy had described as the "want of careful, rational reflection." Next, McGill turned to some of the other claims made in the article that Prentice had circulated for use in the Prop 8 campaign, the kind Cooper was not using to try to justify Prop 8 in court because they fell into the more overtly hostile category.

Among them: that "gender disorientation pathology," as the article described homosexuality, is a sex addiction that "encourages the sexual and psychological exploitation of children" because "the sad truth is, homosexual abuse of children is proportionately higher than heterosexual abuse of children." The term itself, Lamb testified, could be found nowhere in the psychiatric or psychological literature, and studies going all the way back to the 1970s proved that gays and lesbians are no more likely to abuse children than are straight people.

Another of the article's assertions, that the children of gays and lesbians are more likely to be gay themselves, deliberately misled readers, Lamb told the court, by footnoting a study that concluded no such thing. (What the study did find was that there was no difference between the psychosocial outcomes of children of lesbian parents and children of straight couples, a fact not mentioned in the "21 Reasons Why Gender Matters" article Prentice had circulated.) In fact, Lamb told the court, the consensus of the scientific community was that while the children of gays and lesbians tend to be less likely to embrace sex role stereotypes, the sexual orientation of their parents has no bearing on whether they will be gay or straight.

If gay and lesbian parents were allowed to marry, he concluded, the only likely impact on their children would be to improve their chances of achieving the best outcomes in life, in exactly the same way that research showed that the children of cohabitating straight couples benefit when their parents wed.

"In the thousands of books and publications you have written and reviewed in your career, have you ever encountered a sound rationale for purposefully denying a child the opportunity to achieve the best possible outcome?" McGill asked.

"No, I have not."

"I have no more questions, Your Honor."

=====

It was 2:45 P.M. when McGill rose again.

"Dr. Lamb, do you need a break?" he asked, hamming it up a little with the solicitousness of his tone. "Are you all right?"

The courtroom erupted in laughter. For four hours, Lamb had endured a cutting cross-examination by David Thompson. Voice like a jackhammer,

Thompson had thrown out one staccato question after the next in a tone that made clear what he thought of this particular witness's pedigree.

You have been a member of the American Civil Liberties Union, is that correct? And a member of the National Organization for Women, the NAACP, Amnesty International, and the Nature Conservancy, is that correct?

"You have even given money to PBS!" Thompson charged. "So we can agree you are a committed liberal, is that right?"

Thompson never mentioned the damaging Prentice e-mail, or most of its claims, during his cross. Instead, after establishing that Dr. Lamb personally supported allowing gays and lesbians to marry, he had proceeded to phase two of the cross-examination, an attack on science itself. This was the witness Cooper had chosen to make his full-throated Brandeis brief stand, that social science should play no role in determining a constitutional question like this one, and that no matter what studies might say, the impact of allowing gays and lesbians to marry was unknowable.

Wasn't it true that much of the science in his field was funded by government research agencies that, by their nature, were not insulated from political ideology? Thompson demanded.

"Your question presumes that the decisions are being made by governments about what sorts of topics should be studied," Lamb replied. "In fact, certainly in this country, agencies like the National Science Foundation and the National Institutes of Health pride themselves on having peer reviewers evaluate the scientific quality and integrity and importance of the research."

"You would agree that history is littered with scientific theories that were widely accepted within a scientific community and that have proven to be wrong, correct?"

"Well, I'm not sure about that."

Thompson started listing some, beginning with phrenology, a theory developed in the eighteenth century that linked bumps on the head to certain aspects of an individual's personality or character, and ending with the fact that at the beginning of the twentieth century there was widespread consensus among psychologists that homosexuality was a disease.

"And the psychological community was entirely wrong, wasn't it?"

"Well, that portion of the scientific, of the psychological community, that held that belief was wrong, yes."

"You would concede that there are still many differences between men and women in our society, correct?"

"Yes."

"We can also agree that men can't breast-feed, correct?" Thompson asked. "And breast-feeding clearly has benefits for children."

Lamb agreed with that statement of the obvious. But he rebutted Thompson's suggestion that the studies he had relied upon, showing that children of gays and lesbians do just as well as children of heterosexuals, were flawed because the control sample included unmarried heterosexuals. That was appropriate, Lamb said, because the effect that was being studied was whether the gender of parents mattered, not whether marriage mattered.

Thompson then moved to his next point: Hadn't Dr. Lamb once written that children in fact do need a male parent in order to be well adjusted? If a respected academic like Lamb could do a pirouette on this issue, wasn't it reasonable for Californians to believe that too?

McGill had expected this question and had tried to inoculate Lamb by raising it himself during the direct. Lamb had already explained that in the 1970s, in studying the attachments that babies form to mothers and fathers and the different ways that fathers and mothers behaved toward their children, he had studied the importance of fathers in determining child outcomes.

Judge Walker, watching from the bench, smiled as Lamb thanked Thompson for "bringing back these great old memories" of papers he had written as a graduate student, before answering.

It was true that it was important for children of heterosexual couples to have a good relationship with their fathers, Lamb said, but that did not mean that children of same-sex couples needed one. "That is a finding that has not held up in subsequent research."

This was Thompson's "ah-ha" moment: "Well, so science was wrong!"

No, Lamb replied. Science is "a cumulative process."

———

Now Thompson watched, hand on chin, as his old colleague McGill approached the witness. The purpose of a redirect is to undo whatever damage has been done on cross and allow the witness to clarify any points that the opposing counsel had taken out of context. McGill approached the mission with his sardonic brand of humor.

"Let's warm up our time machine and go way back in time, before that cross-examination began, and all the way back to 1975, when you held the view that the presence of a father itself could be a determinative factor in adjustment outcomes," McGill ad-libbed. "Why is it that your views, from before I was born to now"—he paused for effect as people began laughing—"have changed?"

"Well, the body of evidence has been what's changed it. The original view, as I said, was a hypothesis," Lamb replied. "And since then we have had hundreds, thousands of articles that have explored the implications of that belief and found it to be wrong."

McGill had worried from the outset that Thompson would try to use Lamb's testimony to enter all sorts of studies into the record, authored by people he had no intention of calling or allowing to be cross-examined, in an effort to make it appear that scientists were divided on the question of gay parenting. His hunch had proven correct; among the voluminous exhibits that Thompson had entered into evidence were articles suggesting that research in this field was embryonic and a study that concluded that the children of gays and lesbians are in fact less well adjusted than those raised by married, biological parents.

The main problem with that study, Lamb explained when McGill asked about it, was a problem that the author, if not Thompson, had identified when he published it: The children of the gay couples he studied had frequently experienced the recent separation or divorce of their parents, and as such the study was more illustrative of the effects of divorce than the effects of same-sex parenting.

Have those findings ever been corroborated or duplicated in another study? McGill asked.

"No," Lamb replied. "There's no other study that finds that."

Finally, Lamb had "confessed membership" in a variety of groups during his cross-examination, McGill drily noted. "Did the Corporation for Public Broadcasting influence your opinion in this case?"

"No, it did not."

"Did anything other than the social science research in your field influence your opinion in this case?"

"No, it did not."

"Thank you, Dr. Lamb."

———

One reason that trials make for awkward storytelling is that lawyers are not in sole control of their own narrative. Even in a major civil rights trial like this one, experts had to be reordered to accommodate witnesses' scheduling conflicts and teaching schedules. Then there is the problem of the clock.

A witness's direct testimony should preferably be timed so that the cross-examination does not begin so late in the day that it spills over into the next, giving opposing counsel overnight to regroup and refine attacks. At the same time, lawyers need to be ready with a fill-in witness if a cross ends earlier than expected. Judges don't like to see the court's time wasted, and Walker was always urging the lawyers to move things along.

So it was that when McGill finished with Lamb at 3:02 P.M. on the Friday before the long Martin Luther King Jr. holiday weekend, the legal team found itself needing to call another witness.

One way to look at the Prop 8 trial is that it boiled down, essentially, to a war of words, and one word in particular: marriage. The proponents of Prop 8 argued that because California domestic partnership law conveyed the legal benefits of marriage, the plaintiffs were not being denied anything meaningful. That very morning, Thompson had repeatedly noted that as beneficial as marriage may be to adults and children, there had been no extensive research on whether domestic partnership offered similar perks.

Helen Zia was not an expert, and her testimony did not speak to the main, parenting issue of the day. But as a California resident who had married her domestic partner prior to the passage of Prop 8, she could speak to why that one word, "married," matters, in a way that the unmarried plaintiffs could not. And as a Chinese American living in San Francisco, her testimony offered the team an opportunity to try to close an important loop: whether voters in the city's large Asian community had in fact been motivated by the types of messages Tam had disseminated.

Zia was supposed to be Boies's witness. But Terry Stewart, who had found

Zia and lobbied for her inclusion, had taken him aside and asked if he would mind ceding the job to one of the lawyers on her staff. Danny Chou, a former California Supreme Court clerk, had worked hard on the case, and she wanted him to have his moment in the spotlight.

It was not the way that Boies's operation generally worked; the lawyers from his firm were there to prepare him, moons to his sun. But that was the funny thing about Boies. He could be something of a savant, so monomaniacal in his focus that at times he seemed unaware of the feelings of others. But when he dialed back in, he had a gift for making a person feel as though no one in the room was more important. He was unquestionably self-promoting, but he could also be exceedingly generous, whispering advice for which he never took credit during Stewart's redirect of Chauncey, and now readily agreeing to her request and convincing Olson to go along.

"I can't tell you how much real estate he occupies in my heart," Stewart said after she learned the news.

Zia was a former executive editor of *Ms.* magazine and the author of two books, including one about Wen Ho Lee, the Chinese American scientist at Los Alamos National Labs who had been falsely accused of being a spy. Rosanne Baxter, a litigator at Boies's firm who had helped prep her, had been worried that her factual journalistic delivery lacked emotion. "Show a little leg, honey!" she'd wanted to say.

But after fending off the vociferous objections of Cooper's team—this woman had been dragged in "off the street" to testify to what amounted to nothing more than "needlessly cumulative" personal experience with no "probative value," Brian Raum, Cooper's co-counsel at the Alliance Defense Fund, charged—Chou had managed to coax the passion out of Zia.

She was angry when describing how she and her wife, Lia Shigemura, had been treated when they campaigned in their community against Prop 8. "People would just come up to us and say, you know, 'You dyke.' And excuse my language, Your Honor, but 'you fucking dyke.' Or, 'You're going to die and burn in hell. You're an abomination.'

"And while we were handing out fliers, dozens of people, separate people in separate locations, separate times in different cities, would look at the flier, laugh, or just look at us, or say something with a—the most derisive kind of expression, and say, 'No more people. With this, no more people. No more human race.' That we, such abominations, would be the cause of the end of the human race."

All this, she said, because she had married a woman. Her voice softer now, she described the difference that marriage had made, especially in the way her family viewed her relationship. One of her nieces had told her wife, "Auntie Lia, now you're really my auntie."

"My mother, I would watch—my mother is an immigrant from China. English is her second language," Zia told the court. "I would be around her and her friends who—who would look at Lia. And I could hear them say, sometimes in English and sometimes in Chinese, 'Who's she?' You know, and my mother, before we would marry, would just struggle and just say, 'She's Helen's friend.' And then it changed. And she would say, 'This is Helen's—this is my daughter-in-law.' And they would get it. And whether they approved or disapproved, it didn't matter. They got it. It's like, you don't insult someone's wife."

Back at the Gibson Dunn offices after court adjourned for the day, the lawyers from Boies's firm who had been involved in Zia's prep assessed how it had gone. Their boss had already left for the weekend, bound for Las Vegas. The difficult part of Boies's job would start next week, after the plaintiffs rested their case and cross-examination began. Gambling helped relax him, and he planned to spend the weekend hitting the tables at the Wynn casino.

When Zia had been asked under cross-examination about some articles she had authored, she had stumbled a little. "To some gay rights activists, fighting for same-sex marriage is too petty-bourgeoisie, too much about the nuclear family, cocooning, property rights, and all the bad patriarchal things that marriage stands for," she had written. One of the reasons she had married her partner, she wrote, was to express "defiance against the warmongering fundamentalist regime in Washington."

Her response—"That sounds like something I wrote"—had provoked laughter in the courtroom, but the lawyers on Boies's team who had been brought in to ensure that witnesses like Zia were ready for any question that might come their way found it wanting.

"She was prepped seven ways from Sunday on that," said Steve Holtzman, a lawyer who had worked in the trenches with Boies on the Microsoft trial. "She was prepared to say she thought that before."

Olson took a longer view. After working all weekend, he emerged from his office on Monday, January 18. It was Martin Luther King Jr. Day, so the court was not in session, but the trial would resume the following day. Mulling over how the first week had gone with Chad and the rest of the political team in the war room, Olson was in an expansive mood. He likened the trial to a boxing match, except that the judge was keeping score in his own head. But so far, he liked their chances.

Olson and the appellate specialists on his team had been spending a lot of time reviewing the transcripts, checking to ensure that the record included testimony and evidence to back up each of the legal claims he would need to make if the case wound up in the Supreme Court.

The best Cooper had been able to do so far, by Olson's calculations, had been to suggest that the evidence they had put on so far was irrelevant, the word that Andy Pugno, the general counsel of Prop 8, had used during one of the daily dueling press conferences both sides had taken to holding: "The fact that children in other situations are not harmed by other situations is irrelevant," he had told reporters, spinning Dr. Lamb's testimony.

"Nothing they did touched the core of our witnesses' testimony," Olson had said over dinner later that night at his hotel, a sentiment he repeated to Chad and the rest of the media team now. As long as they avoided a "knockdown punch at the end of the final round," they were in good shape, he said.

"Watch out for one another. If you see us going down a bad road, say something," he urged. "We are working on something that every single one of us will remember as one of the finest things we ever did."

FIFTEEN

WHO'S A BIGOT?

T he San Francisco City Attorney's Office overseen by Dennis Herrera had done battle with gun distributors and lead paint manufacturers for deceptive marketing practices, taken on giant financial institutions over credit card scams, and sued some of the state's largest energy companies. His office's aggressive litigation strategy and involvement at every phase of the high-profile marriage fight had allowed him to attract the type of talent typically found at large law firms that pay exponentially more than the city could; he currently had three U.S. Supreme Court clerks working on the Prop 8 case.

But it had been nine years since Herrera had last questioned a witness at trial himself, and he was nervous. Worried about the pounding rain and unable to sleep, he had ordered a car service in the middle of the night to ensure he and his witness would make it to court looking presentable when trial resumed at 8:30 Tuesday morning, then cursed himself for walking out into the downpour without an umbrella. He knew that his distress over the weather was just a proxy for his real concern: All eyes were going to be on him in court today, and not everyone was as sold as he was about the prospect of putting San Diego mayor Jerry Sanders on the stand.

It pays at trial to be risk averse. A witness like Sanders was a gamble, and an unnecessary one at that because he served no imperative legal purpose. "I'm not real crazy about that," Olson had said during one pretrial planning session. "What issue in our case is he relevant to?"

Herrera understood the concern. Olson was thinking two steps ahead, and he did not want anything in the cold hard record of the case that some judge could hang his hat on to justify ruling against them during the appeals phase of the case. What about political power? the Gibson lawyers had asked Herrera. By having an elected official testify in favor of the plaintiffs, would they be giving Cooper ammunition to argue that gays and lesbians have access to the political process and therefore should not be considered a suspect class?

Herrera came at it from a different perspective. As a politician, he felt that the legal team needed to speak to people who did not agree with them, people like his mother-in-law, a deeply religious woman who had spent time in a Catholic convent. Sanders was someone who could do that, a Republican former police chief elected mayor in a conservative part of the state who was prepared to testify about coming to terms with his own unthinking attitudes toward gays and lesbians.

By showing that it was possible to be prejudiced without being a bigot, he thought that Sanders could cause people to examine their own views, while undercutting Cooper's argument that the 52 percent of voters who had supported Prop 8 could not possibly have been motivated by animus in a way that Herrera hoped would speak to Justice Kennedy.

Chad and the rest of the media team agreed, and Boies and Olson had finally given way, despite their reservations. This case had always been as much about public education as it was creating a legal record, and as Yusef Robb put it, "I think the press will like the Republican police chief. He has a story and it should be good shit."

Sanders's moment of reckoning had come in September 2007. The San Diego city council had resolved to file a brief in the California Supreme Court case supporting the right of gays and lesbians to marry. During his campaign, Sanders had opposed same-sex marriage, reasoning that civil unions offered a fair alternative. Should he stick with that position and veto the resolution? He decided to talk the decision over with his daughter, Lisa.

Describing their relationship, he started to choke up. She was sitting in the courtroom now, an attractive young woman with brown hair that fell beneath her shoulders, dressed in a stylish yellow outfit and wearing pearls.

When she was a little girl, "she was basically my shadow," he began, before he was forced to stop. "Trying not to look at my daughter right now," he said, before collecting himself enough to resume telling the court about the call she had made during her sophomore year in college, telling him that she needed to come home to discuss something with him. His reaction, when she told him she was a lesbian, was one of overwhelming love, but also concern.

He recalled how as a young police officer, he had used homophobic slurs in locker rooms and lineups, only stopping after seeing how unfair it was when a sergeant he respected got drummed out of his department for being gay. "I thought it was very tough on gay people in society."

Lisa advised him to veto the resolution. His Republican base could desert him if he came out in support of same-sex marriage, she said, and "she felt that it was important that I be reelected because I was a good mayor."

Comforted by her blessing, Sanders made up his mind to do just that. As a courtesy, he convened a group of gay and lesbian friends to tell them his decision before publicly announcing it. He thought they would understand, given his support for civil unions. Now he recalled that night for the court.

"I remember one of our neighbors, who I have known for quite some time, said, basically, 'I walk by here—my partner and I walk by here all the time, with our children. And you always stop, when you are doing yard work, and say hello to them and talk to them. You know, we're a family just like you're a family.'" Another neighbor told him she loved her children just as much as he did and felt that they deserved to have parents who were married.

"The depth of the feeling was unbelievable. The depth of the hurt," he said. "I could see the harm that I had done by considering the veto."

Herrera then played a clip of the press conference the mayor had held the following day. In it, Sanders haltingly spoke of his own daughter, and of the gay members of his staff, in explaining that he had come to the conclusion that the right thing to do was to come out against Proposition 8 by signing the resolution.

"I simply could not bring myself to tell an entire group of people in our community they were less important, less worthy, or less deserving of the rights and responsibilities of marriage than anyone else."

Rob Reiner could not take his eyes off the screen. The director loved to make movies, but at heart he was an inquisitive policy wonk. During breaks he often played law student, quizzing the lawyers about case law that had been mentioned or the tactics behind what he was seeing. But he immediately

grasped, in a way that Olson and Boies had not, the audience-grabbing potential of this tearful former cop's change of heart.

"Wow," he whispered to Chad.

Even Cooper's wife, Debbie, a slim, dark-haired Alabaman beauty who, like
Olson's wife, Lady, attended trial every day, looked riveted.

"Mr. Mayor, you're obviously very emotional during that press conference,"
Herrera said. "Can you tell us why?"

"I was emotional because of the fact that I felt that I came very close to
making a bad decision, one that would affect, literally, hundreds of thousands
of people. I came very close to showing the prejudice that I obviously had to my
daughter, to my staff, and to the community in San Diego," he said.

Deep down, he knew, as he put it, that "if government tolerates discrimination against anyone for any reason, it becomes an excuse for the public to do
the same thing.

"And yet, the fact that I still believed that civil unions were equal to marriage, I think, really kind of shook me, because I think that the decisions I
made on that were grounded in prejudice.

"It didn't mean I hated gay people," he said. "It simply meant that I hadn't
understood the issue clearly enough."

───────

The cross-examination of Sanders, as Olson and Boies had feared, began with
a focus on political power, with Brian Raum, Cooper's co-counsel from the
Alliance Defense Fund, quickly ticking through various measures of progress.
But Sanders generally gave as good as he got.

He acknowledged that over the course of his twenty-six-year career at the
San Diego Police Department, discrimination against gay and lesbian officers
had lessened, in part because "we worked very hard on that issue," and that as
mayor he had tried to be responsive to the concerns of the gay and lesbian community. But when given the chance on redirect, he also told the court that in
San Diego "it's easier to make a decision against the gay and lesbian community than it is to make it for them," and that he could not think of a group of
Americans that had faced stronger political opposition in recent years.

It was true, he said, that there were three openly gay politicians in San

Diego, two on the city council and one in the state senate, and it was also true that he himself had been reelected, receiving 54 percent of the vote in a six-way Republican primary, despite having taken the position he did and subsequently campaigning against Prop 8.

But the mayor bristled when Raum suggested that his position had not damaged his election prospects, saying, "I can't say it made it easy." In fact, he had told the court during Herrera's direct, the local GOP had threatened to withdraw its endorsement.

People might have voted for Prop 8 for a variety of reasons—religious conviction, a desire to preserve tradition, or the belief that children ought to be raised by, as Raum put it, the "man and a woman whose sexual union brought them into the world," Sanders said, concessions that Cooper would surely use as the case made its way up on appeal. But he never wavered on his fundamental point. The fact that people genuinely believed those things did not mean that they weren't prejudiced, just as he had been in believing that civil unions were an acceptable substitute for marriage. Their feelings, he said, were still grounded in animus. "I don't believe that they realized what they were saying."

But from the war room's point of view, perhaps the best moment of all came after Sanders had stepped down. During the noon press briefing, Sanders addressed an ad put out by proponents of Proposition 8 during the campaign that Raum had played in court that morning. It showed images of vandalized property and portrayed the Yes on 8 supporters as the real underdogs, victimized for holding a politically unpopular view. It was a message that drove Chad crazy, and he had been pressing his team to push back.

"I have to tell you, as a police officer for over twenty-six years, as a mayor, that is not what I've seen," Sanders said, looking straight into the news cameras. "I've seen hate crimes, I've seen people beaten to death, I've seen people almost beaten to death, and never has that been a somebody that was for Yes on Proposition 8. Instead, it's always been the gay and lesbian community."

Chad could not have said it better had he scripted it himself. The war room team's efforts were paying off, with a ton of "earned media" coverage of the case in both local and national outlets. The quotes that Yusef Robb, in consultation with the lawyers, sent out in press releases each day were often those chosen by harried reporters writing on the fly. Journalists who had never set foot in the courtroom were relying on information AFER was posting on its Web site.

Editorial boards were taking their side, influential columnists like the *New York Times*'s Maureen Dowd had made the trip out to San Francisco to see firsthand what was happening in Walker's courtroom, and national network and cable news programs were booking Olson and Boies.

It was still maddening to Chad that talk show hosts like Oprah and Ellen DeGeneres remained noncommittal about having the plaintiffs on their talk shows, despite repeated entreaties. DeGeneres, whose decision to come out as a lesbian in 1997 was considered so bold in those days that it made the cover of *Time* magazine, was particularly baffling.

"I can't figure it out," Amanda Crumley said. "Maybe they are afraid that it will turn off their Middle America audience."

But *People* magazine, after much prodding, had finally bitten, agreeing to do a feature on Kris and Sandy that would reach its forty-three million readers.

It was a huge get. Because *People* is an impulse buy, often plucked off the supermarket shelf at checkout, the magazine's editors test what they put in its pages with focus groups. Kristina took it as a sign that just maybe the country was beginning to move their way.

"The other side puts out statements, but they aren't helping people do their jobs," Robb observed. "Maybe they just figure, 'Fuck the *L.A. Times*, fuck the liberal media.'"

"Press-wise," Chad agreed, congratulating his team that night, "we are clearly outgunning them."

SIXTEEN

A COURTROOM JOURNEY
TO THE NETHERLANDS,
VIA MASSACHUSETTS

E ach evening, the legal team defending Prop 8 would huddle in the cluttered living area of the suite where Chuck Cooper was staying. With no office in San Francisco, the corporate residential apartments they occupied had become cluttered live-work spaces, the floors a tangle of wires leading to rented printers, and available surfaces stacked high with binders and documents.

Cooper, like Olson, had for the most part delegated the actual job of questioning witnesses to his deputies. That freed him up to think strategically about the points his team should—and should not—be making. "How," he would ask himself as he reviewed the lines of questioning in each cross-examination plan, "will this fall on the ear of the one person I care about, Justice Kennedy?"

But some battles are important enough to the outcome of a war that the general needs to climb into the trenches. And that is why Cooper assigned himself the job of cross-examining the expert witness whom David Boies called to the stand after Sanders finished on Tuesday.

Lee Badgett was an economist at the University of Massachusetts Amherst, and the author of *When Gay People Get Married* and another book called *Money, Myths, and Change: The Economic Lives of Lesbians and Gay Men*. She had been an effective witness in a number of the state court marriage cases, and Cooper knew going in that he would need to "rough her up," as he later put it.

Under friendly questioning by Boies, she outlined the three main findings of her expert report for the court.

First, she testified, Proposition 8, far from serving a rational state interest, inflicted substantial economic harm. Keeping same-sex couples in California from marrying cost those couples thousands of dollars a year in higher tax bills and lost spousal health and other employment benefits. That, in turn, harmed the nearly forty thousand children whom same-sex couples were raising in California, she told the court, because "that's thousands of dollars that will not be available to spend on children or to save for their college education."

Nor was its passage in the state's interest, she testified. Not only do struggling families tend to require more government assistance, but by her estimate California stood to lose $40 million over a three-year period alone in same-sex wedding-related tax revenue. That part of her testimony echoed what the chief economist for the city of San Francisco had told the court the previous week. Married individuals, on average, behave in healthier ways than single individuals, Edmund Egan had testified, which translates into greater productivity, lower worker absenteeism, and more payroll taxes.

Second, Badgett offered empirical evidence for the proposition that domestic partnerships do not offer an equitable compromise. Gays and lesbians who would marry do not always take advantage of the benefits domestic partnerships offer by registering, she told the court, in part because the arrangement is seen as "second class" and less valuable. Evidence for that could be seen in what she called the "take-up rate" for the different legal statuses.

In Massachusetts, 37 percent of the state's same-sex couples married in the first year they could do so. By contrast, only 10 to 12 percent of same-sex couples entered into civil unions or domestic partnerships the first year they became available in states that allowed them. In California, that number was even lower. Only 5 percent of same-sex couples entered into domestic partnerships in 2000, when that arrangement became available in the Golden State, versus 21 percent who married during the six-month window when it became legal to do so in 2008. The bottom line, she testified, was that gays and lesbians marry for the same reasons straight people do. In her survey of same-sex couples who had married in Massachusetts, 72 percent reported feeling more committed to their partners as a result of marrying, while 93 percent believed that their children were happier and better off as a result.

And finally, based on quantifiable experience in places where same-sex marriage was already legal, she concluded that there was no basis to believe that any harm would come to heterosexual marriages by allowing gays and lesbians to marry nationwide.

Together, her conclusions formed a formidable legal stronghold for the plaintiffs' argument that Proposition 8 should not survive even the rational basis test, and after beginning his cross-examination with a cordial "pleased to meet you," Cooper tried to attack them from every angle.

He questioned her impartiality, her math, and her assumptions. The *Advocate* magazine had called her "one of our best and brightest activists," had it not? he asked. It had, she answered agreeably. Didn't she agree with the state's fiscal impact statement on Prop 8, Cooper asked, which found that there would be little to no impact on state or local governments? No, she answered, she did not.

What about the fact that hundreds of gay Californians entered into domestic partnerships in 2008, even though that was the year they were allowed to wed? "Do you believe that these California same-sex couples chose domestic partnerships over marriage because they believed it to be culturally and socially second-rate when compared to marriage?" Cooper pressed.

Boies had coached her not to be acerbic: "Your sense ought to be, if I could just explain it to you, you'd understand—not that they are bad people, just a little dense."

"Well," she answered, "I don't know that some of those eighteen thousand couples who married didn't also register a domestic partnership in order to hedge their bets against the outcome of an election. So I don't know exactly what conclusion we could draw."

But it was Badgett's last point, that traditional marriages would not be harmed by allowing gays and lesbians to marry, that was the most potentially damaging to Cooper's case, and it was there that he spent the bulk of his time.

He began in the Netherlands. Badgett had studied marriage trends in that country, both before and after it became the first in the world in 2001 to allow same-sex couples to marry. That data, she had written in her expert report, suggested that heterosexual marriage trends do not change when same-sex couples are allowed to wed.

But Cooper had done some calculations of his own, a tangle of numbers that he now enthusiastically shared with the court. One chart showed that in 1994 there were 5.4 marriages per 1,000 inhabitants in the Netherlands. In 2001, the year same-sex couples began to marry, there were 5.1 marriages per 1,000 inhabitants. By 2008, that had dropped to 4.6 marriages per 1,000 inhabitants.

"It is clear that at least from the time that the Netherlands adopted same-sex marriage until now, the marriage rate has declined significantly, correct?" Cooper asked.

Two other charts looked at the growing number of children born out of wedlock in the Netherlands. In 1994, the percentage of families in which children lived with two unmarried parents was 1.5 percent, in 2001 it had risen to 2.8 percent, and in 2008 it had reached 4.3 percent. The percentage of families in which children were being raised by a single parent had grown from 5.6 percent in 1994 to 6.4 percent in 2008.

Boies had expected this line of questioning, just as he had anticipated that Cooper would be the one doing the asking, and he had prepared charts of his own. They were important enough that the night before, he had personally overseen the finishing touches, even asking whether certain colors could be adjusted to make it more easily understandable and "crisp." ("Well, David, Microsoft, in its infinite wisdom, allows us to do that," joked Steven Holtzman, the lawyer who had done battle with him against the software giant.)

During the cross, Badgett said she did not think Cooper's numbers were statistically significant or unexpected, and that in general what they showed was that trends that had begun before the Netherlands legalized same-sex marriage continued afterward. Looked at over time, she said, there was "no break, whatsoever, to suggest that anything happened of importance in 2001," the year same-sex couples were allowed to marry.

On redirect, Boies used his own handiwork to elaborate on that point, flashing charts onto a large courtroom screen and peering over at them through glasses perched so far down on his nose it was a wonder they did not slide off. He had purposely waited until the redirect to show them, ensuring that he, not Cooper, would have the last word.

One chart showed heterosexual marriage rates all the way back to the 1960s, rather than the 1994 starting point that Cooper had used. "Can you explain what this exhibit shows?" he asked Badgett.

"What we see is a well-known change in the marriage rate in the Netherlands, which peaked in about 1970, and since then has been on a pretty steady decline."

"And there are some yearly variations, is that correct?" Boies asked.

"Yes, there are."

"And, for example, the marriage rate actually goes up from 2001 to 2002," he said, "and goes up again from 2007 to 2008."

"Yes, that's right," Badgett said.

He then offered a different view of the same data, adjusted for year-to-year differences by plotting five-year averages. It showed a smoothly sloping line of gradual declination, the angle of which did not change after 2001. The next slide he showed quoted from the affidavit of an expert witness that Cooper had been planning to call, but had withdrawn after the expert concluded that the Netherlands' declining marriage rate was "no doubt part of a larger secular trend" seen in most Western countries.

That, Badgett said, was the way she saw it too.

Boies then rhetorically spun the globe back to the United States, and specifically to Massachusetts, where same-sex couples had been allowed to marry since 2004. Badgett, during her direct examination, had said that the Bay State offered a better predictor of what might happen to heterosexual marriages than places like the Netherlands and Spain, both of which had made it easier to divorce at around the same time that they legalized same-sex marriage.

Cooper had objected; Badgett's expert report was primarily focused on the experience of the Netherlands, he told the judge, and this was a topic that he had not been given notice she would cover. But after Boies pointed out that it had been raised in her deposition, Walker overruled him, leading Cooper to ask whether it was at least reasonable for people to want to wait for more data from places like Massachusetts before making any kind of firm conclusion.

"I don't think it's necessary," she had answered. "I think we know."

Now Boies flashed more charts across the courtroom's overhead screen, comparing the marriage and divorce rates in Massachusetts to the rest of the nation from 2000 to 2007. Nationally, the marriage rate declined over that period. That was true for Massachusetts as well—until 2004, the year the state legalized same-sex marriage. After that, "the marriage rate actually increased," Badgett told the court, while the overall divorce rate fell at an even greater rate than was true for the rest of the country.

"Well done today, David," Chad said, pulling the lawyer aside after court.

Boies grinned. Some people become bashful when paid a compliment. He was not among them.

"I know," he said. "It was just great."

SEVENTEEN

A JUDGE'S MEMORIES

L istening to the evidence day after day, Vaughn Walker was in what he called his "judge mode." It is not uncommon for a judge to have personal experiences that can inform the way he views a case. But Walker, years later, said that for the most part he compartmentalized his, spending surprisingly little time thinking about how the witness testimony in the trial unfolding before him connected to his own life. As he put it, "I was not on trial," and as someone who had spent years on the bench, he was used to keeping his emotions in check.

Ryan Kendall was different.

Terry Stewart had searched for weeks for someone like Kendall, a twenty-six-year-old Denver Police Department employee, who could put a human face on the harm that can be caused by treating sexual orientation as if it were a choice. When he was thirteen, his parents had read his diary and discovered he was gay. His mother, an evangelical Christian, told him he would burn in hell and forced him to attend two years of sexual orientation "conversion therapy," an experience that left him suicidal.

But before he could take the stand, Stewart's office first had to overcome deep concerns by both Olson and Boies about Kendall's youth and fragility, and then the vehement objections of Cooper's team when Kendall was finally called to testify on Wednesday morning, the seventh day of the trial.

"One man's anecdotal account of his experience with a particular type of conversion therapy is irrelevant to this court's analysis," James Campbell, a lawyer for Cooper's co-counsel, the Alliance Defense Fund, protested to Judge Walker.

Walker glanced down at some paperwork he'd brought to court. "Let me ask you, Mr. Campbell, isn't this an issue that the proponents themselves have raised?" he asked.

"I don't believe that we've—we've raised the issue of forced conversion therapy, Your Honor."

"Well, I'm looking at your trial brief. And you say, 'The evidence at trial will show that many people freely choose their sexual orientation.' [It] goes on, 'The evidence at trial will further demonstrate that however it is defined, sexual orientation can shift over time.'

"And so it seems to me you have raised the very issue to which this witness is going to testify."

The proponents of Prop 8 had indeed made those arguments, to try to prevent the court from applying heightened scrutiny to Prop 8, and so now found themselves in a trap of their own making. Briefs filed by Cooper argued that for gays and lesbians to be entitled to the type of extra judicial protection given to racial minorities and women, sexual orientation must be an immutable characteristic in the same way that skin color or gender was.

As a matter of law, Olson disagreed. The Supreme Court's jurisprudence in this area was not at all clear-cut. It had applied heightened scrutiny to laws that discriminate against a group based on changeable traits, like religion or status as a noncitizen, that the justices deemed fundamental to a person's identity.

But even if Cooper was right, Olson believed that he could satisfy the immutability test, and had lined up an expert witness who could speak to the numerous studies that had been conducted on the subject of human sexuality, a point Campbell now made to Walker.

"If it's relevant, he can testify," Campbell told Walker.

"It is true that this is an issue which largely depends upon expert testimony," the judge replied, but "actual firsthand experience to illustrate points that have been raised is very helpful." And in any event, Walker continued, he was certainly capable of weighing the value of Kendall's testimony against all the other evidence that would be presented.

Motion to exclude denied.

Kendall stood just five foot six, and he looked slight as he sat down in the witness box next to the strapping judge. Listening to Kendall describe how "very, very alone" he felt as counselors tried to suppress his attraction to men, Judge Walker was transported back in time.

———

It was the late 1970s, he confided afterward in a private aside, and he was in his early thirties. He had just made partner at the prestigious law firm where he worked, and his future seemed unlimited, but for one thing.

"I decided to see a psychiatrist about my"—he paused—"affliction."

For years, homosexuality had been considered a mental illness. The American Psychiatric Association had only just removed it from its diagnostic manual, but the profession still viewed people who were "conflicted" about their homosexuality as mentally disordered. It would take another two decades for the group to condemn "reparative" conversion counseling.

Walker did not remember much about those sessions, except that the doctor told him that because he had not yet had sex with a man, he was not actually a homosexual.

"You're normal," the psychiatrist had said.

"And he pronounced me cured."

He wanted badly to believe that was true. Around the same time, he found himself stuck in Chicago during a business trip layover. He called his parents, who lived nearby. Come and meet me at the airport Hilton, he suggested.

They were a reasonably close family. His mom had run an ice business before the era of refrigeration, and his dad had briefly attended law school before winding up in business. After a drink or two, the conversation took a surprising turn.

"I forgot how it came up, but we got around to the subject of their sex life. It was striking how candid and matter-of-fact they were about it. Very honest. Yes, they acknowledged, they'd had their problems in this area, but they'd worked through it. I was kind of telling them that I'd had my problems in this realm too. That would have been the time for me to say, 'It's because I'm attracted to men.'

"But I couldn't admit it to myself because I didn't want to be one of those people, because those people were deviants."

He was sure that his parents would have loved him regardless. But by the time he was ready to tell them, it was too late. "So I never quite took that step."

—————

On the stand, Kendall was talking about his own family, so different from Walker's own. After learning he was gay, his parents yelled at him all the time.

"My mother would tell me that she hated me, or that I was disgusting, or that I was repulsive. Once she told me she wished she had had an abortion instead of a gay son. She told me that she wished I was born with Down's syndrome or I had been mentally retarded."

Walker glanced at Boies. He could see that the lawyer had tears in his eyes, and he was struggling to blink back his own.

Against his will, Kendall was forced to see a local Christian therapist. Then, at age fourteen, he was sent for private and group therapy sessions at the National Association for Research and Therapy of Homosexuality.

NARTH, as the outfit is known, is headquartered in Encino, California, and it had been recommended by Focus on the Family, a politically influential right-wing evangelical group near Kendall's home in Colorado.

NARTH's executive director, Joseph Nicolosi, told him that "homosexuality was incompatible with what God wants for you." The message, Kendall told the court, was that he was "dirty and bad," and must change. But the futility became clear to him one night when a boy whom the therapist had "trotted out [as] his perfect patient" told him he was going to a gay bar later that night, and had just been pretending to be cured for the sake of his family.

After two years, he could take it no longer. Kendall spoke to a state social worker, and she started an investigation that led the state to revoke his parents' custody over him. "I told her that if I went back to that house, I was going to end up killing myself," he said.

And so he found himself on his own at age sixteen, and lost. He wandered in and out of jobs and school, so depressed that at one point he turned to drugs before pulling himself together.

"It's been a—a long hard journey," he said. "But I have fought with every bit of myself to take care of myself, to get a good job, to get someplace to live. And I've been able to do that."

Campbell, the Alliance Defense Fund lawyer, kept his cross short and gentle.

"Your only goal for conversion therapy was to survive the experience, is that true?"

"Absolutely true."

"You didn't have the goal of changing your sexual orientation—" Campbell stopped, aware of his mistake. "I'm sorry, correction. You didn't have the goal of changing your sexual attraction, correct?"

The suggestion was that the therapy had not worked because Kendall had not embraced it, but Kendall refused to bite. "That's correct," he said. "I knew I was gay. I knew that could not be changed."

"The most touching testimony at trial," Judge Walker later said, "was that given by Ryan Kendall."

EIGHTEEN

GOD, GAYS, AND
POLITICAL POWER

T he next witness, Gary Segura, a political scientist from Stanford University, did not pack the emotional punch of Ryan Kendall. But since he was a leading expert on the relative political power of minority groups in America, his testimony went to a critical question in the case: Do gays and lesbians have the political clout to protect their interests in the democratic process, as Cooper contended, or do they require the courts to step in with the type of extra protection the Constitution affords to other vulnerable minorities, as Olson was arguing?

By any measure, Segura told the court, gays and lesbians are relatively powerless to address the discrimination they face. He began with the ballot initiative process that had stripped them of the right to marry in California. As Matt McGill explained, "The other side is going to pound the table and say, 'The people have spoken, the people have spoken!' And we're going to say, 'Yeah, that's part of the problem.'"

Segura told the court that ballot initiatives, which allow voters to bypass their elected representatives and pass laws or amendments to their state constitutions like Prop 8, have historically been a tool for the majority to roll back the legislative or judicial gains of unpopular minorities. When the federal government took steps in the 1960s to protect African Americans from housing discrimination, for instance, California voters passed an initiative allowing property owners to continue to rent or sell to whomever they wanted. More recently, voters in the border state had taken aim at Latino immigrants with an initiative that allowed the state to deny benefits to anyone suspected of being illegal.

But no group in America had been targeted by ballot initiatives more than gays and lesbians; Segura put the number of measures at around two hundred since the 1970s. He said gays and lesbians had lost 70 percent of those contests, and 100 percent of the contests that specifically involved banning them from marrying or adopting children.

"The initiative process has really been the Waterloo of gay and lesbian politics."

Another measure of the political powerlessness of gays and lesbians, he said, could be found in hate crime statistics. National data compiled by the FBI showed that violence against gays and lesbians had increased in the previous five years. In 2008, the last year for which data was available, 71 percent of all hate-motivated murders and 55 percent of all hate-motivated rapes in the nation were of gay men and lesbians. Locally, while hate crimes based on race, ethnicity, or national origin had fallen by 16 percent in Los Angeles from 2007 to 2008, the number targeting gays and lesbians had jumped by 21 percent.

"I have known of individuals who simply don't leave a bar without two people because it's just not safe," Segura said. "There is simply no other person in society who endures the likelihood of being harmed as a consequence of their identity [more] than a gay man or lesbian."

Ted Boutrous, who was handling the direct, turned next to what Segura called a "feeling thermometer." Political scientists ask people to rate, on a scale of zero to 100, how warmly they feel toward various religious, political, ethnic, and other groups. Those test showed that while Americans had grown warmer toward gays and lesbians over time, they were still "not very fond" of them, Segura testified.

Every group has its haters, but what struck Segura was that racial minority groups like African Americans and Latinos that still faced significant discrimination and were afforded extra judicial protection were nonetheless held in higher esteem than gays and lesbians.

The pluralistic ideal, "where I'm trying to persuade you of the rightness of my position and you are trying to persuade me of the rightness of your position," presumes that two groups armed with resources can fight out their disagreements in the democratic process, Segura said. But it does not work when one of those groups is as underrepresented in elected politics as gays and lesbians are, in a climate where not only "fringe" elements of society but sitting U.S. senators and cable talk show hosts feel free to publicly compare the desire of two members of the same sex to marry to a man wanting to marry his turtle, dog, or goat.

When a group is seen as "morally inferior, a threat to children, a threat to freedom, if there's these deeply seated beliefs, the range of compromise is dramatically limited," he told the court. "It's very difficult to engage in the give-and-take of the legislative process when I think you are an inherently bad person."

Olson understood, better than some of the liberal members of the legal team, the pitfalls of talking about the role organized religion played in the passage of Proposition 8. Close friends of his, good people, opposed same-sex marriage out of religious principle. Six of the nine justices, including Justice Kennedy, belonged to the Catholic Church, which taught that homosexual acts are a "serious depravity."

This case was about whether government could discriminate—the Constitution clearly allows churches to refuse to marry same-sex couples—and Olson's gut told him to steer clear of a line of argument that had the potential to drag him into a distracting religious liberties debate and turn off the very people he was trying to bring around.

But as much as Olson wanted to be sensitive to people's religious convictions and not "turn this into God versus gays," as Boutrous put it, his views on the matter evolved as his team dug into the inner workings of ProtectMarriage. com. The discovery documents that Cooper had been forced to turn over, along with materials culled from public sources, made clear that a powerhouse coalition of religious groups had formed the backbone of ProtectMarriage.com's Yes on 8 political operation.

One of the chief architects of the campaign was Catholic archbishop Salvatore Cordileone of San Francisco. He had enlisted Maggie Gallagher, the cofounder of the nonprofit National Organization for Marriage and one of the most vocal opponents of same-sex marriage, to help put Prop 8 on the ballot. NOM, as it is known, became a conduit that allowed donors to anonymously give to the ProtectMarriage.com campaign.

Chief among them: the Mormon Church, which not only raised around half of the nearly $39 million spent to pass Prop 8, but provided twenty thousand volunteers to get out the vote, according to one document. Evangelical ministers and groups like Focus on the Family rounded out what other documents entered into evidence described as "an aggressive grassroots campaign" involving coordination among as many as three thousand pastors.

There was even a "Pastors' Rapid Response Team" to quickly disseminate targeted messages to congregations. An e-mail that Mark Jansson, one of the five official proponents of Prop 8 and the Mormon Church's liaison to the campaign, had been forced to turn over stated that the campaign "was entirely under priesthood direction."

The influence that organized religion wielded in shaping Californians' views on same-sex marriage simply could not be ignored, and a decision had been made to address it head-on during Segura's testimony. But first, why not set the stage by letting two of Cooper's withdrawn witnesses do the talking?

That morning, extended excerpts from the depositions that Boies had taken of the two McGill University religious scholars had been played for the court. In addition to the helpful comments each had made about the children of same-sex couples benefiting if their parents were allowed to marry, both acknowledged that there was a religious component to antigay bigotry, with one even agreeing that it had helped create a climate of physical danger.

"Unbelievable," Rob Reiner told Olson during a break. "Did you kill the guy? Yes! Did you use this knife? Yes!"

"David isn't telling you, but he hypnotized those witnesses," Olson said, as Yusef Robb rushed past to put the finishing touches on a press release entitled "Defendant Experts Undercut Prop 8."

Cooper, listening, had slumped over to one side, a resigned look on his face. Even if he could have convinced his withdrawn witnesses to take the stand, he'd made the determination that it likely would not have helped matters. In the end, all he could do was turn on the experts, entering into evidence those portions of their depositions in which Boies had attacked them for their lack of expertise and knowledge.

Now Boutrous asked Segura for his thoughts on the deposition testimony.

Segura said it confirmed what he had previously believed: "That religion is the chief obstacle to the ability of gays and lesbians to make political progress."

No other minority group has faced such unified opposition from religious organizations, Segura told the court. When African Americans were fighting for their civil rights, virtually every denomination but the Southern Baptist Convention supported them. Gays and lesbians faced the inverse, with most of the major denominations arrayed against them.

"Biblical condemnation of homosexuality and the teaching that gays are morally inferior on a regular basis to a huge percentage of the public makes the political ground, the political opportunity, very hostile to gay interests," he said. "It's very difficult to overcome that."

David Thompson's cross-examination of Segura crisscrossed the American political landscape, searching for signs of political progress that could be turned into a legal negative.

Wasn't it true that the number of openly gay elected officials had risen dramatically in the last eight years, from 257 to 445? he asked. Didn't the fact that California's domestic partnership law had passed over the objections of "biblical literalists" suggest that the church was not as powerful a force as Segura had suggested? What about the fact that gays and lesbians were never disenfranchised in the way that blacks and women were? And how was it possible to conclude that the group had no power in places like New Hampshire and Vermont, where gays and lesbians had legislatively won the right to marry?

Segura was prepared for this line of questioning. Though the Supreme Court had not spelled out exactly how political power should be calculated, it was the legal team's view that "the test under the Constitution was not whether you lack power in a particular state," Boutrous had told him during one prep session. Segura had nodded, telling Boutrous that during the 1940s there were towns run by blacks, but that did not mean that blacks had political power in the era of Jim Crow.

Now Segura told the court that he believed that the question of political power was a national one. Gays and lesbians might be able to marry in Vermont, but the federal government refused to recognize those marriages. Local electoral success needed to be judged in context, he said. The fact that a lesbian was elected mayor in Houston, for instance, was not a reflection of the power of lesbians but rather the racial politics of that city; Segura told Thompson that her sexuality was in fact an issue in the race but she won because she was white and her opponent was black. California might have domestic partnerships, but with the passage of Prop 8 voters had constitutionally established gays and lesbians as "second-class citizens."

Afterward, Boies said he found Thompson's style "perverse." The opposing lawyer was making all the right points, good points like the fact that the Speaker of the California Assembly was an openly gay man, Boies said. But why not wait until he had his own friendly witness on the stand to dump all of that into the record? By raising these issues with the plaintiffs' witness, Thompson was allowing Segura to put them in context and explain it all away.

Thompson had, for instance, found passages on the Web site of the Human Rights Campaign, in which the largest gay rights group in the country boasted of its political muscle. But when he asked Segura about them, the political scientist joked that "I'm beginning to think you are on their mailing list," before adding that the explanation in his view was simple: HRC, as it is known, needs to raise money, and people historically don't give to a group whose motto is, "Donate to us, we are unlikely to make a difference." Thompson had gotten Segura to acknowledge that it was possible that some percentage of voters might have been motivated to pass Prop 8 out of a negative reaction to "activist judges," but then given him the chance to explain why he did not think that was the primary driver.

And Thompson seemed to have annoyed the judge when he wandered into a blame-the-victim line of questioning that suggested that those involved with the "No on 8" campaign had squandered the goodwill of the voters by vandalizing property and boycotting businesses owned by their opponents. Since Thompson was "exploring the subject," Judge Walker said he'd like to know a little more about the role that boycotts and similar tactics played in the civil rights fights of the 1960s.

"It's difficult to imagine the civil rights movement in the 1950s and the 1960s without the Montgomery bus boycott or the boycott of white-owned businesses in certain southern towns," Segura answered, adding that boycotts dated all the way back to the eighteenth century, when the women of Boston stopped drinking English tea. "So I would not group boycotts of businesses in with violence and intimidation."

To the extent that there were isolated incidents of electoral intimidation during the Prop 8 campaign, Segura said, both sides engaged in it; Mayor Sanders, he noted, had told the court that his NO ON 8 sign had been vandalized.

But the most newsworthy moment came when Segura turned the tables on Thompson after the lawyer suggested that gays and lesbians could count on powerful allies, including the current occupant of the White House.

"President Obama, does he count as a political ally to the gay and lesbian community?" Thompson asked.

"No!" Rob Reiner said in a stage whisper. It was a frank assessment by one of Hollywood's most important Democratic donors, and Segura was equally frank in his answer.

A dozen years before he became president of the United States, when Obama was running for the Illinois Senate from Chicago's liberal Hyde Park enclave, he had signed a candidate questionnaire saying, "I favor legalizing same-sex marriage, and would fight efforts to prohibit such marriages." That position had flipped, however, by the time he ran statewide for the U.S. Senate.

It wasn't just that the president now said that he believed marriage should be between a man and a woman, Segura said. It was within the president's power to sign an executive order repealing the policy banning gays and lesbians from openly serving in the military, yet despite a campaign pledge promising to end Don't Ask, Don't Tell, so far he had failed to do so. His promise to work with Congress to repeal DOMA had gone nowhere, which meant that spousal benefits given to married straight couples were still denied to their gay and lesbian counterparts. And while it was true that the president condemned employment discrimination against gays and lesbians, he had expended little capital pressing Congress to pass a federal law to ban it.

Obama was a "good speechmaker," Segura told Thompson, but like many so-called allies of gays and lesbians, his "rhetoric far exceeds his actions."

The headline on the *San Jose Mercury News* article summing of the day's events read, EXPERT IN PROPOSITION 8 TRIAL: BARACK OBAMA UNRELIABLE ALLY OF GAY MARRIAGE MOVEMENT.

Chad, reading it out loud to the war room that evening, was not happy. The day the case was announced, he and Bruce Cohen had tag-teamed the president during a campaign fund-raiser that Chad had helped organize at the Beverly Hills Hilton, telling Obama that they hoped he could find his way to supporting the lawsuit. Chad wanted to create the political space for the president to come out in favor of same-sex marriage, and news coverage like this threatened to force him to dig in further.

Amanda Crumley knew how the White House worked; she was the one member of the war room besides Chad to have worked there. But there was no sense trying to spin what Segura had said, she advised Chad: "He speaketh the truth."

Besides, they had other things to worry about.

Chad had made something of a study of how the religious right became such an effective force in American politics, once even scraping the Clinton sticker off his car and driving down to Lynchburg, Virginia, to listen to Jerry Falwell, the cofounder of the Moral Majority, preach at his megachurch.

The day's testimony on the role that churches played in Prop 8's passage had been powerful, but Chad worried, correctly, that opponents would try to spin it as an attack on the faithful. Yusef Robb, whose job it was to excerpt the best moments of the trial and push them out in a press release, said he would be as careful as the lawyers had been to emphasize that the day's events showed only that "there was this vast, huge, political apparatus" arrayed against gays and lesbians. "We don't have a bone to pick with religion," he said.

Meanwhile, the following day the Supreme Court was expected to hand down its decision in Olson's blockbuster *Citizens United v. Federal Election Commission* case, challenging the ban on corporate spending in federal elections. The case had its genesis in the anti-Clinton documentary aired during the presidential primary by another of Olson's clients, David Bossie, and was a reminder that whatever common ground Chad and Olson had found on same-sex marriage, they were politically far apart on nearly everything else.

"Ted Olson is going to single-handedly bring down the campaign finance system tomorrow," Chad predicted, "a decision we all disagree with."

True, but the upside was that "we can worm our way" into whatever interviews Olson would be giving on the subject, said Robb, and "politics aside, our fucking attorney just won another case."

Yes, Chad mused. That ought to calm the naysayers in the gay rights community.

Less than twelve hours later, as predicted, a sharply divided Supreme Court ruled in Olson's favor, striking down a key provision of the McCain-Feingold law aimed at curbing the influence of special interests in politics, and opening up a floodgate of money expected to disproportionately benefit Republicans.

"Congratulations, I guess," Chad told Matt McGill as the two stood waiting for an elevator in the federal courthouse. McGill, who had worked closely with Olson on the case, did his best imitation of a Dr. Evil laugh and accent.

"Ha-ha-ha-ha! First, the political system. Next, the social fabric of America!"

NINETEEN

THE NAUGHTY BOY

The joke in the war room was that when David Boies removed his glasses, it was time to watch out. He would hold them in one hand near his jaw, then repeatedly plunge them toward the witness in a sharp downward motion that an assassin might use to stab someone in the heart.

Boies's target on the eighth day of trial was Dr. Hak-Shing William Tam, the proponent of Proposition 8 who had done his best to avoid the very situation in which he now found himself, penned into a witness box and forced to explain himself.

Calling a hostile witness can easily backfire, and the team had extensively debated which proponents of Proposition 8 to call. Much consideration had been given to calling Ron Prentice, the executive director of ProtectMarriage. com. Questioning him under oath about some of the campaign documents that had been unearthed through discovery was hard to resist. "If you keep him narrow, if the only point you say is that they carefully coordinated all grass-roots efforts, that everything came with a ProtectMarriage.com stamp of approval, it's worth it," Chris Dusseault said during one discussion.

But Olson and Boies were wary. Prentice was a political pro, and if they put him on the stand he would do his best to try to undermine the case they had already built with the campaign's own documents. "Right now we control our message," Olson said. "If we put him on, they get to tell their side of the story."

Tam was the compromise. By order of the court, he had been sitting in the courtroom for several days running, an older, bespectacled man with tufts of black hair sticking out of the back of his head. During breaks, he kept to himself, looking uncomfortably at his shoes whenever he found himself in the vicinity of the plaintiffs or Chad.

Cooper had expected his opponent to try to pin Tam's views to the entire ProtectMarriage.com campaign, and he had assigned Nicole Moss, a lawyer in his firm, to put as much distance between Tam and the campaign as she could. With her guidance, Tam claimed a minimal role in the campaign, said he had little contact with Prentice and had spoken only "one or two times" to a firm owned by Frank Schubert, the campaign operative who masterminded the Prop 8 victory. He insisted that he did not get the approval of ProtectMarriage.com for the Yes on 8 messages he circulated to the Chinese community. "I acted independently," he said at one point.

But Moss had a hard sell, given that Tam was one of only five official proponents of Prop 8. And that was without the discovery documents that Cooper had been forced to turn over, which Boies proceeded to use to their full advantage.

By Tam's own admission, he had been invited by ProtectMarriage.com to take part in the campaign and worked closely with the organization to collect the more than one million signatures that qualified Prop 8 for the ballot. He supervised the preparation of the ballot language. He acknowledged investing substantial time, effort, and resources in the campaign. Minutes from the weekly grassroots meetings run by Schubert's firm showed Tam in attendance. He appeared at debates and on television at the direction of ProtectMarriage.com. He raised thousands of dollars and was included and referenced in e-mails addressed to the campaign's leadership. "The Chinese coalition with Bill Tam remains strong and he is one of the signatories," read one that Boies introduced into evidence.

E-mails addressed to Tam and another organization showed that ProtectMarriage.com paid for the messages he disseminated. But perhaps most important, the documents showed that Tam had signed a "unity pledge," specifically promising not to pursue independent public messaging strategies. The pledge clearly stated that "public communications by coalition partners in support of the marriage amendment must be approved by the campaign manager."

Most people want to be seen as decent and upstanding, a tendency Boies was happy to exploit. "You consider yourself an honest person, don't you?" he asked Tam.

"Yes," Tam answered, clearly not sensing the menace in the question.

"And when you sign something and make a commitment you take that commitment seriously, don't you, sir?"

"Yes," Tam answered, finally understanding where this was headed, "but later on I—I admit that I violated this, this message principle."

"When do you think you started violating this pledge?"

"What I told the *Mercury, San Jose Mercury News* about homosexuality leads to all kinds of diseases."

"That was right out there in the public, right?"

"Right."

"Did anybody from ProtectMarriage.com come and tell you, 'You shouldn't have said that'?"

"Yes!"

"Who said that? Who told you that?"

Tam hesitated. "I forgot his name."

"Is that in writing anywhere, any record of that?" Boies asked, voice dripping with disbelief.

"No," Tam admitted.

Tam similarly was unable to point to any documentation to bolster his claim that he was not paid by the campaign to place television, radio, and print advertising with Asian media outlets. An October 2008 e-mail from Andy Pugno, the general counsel, addressed to Tam and another pastor stated that "your organizations are spending $50,000" on such efforts.

Boies moved next to a Web site linked to Tam called 1man1woman.net. The team had discovered that Tam was the secretary of a group that administered the pro–Prop 8 site.

Moss had tried to claim that Prentice and others had no knowledge of what was being said on 1man1woman.net, but ProtectMarriage.com had referenced the fact that the Web site was up and running in the minutes of one of its meetings that had been obtained through discovery.

The site was also listed as a cosponsor of a rally that Tam helped organize, featuring both Prentice and Tony Perkins, the president of the Family Research

Council. Boies introduced a flyer promoting the rally. As grammatically challenged as Tam himself, it warned, "It is time for the church rise up against the forces of evil that are destroying families and young souls."

Tam initially tried to deny any knowledge of the incendiary flyer, then hedged and said it "might have been in front of my eyes. But I—"

"You don't remember anything?" Boies interjected incredulously, before whipping out another document that showed that Tam was listed as one of the rally's two press contacts. "Now, does that refresh your recollection that you were more involved in this than you said before?"

Turning to the content of 1man1woman.com, Boies asked whether Tam agreed with the Web site's unsupported assertion that gays and lesbians are "12 times more likely" to molest children. Tam said he did.

"What literature have you read, sir, that says that?" Boies asked, demanding now, like a parent confronting a prevaricating child. "Tell me what it is that you read."

"I don't remember now."

"Who authored it?"

"Some from, apparently academic papers."

"What academic papers, sir?"

"I don't remember."

Boies turned to another of the Web site's claims. "You are saying here that after same-sex marriage was legalized, the Netherlands legalized incest and polygamy?"

"Yeah, look at the date."

In fact, consensual incest was legal before that country began allowing gays and lesbians to marry, and polygamous marriage was outlawed.

"Who told you that, sir?"

"It's in the Internet."

"In the Internet?" Boies contemptuously repeated.

"Yeah."

"Somewhere out in the Internet it says that the Netherlands legalized incest and polygamy in 2005?"

"Frankly, I did not write this, all right?" Tam said, at turns petulant and defiant.

Boies paused for effect. "You just put it out there to convince voters to vote for Proposition 8."

Boies shifted to Tam's "What If We Lose" letter, the one that had convinced the Ninth Circuit to amend its order and forced Cooper to disclose at least a portion of the campaign's internal communications, and its contention that San Francisco was under the rule of homosexuals.

"The mayor was a homosexual, was he, according to you?"

"I don't think so."

"You don't think so? No, I don't think so either, actually."

Several of the mayor's supporters stifled smiles. If anything, Mayor Gavin Newsom was seen as something of a ladies' man, having survived a well-publicized affair, a divorce, and a remarriage.

Boies, meanwhile, was insisting that Tam tell him why he circulated information he knew to be false, leading Tam to protest that the lawyer was trying to "use your legal arguments to pinpoint me."

Tam then offered up a convoluted explanation. First, he said he disagreed with Newsom that homosexuals were a minority in need of protection—"I am a minority," he told Boies. But then, forced to acknowledge that the numbers showed that gays and lesbians were also minorities, he agreed that they should not be discriminated against.

As his five-hour stint on the stand wore on, Tam seemed to become more and more befuddled, as if when forced to explain his views, he could no longer be sure of exactly what he believed.

"You know that domestic partnerships are the same as marriage, except for the name, right?" Boies asked.

"Yeah. That's what I learned."

"You support domestic partnerships?"

"Uh-huh."

"But you think that just changing the name of domestic partnerships to marriage will have this enormous moral decay—"

"Yes."

"Will bring on incest and polygamy, right? And pedophilia, correct?"

Tam said he did.

If the state's decision to offer domestic partnerships to gays and lesbians had not resulted in the legalization of incest, polygamy, or pedophilia, why, Boies pressed, did Tam believe that allowing them to marry would yield those results? He had to reframe the question several different ways before Tam got it.

"Oh, okay. Now I understand your logic."

"You see where I'm going?" Boies feigned excitement, enunciating as if there were an exclamation point after every word.

"Uh-huh."

"Yeah!" Boies egged him on pitilessly.

"All right," Tam said. "Well, the logic is good."

"The logic is pretty good, isn't it?!"

────

It might have been possible to feel sorry for Tam, but for what he was saying and his evasions, Olson said during a recess. Tam, desperate to escape Boies, had pleaded with the judge for a reprieve. "Do you mind if I like to take a break? I'm getting pretty tired."

Chad and Kristina huddled. Chad saw everything that happened at trial through a political lens, and he could practically envision a public education commercial featuring Tam. "I was sitting there thinking that this was such a public service, because his views are so ignorant," he told her. "The more people like him that can be cross-examined, the better."

But not everyone had Chad's ability to view the proceedings with strategic dispassion. Tam might be "going through hell right now," but when he thought no one was paying attention he had no compunction about spreading lies about gays and lesbians, Kris said.

"It's horrible listening to him," she said. "I've been more traumatized by this trial than anything I can remember going through."

Enrique Monagas's dad, Carlos Monagas Sr., was also in the courtroom that afternoon. His son and Enrique's husband, Jason, had been talking about this case since Enrique was dispatched to file it, and he had come to help the couple out by babysitting his granddaughter. A retired air force major, and a practicing Catholic from Puerto Rico, he said during the break that he had met a lot of people like Tam.

"There's a lot of prejudice out there," he said, sadly shaking his head. "He probably felt prejudice against him so he doesn't think it's wrong to be prejudiced. I think that we should be more open because if you are talking about God forgiving everyone, then you cannot say that the entire gay community is going to burn in hell."

He loved his church, but its role in the passage of Proposition 8 and teachings were hard to accept. Pope Benedict, eighty-two, had called homosexuality an intrinsic disorder.

"One of these days we'll elect a pope who is under eighty years old," he said wistfully. "When I was in parochial school, they said the Jews killed Christ and all that stuff. But I don't care. My daughter is married to a Jew, and I'm glad for Enrique and Jason. They have a beautiful daughter."

———

Most lawyers won't ask a question to which they don't know the answer. Then again, most lawyers aren't Boies.

"During the break, did you talk to anybody about your testimony?" he asked Tam when court resumed.

Boies knew that he had—a member of the team had spotted Tam in a huddle in the hallway—but he did not know what was said.

"I talk to my lawyer."

"You talked to your lawyer," Boies said, then, after a pause, "What did you say to your lawyer?"

"I said I felt like a naughty boy being put in front of a classroom and being mocked at."

"And what did your lawyer say to you?"

"He laughed."

"One last question, Dr. Tam. You indicated earlier that you felt like a minority; do you remember that?"

"Yes."

"And you are aware that there were periods, unfortunate periods in our history, when Asian Americans were limited in who they could marry, do you know that?"

"Uh-huh. Yes."

"And I take it if those laws were present today, you would feel very aggrieved by those laws, would you not, if you couldn't marry the person you loved?"

The question prompted another objection, but Tam answered anyway. "Yes."

At that evening's press conference, Boies declared that Tam's testimony was "one of the clearest windows that you have into the minds and hearts and souls of what was really involved in Proposition 8."

Andy Pugno, the lawyer Cooper had designated to handle the press, could do little more than complain about what he called an unwarranted intrusion into protected speech. "You are witnessing history," he told reporters. "For the first time ever in an initiative process, a supporter of an initiative has been put on the stand to be examined about his political and religious views. That is absolutely astonishing."

TWENTY

THE SCIENCE OF SEXUALITY

Midway through Cooper associate Howard Nielson's mind-numbing cross-examination of Dr. Gregory Herek, the plaintiffs' expert on sexual orientation, David Boies whispered into the ear of the lawyer seated beside him. "Gotta give Nielson credit," he said. "He is making sex boring!"

Nielson, a law professor at Brigham Young University and a member of Cooper's firm, had clerked for Justice Kennedy and worked as a deputy assistant attorney general in the second Bush administration. But trial work was not his specialty. His questions rarely deviated from a prepared script, and with his dark suit, wan face, and brooding manner, he looked a bit like an undertaker.

"He ought to be doing wills," Olson told Matt McGill.

To stay awake at the counsel's table, some of the lawyers had begun keeping track of how many times Nielson said "thank you" after the witness answered one of his questions. By midmorning, it was up to 180. Cooper's wife nodded off while listening to the nasal sound of Nielson's voice.

Herek, a professor of psychology at the University of California at Davis, had taken the stand on Friday morning, January 22, at the end of the second week of trial. He was the plaintiffs' last expert witness, and his direct testimony was to the point and lasted just under an hour.

A substantial body of research shows that for the vast majority of people, sexual orientation is not a choice and is not readily changeable, Herek told the court. In his own survey of twenty-two hundred subjects, for instance, 87 percent of gay men and 70 percent of lesbians said they experienced no choice or very little choice about their sexual orientation.

For that reason, the American Psychological Association had concluded, based on available research, that therapists should steer clear of the type of sexual orientation "conversion" therapy that Ryan Kendall—and, unbeknownst to anyone in the courtroom, Judge Walker—had undergone. Not only had it proven ineffective, but it was also potentially dangerous, according to a pamphlet that the group, along with a coalition of other associations representing psychiatrists, pediatricians, teachers, school counselors, and principals, had put together for educators.

A broad consensus had determined that homosexuality is a normal expression of human sexuality. But efforts by religious and political organizations that are "aggressively promoted to the public" have "serious potential to harm young people," the pamphlet read, because by presenting the view that sexual orientation is a curable mental disorder, "they often frame the inability to change one's sexual orientation as a personal and moral failure."

The notion that most people do not choose their sexual orientation seemed so obvious to Boies that he was not sure that the team even needed to put Herek on the stand. "There's no evidence, no study that finds that people wake up and say, 'Today I'll be gay! This seems like a gay day!'" he said.

But Cooper's point was more nuanced. As part of his strategy to keep the court from applying heightened scrutiny, his goal was to try to show that sexual orientation was not as fixed a trait as gender or race. In service of that mission, Nielson spent five hours plodding through everything from the 1935 writings of Sigmund Freud to the work of Alfred Kinsey, a famous sex researcher whose studies in the 1940s and 1950s were credited with bringing taboo subjects like masturbation and adultery out into the open.

Nielson began with what he argued was a definitional problem in establishing gays and lesbians as a new suspect class. Researchers studying homosexuality use different measures for different purposes: whether a person is attracted to a member of the same sex, whether a person engages in sexual activity with a same-sex partner, and whether a person identifies as gay, lesbian, or bisexual.

It is true that some subset of men who have sex with other men do not identify as gay, Herek said in answer to Nielson's many questions on the subject, and it is also true that some people who identify as gay do not engage in gay sex, though that, Herek joked, could also be said of some heterosexuals.

Judge Walker cracked a smile at that one.

But Herek said most people—he put the number at 92 percent—are remarkably consistent in terms of their identity and attractions.

What about studies that showed that a significant percentage of men and women who had a same-sex partner in the past five years also had at least one opposite-sex partner? Nielson asked. And was Herek aware that one of the plaintiffs had once been married to a man?

Sandy was just grateful that her two boys had left by that point. They had wanted to come on a day when there would not be a lot of media attention, but her happiness at seeing them there had turned to mortification when the testimony turned out to be all about sexuality.

Given the stigma attached to being gay, Herek told Nielson, it is not surprising that many people try to have a relationship with or even marry a person of the opposite sex before coming to terms with their true sexuality. That is why researchers generally understand sexual orientation as an enduring pattern of attraction and behavior across a person's life.

Still, "sexual orientation ranges along a continuum, from exclusively heterosexual to exclusively homosexual, correct?" Nielson pressed.

The concept, sometimes referred to as the Kinsey scale, was a useful way to look at human sexuality, Herek answered. But he said that while sexuality can be fluid, more so for women than men, the research showed that most people are bunched up at one end of the Kinsey scale or the other.

"We keep thinking that the judge is going to stop him," Boutrous said during one recess. "We don't even dispute what he is saying. Some people change, but most do not."

But Nielson, seemingly incapable of letting one question suffice when his checklist contained ten, kept going, even, and somewhat oddly, invoking Judge Richard Posner to support his argument that environmental factors, rather than biology, may play a role in determining a person's sexual orientation.

At one level, the invocation made sense: Posner was a Reagan appointee, a prolific writer whose searing intellect had made him one of the most influential appellate judges in the country and an opponent of judicial intervention in the marriage debate. But Posner's writings about the nature of homosexual-

ity actually undercut the point Nielson was trying to make: It is, "if not genetic, certainly innate," he had written, a conviction that had only grown
stronger with time. "It's impossible to change," he said in a phone interview
from his chambers. "If it were changeable, everyone would change, because it
is a big disadvantage." Posner had also rejected as "unlikely" another of Cooper's central arguments, that allowing gays to wed could harm the institution
of marriage.

Still, Cooper on balance thought that Nielson had done what he set out to
do. It might not have been scintillating, but ultimately Cooper believed that
this would come down not to sex, but rather to how the courts applied law and
precedent to this particular set of facts for the purpose of determining the appropriate level of review.

That was not, however, the thrust of the questions that Andy Pugno, Cooper's co-counsel, faced at the midday press conference.

"You say that sexual orientation is a changeable trait," one reporter asked.
"Do you think that your own sexual orientation is changeable?"

"I'm not going to answer a question like that," Pugno angrily retorted.

If homosexuality can be changed, came a follow-up, can the same be said
for heterosexuality?

Pugno, glaring at the questioner, snapped, "I'm not going to argue the case."

━━━━━

Shortly before 5 P.M., Nielson finally called it quits. Ethan Dettmer, the Gibson
Dunn partner assigned to handle Herek's testimony, kept his redirect as tight
as his direct examination, focusing mainly on the definitional issues that Nielson had raised.

Researchers also encounter definitional issues in the context of race, Herek
told the court. A person considered African American for the purpose of membership in that established suspect class might in fact be of mixed race. And
just as it is not always readily apparent that a person is gay, a person's ancestry
may not always be readily apparent from their skin color.

"They may develop an identity as a member of one race or the other race
or as a mixed race individual," Herek said. "So, no, sexual orientation is cer-

tainly not the only area in which things get pretty messy when we are trying to study them."

The second point was more commonsensical. If two women want to marry each other, is it "a reasonable assumption" that they are lesbians, Dettmer asked, just as it would be reasonable to assume that if two men want to marry each other they are gay?

"Yes," Herek said.

"No more questions, Your Honor."

As Herek stepped down, Judge Walker wryly took note of Nielson's long-windedness, telling the witness, "I think you win the long-distance award."

———

"All I kept thinking was, 'When will it end?'" Herek said.

The professor, along with several of the lawyers who helped prepare him, had repaired to Jardinière, a nearby California-style French restaurant, for a much-needed Friday night drink after court.

Terry Stewart was there, as was Sarah Piepmeier, the young lesbian on the Gibson Dunn team who had prepped Kris and Sandy and pushed to have Meyer testify on the effects of stigma. The case was consuming all the lawyers on the team, both physically and emotionally, but especially those who were gay.

"Sarah has slept maybe ten hours this week," Dettmer said.

She just shrugged. She'd caught a quick nap the previous night in one of the conference rooms. "We have to win."

At one point during the trial, Piepmeier had an irrational urge to introduce her wife to the only female lawyer on Cooper's team, Nicole Moss. The two dealt with one another regularly and had a cordial relationship, but Piepmeier could not help but take Moss's position personally. "I wanted to see her reaction to being introduced to a gay woman's wife," she said, "and whether she'd recognize that her whole purpose in this case was to deny me that."

Sitting through the testimony on stigma, Piepmeier had been forced to confront her feelings in a way that she had not done since coming out as an undergraduate at Wellesley College. She had intuitively understood the burdens of being a lesbian. She'd long felt that she was a disappointment to her family; her mother for years had wondered what she had done wrong as a parent, she said. It was only after Olson became involved in the case that she had begun to refer to her daughter's sexuality when discussing her with friends. "That really made a difference," Piepmeier said, "like if he's okay with it, maybe it isn't something to hide."

But to have Meyer, a straight scientist, say, "What you are experiencing is this," giving a name to it, had been cathartic in a way that she could not fully explain. His conclusion that gays and lesbians have a reduced sense of self-possibility particularly resonated. In law school, it had been hard to find a role model who looked like her, someone through whom she could envision her own success. "There's no mirror," she said.

Even now, as a thirty-five-year-old up-and-coming associate at a powerhouse law firm, Piepmeier, with her scrubbed skin, cropped hair, and mannish suits, felt set apart in a way that at times made her think that she did not truly belong. When the driver of one of the minibuses that ferried everybody to and from court called her "sir," she did not even bother correcting him.

"That happens to me all the time," she said. "I'm like, really? In San Francisco?"

Terry Stewart, who did look like her, could relate. Piepmeier could remember watching Stewart argue the California Supreme Court case and thinking, "God, I'd love to meet her someday."

But despite her accomplishments, Stewart also had trouble with self-confidence. After law school, she had clerked for Judge Phyllis Kravitch, one of the first women to serve on a U.S. court of appeals. Stewart recalled the judge, out of concern for her, suggesting she see a psychiatrist, because if she persisted in being a lesbian, it could harm her law career. Though Stewart knew the judge meant well, it was crushing coming from a trailblazing woman she greatly admired.

Now, over drinks, with the second week of trial in the rearview mirror, everyone opened up.

"The first time I heard a friend call his partner 'husband,' I cringed," Piepmeier said. "It sounded—"

"Pretentious?" Herek offered.

"Yes. But then I thought, 'Why am I, of all people, having a problem with this?'" she said. "I know I'm the victim of internalized homophobia."

Herek nodded. Like Meyer, Herek was an expert in stigma, but unlike him he was gay. He confided that he too had trouble calling his husband 'husband,' and for the same reason: It seemed like a word reserved for other people.

Piepmeier and her wife, Emily, had been together for ten years. They had married during the window when it was legal and had made a beautiful home together in Oakland, looking after their five adopted cats and each other. But it was only recently, after becoming involved in the case, that Piepmeier had begun referring to Emily as her wife. She had started with close friends and worked her way up to the lawyers on the team.

She worried that it was not the panacea that the plaintiffs hoped it would be: Restaurant hostesses still raised their eyebrows, she said, when she told them she was expecting her wife to join her. But she forced herself to move beyond her discomfort.

"I know that if we don't claim this language," she told Herek, "it will never be ours."

With the plaintiffs planning to rest their case on Monday, everyone would soon return to the mundane duties of workaday life. Dettmer said he had an actuarial malpractice case. Stewart had a case involving Hare Krishnas at the airport. Piepmeier, who had a patent dispute, kept telling herself to savor these moments.

"Will we ever do anything as important again?" she wondered aloud.

Maybe not, Dettmer said. "But did you imagine a few years ago that you'd be working on a case like this one?"

TWENTY-ONE

THE PLAINTIFFS REST

That weekend, Cooper finished delivering the last of the discovery documents that the plaintiffs were entitled to see. The "web of evil," as Matt McGill liked to call the evidence of animus that the team was compiling from the campaign's internal communications and public sources, was sorted at all hours of the day and night by a team of young associates who divided it into three piles.

Incendiary political messaging went into one pile, to be used as evidence that the procreative argument now being offered in court was not what was used to persuade voters. Documents that helped show the connections between the official ProtectMarriage.com campaign and the groups that acted as its foot soldiers went into a second pile. Evidence that showed that ProtectMarriage.com promoted, funded, and participated in the dissemination of antigay sentiments expressed by those groups went into a third.

The team planned to end their case on Monday morning with a best-of-the-hate video compilation. The idea was to show that whatever the justifications for Proposition 8 now being offered in court by ProtectMarriage.com, an animating feature of the campaign to sell voters on the initiative was a direct appeal to people's discriminatory impulses.

As Chris Dusseault put it, "Don't tell me, Chuck Cooper, that this campaign was all about love and granola, when your campaign paid for this stuff."

The job of refining it all into a concise video reel that Dusseault could present to the court had fallen to Piepmeier and Ted Uno, a forty-one-year-old attorney from Boies's firm. It was intense work, against a suboptimum deadline; under normal circumstances this would have been done months before trial.

"I spent yesterday looking through material of people who are antigay on the Internet," Piepmeier said on Sunday. "By the end of the day, I was in a horrible mood, and it wasn't until later that I realized why. I'm reading all this stuff, and it's different from reading material about semiconductors. They are saying it about me. That I am a sinner, that I am depraved."

Both Dusseault and Terry Stewart were looking forward to seeing the fruits of the two younger lawyers' labor. By now, sleepless nights and shared takeout had given them all a better understanding of one another, and preconceptions had fallen by the wayside.

Piepmeier had been surprised by how passionately Olson felt about this cause. Until the Proposition 8 case, she had assumed she knew everything there was to know about the conservative star at her law firm. "It's reminded me not to judge a book by its cover," she said.

And Stewart now knew that she had been wrong to think that as a straight white guy, Dusseault had no skin in the game. The two had bonded when he shared with her how offended he was by the argument that Prop 8 was rational because children do best when raised by their biological parents. His wife had lupus, which can flare up and cause complications in pregnancy, so their children were adopted.

Still, this was a diverse group, conservative and liberal, gay and straight, and they did not always see things the same way, a fact that became readily apparent after Piepmeier and Uno screened the reel for Dusseault.

"You don't like it," Terry Stewart said afterward.

"There are parts of it I like," Dusseault protested.

The presentation mixed official campaign ads circulated to mass audiences with material from what the team had taken to calling the unofficial campaign, where more pointedly antigay messages were disseminated to targeted groups of voters. Dusseault liked the footage taken from religious rallies in the weeks leading up to the election that had been broadcast by satellite to congregations around the state. The simulcasts featured pastors from some of the biggest evangelical churches in the country. One speaker claimed that same-sex marriage was a tragedy on par with the 9/11 terrorist attacks. Another said that allowing children to be raised by same-sex couples turned "nature on its head." A third wondered how a child with two moms would learn to "change the oil," and a fourth charged that permitting gay couples to wed would result in pedophiles being allowed to marry seven-year-olds, mothers their sons, and even legalized bestiality in which men would be permitted to marry horses.

Other excerpts featured prominent black ministers attacking gays and lesbians for equating their fight with the civil rights battle waged by African Americans. Internal e-mails showed that religious leaders within the Prop 8 campaign understood that, as one article they circulated among themselves put it, "one of the most effective morality-based arguments for same-sex marriage, the one that persuades more people than any other argument, is the one that equates opposition to same-sex marriage with the old opposition to interracial marriage."

In a confidential memo dated one month after the passage of Prop 8, the National Organization for Marriage spelled out its pushback strategy. Religious black voters might vote Democrat, but they tended to be socially conservative, and the organization described its goal in clear terms: "Drive a wedge between gays and blacks—two key Democratic constituencies. Find, equip, energize and connect African American spokespeople for marriage, develop a media campaign around their objections to gay marriage as a civil right; provoke the gay marriage base into responding by denouncing these spokesmen and women as bigots."

The legal team did not have the benefit of that explosive document; it would not emerge for another three years, when it was unsealed as part of a campaign finance investigation into the organization. But the simulcast vividly demonstrated how it worked on the ground in California.

Bishop Harry Jackson, a senior African American pastor of a three-thousand-member Pentecostal church in Maryland, told Tony Perkins of the Family Research Council that it offended him that homosexuals were claiming an affinity with blacks forced to sit on the back of a bus, since "I didn't choose to come into the world and live a deviant lifestyle." Don't compare "my skin with their sin," seconded the Reverend Dwight McKissic, a prominent African American Southern Baptist minister from Arkansas.

It was good stuff, Dusseault thought, but he wanted it cut down. Keep the religious material to the "most crass stuff," he told the other lawyers. "I'm wrestling with this because our position is that the other side can believe whatever they want."

"You can't put discrimination on trial without showing the roots of it," Stewart argued. "I understand that at the beginning we were like, 'We don't want to touch religion—it's the third rail.' But—"

"How do we take it out of the context of religion when a lot of the impetus was religious beliefs?" Piepmeier finished.

Dusseault thought it over and came around. People are entitled to believe what they want, but when they attempt to legislate their beliefs, the courts could certainly scrutinize what motivated them. "Included within animus is moral disapproval based on religious belief," he agreed.

But he was more concerned about some of the official ProtectMarriage.com ads that the group wanted to use as evidence of animus. One featured a pig-tailed little girl telling her actress mother, "Guess what I learned in school today? That a prince can marry a prince, and I can marry a princess!" Another warned that "opponents of Proposition 8 said gay marriage had nothing to do with schools. Then a public school took first graders to a lesbian wedding, calling it a teachable moment."

They all understood Dusseault's hesitation. The danger was that some judge or justice down the line might be convinced by the ads. Prentice himself had boasted of the power of the argument that they now proposed to use against the proponents in remarks to the conservative California Family Council that the team had unearthed. "All it took when we asked someone, do you plan to vote yes, plan to vote no, or are you somewhere in the mushy middle, if they weren't a solid yes, 80 percent of the time all it took was to tell them did you know that every public school child will be taught this?" he said. "Oh, and they would flip."

"We bet the campaign on education," Frank Schubert had told the *New York Times*.

It was Dusseault's job to ensure that the evidence they introduced benefited only the plaintiffs, and the gay lawyers knew that it was harder for them than it was for him to be objective about what met that test. "I'm so personally invested in this case that I take things personally," Piepmeier said. "That's why I think it's great that our team is so diverse."

Uno, like Piepmeier, was gay. He and his partner had been together for fifteen years and were raising five children. He was a Japanese American, a man of faith who said he knew that his grandmother feared for his soul. He had tried to take those varying viewpoints into account when putting together the reel.

Now he told Dusseault how important it was to demonstrate to the court and the public that the very argument that the campaign had found so effective and that Cooper and his team clearly believed could pass the animus smell test—they had played similar ads himself for the court—was in fact discriminatory. "If you get rid of the more moderate messages, you don't understand how insidious the discrimination is," he said.

Stewart tried to put herself in Dusseault's shoes. "Chris is, well, he's not queer."

"Not yet!" Uno said with a laugh.

So the three of them stepped back and tried to explain to him what seemed so obviously hostile to them.

"Maybe this comes from my being a homosexual," Uno said, "but if I were to say to you that it offends my sensibilities for you to teach children that it's okay for blacks to marry whites, you'd think that I was the most racist person in the world."

Dusseault also found the ads offensive. But he worried that not everyone would. Children that age aren't taught about straight marriage, he said.

That set the gay attorneys off. They all began talking at once about how marriage is ubiquitous in the cultural lives of children, in the fairy tales that they read, in the roles they play as ring bearers and flower girls. No one would think twice about bringing a five-year-old to a wedding, Stewart said. What's different here, Uno chimed in, is that otherwise reasonable people don't want children to know about one specific type of marriage.

"Some of our own family members," said Piepmeier.

"And if you are in mine, many," Uno said.

Suddenly, it clicked for Dusseault in a way that it had not before. What explanation could there be for the fact that people treated two similar events, the wedding of a straight couple and the wedding of a gay couple, so disparately? As Uno put it, "People may not see it as bigotry, but that is prejudice."

Framed correctly, the ads offered powerful evidence of animus, Dusseault realized. He would recommend to Olson that the ads could—and should—stay.

━━━━━

The following morning in court, Cooper's team focused on distancing Prentice and the rest of the proponents from the religious simulcasts, which clearly worried them more than the official ads that Dusseault played. The campaign had not "produced" the simulcast events, and Ron Prentice had not attended them and did not know what was said there, protested Nicole Moss, the lawyer from Cooper's firm who had been tasked with distancing Tam from the campaign.

"The campaign does not dispute that these simulcasts were paid for with money that was raised by ProtectMarriage.com," she said. "But there is no evidence that they had control over the content."

Dusseault had anticipated this line of attack, and had a slew of documents at the ready. In his deposition, Prentice had acknowledged that the simulcasts had been organized by the "Pastors' Rapid Response Team," which the plaintiffs had already established was a crucial component of the campaign's grassroots apparatus. ProtectMarriage.com had paid close attention even to small details involving the simulcasts: In one e-mail that Cooper had been forced to turn over, Andy Pugno complained that another group was incorrectly being given credit for the simulcast in advance promotional material. "All of the CWA references needed to be taken out," Pugno wrote. "'CWA presents' should read 'ProtectMarriage.com presents.'"

Another e-mail exchange showed that Prentice had been given an advance four-page outline of the agenda of one of the simulcasts by its chief organizer, an evangelical megachurch located just outside of San Diego headed by Pastor Jim Garlow. Garlow had acted as the master of ceremonies, charging that if same-sex marriage passed, polygamists would be "waiting in the wings."

But it was a postelection e-mail, between Prentice and Garlow, that was perhaps most damaging. Moss, jumping up to object, protested that the document was irrelevant given that it was dated on November 16, 2008, days after the election.

"Yes," Judge Walker said. "I noticed that."

"Your Honor, if I may, I think I can explain the relevance," Dusseault said. "It *is* a postelection document. And it's a postelection document in which the head of ProtectMarriage.com is trying very hard to make sure that these simulcasts don't get out to the public.

"And this is about a *Dr. Phil* show, and what's going to happen on a *Dr. Phil* show," Dusseault continued. "And what Mr. Prentice says is, 'We must control the message from the simulcast, Jim. I don't see how using any portion of it will not permit the show to direct the message to the religious bias.'

"We think it's directly relevant, Your Honor, that ProtectMarriage.com, after the election, was trying to make sure that a national audience, like an audience of the *Dr. Phil* show, didn't learn of this religious bias. And that's Mr. Prentice's word for it, not mine."

Walker agreed. The document was in.

At 11:06 A.M., Dusseault signaled that his presentation had come to a close. "Thank you, then, Your Honor, I will hand over the reins to Mr. Boies."

"Very well," Judge Walker said. "Mr. Boies?"

"Purely ceremonial, Your Honor," Boies said. "The plaintiffs rest."

TWENTY-TWO

COOPER'S TURN

Like Olson, Cooper had thought hard about putting Ron Prentice, the executive director of ProtectMarriage.com, on the stand. Over the weekend, he had also notified the plaintiffs that he might call Frank Schubert, its chief political operative. Having someone other than Tam speak on behalf of the campaign and its motivations had its attractions. But Cooper ultimately decided against the move for two reasons.

First, he did not want to take a position that was inconsistent with his overarching legal argument, which was that seven million California voters could not all have been irrational or bigoted. The campaign's messages, the mindset of its proponents and operatives—all meaningless, in Cooper's view. The Supreme Court's jurisprudence in this area was hardly a model of clarity, but as he read the *Romer* decision, as long as he could show that banning same-sex marriage served some legitimate interest, it should not matter whether the campaign was run by "the devil incarnate" or "supported by some people for completely evil reasons."

Second, Cooper did not want to give his opponents an opportunity to go on a fishing expedition. That very morning, Ted Boutrous had argued that the claims of privilege that had shielded Schubert's documents and that Schubert had invoked seventy-six times in refusing to answer questions during his deposition would go out the window if he took the stand. The limited rebuttal value of calling either man could be offset if it entitled the plaintiffs to a wide-ranging cross. "Whatever good we could get out of Prentice or Schubert," Cooper later explained, "wasn't worth the risk we were running."

And so shortly before noon on the tenth day of trial, Cooper's team called the first of only two witnesses: Kenneth Miller, an associate professor of government at Claremont McKenna College.

Cooper's top priority remained keeping the court from determining that gays and lesbians met the test for heightened scrutiny. His first line of defense was precedent: The Ninth Circuit, in a 1990 case called *High Tech Gays v. Defense Industrial Security Clearance Office* challenging the Pentagon's policy of denying security clearances to people who were known or thought to be homosexuals, had ruled that the proper standard of review for laws that target gays and lesbians was the lower, rational basis bar: "Homosexuality is not an immutable characteristic," the court had found, but rather a behavioral choice, and "homosexuals are not without political power."

But with Olson arguing that the appeals court decision predated the Supreme Court's two landmark gay rights rulings—indeed, it cited the since overturned *Bowers v. Hardwick* case upholding laws criminalizing sodomy—Miller was Cooper's insurance policy. He was there to rebut Segura's testimony that gays and lesbians lacked the ability to seek redress in the democratic process.

It did not get off to a smooth start.

Miles Davis, the legendary jazz musician, once said, "Don't play what's there, play what's not there." It might have been Boies's motto as well.

Miller specialized in the politics of California and was the author of two books, one on the initiative process called *Direct Democracy and the Courts,* and another called *The New Political Geography of California.* But he had written very little about gays and lesbians, and compared to Segura's twenty-five peer-reviewed articles and his position as the codirector of the Stanford Center for American Democracy and a member of the editorial board of the *American Journal of Political Science,* his curriculum vitae was lacking.

"He's not an expert—I want to have everything we can say about that," Boies had told his team over the weekend. "What he hasn't been. What he hasn't studied."

Because juries tend to give expert opinions great weight, courts are required to act as gatekeepers to ensure that expert testimony is helpful to understanding the matter at hand and based on a reliable, intellectually rigorous foundation. Now, armed with the information he had requested, Boies challenged Miller's qualifications.

Miller acknowledged to Boies that he had not written any peer-reviewed articles on the subject of gay and lesbian political power besides one piece in a French journal; there, he had taken the counterintuitive position that the losing battle they had fought against Proposition 8 actually demonstrated their political muscle. He had not extensively studied the history of discrimination against gays and lesbians. And during his deposition, he had been unable to name the first openly gay officials elected to office.

"He doesn't even know many of the key facts and people involved," Boies protested.

Walker, though, was understandably reluctant to knock the witness out. The Supreme Court had made clear that such a move should be the exception, rather than the rule; vigorous cross-examination and presentation of contrary evidence "are the traditional and appropriate means of attacking shaky but admissible evidence," the justices had said. Implicit in Miller's knowledge of California politics and initiatives was an understanding of the different groups that made up the electorate, the judge decided. That qualified him to speak to the subject at hand.

"You may proceed," Walker said.

But the seed had been planted, and the spat over Miller's qualifications was featured nearly as prominently as the substance of what he had to say in much of the media coverage of the defense's opening day. And the testy credentials confrontation was just a taste of what Boies had in store for Miller, "the equivalent of David Boies saying at recess, 'I'll see *you* after school,'" as Yusef Robb put it later that night in the war room.

———

Miller's thesis was that the political power of minority groups should be measured in terms of money, access to power, and the ability to build alliances. Gays and lesbians, he told the court, had demonstrated all three.

Where Segura had looked at indicia such as the fact that gays and lesbians were more likely than any other minority to be the target of hate crimes, Miller noted that a record $83 million was spent on the Proposition 8 campaign, with supporters of same-sex marriage slightly outspending opponents. A "who's who of Silicon Valley" that included corporate giants like Google had sided with gays and lesbians in opposing Proposition 8, he told the court, as had some of the state's most powerful unions, the state Democratic Party, and twenty-one of twenty-three of the state's largest newspapers.

Rather than focus on the repeated political losses that gays and lesbians had suffered in ballot initiatives across the nation, Miller talked instead about the ballot measures they had been able to beat back in California. One was a 1970s initiative that would have allowed public schools to fire teachers who promoted homosexuality; another was a 1980s push to quarantine people with HIV/AIDS.

Another measure of progress in California, according to Miller, was the fact that Proposition 22, the law voters passed in 2000 to ban gays and lesbians from marrying, passed by a wider margin than Proposition 8, which changed the California constitution after that law was struck down.

One measure of political powerlessness, according to the Supreme Court, is the inability to attract the attention of lawmakers. Where Segura had noted that gays and lesbians had been unable to secure federal legislation that would protect them from discrimination in the employment, housing, and public accommodation arenas, Miller talked about the numbers of large companies that provided benefits to same-sex partners.

And where Segura had focused on the failure of Congress to repeal the law banning gays and lesbians from serving openly in the military, Miller pointed to the 100 percent rating given to more than half the California Legislature by the largest gay rights groups in the state, and the recent passage by Congress of the Matthew Shepard and James Byrd, Jr. Hate Crimes Prevention Act.

That last reference infuriated Mary Boies, herself a lawyer, who had a note passed to her husband. The law, which provided for additional federal penalties for hate crimes based on sexual orientation, was named in part after a Wyoming college student who was taunted, beaten, and left to die after attending a gay awareness meeting on campus. Witnesses said he was found tied to a ranch fence post, his head bathed in blood except where tears running down his face had washed it away. It had taken Congress multiple tries and more than a decade to pass the statute. If anything, the need for such legislation was an example of gay vulnerability, she thought.

"This witness cites the Matt Shepard hate crimes act as one indication of gay political power," she wrote. "Does [*sic*] statutes like Megan's Law indicate that little girls who are raped and killed have political power?"

———

Boies once told Terry Stewart that the key to a good cross-examination is to attack the witness's credibility, win whatever concessions you can that help your case, and then get the person off the stand. "You have to control the witness on cross-examination," he had explained as he prepped over the weekend, "and the only way to control the witness is by keeping your question precise."

Over lunch, he held forth on his plan for Miller. While Olson craved solitude before performing in court and often retreated to the lawyers' lounge to eat, Boies rolled with an entourage that included a driver and his own press person. He spent most days at a round table in the cafeteria, talking to reporters and fans while consuming a peculiar and never-deviating meal: the torn-off crust of a loaf of round sourdough bread fetched daily by the driver, and a slice or two of apple pie.

"Everything that they've said so far can be taken care of with a few questions," he said. "All those groups of allies they mentioned—they also were supportive of African Americans, weren't they? Yet you don't have any doubt that African Americans lacked political power, do you? Gays and lesbians lost Proposition 8, didn't they? And not only did they lose in California, but they have lost in every single state where there's been a ballot initiative over marriage, correct?"

Boies organized his cross-examinations by the points he wanted to make, with backup material readily accessible in tabbed and color-coded binders. Any attempt at evasion was interrupted with a curt command to answer "yes, no, or I don't know," and, when Boies was truly excercised, a demand that the witness repeat his question. Miller got the full treatment when court resumed that afternoon.

The first slip-up came within minutes. Expert witnesses must prepare a report summarizing their conclusions and analysis for the court. Boies was in the midst of listing all the facts that Miller had not known when his deposition was taken prior to the start of the trial, but that were now contained in the expert report Miller had since submitted.

When Miller was deposed, he had not known whether gays and lesbians were underrepresented in political office, had not accurately described the term "gay bashing," had not been able to say how many states (just twenty-one of fifty) had acted to prohibit employment discrimination against gays and lesbians, and had not reviewed academic books dealing with minority prejudice, to name a few.

Listening, Miller grew defensive. "What I wrote in my report is something I investigated myself," he insisted.

Something about the wording stopped Boies. It is a given that expert witnesses are supposed to conduct independent research; they cannot simply be a paid mouthpiece for one side or the other.

A willingness to deviate from his preestablished plan was a Boies trademark. He likened questioning a hostile witness to skeet shooting: "You've got your gun cocked, but you have to wait until the target is up in the air to decide exactly when and how to take your shot." Now, taking aim, he probed further.

"And you didn't go over it with counsel at all; is that your testimony?"

David Thompson was on his feet, objecting. Generally, communications between a lawyer and an expert witness are considered privileged, meaning that they do not have to be disclosed. But Judge Walker agreed that Miller had "opened up the door to the issue of what it is that he himself investigated and did not personally investigate."

Thompson sat down. "No objections to that, Your Honor."

"I investigated everything that was in my report," Miller answered.

"Personally?" Boies asked.

"Personally."

Boies flipped through his binder until he found the materials that Miller had relied upon. "Were some of these materials provided you by counsel, or did you find all of them yourself?"

Miller was looking increasingly uncomfortable. "Um, most of these I found by myself."

"That wasn't my question, sir," Boies said, managing to make the honorific sound like a four-letter word. "Remember my question?"

By now, Boies had closed the distance between himself and the witness. "Circle the ones that were—that you found yourself, were not provided by counsel," he demanded.

More than fifteen excruciating minutes ticked by, the sense of suspense building as Miller sat hunched over his report, pen in hand, Boies crowding him from the front and Thompson at his side. The only sound in the courtroom was the rustle of pages as Miller flipped through them, save for thirty seconds of crunching noises that resulted in a deputy scolding Rob Reiner for smuggling snacks into the courtroom.

At one point Miller told Boies he was having difficulty recalling who had found what. Chad grinned. "Like a sitting duck in front of a machine gun" was the way Chad would later describe Miller's demeanor to the rest of the war room.

"Just put a question mark next to those," Boies instructed.

Finally, Miller handed the marked-up report back to Boies. It is not unusual for a lawyer to suggest that a witness consider a work of scholarship before finalizing an expert report. But Miller's scribbles indicated that the legal team defending Proposition 8 had provided him with the vast majority of the materials he had considered; of the 427 citations undergirding his report, he could only be sure that he had personally identified ninety-eight.

Even Cooper had to admit that it made for good courtroom theater. "There were some rough spots in his testimony," he said later.

Boies paced his cross so that it lasted into the next day, giving him overnight, that "golden time," as he called it, to sharpen his attack.

Miller, in an effort to undercut the plaintiffs' evidence on religious animosity, had listed churches that supported same-sex marriage in his expert report. But Boies forced him to acknowledge that the largest denominations, with congregations totaling eighteen million people in California, supported the ban. Confronted with exit poll data that showed that 84 percent of weekly churchgoers voted yes on Proposition 8 and his own past writings, Miller wound up agreeing with Boies that religion played a critical role in Proposition 8's passage.

Boies similarly sought to impeach Miller's testimony that gays and lesbians had powerful allies in the labor movement by confronting him with exit poll data that showed that 56 percent of those with a union member in their household had voted in favor of Proposition 8.

By the time Miller stepped down on Tuesday, January 26, he had made so many useful concessions that Boies (correctly, as it turned out) predicted that Cooper would not quote him in his closing arguments or subsequent briefs. Olson, for his part, kept a running tally, jotting notes on his yellow legal pad and already envisioning how he would use the admissions as the case made its way up on appeal. Among them: that "gays and lesbians currently face discrimination"; that discrimination is relevant to assessing a group's political power; that gays and lesbians possibly face as much discrimination as African Americans and more than women, both groups that the Court considers deserving of heightened scrutiny; that he had not investigated the extent of antigay harassment in the workplace or schools or the way that antigay rhetoric might have influenced Proposition 8 voters but that "at least some people voted for Proposition 8 on the basis of antigay stereotypes and prejudice"; and that laws like Proposition 8 and DOMA were examples of state-sponsored discrimination against gays and lesbians.

And then there was this back-and-forth:

"You have actually written about why minorities who have a lot of political allies nevertheless suffer defeats in the initiative process, correct?" Boies asked.

"I don't know if I phrased it quite that way," Miller replied.

Boies proceeded to read aloud from an article Miller had published in 2001, in which he wrote about what can happen when voters are allowed to bypass legislatures and engage in direct democracy: "'The direct initiative can be and has been used to disadvantage minorities.' That's what you wrote, correct?"

"That's correct."

"And you believe that today, correct, sir?"

"I do."

"And then you next write, 'The checks-and-balances system of representative government is designed to harmonize majority rule with protection of minority rights.' You believe that today, correct?"

"Yes, I do."

"You then write, 'In contrast, the direct initiative system, by bypassing checks and balances, is weighted heavily toward majority rule at the expense of certain minorities. Racial minorities, illegal immigrants, homosexuals, and criminal defendants have been exposed to the electorate's momentary passions as Californians have adopted a large number of initiatives that represent Populist backlash against representative government's efforts to protect or promote the interests of racial or other minorities.'"

"That's what I wrote at the time," Miller said. "I no longer believe that."

"You no longer believe that," Boies acidly repeated. "Well, sir, let's see about that."

He referred Miller to his deposition testimony, taken just before the start of the trial, and began reading from it:

"'QUESTION: Do you agree that the direct initiative can be and has been used to disadvantage minorities?'

"'ANSWER: I believe that's a fair interpretation of the history of the initiative process.'

"Did you give that testimony under oath on December 9, 2009?"

"Yes," Miller said. "And I would say the same thing today."

"Thank you," Boies said, making no effort to hide the note of triumph in his voice.

David Thompson tried his best during the redirect to clean up the mess that Boies had made of his witness. Miller told him that he had "tried to review" all of the materials he had referenced in his expert report, regardless of who found them. But when, in answer to another of Thompson's prompts, Miller said he had come to believe that ballot initiatives like Prop 8 act as a useful check on "judicial activism," it was Judge Walker who jumped in to play the role of cross-examiner.

"Are you saying that it is never appropriate for the judiciary to intervene in the initiative process?" the judge asked.

"No, Your Honor."

"When is it appropriate?"

"In my view, it's appropriate when an initiative, just like any other statute enacted by the legislature, violates in this case the federal Constitution."

"And who is to make that determination?" the judge asked.

"That's ultimately a question for the courts to decide."

What a remarkable exchange, Olson thought. "I never like to guess what a judge is thinking, especially in the middle of a case," he said during a break, "but I liked that question."

Ted Boutrous, whom Olson joked had become the "sound bite king" of the operation, was even more bullish at the midday press conference. "A nail in the coffin of Prop 8" was how he described Miller's performance.

———

The muttering man barged through the courtroom doors, and before anyone could stop him he had made it midway up the court's center aisle, within striking distance of the four plaintiffs.

"Return the family to Jesus!" he shouted.

Deputies rushed to restrain the disheveled intruder, and removed him within moments. But everyone was shaken by how close he had managed to get, especially Kris and Sandy.

Since the start of the trial, a stranger had been harassing them. The phone calls would begin just after 4 A.M., and had kept them in a near-constant state of anxiety. "You make me sick," the man would say. "I hope you burn in hell."

Chad wanted to book Kris and Sandy on every television show he could; Americans on the fence about same-sex marriage needed to hear the plaintiffs' stories. But the two women worried that the exposure could invite violence. The upcoming *People* magazine interview that the war room had pushed so hard to land had almost fallen apart when editors insisted that the spread include a family photograph with the twins, now freshmen in high school; only after they had agreed to shoot the boys from behind had Kris signed off. But she had not been able to shield them from the caller.

One day while they were in court, Elliott had been home alone when the man rang. "'Tell those faggots they should be dead,'" he recalled the caller saying. "He listed all these terrible things about my parents. He kept calling. He persisted for four hours. I had to sit there and try to do my homework. English, math, and chemistry. I just closed my door. After a while it turned into white noise."

Kris had been so worked up when Spencer answered another of the man's calls—"Hang up, hang up," she'd cried—that he had not wanted to add to her worries by telling her that someone had found his e-mail address on his Facebook page. "It's okay to not be okay with this," the anonymous writer had said. "It's okay to seek help."

What was not okay with Spencer was the writer's presumptions. He and Elliott were among the brightest kids in their class. Sure, as Elliott later said, it might have been nice to have a guy around to teach him to shave, but "those are hiccups in the greater scheme."

"There was never a time when I thought I would be better off having a dad," Spencer said. "What's the real benefit of having a football thrown?"

He would have liked to e-mail back: Think logically about everything gays and lesbians have to go through to have children, how much they have to want them. "Because of that they are more devoted," he would have told the writer.

But over the years he had learned not to respond. "People who feel this way, it's the result of years of conditioning," Spencer said.

Kris called the Berkeley police, who responded by putting their home on a frequent-patrol list. (The caller, it turned out, was later sentenced to eighteen months in prison for threatening House Speaker Nancy Pelosi.) AFER paid to have a home alarm installed. For a while, court deputies escorted both women to and from the bathroom during breaks. And Sandy began watching out of the corner of her eye each morning when she stepped outside to pick up the paper.

Meanwhile, the proponents were talking about how their witnesses would not testify because they feared being harassed.

"We just sat there thinking, 'Come on,'" Sandy said.

Kris had tried to adopt a "what will happen, will happen" attitude. But her attempt at fatalism was often overpowered by a single thought: "Please, God, don't let anything happen." She was tired of being scared. Hang in there, she told herself, after the courtroom intruder was removed. Just one more witness, and at least this phase of the case would all be over.

TWENTY-THREE

"A HIGH OL' TIME OF IT"

When court resumed that afternoon, Chuck Cooper called his final witness.

Afterward, Olson and Boies would wonder aloud why Cooper had even bothered with someone who spent so much time extolling the many virtues of same-sex marriage that it was easy to forget that he was there to defend the voters' decision to ban it.

Cooper would counter that his opponents had missed the entire point of the testimony. And the witness would recall the sheer exhilaration of his star turn on the stand, the "stroke to the ego" he had experienced "going head-to-head with a skilled interrogator" like Boies.

"You know what I enjoyed?" David Blankenhorn said. "The combat."

He did not have to wait long for it to commence. Blankenhorn was the founder of the Institute for American Values, a nonprofit dedicated to strengthening marriage, and he was there to rebut the testimony of the plaintiffs' experts that no harm would come from allowing gays and lesbians to wed. But before Blankenhorn could proceed, Boies, as he had with Miller, challenged his qualifications to opine on those topics.

Boies began with Blankenhorn's actual area of academic expertise—the Victorian cabinetmaker thesis that Chad's team had dug up—then listed all the qualifications he lacked. He did not have a degree in sociology, anthropology, psychiatry, or any other field relevant to the study of marriage, children, or families. He had never taught at a university.

"Boies made a big thing that I was incompetent, that I couldn't walk and chew gum at the same time," Blankenhorn later recalled. "Peer review this, publish that—he just had a high ol' time of it."

Judge Walker made clear that Blankenhorn was a tougher call than the previous expert witness, Professor Miller. To his credit, Blankenhorn had written two books, one on fatherhood and another called *The Future of Marriage*. His views on same-sex marriage were frequently quoted in the press and he had testified before a congressional committee on the subject. And in the Ninth Circuit, where the trial was being held, the rules on expert testimony were fairly lax; there were no minimal academic requirements, for instance.

But experts must be informed by scientific or other specialized knowledge that gives them a command of the subject beyond what an informed layperson might have. In this case, Blankenhorn acknowledged that he had conducted no independent studies to test his contention that allowing same-sex marriage would have a deleterious societal impact. He was merely a "transmitter of the findings of eminent scholars," as he described it in his deposition.

"I have just read articles and had conversations with people, and tried to be an informed person about it," Blankenhorn told the court. "But that is really the extent of it."

Walker decided to hear Blankenhorn out before rendering judgment on his qualifications. But "were this a jury trial, I think the question might be a close one," he said.

Amir Tayrani, who had spent most of the trial back at the office looking through the transcripts with an eye toward the appeal, was in court that day to watch the action. "They might as well have got someone off the street," he said to Kristina. "He's going to get eviscerated up there."

Kristina nodded her agreement. "Good times, good times!"

A Mississippi native, Blankenhorn had the accent and thundering cadence of a tent revivalist preacher, and he used both to ponderous effect during Cooper's direct examination. "How's Pat Robertson doing in there?" joked Olson, who had left the courtroom to stretch his legs.

Blankenhorn saw himself as an anguished warrior in the debate over same-sex marriage, someone who had only reluctantly concluded that the rights of gays and lesbians must take a backseat to the needs of children. He had come to Cooper's attention because he ran in the same circles as Maggie Gallagher, whose National Organization for Marriage was one of the driving forces behind Prop 8's passage. She had worked at his Institute for American Values, but had struck out on her own because for years he had refused to involve himself in a gay marriage debate he viewed as divisive. Eventually, though, the "issue just hunts you down," as he later put it, "and you realize that silence is not an option."

Blankenhorn had founded his nonprofit out of concern over the growing number of children being raised in fatherless households. Now he shared with the court his fear that allowing gays and lesbians to wed would further devalue an institution already weakened by the prevalence of out-of-wedlock births and no-fault divorce. Marriage, he told the court, is a "gift to children" that exists to "regulate filiation"—or, in plainer terms, to make it as likely as possible that that they are claimed and raised by the biological parents who brought them into the world. "That is the lodestar," he said.

"Why does it matter whether the child is raised by his or her own biological parents?" Cooper asked.

"The scholars have given it a name, called 'kin altruism,'" Blankenhorn said. "And it really means, you know, you care a lot about who you are related to. You care about your relatives. You care about who your parents are, who your child is. And you would be—they have measured this with great precision. You typically sacrifice more for people to whom you are related."

So, he continued, "If you wanted what was best for the child, you would want that child—other things being equal, of course—you would want that child to be cared for by the two individuals who are most closely related to the child. And that would be the child's mother and the child's father."

Concern about the "deinstitutionalization" of marriage and the potential impact that could have on children was, Cooper believed, reason enough for Californians to vote to ban gay couples from marrying—even if it never materialized. This was, in essence, his "I don't know" and "science can't say with the kind of certainty required for setting constitutional precedents" defense, which he alluded to in a question aimed at inoculating his witness against charges that there was no definitive proof to back up his dire predictions.

"Mr. Blankenhorn, how confident are you that redefining marriage to include same-sex marriage, same-sex couples, would further the deinstitutionalization of marriage?"

"It's impossible to be completely sure about a prediction of future events," Blankenhorn answered. "But . . . if you change the definition of the thing, it's hard to imagine how it could have no impact on the thing."

———

Blankenhorn had studied Boies during his cross-examination of the defense's previous witness, Kenneth Miller. He admired the way he always seemed to be reassessing the situation, searching in an unscripted way for a genuinely human interaction. But Blankenhorn was determined not to fall for the lawyer's traps, and particularly not to be forced into giving the type of simplistic "yes, no, or I don't know" answers the lawyer demanded to questions he considered to be far more complex. "I wasn't going to be bullied by him or anyone into choosing three words," he said later.

The result was a confrontation that at times saw the two men shouting over one another, and the judge growing so exasperated by Blankenhorn's repeated attempts to reframe Boies's questions into ones more to his liking that at one point he said, "That's how it works. There's a question, and there's an answer."

In one representative exchange, first Boies, then Walker pressed Blankenhorn to say whether the long list of academics he had reeled off during his direct testimony actually agreed with him that allowing same-sex couples to marry would lower the rate of heterosexual marriage. "He is giving you three choices, 'yes, no, or I don't know,'" Judge Walker told Blankenhorn.

Repeated queries finally yielded this: "I do not have sure knowledge that in the exact form of words you are asking me for they have made the direct assertion that permitting same-sex marriage would directly lower the marriage rate among heterosexuals."

Boies treated Blankenhorn with deliberate disdain, his tone alternatively sneering and bullying, "like an abusive parent," Yusef Robb said. He repeatedly mispronounced the witness's name, as if to say he could not be bothered with someone of his caliber, and neither should the court.

"Mr. Blanken*thorn*," Boies would say.

"Horn!" the witness would protest. (Rob Reiner joked that either version sounded like a character out of a Groucho Marx movie.)

Boies even offered the witness a "gold star" when he managed a simple, declarative answer. It got so bad that Blankenhorn at one point complained that Boies was making fun of him.

"I don't think he's laughing at you," Judge Walker said. "He's amused at the back-and-forth. As I think many of us who are observing this are."

By defining marriage as a union between a man and a woman and then arguing that allowing gays and lesbians to marry would deinstitutionalize it, Olson felt Cooper was playing a tautological game, like saying that the right to vote was deinstitutionalized when women were allowed into polling booths. He wanted Boies to deconstruct it by getting the witness to make concessions drawn directly from the Supreme Court's prior marriage rulings that he could then use on appeal.

"Pull him back—get him to say that marriage is a fundamental right," said Boutrous, conveying Olson's wishes during one prep session. "And on deinstitutionalization, Ted was thinking, when blacks and whites were allowed to marry, did that deinstitutionalize marriage? How about when prisoners were allowed to marry?"

Boies agreed with Olson. "They are saying you shouldn't make any change until you've had time to see whether there is any impact, but if everybody took their position then there would never be any change to study."

But Blankenhorn's stubborn evasiveness—"Your Honor, Your Honor, he keeps doing this!" Boies protested at one point—prevented the lawyer from eliciting some of the concessions that Olson most wanted.

Still, over the course of the cross-examination, Boies forced Blankenhorn to acknowledge that marriage "evolves over time," is a "public good," and that to the extent it was being deinstitutionalized, that was a phenomenon attributable to heterosexuals, not gays and lesbians. Blankenhorn also conceded that, notwithstanding his testimony about "kin altruism" and the superiority of the genetically related family, studies showed that adoptive parents can actually outstrip biological parents in providing for their children because of the rigorous screening process they undergo.

But the moment that Boies would crow about for years to come, the moment in which he confronted Blankenhorn with words from his own book, words about how allowing gays and lesbians to marry would be a "victory for the worthy ideas of tolerance and inclusion," was not quite the gotcha moment that it seemed.

In fact, as incredible as it might have seemed to Boies and Olson, it was Cooper's entire reason for putting Blankenhorn on the stand.

━━━━

If Cooper could have, he would have called the president of the United States. He was betting the case on the proposition that in a rational-basis world, "if I can point to a single nonbigoted person" who favored keeping the traditional definition of marriage, "I have to win."

"So, Exhibit A was Barack Obama," he later explained. "And Exhibit B was David Blankenhorn."

Cooper had known all along that Judge Walker was gay. When David Thompson first approached Blankenhorn about testifying, he told him about the judge's sexual orientation. "The impression he conveyed to me was that it was widely believed that he was gay but he hadn't ever publicly said so," Blankenhorn recalled. "He also told me that they were under no illusion that they would win in Judge Walker's courtroom."

But with the case headed for the Supreme Court, it was critical to Cooper that the expert called by Proposition 8's defenders have nuanced views about gay people. "Olson and Boies want to make this about being homophobic," Blankenhorn recalled Thompson saying. "We're going with you because we think on the whole you'll be more credible for us. You're not a cartoonish figure, and your views aren't easily pigeonholed."

Cooper had a team of volunteers from a Utah law firm go over everything that Blankenhorn had ever written or said. Boiled down, his take was that while there were plenty of very good reasons to be for gay marriage, there were more important reasons to oppose it. Cooper had read every word of it.

So Blankenhorn said he had to laugh when Boies began throwing quote after quote from his book at him, "cleverly, manipulatively using what I wrote as some sort of victory dance.

"It wasn't like he caught me in some big, 'oh my gosh' thing," Blakenhorn said.

Indeed, Boies overlooked the piece of evidence that actually did worry Cooper, he said: a video clip in which Blankenhorn had declared that domestic partnerships relegated gays and lesbians to back-of-the-bus status.

"You're a helluva good witness," Blankenhorn said Cooper told him at the end of the first day. "And I thought, 'Gee, Chuck, I kinda agree.'"

But from where Olson was sitting, it did not seem that way at all. "Prop 8 Case Heads to End with Defendants' Own Witnesses Making Plaintiffs' Case," read the press release the AFER war room sent out that night, followed by a list of "Blankenhorn Admissions" cherry-picked in conjunction with the legal team.

"Homophobia is a real presence in our society," the witness had told the court. Permitting gays and lesbians to marry would "signify greater social acceptance of homosexual love, and the worth and validity of same-sex intimate relationships." That "might contribute over time to a decline in antigay prejudice, as well as, more specifically, a reduction in antigay hate crimes." Gay marriage would also "extend a wide range of the natural and practical benefits of marriage to many lesbian and gay couples and their children." Not only would it contribute to "longer-lasting relationships," but also more economic stability. It would also "probably reduce the proportion of homosexuals who marry persons of the opposite sex, and thus would likely reduce instances of marital unhappiness and divorce." And "by increasing the number of married couples who might be interested in adoption and foster care, same-sex marriage might well lead to fewer children growing up in state institutions and more growing up in loving adoptive and foster families."

And this jaw-dropper: "I believe today that the principle of equal human dignity must apply to gay and lesbian persons. Insofar as we are a nation founded on this principle, we would be more American on the day we permitted same-sex marriage than we were on the day before."

"You wrote those words, did you not, sir?" Boies asked. "And you believed them then, correct?

"That's correct."

"And you believe them now, correct?"

"That's correct."

Years later, Cooper had no regrets about Blankenhorn's testimony. "Everything he wrote, it makes my point," he said. But underscoring just how differently the two men saw the law, Olson simply could not discern the method to his opponent's madness, then or later.

How could it be rational to toss aside all the good that Blankenhorn had just outlined, simply because of some unproven fear of deinstitutionalization? From Olson's perspective, it was the perfect ending to the trial, showing just how indefensible the kind of arguments that might work in a campaign are when they must be defended in court. Shaking Boies's hand outside on the steps, Olson was positively gleeful.

"God, their witnesses were so awful!"

"This is too easy," Boutrous said.

"I know," Boies answered.

The following day, on the afternoon of January 27, Chad and Kristina packed up the war room and headed their separate ways. Their firm's paying clients were clamoring for attention, and Chad needed to take care of business in Los Angeles while she tended to First Lady Maria Shriver in Sacramento.

After the intensity of the last two weeks, the abruptness of the ending was jarring. Walker had decided to put off closing arguments indefinitely, both to give himself time to study the record first and because he had granted a request by Cooper that he be allowed to root through the sort of "No on Prop 8" campaign material that his clients had been forced to turn over. So there was no satisfactory summation of what had transpired, no real denouement, just a lovely speech from the judge in which he shook hands with all the lawyers and thanked them for a job well done. "Congratulations to the lawyers in the case for, obviously, a fascinating case," he told them. "Extremely well presented on both sides."

Kristina was heading straight to the Sundance Film Festival from the state Capitol, and wasn't going to see Chad for a few weeks. Like election day after a hard-fought campaign, there was little else to do but wait for the verdict.

"I guess I'll see you later," she told Chad.

She was running late for a meeting with the first lady's staff. But instead of heading straight for the Capitol, she found herself in Nordstrom, buying a pair of high heels. It was the only thing she could think to do that would make her feel better. Chad felt equally strange and unsettled. When Kristina arrived in Sacramento, there was an e-mail from him. "That was that ☺," was all it said.

The night before, a number of the younger Gibson Dunn lawyers had joined the plaintiffs and the war room team for a party at a nearby restaurant, followed by some karaoke. Everyone had been in high spirits. Matt McGill surprised everyone by rocking a version of Bruce Springsteen's "Thunder Road" to get the group started. Enrique Monagas was next, then he and McGill teamed with Adam Umhoefer and got into a Journey face-off with some random people at the bar. As the drinks flowed, "Name Your Favorite Blankenhorn Quote" became something of a parlor game. Hands down, it was when he said that allowing gays and lesbians to marry would benefit their children. "Check please!" Jeff said.

"Twenty years from now," Adam said, "people will look back at what happened in that courtroom as a turning point."

Chad, though, had quietly sat apart, dreamily holding up his iPhone and snapping pictures. Photography was his passion. "I can disappear and be in another world, be an observer of life," he explained one afternoon. "As a kid, my mom would say, 'Go play with the other kids.' But I liked to watch and listen to the adults. To take a picture—it freezes that one moment."

Chad knew enough to want to capture this one, could sense its historic implications, but his subconscious wouldn't allow him to reflect on his own role in choreographing it. Some part of him would always be the closeted gay guy from Arkansas, deflecting attention onto others, lest someone find out his secret.

"He doesn't think of himself as a player," Kristina said. "I think he always just thinks, 'It's a war and we're foot soldiers in the thick of the fight.' I can't imagine Chad sitting in Washington, D.C., in an office being the leader of some gay rights group. He likes to be in the trenches, fighting."

When Chad awoke the following morning, his camera roll contained images of everyone but himself.

TWENTY-FOUR

VICTORY

The e-mail went out at 4:12 P.M. Pacific time on August 3, 2010: "It's happening!" Six months after the trial ended, Judge Walker planned to issue his decision the following day.

David Boies was already in California, taking a deposition in his latest blockbuster case, an ugly divorce with $130 million and the ownership of the Los Angeles Dodgers on the line. Ted Boutrous, when he got word, had just picked up a pair of diamond chandelier earrings for his wife's birthday and the fixings for a dinner party he was throwing her that night.

He and Olson began e-mailing like crazy. But they could see no way that Olson, given the time difference and the remoteness of his Wisconsin lakeside home where he was vacationing, could catch a commercial flight to San Francisco and be there in time for the decision. Boutrous rushed back to his home in Brentwood, turned over the barbecuing to his brother-in-law, and called AFER. Within an hour, a private plane had been chartered to pick Olson up.

In Los Angeles, Chad, Kristina, and the rest of the war room threw their things in bags and jumped on shuttle flights to San Francisco. Adam Umhoefer told everyone he had recently dreamed about Judge Walker.

"Are you sure this is for public consumption?" Chad joked.

Adam gave him a "very funny" look before describing the dream. The entire team arrives at the federal courthouse, where they are directed to an entrance that does not actually exist in reality. When they walk in, what they find is an amphitheater with flowing red curtains. Ushers take them to their seats. A voice booms, "I now present Judge Walker." The curtain rises and out walks Walker, dressed in a tux, as a symphony starts playing and a gospel choir sings "God Bless America."

"There's a lot going on there," Chad said with a laugh. "We have to analyze!"

Chad was not a superstitious person. But now, alone in his hotel room, even he started to believe that maybe the universe was trying to tell them something. Earlier, he and Adam had walked through the Martin Luther King Jr. Memorial in San Francisco. More than a hundred thousands gallons of water flow over a sharply angled fountain before dropping twenty feet, echoing off the Sierra granite, and traveling through a wishing well channel to a moat where the water becomes still as glass. "No, no, we are not satisfied, and we will not be satisfied until justice rolls like water and righteousness like a mighty stream," reads the King quote inscribed at the west entrance.

When he opened his curtains, Chad was surprised to see the entire vista lit up beneath his window.

———

Much had happened, in people's lives and the world around them, since everyone had split up in January.

Olson and Boies had made the *Time* 100 list of most influential people, along with pop diva Lady Gaga. "Madonna has to be jealous. Congrats!" Chad e-mailed. Chad, for his part, had been named to the *Advocate*'s 40 under 40 list of young movers and shakers in the gay community, a sign that the success of the trial was starting to bring the establishment around. The movie theater chain that employed Jeff had named him general manager of the year. Rob Reiner's latest film, a sweet coming-of-age tale called *Flipped*, was about to be released.

But the biggest news concerned the man who now held all of their fates in his hands. Less than two weeks after the trial had ended, Judge Walker had been outed by the *San Francisco Chronicle*.

Chad and Kristina knew it was coming because the writer had called in an unsuccessful attempt to get them to comment. Both wished it had held until after the ruling, but what was done was done. Kristina summed up the going-forward strategy in an e-mail:

"All that matters is focusing on ensuring that this doesn't improperly [taint] the ruling coverage and remembering that our key audience is actually a very small group in DC," she wrote. "Important that we are never on the record and that we don't engage the gay groups—most credible people on this are conservatives and legal voices."

The opposition researcher AFER had hired pulled every editorial and article written after Walker was nominated saying he was too conservative, as well as quotes from all the gay groups that had opposed his nomination. A public records request to the Reagan Library had yielded gold: Former attorney general Meese, who had penned the op-ed in the *New York Times* slamming Walker, had recommended that he be put on the bench. The late Strom Thurmond, the long-serving Republican senator of South Carolina known for his early segregationist campaigns and his vehement opposition to the Civil Rights Act, had shepherded Walker through his nomination. The war room put all of it together in a package it provided to reporters on background.

Pete Wilson, former Republican governor of California, had been Walker's chief sponsor when he served in the U.S. Senate. Kristina, who knew his former chief of staff, put in a call. Could the governor talk Walker up on background calls with reporters, she asked, or at least not join the chorus of voices criticizing him? Remember, she recalled telling her friend, this reflects on him as well: "Pete put him there."

The official position of ProtectMarriage.com on the judge's sexuality was that "we are not going to say anything about that," as Andy Pugno, the group's general counsel, told the *Chronicle*. But surrogates like Ed Whelan, the former Scalia clerk, were questioning his impartiality, in scathing blog posts for *National Review Online* with titles like "Judge Walker's Wild Witchhunt—Part 5" that criticized Walker for "scorched earth document and deposition discovery" orders and an "insane inquiry into the subjective intentions" of voters that threatened "severe damage to citizen participation in voter initiatives." On that front, the war room got some indirect help from an unlikely source.

In an 8–1 decision in a case called *Doe v. Reed*, making public the names of petition signatories to a ballot initiative aimed at gutting Washington State's domestic partner law, Justice Scalia effectively said that if people can't stand the heat, they ought to get out of the kitchen.

"Requiring people to stand up in public for their political acts fosters civic courage, without which democracy is doomed," Scalia wrote in his concurrence. "For my part, I do not look forward to a society which, thanks to the Supreme Court, campaigns anonymously and even exercises the direct democracy of initiative and referendum hidden from public scrutiny and protected from the accountability of criticism."

Other justices were put to different use. The team worked the phone, asking surrogates and opinion columnists to help bat down any suggestion that Judge Walker was biased because he was gay by putting it in historical context. Thurgood Marshall, the nation's first black justice, took part in landmark civil rights decisions. No one would say that a black or woman judge was biased simply because of their gender or skin color, but it is "perfectly acceptable to say it about a gay person," Kristina wrote in an e-mail. "It proves how discriminated against gays are," she wrote. "At the end of the day this is an opportunity. We are back in the news and can go back to how strong our case is. They can't win under oath so they have to resort to these things."

The months since Walker's outing had crawled by, with a mixed bag of news.

In Virginia, Republican governor Bob McDonnell issued an executive order reversing a policy supported by his two predecessors that had barred discrimination in the state workforce based on sexual orientation. And in the nation's capital, Justice Stevens, the man Olson had believed would be helpful in swinging Justice Kennedy's vote their way, had announced his retirement. Elena Kagan, President Obama's solicitor general and pick to replace Stevens on the Court, had stated that "there is no federal constitutional right to same-sex marriage" in her Senate questionnaire.

That could be read in multiple ways, one being that the Supreme Court simply had not as yet declared any such right. Still, Terry Stewart found the answer, as well as the White House's furious response to a post on CBS News's Web site that published rumors that Kagan was gay, telling. The White House had forced CBS to take down the post after charging that it had become "en-

ablers of people posting lies." But true or false, Stewart said the language officials used to attack the post made it seem as though there could be no bigger
slur than being called a lesbian. "It shows you where we are still at in our culture, especially at the federal level."

Still, it did seem that something was stirring out there, a building sense of
momentum. The District of Columbia became the first jurisdiction below the
Mason-Dixon line to begin issuing marriage licenses to same-sex couples.
Mexico City legalized same-sex marriage over the objections of the Catholic
archdiocese. Laura Bush told CNN's *Larry King Live* that she favored giving
gay couples the same rights as straight couples.

On the legal front, a new study, the first to track children raised from
birth to adolescence by lesbians, bolstered the case the plaintiffs had made at
trial. Published in *Pediatrics,* it showed that the children of lesbians did just as
well in terms of social development and adjustment as children of heterosexuals, and actually had more self-esteem and confidence, did better academi-
cally, and were less likely to have behavioral problems than kids with straight
parents.

And an expert witness who had testified in a number of state court cases
that homosexuality was a "perversion" and that gay couples should not be allowed to marry or adopt had been caught with a male prostitute hired from a
Web site called RentBoy.com; George Rekers was not only a founding member
of the Family Research Council, the Christian lobbying group that had been
part of the coalition to pass Prop 8, but he also served on the board of NARTH,
the gay conversion therapy outfit that Ryan Kendall had been forced to attend.

———

Closing arguments had come and gone two months earlier. The judge had
given each side a little over two hours to make their final case in June, timing
he said he found appropriate: "June is, after all, the month for weddings."

Olson summarized the arguments the plaintiffs had been making throughout the trial, with a court stenographer AFER hired live-blogging it. But this
time around he also took note of a Supreme Court case he had lost: *United
States v. Virginia,* which struck down the Virginia Military Institute's policy of
excluding female cadets.

The case stood for two important propositions. The first was that the name one calls something and the prestige that it confers matter for the purpose of evaluating the constitutionality of separate but supposedly equal institutions. In the Proposition 8 case, Olson was arguing that the name, marriage, had a societal meaning that domestic partnerships could never equal. In its 1996 Virginia Military Institute opinion, the Court found that Virginia's offer to form a women-only academy similar to the male-only Virginia Military Institute was an inadequate remedy, not only because the Court judged its proposed curriculum, funding, and faculty to be inferior, but also because the new academy would lack the prestige and stature that the name Virginia Military Institute conferred.

The second proposition the case stood for was that in cases where heightened scrutiny applies and the government must prove that a discriminatory law serves an important or compelling governmental purpose, the rationale it offers the Court must, as Justice Ginsburg wrote, be "genuine, not invented post hoc," or after-the-fact, "in response to litigation." The argument Olson made on behalf of the state of Virginia—that the state was interested in creating diverse educational opportunities—did not meet that test, the Court concluded.

Olson had at the time criticized that opinion, calling Justice Scalia's dissent "one of the most elegant and moving opinions I have ever read." But he didn't hesitate to use the decision in service of this cause. Cooper's deinstitutionalization theory—"whatever in the world that is"—was exactly the kind of post hoc rationalization that the Virginia Military Institute case had made clear was prohibited, Olson charged in his closing argument, and one need only look at what the proponents in Proposition 8 put into the hands of voters to see that.

"'Protect our children' from learning that gay marriage is okay. Those are the words that the proponents put in the ballot—in the voter information guide that was given to every voter. That was not a very subtle theme that there is something wrong, sinister, or unusual about gays, that gays and their relationship are not okay, and decidedly not suitable for children," he said.

"For obvious reasons, the 'gays are not okay' message was largely abandoned during the trial in favor of the procreation and deinstitutionalization themes. And after promising proof that people might stop marrying and cease procreating if Proposition 8 were overturned, the proponents switched course from that as well, and affirmatively argued that they actually had no idea and certainly no evidence that any of their prognostications would come to pass if Proposition 8 were to be enacted."

Cooper, when he rose, noted that demographers in the 1930s failed to predict the baby boom, while sociologists in the 1960s failed to forecast the upcoming rise in the number of couples living together outside of marriage. Those were two "extraordinary sociological phenomenon," he said, that "no one had a clue was coming." And he used the "no one predicts the future that accurately" quote from Professor Cott's testimony to argue that a "change as profound as this one" would have unpredictable consequences. "The plaintiffs think that the consequences dominantly will be good consequences," he said. "And again, we respect that point of view, but it's not something that they can possibly prove."

Chad's favorite moment came when Cooper inadvertently paid him a huge compliment by revisiting his infamous "I don't know" answer. "I have heard this and read this more than any three things, three words, that I have ever spoken, 'I don't know,'" Cooper said. "I don't know how many times, Your Honor, I had wished I could have those words back. Because, Your Honor, whatever your question is, I damn sure know, whatever it is!"

"I had this moment of *yes!*" Chad said afterward. "If you are feeling the pain now, just wait. This drumbeat isn't going to stop."

But for the most part, it had been Judge Walker's show. The questions he posed to both Olson and Cooper offered a window into his thinking. He seemed skeptical of the evidence that Cooper had put on to prove his point that allowing same-sex couples to wed could damage an institution whose primary purpose was to channel responsible procreation.

"Why only one witness?" the judge asked, before adding, "And I think it fair to say that his testimony was equivocal in some respects."

When Cooper replied that the witness and, implicitly, the trial itself were "utterly unnecessary" to prove what to him seemed obvious, the judge did not disguise his dissatisfaction: "This goes back to the *you don't need any evidence* point."

On the other hand, Walker told Olson to assume the rational basis standard applied, and assume that voters had a genuine belief that children do best when raised by their biological parents, or that heterosexual marriage would some-how be harmed by allowing gays and lesbians to wed. Even if science says that is not so, is that good enough to pass constitutional muster, as long as voters could have reasonably believed that to be the case at the time of enactment? Didn't the Supreme Court, in a 1981 equal protection case called *Minnesota vs. Clover Leaf Creamery Company*, effectively say the rational basis standard is so deferential that "any debatable" state interest will suffice?

"Well, it has to be a debatable proposition," Olson said. Cooper, the "propo-nents' counsel, said it came down to this: 'Same-sex marriage is simply too novel an experiment to allow for any firm conclusions about its long-term ef-fect on societal interests. They just don't know.' That is the essence of the case as it comes to the end of the trial and to the closing arguments. They just don't know whether same-sex marriage will harm the institution of heterosexual marriage.

"And I submit that the overwhelming evidence in this case proves that we do know. And the fact is that allowing persons to marry someone of the same sex will not, in the slightest, deter heterosexuals from marrying, from staying married, or from having babies. In fact, the evidence was from the experts that eliminating invidious restrictions on marriage strengthens the institution of marriage for both heterosexual and homosexual persons and their children."

"Very well," Judge Walker said after both sides were finished. "The matter is submitted."

———

And then, silence. June became July, and still no decision. Everyone took to obsessively checking their e-mail. Any word yet? Olson would ask Boutrous. Chad refused to get on an airplane to anyplace other than San Francisco. "I feel like a doctor waiting for our baby to be born," Enrique Monagas said.

The AFER team tried to put the downtime to use. Chad and Olson worked together to expand the team's bipartisan brand, convincing two heavy-hitting Washington insiders from opposite sides of the aisle to cochair AFER's advi-sory board. John Podesta, the founder of the progressive Center for American Progress, and Robert A. Levy, the chairman of the right-leaning Cato Institute, had announced the news in a joint op-ed in the *Washington Post*: "We have

come together in a non-partisan fashion because the principle of equality before the law transcends the left-right divide and cuts to the core of our nation's
character. This is not about politics; it's about an indispensable right vested in
all Americans."

A major Hollywood fund-raiser was in the works. Olson's and Boies's legal
fees didn't include expenses. The trial had been costly, with experts to fly in
and pay and a legal army to put up and feed. By the time it was done, AFER had
incurred more than $1 million in unexpected costs. Ron Burkle, the billion-
aire friend of the Clintons who had helped Chad and Kristina with the seed
money, had agreed to open up his storied mansion, but they needed an A-list
act to draw a red-carpet crowd that would not only replenish the coffers but
also generate headlines.

Chad called Bruce Cohen, who had recently been named coproducer of
the eighty-third Academy Awards show, to toss around ideas. Could Rob
Reiner ask Lady Gaga? No, Cohen said: Rob was no longer represented by
William Morris, Gaga's talent agency, so he had no in. (Eventually, Michele
Reiner would suggest Elton John. The singer, lambasted by liberal fans for performing at the wedding of conservative talk show host Rush Limbaugh, readily
agreed.)

Celebrities have huge online followings, and Chad also worked his contacts
to build out the team's social media presence prior to the decision. When Alicia
Keys, a client, agreed to his request to tweet about the case, it generated four
thousand individual visits to AFER's Facebook page. AFER's fan base, measured in Facebook "likes," climbed from ten thousand to eighteen thousand in
the space of a week.

Managing the politics of decision day, win or lose, required advance work.
Walker's decision would land in the middle of a hotly contested governor's
race. California attorney general Jerry Brown, already firmly on their side, was
running on the Democratic ticket. Meg Whitman, the president and CEO of
Hewlett-Packard, was the Republican nominee. Kristina had dated Mike Murphy, the Republican political strategist running her campaign, and she called
him shortly before Whitman locked up the GOP primary. Would he take a
confidential call from Chad?

"He said that her public position is that she supports Prop 8," Chad said,
relaying the conversation to Kristina afterward. "I said, 'Look, from what I

hear her public position isn't the same as her private. Our hope is that we can work with you on messaging and maybe she can moderate her position.' He said, 'We're not looking for controversy.'"

The Prop 8 fight had been a close one, and Murphy understood that many Californians, whose votes Whitman might need to win in the general election, backed the right of gays and lesbians to marry. "Her position is her position," he recalled telling Chad. "But Meg has friends on both sides of this issue. Tonally, we will be respectful, and we are not going to make it a centerpiece of the campaign."

Knowing that friends can sometimes be a campaign's worst enemy, Chad did what he could to impose message and image discipline in the gay community. The AFER team reached out to the Los Angeles Police Department to talk about crowd management strategy should Walker uphold Prop 8 and massive protests erupt. "We want to be sure that the images that come out of California are appropriate and help us win hearts and minds," Chad said.

He also held a conference call with thirty gay rights groups, many of whom had been outspoken opponents of the lawsuit, and met personally with community organizers in California to share AFER's talking points. Minutes from a June 24 meeting Chad attended at San Francisco's LGBT Center summed up some of the dos and don'ts:

In the event of a victory, be graceful winners: "Fairness has prevailed (NOT 'We Won, ha ha!')." Stress that the case was not about new rights: "To some people, change is scary, but it has been an enduring American tradition to extend civil rights to all people, and today is just another example of that tradition." And in the event of a loss, share stories of how discrimination against gays and lesbians affects families and kids in their everyday life. Ask, "How would you feel if you could not marry the person you love?"

———

Judge Walker's plan was to release his opinion to the public sometime between 1 P.M. and 3 P.M. Pacific time. He had sent word that he would give the lawyers and the parties in the case an advance copy at 11 A.M., but they were under strict orders to share it with no one else.

In Washington, Cooper had resigned himself to a loss. The night before, he had taken the extraordinary step of filing for an emergency stay preventing marriages from resuming while he appealed a ruling that Judge Walker had yet to hand down.

In San Francisco, David Boies and Ted Boutrous swapped stories about their latest cases while they waited. Olson arrived at 10:40 and joined them in a corner conference room overlooking the bay. His wife, Lady, sat down with the plaintiffs and Michele Reiner in an adjacent room. Olson had been episodically irritable the night before, which was how she could tell he was nervous.

"It'll be good either way," Michele said.

"Yeah, but it'll be better when we win," Sandy, dressed in pink again, replied. "Winning is better than losing."

The 11 A.M. deadline passed with no word from Walker. To pass the time, Michele took pictures of everyone with a new iPhone camera "fat" app that makes people look as though they have packed on the pounds:

"It's so cruel, this thing."

Snap, snap.

"It's pretty funny."

Boies, briefly emerging from the lawyers' conference room for a soda, was at a loss to explain the delay. "I think the son of a bitch is still editing the opinion," he said. "Going over it one final time."

And then, with no warning, bang, in it came. At 12:26 P.M. the lawyers told Chad to gather the plaintiffs. Mindful of the judge's order to keep the advance copy under wraps, everyone else was ordered out of the lawyers' conference room, "spouses, everyone but the lawyers and the clients," Ted Boutrous said before closing the thick wooden door firmly behind him.

Chad, Kristina, Michele, and Adam stood just on the other side, straining to hear what was being said. "Somebody's weeping," Adam said. "I can't tell if it's happy or sad!" He held his hand up for everyone to see. "Shaking." Chad tried pressing his ear against the door before Boutrous finally took pity, sending him an e-mail at 12:31 P.M.: "You can come in, but only you."

Finally, the door opened wide and everyone emerged. "If we can all go into one room," Chad said.

Boies was hugging Lady. Paul was crying, talking about how Boutrous had told him he could not say much but that he could say, "I'm happy." He ripped up a copy of the statement he would have given had they lost, so it was clear that the news was good.

But how good? Not knowing the details was driving Michele Reiner nuts. By this point, everyone had become a student of the case. What level of scrutiny applied? Was it a due process or equal protection decision? Was his decision California-specific, or nationwide?

"This is kind of anticlimactic," she complained, begging for some specifics. "Come on!"

"You'll have to wait to climax," Boutrous joked.

Paul cracked up. "Said like a man."

Across the city, Judge Walker was in his chambers, already at work on another case. He had just handed the gay community—a community that had vigorously fought his nomination to the bench more than two decades earlier—a sweeping and historic victory. For the first time, a federal court had held that the right to marry is a fundamental right that must be extended to gays and lesbians, a rationale that if upheld would mean that all fifty states must recognize same-sex marriage.

The plaintiffs won on every count. Laws targeting gays and lesbians should be subject to heightened scrutiny, the judge had ruled, because the evidence showed that sexual orientation was not readily changeable and that gays and lesbians faced historic and ongoing discrimination and were not powerful enough to fend off majoritarian disapproval. But in this case, he had written, that was not even necessary because Proposition 8 failed even the rational basis test. For no good reason, he found, "it places the force of the law behind stigmas against gays and lesbians."

As was his habit in controversial cases, Judge Walker and one of his clerks had swapped the opinion back and forth numerous times. Before signing off, he had organized sessions in which his clerks read it aloud. "We did that three or four times. You'd be surprised at what comes up when you do that," he said, recalling the process afterwards. "The case was so prominent that you didn't want to dash it off."

Grounded in the Constitution's right both to due process and equal protection, the 136-page opinion rested not only on the law but also on forceful factual findings drawn from the trial record.

"Marriage," Walker wrote, "is the state recognition of a couple's choice to live with each other, to remain committed to one another and to form a household based on their own feelings about one another and to join in an economic partnership and support one another and any dependents." He quoted liberally from the Supreme Court's own precedents, as when he said that while "the Constitution cannot control [private biases], neither can it tolerate them.

"In the absence of a rational basis, what remains of the proponents' case is an inference, amply supported by evidence in the record, that Proposition 8 was premised on the belief that same-sex couples simply are not as good as opposite sex couples," Walker wrote. "Whether that belief is based on moral disapproval of homosexuality, animus towards gays and lesbians or simply a belief that a relationship between a man and a woman is inherently better than a relationship between two men or two women, this belief is not a proper basis on which to legislate."

Throughout the trial, the judge had puzzled over why Cooper was not mounting a more robust defense of Proposition 8. It puzzled him still. The plaintiffs had called seventeen witnesses. He still couldn't get over the fact that Cooper had called only two.

Walker had, for instance, expected Cooper to put the proponents on the stand. Maybe even some Catholic bishops or religious leaders. Certainly someone who could offer a better explanation of the campaign's motives than, as he put it, the "pathetic" Dr. Tam, and a more plausible rationale for how the ban served the purposes of the state than the "hapless Blankenhorn."

"Chuck spent most of the trial looking like he'd rather be anywhere else," Walker said. "He could have put on historians. Instead he quoted philosophers. The problem he had is there is not secular evidence to support his position."

———

Back at Gibson Dunn, Chad, suddenly realizing that he had not yet hugged Kristina, went looking for his best friend. She was in the war room, helping Adam oversee the press rollout. He couldn't imagine doing this case without her. She was the most determined person he knew, calm and cool when he got excited. He avoided issues he didn't want to address; she confronted them.

"We made all these decisions together," he said. "I joke with her, 'You do know that you're going to have to spend the rest of your life coming out as a straight person.'"

In the lawyers' conference room, everyone was reading aloud their favorite passages from the opinion. Walker had dissected each of Cooper's arguments. Olson loved that the judge picked up on his citation of *Williams v. Illinois,* a 1970 Supreme Court ruling that found that the "antiquity of a practice" cannot insulate it from constitutional attack, to rebut Cooper's argument that marriage had always been between a man and a woman.

"It's Ted's favorite quote of all time," Boutrous said. "He's probably cited it in twenty different briefs over the years."

Matt McGill was happy to see that the judge cited a Supreme Court case that had been handed down six days earlier, called *Christian Legal Society v. Martinez.* The 5–4 decision, in which swing voter Justice Kennedy joined the liberal justices in an opinion written by Justice Ginsburg, upheld the right of a public law school to refuse to recognize a Christian student group that excluded gay students. It was a First Amendment speech case that, in and of itself, had nothing to do with marriage.

But on the day it was handed down, McGill's wife, Lori Alvino McGill, a former Ginsburg clerk, had spotted a line in the opinion that she thought could be applicable to the Prop 8 case. The justices rejected the argument by the Christian group that it was not discriminating on the basis of sexual orientation, but was merely excluding gays and lesbians because they refused to acknowledge that their conduct was wrong. "Our decisions have declined to distinguish between status and conduct in this context," Ginsburg wrote.

McGill's wife was overdue to give birth to their second child, and the two were walking around their neighborhood later that evening in the hope of inducing labor when McGill jumped on his cell phone to explain the significance to the AFER team. The Court, for the first time, had identified homosexuality as a status, a characteristic like race, gender, or heritage. Laws or, in this case, policies that treat gays and lesbians differently, the justices seemed to be saying, target them not based on what they do *but who they are.* That had substantial implications for the Proposition 8 case, potentially increasing the likelihood that the Court would apply some form of heightened scrutiny to laws that discriminate on that basis.

The lawyers immediately fired off a letter bringing the case to the judge's attention. Walker cited it in finding that "homosexual conduct and attraction are constitutionally protected and integral parts of what makes someone gay or lesbian."

Boutrous was struck by the judge's analysis that bans on same-sex marriage discriminated not just on the basis of sexual orientation but also on the basis of gender. His ruling effectively said that the reason that Jane cannot marry Jill is because Jane is a woman, an inarguably immutable characteristic. It was not an argument that had featured heavily in their briefs, but if upheld it would automatically subject all bans to heightened scrutiny, without the need for the court to create a new suspect class.

Boies was gratified to see that the judge had granted his motion to disqualify Blankenhorn, though he joked that he should have withdrawn it given how helpful the witness had turned out to be for the plaintiffs. Blankenhorn's opinions were "not supported by reliable evidence or methodology," the judge wrote, and therefore "entitled to essentially no weight."

The gay lawyers on the Gibson Dunn team were just gratified. Sarah Piepmeier had sent the opinion to Enrique Monagas, who was in Puerto Rico for the funeral of his grandmother. The subject line was a smiley face.

"I yelled, I screamed I was so excited," Monagas said. "I thought about my daughter, who is named after my grandmother. I thought, 'Whatever happens in your life, you've made a difference.'"

———

At 2:04 P.M., Judge Walker's decision was posted on PACER, a service that provides online access to federal court records nationwide. Kristina popped out to tell Michele that she could finally call Rob, who everyone knew could not have kept the secret. He was in Hollywood, promoting his new movie, and when Michele reached him he was sitting at the same table at the Polo Lounge where it had all begun.

He started whooping. "Great news!" he told *Saturday Night Live* producer Lorne Michaels, who was at the next table. "Congratulations!" Michaels exclaimed.

In her office at San Francisco City Hall, Terry Stewart found it difficult to feel anything at all. She was happy, but she had been down this road before, winning, only to see it snatched away.

Lance Black was at Bruce Cohen's house in Los Angeles, glued to CNN, when the news broke. As the reporter began reading from the opinion, the two men started crying and hugging. Cohen then called his husband, Gabe, who was in New York. His assessment: "It's like a love letter to the Supreme Court. And a dare."

Over the television, Maggie Gallagher, of the National Organization for Marriage, and Freedom to Marry's Evan Wolfson, who not so long ago had been berating Black at the OutGiving conference, debated the ruling. Wolfson praised the decision, though he warned supporters not to get too excited. "We'll have to see what the Supreme Court does," he said. "There are many twists ahead."

Cohen realized just how big the decision was when CNN cut to a live shot of Chad speaking at a press conference in San Francisco. He had thought he would have to go to some obscure Web site to find that.

"Today's decision gives gay Americans the hope and strength and comfort that they too can have a future filled with love, commitment, and shared responsibility," Chad said, managing not to choke up the way he had when he practiced the speech with Kristina. "Today we begin the process of saying to the millions of people who are made to feel ostracized, besieged, bullied, and ashamed of how God made them, 'Be who you are. Love who you love, and marry who you wish to marry.'"

Back in San Francisco, two small private planes sat on the airport tarmac, waiting to ferry the plaintiffs and most of the legal team to Los Angeles, California's biggest media market. The plan was to hold a rally in West Hollywood, near where protesters had gathered following Proposition 8's passage, in time for the nightly news.

Chad, in his usual plan-for-the-worst mode, had insisted on splitting up the team in case one plane fell from the sky. His mind had already skipped ahead to the next phase of the case.

The Ninth Circuit Court of Appeals was still considered the most reliably liberal in the country, but in recent years it had become decidedly less so. President George W. Bush had appointed seven of the court's twenty-seven active members during his tenure. A randomly selected panel of three judges would hear the Prop 8 case. Everything would depend on the draw.

Kristina, checking her e-mail, saw the reaction statement Meg Whitman's campaign had released and smiled. It was a bland nothing-burger, better than she could have hoped. "Today's ruling is the first step in a process that will continue," the candidate said.

In West Hollywood, Rob Reiner was waiting when their bus pulled up to the rally. He engulfed Chad in a bear hug, the way a father would his son.

"That speech—I was so proud," he said.

Amanda Crumley had hired an advance team, political veterans she knew from the Clinton administration, to deck out the West Hollywood stage with American flags. Bruce Springsteen's "Born in the USA" was booming out of speakers, making the event feel like a campaign rally. (The Clinton playlist, she joked, is a small one.)

The crowd went wild when Olson, their conservative champion, took the stage. He and Boies lingered behind long after Chad and the plaintiffs stepped down, working the rope line like rock stars, shaking outstretched hands and reaching out to touch the shoulders of people farther back.

"They're on a roll," Kristina said to Matt McGill.

He laughed. "Like they're running for gay Congress."

Chad, looking back on the day later, didn't remember much except the sound of news helicopters overhead and the brightness of the lights. Squinting out at the crowd through his glasses, he saw that people were openly crying, and that's when it hit him.

"Oh my God—Prop 8 is unconstitutional. That's why all these people are here."

Section III

TWENTY-FIVE

A TRUMP CARD,
RELUCTANTLY PLAYED

Watching Ted Olson craft his arguments for an appellate court was a lot like watching a world-class bridge player. Olson loved the card game, and over drinks one night, David Boies compared him to Charles Goren, one of its all-time champions.

"At tournaments, people can sit behind someone and watch as long as they don't talk. And so at the end of the game, a woman says to Goren, 'You didn't make a single play all night I couldn't have made.' He said something like, 'That's probably right. But could you have made all of them with the consistency that I did?' That is what Ted does."

Boies knew better than most. In the *Bush v. Gore* case that had pitted the two men against one another, Olson had made one deft play after the next. He focused on the Supreme Court, arguing that the recount in deadlocked Florida was unconstitutional on numerous grounds. Another team prepared a pragmatic set of pleadings in the event that the justices declined to step in and stop it, aimed at ensuring that ballots likely to favor Bush were counted and those likely to favor Gore were thrown out. A third group of lawyers that included Chief Justice John Roberts, who was in private practice at the time, did the legal spadework on a plan to have the Florida Legislature declare Bush the president regardless of the recount outcome.

It was a scorched-earth litigation model designed to produce a Bush win under almost any scenario. And it was one that Olson replicated in his multi-pronged approach to tearing down Proposition 8, as the case moved into its next phase at the Ninth Circuit.

The court could rule in his favor on due process grounds by finding that Proposition 8 violated the plaintiffs' fundamental right to marry, on equal protection grounds by finding that Proposition 8 discriminated against a vulnerable minority group and could not meet the court's heightened scrutiny test, or it could find that bans like Proposition 8 were born out of animus toward gays and lesbians and could not survive even the rational basis test because they served no legitimate state purpose.

But the team's trump card involved a relatively arcane legal doctrine called "standing" that had nothing to do with marriage or discrimination. Under Article III of the Constitution, the U.S. Supreme Court may only decide actual "cases or controversies." The idea behind that limitation is that unelected judges should be constrained from injecting themselves into the political process by offering freewheeling legal advice to the democratically elected branches about how the government ought to run. What it means in practice is that before a federal court can decide the merits of a constitutional challenge, it must first decide whether the party invoking its jurisdiction has the right to be in court.

In order to have what is called "Article III standing," a party must have a particularized stake in the outcome of a case, meaning the party must show actual or imminent injury if the court does not step in to redress it. At the district court level, the burden was on the plaintiffs, because they were the ones asking the court to overturn the law. Their stake was clear-cut and undisputed: Kris and Sandy and Jeff and Paul wanted to marry, and Proposition 8 barred them from doing so. But once the plaintiffs prevailed in Judge Walker's court, the burden shifted to the party seeking to overturn that decision.

The state clearly had standing to defend a law passed by its citizens. But did Cooper's clients? Before the trial had even begun, some of the younger members of the Gibson Dunn appellate team had concluded that Cooper's ability to have a higher court consider the merits of his argument if he lost at trial was in serious doubt, thanks to two Supreme Court decisions.

A 1986 opinion in a case called *Diamond v. Charles* made clear that the mere fact that a party had been allowed to intervene at the trial level to defend a law did not automatically confer standing to appeal. At issue in that case was a decision striking down a restrictive Illinois abortion law that the state had declined to appeal. The court found that the "conscientious objection to abortion" expressed by a trial court intervener was not sufficient to confer standing on appeal: A party must show "a direct stake in the outcome" if the decision is not overturned.

And in a unanimous 1997 opinion in a case called *Arizonans for Official English v. Arizona*, the Supreme Court had cast "grave doubt" on whether ballot proponents like Cooper's clients could meet that test, saying it was not enough to share a generalized interest with members of the public in the proper application of the Constitution. The comment by Justice Ruth Bader Ginsburg was made in passing, in what lawyers call dicta, and as such was not binding. (The Court ultimately dismissed the case, which involved a ballot initiative mandating that state workers speak English only, on other grounds, ruling that it was moot because the Spanish-speaking employee who had challenged the law had left her job by the time the appeal was filed.) Still, Justice Ginsburg's words seemed like a pretty good indication of where the justices might wind up in this case.

"If the governor and the attorney general decline to defend the law, that could be it," McGill recalled telling Olson one day over lunch at Spezie, a restaurant near the firm's Washington, D.C., headquarters. "This case could be over."

It was not the way either Olson or Chad wanted to win, and both were conflicted. They wanted the courts above Walker's to uphold his ruling and strike down same-sex marriage bans across the nation. If Cooper could not appeal, Walker's ruling that Proposition 8 was unconstitutional would remain in force, but have no precedential impact beyond California's borders. But given that the courts were duty-bound to decide the standing question anyway, they would be derelict if they did not make the argument themselves. And if the case made it past the Ninth Circuit to the Supreme Court, the standing argument would likely find a receptive audience in Chief Justice Roberts. He had a particular interest in standing doctrine that dated back to his days as a young lawyer in the Reagan Justice Department, when he was a forceful advocate for challenging the standing of litigants who were trying to drag the administration into court over its environmental policies.

The thinking was that Olson could continue to emphasize the broad arguments designed to produce a fifty-state victory, while offering the Supreme Court an alternative that might be attractive to some of the Court's conservatives unlikely to be with them on the merits.

"This is the way I get to nine votes," Matt McGill explained one day during the trial. "The chief hates big, controversial cases, and this is one."

Which is why, on the day Judge Walker's decision came down, two phone calls had been placed. Chad had called Governor Schwarzenegger's chief of staff. Boies had called Attorney General Jerry Brown, whom he knew personally.

Both were assured that they need not have bothered. The state had no plans to appeal Judge Walker's decision in the Proposition 8 case.

⸻

The team that reassembled at Gibson Dunn's San Francisco offices on Saturday, December 3, 2010, was a pared-down version of its former self. Boies was there, fresh off of another big win; he had recently won a record $1.3 billion in damages on behalf of the Oracle Corporation in a software piracy case. But with the Gibson Dunn team set to take center stage now that they had reached the more cerebral appellate phase of the case, most of the trial lawyers from Boies's firm had moved on to other cases.

Trial courts resolve factual disputes while appellate courts look only at whether the law was correctly applied. The result was an operation that felt less kinetic and more Socratic.

Olson was spending most of his time holed up in his office, restudying the case law, honing his argument, and sending out requests for information via Ted Boutrous, who joked that he sometimes felt as though he were managing a Triple Crown racehorse: "Water! Carrots!"

They had brought along Gibson Dunn's appellate A Team to play devil's advocate during preargument prep sessions: Olson's two Supreme Court wingmen, Matt McGill and Amir Tayrani, were joined by Theane Evangelis, a former clerk to Justice Sandra Day O'Connor who worked closely with Ted Boutrous and had been hovering quietly in the background since the inception of the case, drafting the initial complaint and portions of every brief filed since.

Question to Olson: What would happen if the evidence showed that divorce rates climbed in Massachusetts after it recognized same-sex marriage? We know that it did not show that, but what if it had?

Answer: The proponents can't prove cause and effect. It would be like outlawing football because it makes the weather grow cold.

Better answer: If divorce rates rose after slaves were freed, would that make prohibiting ex-slaves from marrying constitutional?

McGill was so tough on Olson at one session that Chad pulled him aside afterward. "Nice job, Justice McGill," Chad said. "You'll make a good Supreme Court justice someday. We just have to liberal you up between now and then."

McGill laughed. "I think this case is going to take care of that."

Arguments were set for December 6. The Ninth Circuit had given each side an hour to make its case, half of which had to be devoted to the standing question. Boies was going to handle that portion of the argument, leaving Olson free to focus on the merits of the constitutional challenge. The three-judge panel that would hear the case had been named the previous week.

Judge Randy Smith, sixty-one, was a Mormon from Idaho appointed by President George W. Bush as part of Bush's quest to change the makeup of the Ninth Circuit. He was conservative, though not in a chest-thumping kind of way. Stephen Reinhardt, seventy-nine, was considered the liberal lion of the court. His past rulings made it clear that he believed laws targeting gays and lesbians should be subject to heightened scrutiny. And he made no apology for the fact that his fondness for big, sweeping opinions had made him one of the most reversed judges on the appeals court bench.

As Terry Stewart put it, "A lot of times he doesn't give a fuck what the Supreme Court thinks."

On the surface, then, the question appeared to be whether Reinhardt could bring Michael Hawkins, a cautious Clinton appointee who viewed himself as a moderate, along for the ride. But there was a wrinkle.

Cooper had filed a motion demanding that Judge Reinhardt recuse himself, citing the fact that Reinhardt's wife was an outspoken supporter of same-sex marriage who had worked to defeat Proposition 8, as well as a news report that she had engaged in "confidential discussions" with the plaintiffs' attorneys.

Reinhardt had curtly denied Cooper's request the day before. Justice Clarence Thomas's wife had done work for a conservative think tank that was challenging the constitutionality of Obamacare, the president's overhaul of the nation's health care system, and Justice Thomas had no intention of recusing himself from that case. Reinhardt chastised Cooper for an "outmoded conception of the relationship between spouses" in a follow-up order explaining his decision. The court's rules had changed since the days when judges were told to ensure that their wives not participate in politics, in part at Reinhardt's urging: "I wrote the ethics committee and suggested that . . . even if it were desirable for judges to control their wives, I did not know many judges who could actually do so." His wife's views, he said, "are of no consequence," and "cannot be imputed to me, no matter how prominently she expresses them."

Chad and the rest of the team found the entire exchange more than a little ironic. Reinhardt's wife was Ramona Ripston, the longtime executive director of the ACLU of Southern California. And the "confidential discussions" vaguely referenced in the article Cooper cited took place over that lunch at the Reiners' home a year and a half ago, the one where Ripston and her colleagues from the ACLU and Lambda Legal had denounced them as misguided outsiders whose inability to count to five votes on the Supreme Court could set the movement back decades. If anyone should worry about Reinhardt's presence on that panel, it was the plaintiffs.

———

Just four months had passed since Judge Walker had issued his ruling, but it felt like much longer.

"It's been such a blur for me, this year," Boies said.

The fall had been a trying time for many on the team. Few knew it, but David Boies's forty-eight-year-old daughter was in the end stage of her battle with cancer, and had only weeks left to live.

Chad had suffered a double loss. His father had died in October. Chad's parents had divorced when he was small, and the two had never been close. But that made it difficult in its own way. Chad could still remember how frightened he had been as a boy when his father dropped him at a hunting stand with a gun before dawn one morning, then drove off, leaving him alone with the sound of the animals. He had cried after shooting his first deer, but when his father returned, he had pretended to enjoy it, bragging about how he "got him." His mom had supported him from the moment he came out. But David Griffin, who was sixty-two when he passed away at a hospital in Arkadelphia, Arkansas, had never told his son how he felt about him being gay, or about the case that Chad had made his life's work. Now Chad would never know.

And just the day before, Chad had said goodbye to Kristina. First Lady Michelle Obama had offered her a job as her communications director. Chad had pushed Kristina to take it, just as she had pushed him to file the case. The two friends looked after one another, and Chad, having once worked at White House himself, knew it was too good an opportunity to pass up.

He had dropped her at the airport before heading to San Francisco. In her bag was a leather-bound copy of Judge Walker's opinion, Chad's going-away gift. They had both cried. Driving off, he was out of sorts. Who would accompany him to the antique flea markets he liked to haunt, or to Starbucks?

"I thought, I don't know where I am going. Because I would always plan my day with Kristina."

The war room felt empty without her. Yusef Robb, who might have filled the silence with his tough-talking banter, had left AFER to work on the campaign of Eric Garcetti, the man who would soon become Los Angeles's next mayor. Adam Umhoefer and Amanda Crumley were e-mailing op-ed columnists and trying to book the plaintiffs and lawyers on news programs, but it was a harder sell this time around.

To the extent that anything related to gay rights was breaking through the wall-to-wall coverage of the explosive release by WikiLeaks of 250,000 secret U.S. diplomatic cables, it was the fate of the military's Don't Ask, Don't Tell policy. A federal district court had declared the policy unconstitutional and ordered the military to cease enforcing it worldwide, and a White House effort to repeal the law was coming down to the wire in Congress. News organizations tend to shy away from incremental developments, and everyone knew that the Ninth Circuit panel likely would not have the last say on Proposition 8.

"We're in the messy middle," Amanda Crumley complained.

Still, momentum continued to swing their way. The first national poll to show majority support for same-sex marriage had been released in the weeks following Judge Walker's ruling; Americans were still closely divided on the subject, the CNN survey found, but 52 percent now believed that gays and lesbians should have a constitutional right to wed.

And in California, where coverage of the trial had been heaviest, Jerry

Brown had defeated Meg Whitman in the governor's race. That was significant because despite Chad and Kristina's efforts, Whitman had eventually been forced to clarify that if elected she would defend the constitutionality of Proposition 8. Democrat Kamala Harris, who had vowed during her campaign not to waste the state's "precious resources" appealing a law that had been found to be unconstitutional, had replaced Brown as attorney general, besting an outspoken supporter of Proposition 8.

But the team's sense of triumph over those milestones had been tempered by a series of tragedies around the country. In the space of four weeks, four teenagers had committed suicide after being tormented by classmates because they were or were perceived to be gay.

In California, thirteen-year-old Seth Walsh hanged himself from a tree in his backyard rather than endure more fear-filled walks to school with the sound of "queer" ringing in his ears. In Texas, thirteen-year-old Asher Brown shot himself with his stepfather's handgun after two years of being taunted and tripped down stairs by bullies. In Indiana, fifteen-year-old Billy Lucas hanged himself in the family barn after being kicked, called a fag, and told hours before his death that he didn't deserve to live. And in New Jersey, eighteen-year-old Rutgers University student Tyler Clementi threw himself off the George Washington Bridge after his roommate secretly recorded him in an intimate moment with another male student and broadcast it online.

The news had hit Chad and some of the gay lawyers on the team particularly hard. "I am hopeful our case has had an effect, but then something like this happens, and you wonder," Enrique Monagas said. "The Tyler Clementi case kills me. Because I'm sure when Judge Walker's decision came out, I'm sure he had a moment of happiness. And still it made no difference to him."

"Once again we are in a twenty-passenger bus, heading to court," Chad said.

It was early in the morning of December 6, and the plaintiffs had just boarded. In a singsong, highly caffeinated voice, Sandy started making up her own words to an old children's camp song as they made their way across town: "Here we sit like birds in the wilderness, birds in the wilderness, waiting for our rights."

Chad groaned. "She has too much energy this morning."

Everyone had settled into a groove, and the mood was far more relaxed as the bus pulled up to the court of appeals than it had been on the drive over to the district courthouse on that first day of trial, nearly a year earlier. As Chad put it, high-fiving both couples, "We're going in there winners."

CNN was waiting at the courthouse to interview all four plaintiffs, and camera crews from other networks were ready to go live with the short statement they each gave before heading inside. But what had once been anxiety inducing was becoming old hat.

"Government discrimination hurts everyone," Kris said in perfect sound bite–ese. Jeff added, "The truth and the law are on our side."

Chad checked his e-mail as they headed up the steps. No word yet from Kristina. He had sent her a note earlier to wish her luck on her first day at the White House: "I miss you. I love you."

No one seemed particularly fazed by the truck plastered with signs like PERVERSION and PREPARE TO MEET THY GOD that was circling the courthouse. Kris just shrugged when one of the courthouse guards apologetically commented that "there are a lot of crazies out there" as she and her two boys passed through the metal detector.

Inside, the courtroom was packed. A number of judges who had not been chosen to hear the landmark case were sitting in the audience, adding to the historic atmospherics. The chief judge of the Ninth Circuit, Alex Kozinski, made a special appearance to welcome the lawyers. "Well, Olson," he boomed, "after arguing so many cases before the Supreme Court, it's good to see you've graduated and come to the Ninth!"

Alone and unnoticed, Terry Stewart slipped by and took her seat at the plaintiffs' table. Tensions between Stewart and the Gibson Dunn team had been running high ever since she filed a separate brief with the Ninth Circuit on behalf of the city of San Francisco, which was still a party to the case. Her decision to file separately, rather than to simply sign on to the brief filed by Olson, had caused the first serious strategic rift on the team, and harsh words had been exchanged as the Gibson Dunn lawyers tried to force her to back down.

Cooper had always believed that one of the strengths of his case was that California offered so many protections for gays and lesbians, arguing during

trial and in briefs that it meant that the initiative could not have been motivated by prejudice. The brief Stewart had filed attempted to turn that argument
on its head, arguing that Prop 8 was peculiarly irrational precisely because
California's gay-friendly laws neutered Cooper's argument that the state had an
interest in promoting one type of family structure over another.

The state's domestic partnership law contemplates that gays and lesbians
will form families, and it encourages them to become parents. The state, for
instance, prohibits discrimination based on sexual orientation in adoption and
foster care placement decisions. Stripping gays and lesbians of the ability to
marry while leaving those policies in place, she argued, irrationally under-
mines the state's interest in protecting the welfare of children by stigmatizing
those being raised in same-sex households.

It was not that Olson thought it was a bad argument. His brief touched on
several similar themes. It was the way she made it, and her motivations for
doing so. Making the standing argument was one thing, since the court had to
consider the procedural question of standing in any event before it could address the merits of their claim that Proposition 8 was unconstitutional. But if
the Ninth Circuit panel found that Cooper's clients did have a right to defend
the initiative on appeal, Olson wanted it to adopt Judge Walker's rationale,
with the result that same-sex marriage bans across the Ninth Circuit, in conservative states like Idaho and Alaska, would fall. But Stewart was urging the
court to adopt a California-specific line of reasoning that would result only in
a finding that Proposition 8 was unconstitutional, and she was doing it with
the express hope that the Supreme Court would decline to review a narrower
ruling limited to just one state.

And therein lay the crux of the clash. The entire point was to bring this case
to the Supreme Court so that gays and lesbians nationwide could marry. Unbeknownst to Stewart, Chad already had the Gibson Dunn and Boies lawyers
working on a plan to file a new case challenging another state's ban if Cooper's
standing problem or a California-only ruling by the Ninth Circuit prevented
that from happening. The recent rash of suicides had only strengthened Chad's
resolve.

"These are the consequences to discrimination," he had told the lawyers
during one planning call. "It's not just a ceremony in which we all wear a suit
and call ourselves married."

Ted Olson, on the left, and David Boies share a laugh as the team readies for trial. The odd-couple pairing—Olson represented George W. Bush and Boies served as Al Gore's lawyer in the disputed 2000 presidential election—generated headlines and helped change the nature of the debate over same-sex marriage.

Kristina Schake and Chad Griffin plot strategy in the war room as David Boies, on the right, looks on. The constitutional challenge to Proposition 8 was always intended to be a vehicle for public education, and the legal and political operation worked hand in hand to convince both the courts and the public as the case made its way up to the Supreme Court.

The four plaintiffs in the Proposition 8 case were a bundle of nerves on the morning of the first day of trial. From left to right: Paul Katami, Jeff Zarrillo, Kris Perry, and Sandy Stier.

"Any case has its trying elements and its challenges," Chuck Cooper remarked, regarding his defense of California's Proposition 8, "and this one had more of them and at different kind of levels than any case, honestly, that I've been involved in."

"Prove it," Judge Vaughn R. Walker thought as he read through the competing filings in the Proposition 8 case. The result was a first of its kind federal trial, with evidence and testimony that delved into the history of marriage, the science of sexuality, parenting, and the long record of discrimination against gays and lesbians. By deciding to hold a trial, the judge subjected all the rationales offered by supporters of same-sex marriage bans to the crucible of cross-examination.

"A standing ovation for our plaintiffs!" Olson exclaimed when everyone arrived back at the war room after the emotional, and draining, experience of testifying. Here, he hugs Sandy and Jeff talks with Boies while Kris looks at Olson's cover essay for *Newsweek* entitled "The Conservative Case for Gay Marriage," which had just hit the newsstands.

During the trial, some of the younger members of the legal team managed only a few hours of sleep each night. Pictured here, from left to right: Ted Boutrous, Ted Olson, Olson's wife, Lady Booth Olson, David Boies (with his back turned), Chris Dusseault, Matt McGill, and Amir Tayrani.

From left to right: Kristina, Adam Umhoefer, and Chad and Michele Reiner strain to hear what is happening behind closed doors. Minutes earlier, Judge Walker had released an advance copy of his historic ruling, and inside the lawyers were explaining it to the plaintiffs.

Enrique Monagas, the young lawyer who filed the original complaint in the case, holds up his smartphone so everyone can watch the plaintiffs' appearance on the nightly news. From left to right, Paul's sister, Maria McGuire, AFER board member and AIDS quilt creator Cleve Jones, Paul, Enrique, Jeff Zarrillo, and Jeff's parents, Linda and Dominick, look on. "I couldn't do this," Monagas, who is gay, said. "I couldn't put myself in this situation of being the face of this movement."

After her husband took the case, joked Lady Booth Olson, the Olsons' social circle changed. Here, Ted Olson talks to top White House adviser Valerie Jarrett and Chad at a cocktail party in honor of the plaintiffs in Georgetown. The party was held after intense internal White House deliberations over whether the Obama administration should file a brief with the Supreme Court that Prop 8 was unconstitutional.

Jeff and Paul share a kiss at Chad's apartment on the morning of the Supreme Court arguments. Also pictured are Kris, Sandy, and AFER staffers Elizabeth Riel and Melissa Gibbs.

Before the challenge to Proposition 8 was even filed, Rob Reiner made a prediction: "We are going to the Supreme Court! And we are going to win!" Here, the movie director stands outside the nation's high court on the morning of oral arguments with his wife, Michele Reiner, Adam Umhoefer, and AFER board members Lance Black and Ken Mehlman, who ran George W. Bush's reelection campaign and played a critical role in galvanizing Republican support for same-sex marriage.

Edie Windsor after her case challenging the federal Defense of Marriage Act was argued before the Supreme Court. Though they were legally married, Edie and her wife, Thea, were treated by the government as legal strangers after Thea passed away, sticking the widow with a $363,000 estate tax bill. Her lawsuit, like the one challenging Prop 8, was filed against the better judgment of the gay rights legal community, which worried that a premature challenge could lead to a Supreme Court setback.

The Proposition 8 plaintiffs arrive at the Supreme Court to hear the decision of the justices. "No matter what happens, we won," Kris said on the bus ride over.

Days after the Supreme Court ruling, a record 1.5 million celebrated equality at the San Francisco gay pride parade.

For Chad and the plaintiffs, it was the gay equivalent of a ticker-tape parade after winning the Super Bowl. Here, Chad snaps a photo of signs featuring the stick-figure family that supporters of Proposition 8 had used as a logo during the campaign to reinforce their "Protect Our Children" motto, only now the figures were standing on their heads, beneath a single word: "Overturned."

Marriage is the "principal happy ending in all of our tales," one expert witness testified during the trial. Here, Kris and Sandy finally get theirs, exchanging vows on a balcony at San Francisco City Hall.

The lawyers were looking for states that offered virtually no protections for gays and lesbians and where the governor and the attorney general were guaranteed to fight them. Chad, being Chad, wanted them to choose one with a major media market.

Over a tense phone call Thanksgiving week, Stewart had tried to explain to Ted Boutrous that she was not trying to sabotage the broader case Olson was making, and indeed wanted it to succeed. She just wanted to hedge the team's bet. "You guys have always been optimistic that the sweeping fifty-state argument will prevail in the Supreme Court," Stewart recalled telling Boutrous. "But I am anxious. I respect that you are not. But I am."

Boutrous had responded by telling her that she was no better than the groups that had opposed them at the outset. The word "traitor" crossed his lips before they both hung up.

Chad had been enlisted to call Stewart's boss, Dennis Herrera. This was no time to get cold feet, from his perspective. The only thing that had happened between the time they filed the case and now was that they had won big in the district court.

The Ninth Circuit had allotted Stewart fifteen minutes to make her narrower argument. Olson wanted her to cede it to him so he could spend the limited time they had making the broad arguments that would require the panel to reach the same conclusions that Walker had, Chad told Herrera. The judges understood they had other, narrower options, without the team negotiating with itself.

When that failed to produce the desired result—"Dennis has my back," Stewart said—Boies had called. Privately, Boies shared Stewart's concern about the Supreme Court. In his perfect world, the plaintiffs would win the right to marry in a California-specific decision, show the justices and the country that allowing same-sex couples to wed in the country's most populous state would not cause the institution of marriage to implode, and file another case somewhere else. But he was not in charge. Couldn't she make her argument in five minutes, he asked, and give Olson the rest of her time? In the end, she had found it impossible to say no to Boies, but the episode left her feeling bruised.

"I adore David," she said after hanging up the phone. "But with Ted, sometimes I feel like he thinks I'm an idiot and a jerk."

In any oral argument, time is of the essence. One key to Olson's success as an appellate advocate was that he did not waste his time giving elaborate answers to questions that diverted him from the points he wanted to make. And no matter who was doing the asking, he kept his ultimate audience in mind.

So as the argument got under way, Olson kept returning to the broad constitutional arguments he believed would sway Justice Kennedy, namely that "the right to marry is a central aspect of the right to liberty, privacy, association, and identity," that California "engraved discrimination on the basis of sex and sexual orientation into its governing charter" when it stripped over one million gays and lesbians of that right, and that it did so simply because they engaged in intimate sexual conduct that the Supreme Court found to be constitutionally protected in its *Lawrence* decision.

"California has built a fence around its gay and lesbian citizens. And it has built a fence around the institution of marriage, which the Supreme Court says, not based upon sex or procreation or anything else, is the most important relation in life. And the citizens of California within that one fence, because of their sexual orientation, are denied access to what every other citizen in California has," Olson said. "That is a violation of the equal protection clause, and it's a violation of the due process clause."

But each time his rhetoric soared, the panel pulled him back down to earth, and specifically to California and the kind of state-specific arguments that Stewart had made with the hope of avoiding Supreme Court review.

Reinhardt, particularly, seemed to have lost his usual taste for boldness. This was a judge who had found that there was a constitutional right to doctor-assisted suicide and written that the right to bear arms is not an individual one, and his penchant for opinions that practically begged the Supreme Court to reverse him had led the satirical Web site *Onion* to joke that Reinhardt had struck down Christmas "in accordance with my activist agenda to secularize the nation." Now here he was lecturing Olson on the doctrine of judicial restraint, using the Court's opinion in a case Olson had argued before the Supreme Court called *Plaut v. Spendthrift Farm, Inc.*

Olson's arguments in the Proposition 8 case would "require a holding that any state that did not permit gay marriage would be in violation of the Con-stitution," Reinhardt said, but "as you well know"—and as the Court held in the *Plaut* case—"we are advised not to reach a constitutional question unless we have to."

Instead, both Reinhardt and Hawkins focused on the similarities between Proposition 8 and the Colorado initiative that the Supreme Court had struck down in *Romer v. Evans.* Wasn't it true that in both cases, voters had stripped gays and lesbians of rights and protections that they had previously enjoyed? Hawkins had asked Cooper earlier. Why shouldn't the court resolve the case based on those grounds—that a right, once given, cannot be rescinded—alone? Reinhardt now asked Olson.

If the Ninth Circuit panel did that, it would not have to address whether gays and lesbians constituted a suspect class deserving extra judicial protection because of the historic discrimination against them, or the immutability of sexual orientation. It would not have to grapple with Judge Walker's finding that bans like Proposition 8 could not be justified by an interest in promoting an ideal child-rearing environment, because the children of gays and lesbians do just as well as those raised by opposite-sex parents. And it could strike down Proposition 8 without addressing whether bans elsewhere were unconstitu-tional, because only in California had the right to marry been given to gays and lesbians, then taken away.

The way Reinhardt was talking, it was as though the entire trial, with its mountain of evidence and expert testimony, had never taken place.

"This panel makes me nervous," Enrique Monagas said to Sarah Piepmeier afterward. "It would be such a waste if they go narrow."

———

Walking into court that morning, Chuck Cooper had shaken Olson's hand and clapped his old employee, Matt McGill, on the back. But inside, he was seething.

It was bad enough that the state had declined to defend Proposition 8 in Judge Walker's courtroom. But he had known all along that standing could be a problem for his clients if the state did not at least file an appeal, then delegate the actual responsibility of defending the law to the initiative's proponents. If no one had the authority to appeal Judge Walker's decision, then it would stand, unchallenged, and he would lose on a procedural technicality.

"I thought that was incredibly irresponsible and incredibly inappropriate," Cooper said later of what he regarded as the state's negligence. "Fifty-two percent of the people of California deserved to have their views considered and the validity of their constitutional amendment tested by more than one federal district court judge."

Cooper believed that Supreme Court precedent was on his clients' side. California's ballot initiative process effectively allows the people to act as lawmakers. And in a 1987 case called *Karcher v. May,* the Supreme Court had allowed members of the New Jersey Legislature to appeal a decision striking down a school prayer law when the attorney general declined to do so.

But the *Karcher* decision predated Justice Ginsburg's comment in *Arizonans for Official English.* So, with his case potentially hanging in the balance, shortly after Cooper was hired to defend Proposition 8 he had hatched a backup plan.

The California Supreme Court had held that the regulation of marriage is a state function. But because county clerks actually issue marriage licenses on behalf of the state, they arguably might have the type of direct stake in the outcome of the case that the Supreme Court requires. Find a clerk willing to defend Proposition 8 on appeal, Cooper had directed his co-counsel, the Alliance Defense Fund, in the event the initiative's backers could not.

But in what now appeared a serious misstep, the group had signed up the deputy clerk of Imperial County, rather than the actual clerk. Her motion to intervene had been denied by Judge Walker, and judging by the way the three-judge panel was now manhandling her lawyer, it was clearly not going to fare any better here.

The problem was that under California law, deputy clerks have no independent power, and in this case there was nothing to indicate that Imperial County's clerk had authorized the deputy's motion to intervene.

"We're left completely at mystery to know why *the* clerk is not before us," Judge Hawkins said.

"If the clerk isn't here, we have a problem," Judge Smith agreed.

Over the weekend, Boies had talked about how "it's easy in the give-and-take of oral argument to seize on whatever arguments sound good, without thinking about the implications for the rest of your argument." But knowing the trap and not falling into it are two different things.

Part of Boies's job was to keep Imperial County out of the case; he and Olson knew full well that that was Cooper's plan B in the event that his own clients did not have standing. To that end, Boies argued that Imperial County had no stake in the matter because the only clerks directly bound by Judge Walker's order were the two named in the lawsuit, the clerks of Los Angeles and Alameda counties who had denied Jeff and Paul and Sandy and Kris their licenses. But Boies's argument took a complicated turn when Judge Reinhardt wondered aloud whether all fifty-eight clerks should have been named as defendants, or the case filed as a class action, leading to a tangled discussion over whether Judge Walker's decision would apply statewide if no one had the standing to appeal it.

Reinhardt then rebuked Boies, "a lawyer with your ability and fame and, uh, whatever else you have—even if you lost to Mr. Olson," for failing to think all of that through.

To be fair, Reinhardt's question was completely unexpected, and Boies had not been given much time to prepare; Olson had assigned the standing argument to his partner at the last minute because he wanted Boies to have a role. Olson, scribbling on his notepad, thought Reinhardt was wrong on the law. The plaintiffs had sued the governor and the attorney general because marriage in California is a state function; it was not necessary to sue anyone else. But there was little he could do but watch as Boies tried to rebound.

In practical terms, Boies told the judge, the governor and the attorney general had the authority to force the clerks in all fifty-eight counties to resume issuing licenses to same-sex couples. But in answer to another of Reinhardt's questions, he conceded that another round of litigation might be necessary first.

As the half hour came to a close, it was clear that the panel had concluded that the best way to resolve the problem was to eliminate it, by finding a way to rule that Cooper's clients had the right to appeal Judge Walker's decision.

Judge Smith noted that the governor has no veto power over voter initiatives, and the California Legislature may not amend them. "I guess my problem is that in fact the governor's actions and the attorney general's actions have essentially nullified the considerable efforts that were made on behalf of the initiative to be placed on the ballot and obtain passage," he said. "If they don't appeal, and therefore no one can appeal, haven't they effectively nullified the effect?"

During the prep sessions, Boies had answered similar questions by pointing out that the proponents of Prop 8 had already had their day in court. Now, though, he found himself deep in the weeds, arguing that was true "only in the sense, Your Honor, that in every standing case, if a state official does not appeal, it, quote, nullifies it."

"The answer then is yes," Judge Reinhardt declared.

Reinhardt and Hawkins seemed unlikely to uphold Proposition 8 as constitutional: The lawyer's contention that Proposition 8 was about ensuring that children were raised in two-parent household "sounds like a good argument for prohibiting divorce," Judge Reinhardt said, "but how does it relate to having two males or two females marry each other and raise children?"

But like Smith, they were sympathetic to Cooper's argument that his clients had a right to defend the initiative. Both men had, as Hawkins put it, been on the "wrong side" of the *Arizonans for Official English* case when it passed through the Ninth Circuit, reaching the merits of the challenge to the Arizona initiative only to be reversed by the Supreme Court. "I thought it was the right side!" Reinhardt interjected.

It bothered Reinhardt that the court kept putting up procedural roadblocks that barred the courtroom door to people. This case offered a way to claw back some of the ground they had lost, if they could find a way to distinguish California from Arizona.

In the *Arizonans* case, Justice Ginsburg had noted that the court was "aware of no Arizona law appointing initiative sponsors as agents of the people to defend, in lieu of public officials, the constitutionality of initiatives." Now, again out of left field, Reinhardt threw a question at Boies. "Why shouldn't we ask the California Supreme Court what the law is in California?" Reinhardt asked. "Rather than kill an initiative that the voters have passed, wouldn't it be advisable to attempt to get a legal answer to this question?"

Chad wanted to scream. He still worried that another case could overtake this one and reach the Supreme Court first; he wanted Olson to be the one to frame the argument for the justices. This would delay them for months, maybe even years. But when a judge is as hell-bent on a course as Reinhardt seemed to be on this one, there is little to be done. By the time court wrapped up, the legal team had resigned itself to a new and unwelcome reality: Their case was about to take a detour.

"What a mess," said Theane Evangelis.

TWENTY-SIX

"SOMETIMES PRAYERS WORK"

By White House standards, the party that took place on February 6, 2011, was an informal one. The Obamas had set up big-screen televisions in the State Dining Room and invited some friends over to watch the Green Bay Packers play the Pittsburgh Steelers in the Super Bowl.

Stepping out into the hallway for moment, Attorney General Eric Holder was surprised to find Obama standing there, near a portrait of John F. Kennedy. It was rare to catch the president alone, and he decided to take advantage of the moment.

While the Proposition 8 case had been perking along, a number of other federal lawsuits involving the rights of gays and lesbians had been filed in federal courts around the country. These lawsuits did not challenge same-sex marriage bans. Rather, they were the more narrow challenges to the provision in the Clinton-era Defense of Marriage Act that denied spousal benefits to same-sex couples who had married in states where it was already legal. And that presented a challenge for the Obama administration.

Except under extraordinary circumstances, the Justice Department has a duty to defend laws passed by Congress, regardless of whether the occupant of the White House likes them or not. For that reason, Obama and Holder were dutifully arguing to uphold DOMA, as the law was known, and taking incoming fire from gay rights groups that reminded Obama at every turn that he had promised to repeal, not defend it.

Holder thought he had found a way out. But before he could tell the president about it, Obama beat him to the punch. Before his career in politics, Obama had taught constitutional law, and now he shared what he believed to be an elegant solution to the DOMA problem.

Listening, Holder had to laugh. "I was going to tell you exactly the same thing!" he recalled telling the president. "And I remember telling him this was one of the reasons why I was proud to serve in his administration, because what he was saying was not going to be without controversy. But it was the right thing to do.

"And, as is typical of him, he just kind of said, 'Yeah, it is right. I think it's the right thing to do, Eric, so let's get back to the game.'"

The quest for a solution had begun twenty months earlier when the Justice Department filed a brief defending DOMA in a case called *Smelt v. United States*.

The Civil Division of the Justice Department, which defends cases brought against the government in the lower courts, had inherited its defense of DOMA from the Bush administration. Tony West, the political appointee who headed the division, went through the brief before it was filed, stripping out arguments that he felt were inconsistent with the new administration's values or unsupported by evidence. Gone was the argument that states had a right to make judgments consistent with prevailing "societal mores." Relying on the same kind of sociological evidence Olson had used in the Prop 8 trial, West also abandoned the argument that DOMA was justified because it promoted an ideal child-rearing environment. But his effort to strike a balance was overshadowed by the arguments the brief did make.

Instead of simply outlining the procedural flaws with the case that would eventually result in its dismissal, the Justice Department had mounted a multifaceted defense of the law's constitutionality. Echoing Cooper's argument in the Proposition 8 case, the brief argued that adopting a "cautious, wait-and-see approach" to same-sex marriage was perfectly rational. The biggest uproar, though, was caused by a citation West had overlooked buried deep within the brief. In defense of the law's provision that states did not have to recognize same-sex marriages performed elsewhere, it referenced a decades-old Supreme

Court decision that held that states do not have to recognize marriages between cousins or an uncle and a niece.

The June 11, 2009, brief instantly became a flashpoint for activists who were
already disappointed with a president they felt was an "unreliable ally," as Segura had put it during the Prop 8 trial. OBAMA DOJ COMPARES GAY MARRIAGE
TO INCEST, read one headline.

At the White House that Saturday, the president hit the roof as he read
through his daily package of news clips. West had consulted with the White
House Counsel's Office and given lawyers there a copy of the brief before it was
filed, but apparently no one had filled in the president.

Obama fired off an e-mail to Valerie Jarrett, one of his oldest friends and
closest White House advisers, and his primary liaison to the gay community.
Jarrett was attending the wedding reception of the president's domestic policy
adviser when she checked her BlackBerry and saw the president's sharply
worded message. At her table was Rahm Emanuel, Obama's chief of staff at the
time, and Hilary Rosen, a powerful and openly gay Democratic consultant,
who recounted the conversation this way:

"The president has just gotten around to doing his weekend reading, and
he's not happy," Jarrett told Emanuel.

Rosen wasn't sure what had irked the president, but she sensed an opportunity. "I'll tell you what he shouldn't be happy about," she said. "He shouldn't be
happy about this DOMA filing."

"That's exactly what he isn't happy about," Jarrett replied.

Turning back to Emanuel, Jarrett said, "He's going to do want to do something about this."

"I don't know what he can do about it," Emanuel replied.

"Well, we are going to have to figure something out."

———

On a personal level, Eric Holder had never liked DOMA. Neither had Tony
West. Both were African Americans who saw distinct parallels between the
civil rights battles of the past and the present-day struggle for marriage equality. Standing up for a law both felt was discriminatory felt, as West put it, like
standing "on the wrong side of history."

So when the president's displeasure filtered back to the Justice Department, neither man was averse to taking a second look at the department's position. But it was not as easy for them to drop the defense of a law passed by Congress as it been for the governor and the attorney general of California to cease defending a law passed by state voters.

The ethos of the department is that the rule of law and the founders' vision of three coequal branches of government require the executive branch to strongly defend laws passed by the legislative branch. Both men were steeped in the department's traditions, having landed their first jobs there when they were fresh out of law school. However personally distasteful they found DOMA, both knew that if the Justice Department was going to take the momentous step of declining to defend a duly enacted law of Congress, it had better have a damned good legal reason.

To avoid any perception that the department's legal judgments are politically motivated, appointees like West generally, though not always, defer to the recommendations of civil service line lawyers. The line lawyers' initial take was that the department had a duty to make any and all arguments in defense of DOMA. So West arranged a series of meetings with gay activists so they could hear the critique of the law's constitutionality directly from the community that it impacted.

Since the *Smelt* dustup, three other DOMA challenges had been filed. But all were in circuit courts of appeal that had already decided that the highly deferential rational basis test—requiring only that the law be rationally related to some legitimate government purpose—was the proper standard of review for laws that target gays and lesbians.

The department had been arguing for years that DOMA was rational. It would be burdensome for the federal government to have to administer benefit programs on a state-by-state basis, depending on the marriage laws in effect, the argument went, and so it was rational to want a uniform rule that simply defined marriage as a union between a man and a woman. The courts would not give the department's position much, if any, weight if it suddenly did an about-face, especially given the leniency of the standard. And it could damage the institution's credibility in other cases.

But as West put it, "it didn't take a rocket scientist" to know that one of these days someone was going to file a challenge to DOMA in a circuit that had yet to decide whether gays and lesbians should be considered a suspect class, where it could be argued that heightened scrutiny applied, as Walker had found it did in the Prop 8 case. When that happened, they could reassess.

Unbeknownst to West, the hypothetical case he envisioned was already in the works.

———

Robbie Kaplan said it took her "all of a few seconds" to decide to help Edie Windsor get her money back from the federal government, about the same amount of time Edie said it took her to decide she wanted Kaplan as her lawyer.

Sitting in Edie's apartment overlooking Greenwich Village one morning, the two women took turns telling the story of their first meeting, in 2010. Edie's wife, Thea Spyer, had recently died. Grief-stricken, Edie had been hospitalized with a condition called cardiomyopathy, also known as "broken heart syndrome" because it can be brought on by stressful situations like the death of a loved one. When she was released, she found she owed the federal government $363,000 in estate taxes.

Had she married a man, his estate would have passed to her tax-free. But because DOMA prohibited the federal government from recognizing her marriage, Edie had to pay taxes on her wife's half of the apartment they owned in New York City's Greenwich Village and a cottage they had bought years earlier in the Hamptons.

In the hospital, Edie had been quite prepared to die. She was seventy-nine years old, and she missed Thea desperately. But the tax bill made her mad. It made her want to fight.

First, she called Lambda Legal, the group that had so vehemently opposed the filing of the Prop 8 case. No one returned her call. She tried again. Finally, a lawyer got on the phone. Would the group be willing to challenge DOMA on her behalf? she asked.

"No," the lawyer answered. "Wrong time for the movement."

"But I have a documented marriage," she said.

"No. Wrong time."

It was then that a friend of a friend referred her to Kaplan. A corporate litigator at the Manhattan-based firm of Paul, Weiss, Rifkind, Wharton & Garrison, she typically represented clients like JPMorgan Chase. But she was an outsider who might not mind bucking established gay rights groups. Though the initial DOMA case filed by Mary Bonauto on behalf of plaintiffs from Massachusetts was going well, many within the movement remained deeply wary about bringing federal cases of any kind. And Kaplan, like Bonauto, had experience; a few years back, Kaplan had unsuccessfully challenged New York's ban on gay marriage in state court. Edie placed the call.

"And the following day, *that* walked into my life," Edie said, pointing at Kaplan, who laughed uproariously before recounting her own impressions.

Edie was the perfect plaintiff, Kaplan thought, glamorous in an old-fashioned way. Her hair framed her face in soft blond waves, her oval nails were perfectly manicured, and she wore pink lipstick and the same strand of pearls that she had on her wedding day. Though she was a frail slip of a thing, she carried herself with the confidence of a woman used to being admired, and her life story was a vehicle to tell the broader history of discrimination against gays and lesbians.

Edie had known ever since she was a small girl that she loved women. She was born in 1929, in Depression-era Philadelphia, and she could still remember her shiver of delight when, at age seven, she put her arm around another little girl after a day of roller skating. She tried to fight it, dating loads of boys in high school and eventually marrying one in 1951.

"I wanted to be straight," she explained.

It lasted less than a year.

"Honey, you deserve someone who thinks you are the best thing in the world," she said she told him, "and I can't be that."

The two divorced amicably, and Edie moved to Manhattan. Her apartment was on the fourth floor of a walk-up building, with room for just a bed and a sink, and bathroom she had to share with a guy down the hall. But the city was just as it had been described in a lesbian pulp fiction paperback she'd purchased, a place where "anything could happen," where "you could even kiss a girl."

"I remember thinking, 'Where?!'" she said, laughing.

Edie boarded a bus to Washington Square Park and stopped a woman wearing a trench coat and pink button-down shirt. These were the years leading up to the Stonewall riots that Chauncey had described in the Prop 8 trial, when the police still regularly sent snitches into gay bars. Undaunted, Edie boldly asked the stranger if she knew where women went to meet. The woman showed her the way to a bar she called "Ls."

Being a lesbian meant being a career woman at a time when that was still exceptional. With no man to take care of her, Edie worked first as a cosmetologist, then as a bookkeeper, then put herself through New York University's master's program in applied mathematics. To support herself, she worked as a programmer on one of the world's earliest computers for the Atomic Energy Commission and, after she graduated, for IBM.

But it was Edie and Thea's love story that had Kaplan from the minute she walked into Edie's small apartment. Every available surface was cluttered with photographs, a visual ode to the forty-two years they spent together.

There they were in black and white, young and beaming not long after they met in 1963. They had run into one another at Portofino, one of the few restaurants where lesbians were welcome. It was owned by Elaine Kaufman, whose Upper East Side saloon Elaine's became a famed haunt of New York's literary crowd.

In another shot, Edie is wearing the circular diamond brooch Thea gave her four years later when she proposed. The two women had been driving to the Hamptons, and Edie said yes immediately, though of course back then it was completely impossible. Both knew a traditional wedding band would have raised too many questions; if anyone at work found out that Edie was a lesbian, she could lose her job. President Eisenhower's executive order prohibiting federal contractors from hiring homosexuals was still in effect, and Edie still shuddered thinking back to her first security clearance interview.

They spent much of their courtship dancing. They never stopped, even after Thea was diagnosed with multiple sclerosis in the 1970s. The photos document her decline: Edie holding Thea tight on the dance floor as the disease began to take its toll, and later, sitting on her lap as Thea spun them both around in her wheelchair.

In 2007, Thea's doctor told her she did not have long to live. "Do you still want to get married?" Thea asked Edie. She did. Enlisting friends and medical assistance, they managed to fly to Canada, which two years earlier had become the fourth country in the world to allow gays and lesbians to wed. A documentary crew followed them. In the footage, both look joyous, though by then Thea was so crippled she could barely lift her arm.

"Now that is a marriage," Kaplan thought.

Walking over to a computer, she played Edie a clip of her argument in the New York Court of Appeals. Kaplan wore a suit and a Rolex watch. Her chin-length hair was cut in layers and expertly colored, and she exuded confidence. And like Edie, the lawyer was a lesbian, who knew firsthand what discrimination felt like. Edie was sold, but between the tax bill and the beating she had taken during the 2008 financial market crash, her savings were depleted.

"How much will it cost?" she asked.

Kaplan made a zero with her thumb and middle finger. Her firm would handle the case pro bono, she explained.

"It's not just for you," Kaplan told Edie. "I have a wife, and a son, and I care."

"I thought, if anyone can do this, she can," Edie said.

On November 9, 2010, Kaplan filed a lawsuit on her client's behalf in the U.S. District Court for the Southern District of New York. To fend off criticism from gay rights legal groups, Kaplan brought in James Esseks, the new director of the ACLU's Lesbian Gay Bisexual Transgender & AIDS Project, and she deliberately kept her argument narrow.

Windsor's brief made clear that the court did not have to decide the larger question of whether the Constitution contained a right for gays and lesbians to marry. It did not challenge a provision of the law that gave states the authority to decline to recognize same-sex marriages performed elsewhere. It demanded only that the federal government refund the estate taxes Edie had paid, on the grounds that DOMA treated married same-sex couples differently than their straight counterparts for no good reason. The opportunity that the Justice Department had been waiting for had arrived.

With a deadline looming to file a response in both the *Windsor* case and a related DOMA challenge out of Connecticut, Holder convened a working group involving multiple divisions of his department to take a fresh look, unshackled from precedent, at whether the defense of DOMA ought to be abandoned.

Did gays and lesbians meet the Supreme Court's test for heightened scrutiny? It was possible to take the position that it did, because the *Windsor* case was filed in the Second Circuit Court of Appeals, which had yet to consider what standard of review was appropriate when considering laws that target gays and lesbians for disparate treatment. If so, could the department still mount a plausible defense that the law was constitutional? That was an equally important question, because the Justice Department had on rare occasions abandoned the defense of a law when none could reasonably be made.

Line lawyers in West's shop considered the same questions that Judge Walker had: the history of discrimination against gays and lesbians, the immutability of sexual orientation, and their relative power to protect themselves in the democratic process.

West was in Milan on vacation with his family when the lawyers called for one last group discussion. It was an intense, hour-and-a-half call, and not everyone agreed. But by the end, a consensus had emerged: Heightened scrutiny applied, and under that standard, DOMA could not pass constitutional muster. As such, the department did not have to defend it.

"I was never so proud of those line lawyers as I was that night," West said.

The Civil Division's recommendation carried a lot of weight, because it is the government's defense shop. But other divisions were also involved in the debate, and one very important one remained adamantly opposed.

The Office of the Solicitor General argues cases on behalf of the government at the Supreme Court. Elena Kagan, Obama's first solicitor general, had recently left to take her place on the Supreme Court. It was currently run by Kagan's deputy, Neal Kumar Katyal, while the president searched for her permanent replacement.

Four of the justices of the Supreme Court had served in the Justice Department, including Chief Justice John Roberts, and would understand what a break from tradition this would be. The Justice Department was not in the habit of arguing that the laws of the United States should be subject to heightened scrutiny. It made it harder to defend them, which was their job. Katyal worried it could damage the department's credibility at a critical juncture: The Office of the Solicitor General was gearing up to defend one of President Obama's signature, and most controversial, accomplishments: a massive overhaul of the nation's health care system, nicknamed Obamacare.

"The context was, what happens if President Bachmann gets elected and doesn't want to defend health care?" West recalled, referring to Congresswoman Michele Bachmann, who, like the rest of the Republican field of presidential candidates, was campaigning against Obamacare in the hope of denying the president a second term.

The debate culminated in a conference call just before Super Bowl weekend that one official who participated called a "knock-down drag-out." Both sides made their case to the attorney general.

"There was a split, strong feelings," Holder recalled. "At the end of the day, this was something I had to resolve."

===

Robbie Kaplan was waiting for the government to file its reply brief in the *Windsor* case when one of the Justice Department's line attorneys called her office. Would she be willing to agree to a thirty-day delay?

The Justice Department had kept a tight lid on its deliberations, and Kaplan still saw it as her adversary. Not happening, she replied. Edie's health had worsened, and she could easily die before the case was resolved.

West then called her personally. "We are thinking about what we going to say," he told her. "We need time to decide how to respond."

Kaplan found that hard to believe; she fully expected the government to file its pro forma defense.

"Please," West begged. "The attorney general of the United States is asking you for time."

"I said, 'Okay, if that's what is really going on, and you really are thinking about this, then please tell the attorney general and the president that I am going to be praying for them.'"

===

"There are lot of important decisions that you make as attorney general," Eric Holder said, reflecting back on those days of deliberation. "But there are a few that even when you are in the process of making them or deciding them, you understand that they are going to be potentially historic. This was certainly one of them."

In deciding the way forward, Holder said he kept thinking about the past. He went back to 1996, to a congressional record that explicitly stated that the intent of DOMA was to express moral disapproval of homosexuality and prevent "wavering children" from experimenting. Then he went further back, to the era of Jim Crow, and separate water fountains.

"The way in which gay people through history have been discriminated against, opportunities denied them, the parallels are very striking. There are stereotypes drawn, negative stereotypes, and policies based on those stereotypes, laws based on those stereotypes. And it seemed to me that you could not help but compare that treatment, that history of discrimination, with the way in which African Americans had suffered. The inability to obtain basic rights, basic American rights, because of who you are."

He considered the arguments about political power, and those same parallels kept coming up. The election of the first African American president, the appointment of the first African American attorney general, showed that "we are in a fundamentally differently place than we were fifty years ago when it comes to black people," yet African Americans were still considered a suspect class.

All of that argued for applying heightened scrutiny. But what about the institutional concerns that had been raised by some of his top lawyers? Again, he felt the weight of a shared history. When the Supreme Court issued its *Brown v. Board of Education* decision, it did more than just desegregate schools. "It was an affirmation of black life. To say that the policy was inherently unequal necessarily meant that black people were the equal of white people and need to be treated that way."

Didn't gays and lesbians deserve the same? Under Article II of the Constitution, which mandates that the president "take care that the laws be faithfully executed," the executive branch has a duty to enforce the laws of the United States. But it does not have to defend those that cannot pass constitutional muster.

And that was what he was about to recommend to the president when he ran into him outside the State Dining Room, only Holder said the president started talking first, about how he thought DOMA ought to be subject to heightened judicial scrutiny, and how, given that, he did not think that the administration's legal position was what it should be.

"He was where he was, and I was where I was, and we just met at that Super Bowl thing," Holder said.

Seventeen days later, on the morning of February 23, 2011, Robbie Kaplan got another call from West. As a personal matter, the president remained opposed to same-sex marriage, though he now said that his view that civil unions were adequate for gay couples was "evolving." But that afternoon, the Justice Department planned to notify Congress that while the administration would continue to enforce DOMA, it would no longer defend a federal law that treated married gay couples differently than their straight counterparts.

"Remember when you said you would be praying?" West asked. "Well, sometimes prayers work."

TWENTY-SEVEN

WHEN A NIGHTINGALE SINGS

It was a festive group that stood in the sunshine in midtown Manhattan a few months later on Sunday, June 26, 2011, waiting for the city's forty-second annual gay pride parade to start. Two days earlier, in a nail-biter of a vote, New York lawmakers had made their state the sixth, and by far the largest, to allow gays and lesbians to wed.

Chad had planned to spend the weekend in Palm Springs, but when the law passed the Republican-controlled state senate late Friday night, he and Adam had jumped on a red-eye flight. They had headed first to the Stonewall Inn, to celebrate a momentous political victory in a state that had birthed the modern gay rights movement, one with profound implications for the country and the case. Rob and Michele Reiner, who were in town on business, joined them at a prearranged parade meet-up point with their daughter, Romy. Rob's producing partner, Alan Greisman, and his son with actress Sally Field came with them. Bruce Cohen and his husband, Gabe, arrived last, pushing along their newly adopted two-month-old baby girl, Ilaria, in a stroller.

Once the law went into effect, the number of people living in states where same-sex couples could marry would double overnight, an inflection point that would make what was once deemed remarkable, even radical, quite ordinary.

Pending the outcome of the marriage litigation, the federal government and states with Proposition 8–like bans would not have to recognize the marriages of gays and lesbians performed here. But just two years after a state senate then under Democratic control easily rejected a similar bill, the traditional political dynamic had been upended by a campaign that harnessed Wall Street money, bipartisan muscle, and newfound political savvy to overcome stiff opposition from the Catholic Church and other religious leaders. The cause had gone mainstream, in a way the lawyers hoped would convince the justices that the country was ready.

"Now that the winds are shifting," Rob Reiner exclaimed, "I don't see how the Supreme Court is going to rule against us!"

Just then, Christine Quinn, the first openly gay speaker of the New York City Council, wandered over. "Happy Pride!" she said. Cohen had recently thrown her a fund-raiser, and now she introduced her longtime partner, Kim Catullo, to the group. The two women planned to marry now that it was legal. "Chad's been, like, leading the effort legally," Quinn told her fiancée.

The case, however, had ground to a standstill. As expected, the Ninth Circuit had denied Imperial County's motion to intervene and asked the California Supreme Court for guidance on whether ballot proponents like Cooper's clients have the authority under state law to defend the validity of initiatives such as Proposition 8. But arguments weren't scheduled to take place until September, more than two months away.

With the case in legal limbo, Adam and the team's Hollywood contingent were working with a nonprofit group of theater artists called Broadway Impact on a unique plan to carry the story of the plaintiffs' trial victory to an audience beyond the courtroom. AFER's in-house screenwriter, Lance Black, was writing a play, with nearly all the lines drawn verbatim from the trial transcripts, that the Reiners were helping to cast. The Supreme Court may have prevented the American public from seeing the trial, but it could not stop them from re-creating it. Black's play, 8, would open for a one-night fund-raiser on Broadway, followed by another in Hollywood. AFER would then make the script available to anyone who wanted to put it on a stage.

Standing on the corner, the Reiners went over the various roles with the rest of the group.

"Kevin Kline would be a good one to play David," said Rob, whose shirt was festooned with gay rights stickers, including one that read POWER IS SEXY.

"I like Rob for Blankenhorn, don't you?" Michele asked.

"Oh my God—that's good!" Chad gasped. "Would you do it?"

"I would do it, sure."

Michele was a little worried about Paul and Jeff; Kris and Sandy had larger roles in the play. And someone needed to talk to Ted Boutrous and explain that for creative reasons the only lawyers featured would be Olson and Boies.

"Chad and I were talking about Ted," Adam said. "We said, you know who would be perfect to play him? Robert Redford."

The throngs around them began growing larger and louder, cutting off discussion. Ilaria was sleeping through the din, "but if I sneeze, she'll wake up," Gabe said, proudly fussing with her blanket. A young man wearing a NEXT MARCH, DOWN THE AISLE T-shirt offered to help the new fathers by clearing the way for her stroller. As the march began to move, Bruce hugged both Reiners. "Rob and Michele, for the gays!" he cheered.

But the one AFER board member who had as much to do with the passage of same-sex marriage in New York as anyone was nowhere to be found. Ken Mehlman, one of the Republican Party's shrewdest political operatives, was sitting out the march at his apartment downtown. He didn't want any credit. Besides, he told Chad and Adam when he begged off, he was not entirely sure his presence would be welcome. Marching in the parade was for people who had been waging these battles for years, not a newcomer like himself. "I didn't think I had earned that right," he said afterward.

━━━━━

Mehlman liked to think of himself as a stand-up guy. As the chairman of the Republican National Committee under President George W. Bush, he had made headlines by apologizing to the National Association for the Advancement of Colored People for the Republican Party's exploitation of racial strife to court southern white voters. He had taken on his party's anti-immigration wing, publicly charging that it was jeopardizing years of outreach to Latino voters.

But as the man responsible for reelecting Bush in 2004, Mehlman had not spoken out against his party's use of antigay initiatives to drive evangelical voters to the polls for political gain. Eleven states passed same-sex marriage bans that year, including Ohio, a battleground Bush needed to win. And he had been evasive and misleading in his attempts to quash the widespread rumors about his own sexuality. He knew he was gay, but he had not come to terms with it. It took him forty-three years, and Olson's involvement in the Proposition 8 fight, to come out and speak up.

"I call Ted the nightingale, because when one nightingale sings, others start singing too," he said one night over dinner, prior to the parade. "Before, whenever this issue would come up, I would just not engage. It was the one area of my life where I had been unwilling to take a risk or a chance."

Like nearly everyone else in Olson's circle of Republican friends and colleagues, Mehlman had been intrigued when the lawyer challenged the constitutionality of California's same-sex marriage ban. He had followed the trial coverage carefully, and been impressed with the public education component of the litigation. He wanted to help. But first he wanted to be reassured that the case did not constitute the kind of judicial activism that, as a conservative, he had long deplored.

Olson's answer—that marriage was not a new right, and that the courts were there to protect against the tyranny of the majority—satisfied Mehlman. He wanted to hold a fund-raiser to benefit AFER, he told Olson, and not just any fund-raiser but one filled with big-name Republicans whose support for marriage equality would make headlines. Talk to Chad, Olson said, introducing the two via e-mail.

There is a team-building exercise that Mehlman had always hated, the one where one person tumbles backwards and trusts another to break the fall. Meeting Chad for the first time felt a lot like that. Chad had been one of several producers behind a documentary called *Outrage*, about the political hypocrisy of closeted gay Republicans and the media's role in covering it up. The film featured a clip of comedian Bill Maher referring to Mehlman as a closeted gay man on *Larry King Live*, a comment CNN edited out of later taped editions and that the Republican operative had denied.

But the two operatives liked one another immediately. Though they came from opposite ends of the political spectrum, they were both obsessive, Type A workaholics. When Mehlman embarked on a task, he employed what he called "command focus" to shut out all distractions.

"Anyone who can get George Bush elected and reelected is a fucking genius I want on my team," Chad joked after their first meeting.

Both men believed that big social change does not happen unless people with multiple perspectives come to believe that it is consistent with their values. As Mehlman put it, selling the American public on same-sex marriage involved Republicans arguing that it was consistent with conservative values of fidelity and commitment, athletes arguing it was consistent with fair play, CEOs arguing it was good for business and the economy, religious leaders calling on people to "love thy neighbor as thyself," and foreign policy hawks pointing out that some of the most antigay countries in the world were also the most vehemently anti-Western.

It also, Mehlman understood, involved him finally being honest about who he was. He was living in New York, working as partner at the private equity giant Kohlberg Kravis Roberts and Company, or KKR as it is known, and was in the process of quietly coming out to family and a few close friends. But joining up with AFER for a big-name fund-raiser would require something more public, and not just because the event was bound to renew all those old questions about his sexuality.

"People told me, and I didn't believe it then, but I do now, that one of the most powerful things you can do is come out," he said. "People's views change because they come to know that their brothers and their sisters or their friend, who put on their pants one leg at a time just like them, who pay taxes and salute the flag just like them, just so happen to be gay."

He planned it with the meticulousness that he had brought to plotting Bush's second term in office. In August 2010, he had sat for an interview with the *Atlantic* magazine titled "Bush Campaign Chief and Former RNC Chairman Ken Mehlman: I'm Gay." One month later, Mehlman opened up a new spigot of Wall Street money for the marriage equality cause, raising $1.3 million for AFER at a fund-raiser at the Mandarin Oriental Hotel overlooking Central Park. GOP megadonors like hedge fund billionaires Paul Singer and Peter Thiel mingled with two former Republican governors, several leading GOP political strategists, high-ranking officials from the Bush administration, and a surprise guest, President Bush's daughter Barbara.

"Ken's all in on everything he does, but there's all in, and then there's all in," said attendee Mark Wallace, a close friend and Bush's deputy ambassador to the United Nations. "This was more important to him than anything he had ever done. He wanted to get it right, because he wanted it to be the beginning of the best campaign he would run in his life."

The event generated huge press buzz, but afterward AFER's Facebook page was awash with negative comments. "Ken Mehlman set gays and lesbians back ten years," read one. "The damage is done by his precious GOP and suddenly he has an attack of conscience?" read another. Undaunted, Chad announced Mehlman would be joining the AFER board.

Olson's embracement of the marriage equality cause had been important both legally and symbolically, but Mehlman's offered an opportunity to engage with the entire Republican Party political apparatus and electorate on an operative level. He was also a genuinely nice guy, Chad told Kristina, still awkwardly trying to find his way as a gay man in a world that was largely unfamiliar to him. "Coming out is hard," he told her. "No matter who a person is, you have to support him. We have to be there for him."

Mehlman quickly set about proving his usefulness. Nearly two years into his presidency, Obama had finally made congressional repeal of Don't Ask, Don't Tell a priority, following a painstaking campaign to enlist the support of top military brass. Weeks after the AFER fund-raiser, the Pentagon released a survey of active member and reserve military. More than 70 percent said the effect of repealing the ban on gays and lesbians serving openly would be positive, mixed, or nonexistent, leading the study's authors to conclude that the ban could be lifted with minimal risk to the current war efforts in Iraq and Afghanistan. The repeal had passed the House, but with the chamber set to flip to Republican control in January 2011, the administration had only weeks to move it through the Senate.

Mehlman offered to help during a White House visit with Valerie Jarrett, the president's friend and top aide. He then threw himself into rounding up the Republican votes that the president's advisers said were critical to the bill's passage, acting as a trusted translator during negotiations with the White House.

"Ken spent a lot of time talking to them. He was very helpful in terms of figuring out what they wanted and communicating that to us," said Jim Messina, then the White House deputy chief of staff. "We were trying to get rid of excuses, redlines, and the Republicans gave Democrats cover."

Mehlman devoted even more energy to the effort to legalize same-sex marriage in New York. To avoid a repeat of the infighting and disorganization that had contributed to defeat two years earlier, Democratic governor Andrew Cuomo had insisted that gay rights groups work together in a coalition that reported up to a top-notch campaign manager of his choosing, former labor leader Jennifer Cunningham. Cuomo, who had made the legalization of same-sex marriage a top priority, committed to holding Democratic lawmakers' feet to the fire. But it was going to take Republicans in the GOP-controlled Senate to pass the bill, and that was where Mehlman came in.

He reached out to Bill Smith, the national political director for the Gill Action Fund, which was deeply involved in the New York battle, and invited him to a meeting in Paul Singer's office with some of the GOP megadonors who had attended the AFER fund-raiser. The deep-pocketed nonprofit Gill Action Fund, formed to advance LGBT causes through the political process, was working to make the movement more effective by insisting that the groups it funded employ polling, focus groups, and other tools of modern politics. Smith had worked for Bush strategist Karl Rove and at the RNC, and had been one of the people Mehlman consulted when he came out. The donors Mehlman brought to the meeting were sold.

"Over a million dollars came from that one meeting, more than from all the other donors combined," Smith said. "It completely changed the equation. Gill Action had a right-of-center strategy, but Ken put it on steroids."

Working in coordination with Cuomo, they began building a model they hoped could be exported to other states. The Republican Wall Street money went toward hiring a Republican lobbying team that lawmakers in Albany knew and trusted. Wavering Republicans senators were assured that there would be plenty more money to protect them if their vote in favor of same-sex marriage caused them problems in the next election cycle. Mehlman also arranged a confidential meeting with Republican state senate leader Dean G. Skelos and some of the Republican donors who were now backing AFER. If Skelos imposed party discipline and refused to allow his members to vote their conscience, the bill was doomed.

"We said, 'We want to build this party, we want you to be in the majority in the future,'" Mehlman recalled afterward. "We said to him, 'In every competitive district, we will hire polling guys that had polled for Republicans in the past to do polling on the issue. And we'd like to share that with you. So your guys know we're not asking them to take a flier, we think it's in their interest.'"

Next came the enlistment of the business community. Mehlman, City Council Speaker Quinn, and Kathryn Wylde, the CEO of Partnership for New

York City, a nonprofit organization of the city's corporate leaders, split up a list of names. The result: an open letter to Albany, signed by business titans like the CEOs of Goldman Sachs and Morgan Stanley, arguing that passage was important to their ongoing ability to recruit talent. New York mayor Michael Bloomberg was a also forceful advocate, lobbying lawmakers and appearing in an advertising campaign that also featured iconic New Yorkers like former mayors David Dinkins and Ed Koch and former police chief Bill Bratton.

Republicans held thirty-two of sixty-two seats in the state senate. Seventeen would have to vote to put a bill on the floor. With all but one Democrat committed to voting for it, at least three Republican senators would have to cast votes in favor. Mehlman went to Albany to personally lobby lawmakers, assuring them that they could count on financial backing to fight off primary challengers.

But with New York's Catholic archbishop Timothy Dolan charging that passage of the bill would put New York in the category of North Korea and China, where "government presumes daily to 'redefine' rights, relationships, values, and natural law," only two Republicans had publicly committed to supporting the bill, one short of the number needed. Under pressure from both sides, it had not been an easy decision for either of them.

"You get to the point where you evolve in your life, where everything isn't black and white, good and bad, and you try to do the right thing," state senator Roy McDonald told reporters, explaining his decision to vote in favor of allowing gays and lesbians to wed. "You might not like that. You might be very cynical about that. Well, fuck it. I don't care what you think. I'm trying to do the right thing. I'm tired of Republican-Democratic politics. They can take the job and shove it."

With only one more Republican senator needed, Mehlman kept at it. He called Senate Majority Leader Skelos repeatedly, and updated Chad via e-mail. Finally, on June 24, Skelos called him. Mehlman had spent a sleepless night at the Ritz-Carlton in D.C., where he was staying on business. "The vote is going to happen tonight," Mehlman recalled Skelos saying. "I think you'll be pleased with the outcome."

After six hours behind closed doors, the Republican state senate caucus emerged. The governor had agreed to a broad exemption, ensuring that religious institutions and nonprofits could not be sued for refusing to take part in same-sex marriages. "After many hours of deliberation and discussion over the past several weeks among the members, it has been decided that same-sex marriage legislation will be brought to the full Senate for an up-or-down vote," Skelos said in a statement.

When the vote was called, four Republican senators voted aye, putting the bill over the top.

———

Back along the parade route, "Here Comes the Bride" was playing out of unseen speakers. Just up ahead, the crowd chanted, "Bloomberg! Bloomberg!" as the mayor passed by. Volunteers pressed THANK YOU, GOV. CUOMO signs into revelers' hands.

"Printed those fast, didn't they?" Chad said to Adam.

"I keep thinking about those four Republican senators," Adam replied. "When they went home they must have felt so good. Whereas some of these other guys . . ."

Rob Reiner shook his head. "What about Obama?"

The president, in town for a $1,250-per-head fund-raising dinner with gay activists while the bill was being debated the previous week, had referenced the "deliberation about what it means here in New York to treat people fairly in the eyes of the law," without committing himself to one view or the other. Then, after the bill passed, a White House spokesman had put out a statement that echoed the case segregationists had made in the South half a century ago, that civil rights should be decided by the political process. "The states should determine for themselves how best to uphold the rights of their own citizens," the president's spokesman said. "The process in New York worked just as it should."

"He should've stuck with 'my views are evolving,'" Rob told Chad. "Whoever told him to message states' rights ought to be fired. For a black man to evoke states' rights? It's unbelievable."

"It was a ham-handed attempt to try to say something nice about New York, since his views are still 'evolving,'" said Chad, who had called the White House to complain. "They did not think through the fact that it flew in the face of our case, and their own constitutional reading of DOMA that gays and lesbians deserve heightened scrutiny."

But as they made their way down Fifth Avenue toward Greenwich Village, the president was largely forgotten. An elderly lady in a straw boater hat handed out cups of water. Kids waved bubble wands. Chad, who badly wanted children of his own someday, peeked back at Ilaria.

"I just want to take her off the parade route and go hang out somewhere," he said.

Here and there, a reveler could be spotted in an outlandish outfit, but overall the crowd was much tamer than either Chad or Adam had expected.

"Maybe because marriage is a more serious thing to celebrate," Chad said.

"Or, now that we can get married, we're boring!" Adam replied.

Chad smiled. Seven months earlier, he had begun dating Jerome Fallon, a corporate sales manager at Anthem Blue Cross. Jerome was a six-foot-six-inch gentle giant, kind, as calm as Chad was high-strung, and cute to boot. For the first time, Chad was planning to bring someone he was dating back home to Arkansas, and to his twentieth high school reunion at that. Fishing out his iPhone, Chad sent him a text and some photos of the celebration. Then he turned back to Adam.

"I wonder what the parade will look like when we win the case?"

TWENTY-EIGHT

SOME "GRIST FOR JUSTICE KENNEDY"

C had was working on four hours of sleep when he arrived at Gibson Dunn's Los Angeles office at 7:45 A.M. on Wednesday, February 8, 2012. More than a year after the case had been argued in the Ninth Circuit, the three-judge panel was at long last about to hand down its decision. Joining the plaintiffs in a conference room, Chad read the statement he would deliver in the event of a win.

"Should I read the losing one?" he asked.

"*No!*" Paul and Jeff shouted at once.

But in truth, they were all feeling confident, and relieved that the case finally seemed to be on the move again.

"I slept like a baby last night," Sandy said.

In November, a unanimous California Supreme Court had finally issued the standing-related decision that everyone had been waiting on. The court found that as a matter of California law, it was essential to the integrity of the initiative process that proponents like Cooper's clients be allowed to assert the state's interest in defending a ballot measure when public officials refused to do so. The decision was not unexpected, given the tenor of the arguments, and in fact was welcomed by the plaintiffs and their legal team, even though it seemed to foreclose any possibility that they could win on a technicality; as a general rule, federal courts defer to state courts on questions of state law.

As Kris and Sandy explained to their boys, "bad news is good news," because only if Cooper's clients had standing to appeal would the Supreme Court be able to settle the question of whether gays and lesbians had a right to marry by ruling on the constitutionality of Proposition 8 and bans like it. Olson compared the outcome to the folkloric strategy employed by the fabled Brer Rabbit to avoid being killed by a fox.

"He said, 'Eat me if you want, but please, please don't throw me in the briar patch.' And as a result of the importuning they threw him in the briar patch, and the rabbit easily escaped. That was exactly what the rabbit wanted. And in a way, this is exactly where we want to be. We now have an opportunity to change the law of the land, which is what we said we wanted to do."

The California Supreme Court decision should have cleared the way for an immediate ruling by the Ninth Circuit, but Cooper had thrown a wrench into the works. Rather than rule on whether Judge Walker had reached the correct legal decision in the case, he had asked the appeals court to throw Walker's opinion out altogether, a ploy that if successful would land everyone back at square one.

Cooper had been under pressure to make Walker's sexuality an issue ever since the judge was outed in the *San Francisco Chronicle,* but he was not given to quixotic gestures, and a judge is presumed under the law to be impartial. But an interview that Walker gave after announcing his retirement from the bench gave him an opening. In it, the judge had talked openly about his longtime partner. Cooper filed a motion arguing that while the fact that the judge was gay was not disqualifying, the fact that he was in a long-term relationship with a man potentially was, and should have at least been disclosed.

Even observers who disagreed with Walker's ruling striking down Prop 8 had criticized the attack on the judge's impartiality: bordering on "frivolous," Richard Painter, a law professor who served as chief White House ethics lawyer under President George W. Bush, told the *Los Angeles Times.*

Judge James Ware, who had been appointed to the bench by the first President Bush and had replaced Walker as chief judge of the Northern District of California, had dismissed the claim. Not only had Cooper failed to produce any evidence that Walker in fact wanted to marry and therefore had an improper interest in the outcome of the case, Ware wrote, but simply because a judge might be affected by a ruling in the same way as other members of the public is not a basis for recusal or disqualification. Forcing judges to disclose irrelevant, intimate details about their future intentions would set a dangerous precedent, he said. Should female judges of childbearing age, for instance, be required to recuse themselves from a case involving abortion, or disclose whether they might in the future someday want to have a child?

"The mere fact that a judge is in a relationship with another person—whether of the same sex or the opposite sex—does not ipso facto imply that the judge must be so interested in marrying that person that he would be unable to exhibit the impartiality which, it is presumed, all federal judges maintain."

Undeterred, Cooper had appealed. That had resulted in yet another round of arguments before the Ninth Circuit panel in December, frustrating both Olson and Chad. Time, both felt, was Cooper's friend, not theirs. They wanted to beat the DOMA cases to the Supreme Court. And, by both Chad and Mehlman's assessment, there was only a fifty-fifty chance that Obama would be reelected.

What if one of the liberals on the Supreme Court retired or died? At age seventy-eight, Justice Ginsburg had twice been diagnosed with cancer. A replacement named by a Republican president could tip the balance against them, Chad worried. What if, instead of acting too soon, as their critics contended, they had waited until too late?

Living with the extended uncertainty had also worn on the plaintiffs. Paul, worried that the case was starting to define him, was trying to force himself to stop posting case-related news on his Facebook page. Jeff kept thinking about the children he and Paul wanted so badly, once the case was decided. Adopting or finding a surrogate does not happen overnight, and he could not help but do the math. He was thirty-eight; in the best-case scenario, he would be forty by the time they had a child, meaning he would be fifty-eight by the time their son or daughter graduated from high school.

Kris had started to give up hope that she and Sandy would be able to marry before the twins, now sixteen, reached adulthood. Spencer and Elliott had shot up inches since the beginning of the case, and planned for the first time to take part in the postdecision press conferences, along with Jeff's dad. Elliott did his advanced placement environmental homework in one corner of the conference room, while Spencer showed Adam the remarks he had written the night before.

"I'm here today because I have a chemistry test and I don't want to take it," Sandy joked.

Chris Dusseault and Theane Evangelis were on hand in the conference room with the plaintiffs to explain the opinion. Olson and Boutrous were downstairs, waiting for it to come in. Terry Stewart was in San Francisco, in her office at City Hall. Boies was in New York, receiving an award from the American Friends of Hebrew University.

At 9:40 A.M., Lance Black joined the plaintiffs in the conference room. He was pale and drained. His oldest brother Marcus had recently died, eight weeks after receiving a diagnosis of bone cancer. Marcus had always been his protector growing up, but he was too weak to walk by the time Black arrived in Michigan to drive him to their mother's home in Virginia for Christmas.

"A lot of nervous people," Black observed.

"So, we lost," Chad deadpanned, "but we're going to appeal."

Black stopped short, a horrified expression on his face. "Is that true?"

Everyone burst out laughing.

"That was so horrible!"

Then the group dialed in to the AFER office, where several new members of the recently expanded war room team were stationed that day, and waited.

"Here we go!" Chad said, as the opinion popped into his in-box.

Silence.

"It's not letting me open it."

"Reinhardt wrote the opinion," someone back at AFER could be heard saying over the speakerphone.

"Looks narrow," Evangelis said, reading portions aloud.

"'Whether under the Constitution same-sex couples may *ever* be denied the right to marry, a right that has long been enjoyed by opposite-sex couples, is an important and highly controversial question. It is currently a matter of great debate in our nation, and an issue over which people of good will may disagree, sometimes strongly. . . . We need not and do not answer the broader questions in this case.'"

Kris clasped her hands together. Spencer cracked his knuckles. The two lawyers scrolled through the opinion as fast as they could. The panel was unanimous in rejecting Cooper's attack on Judge Walker's impartiality, and in finding that his clients did have standing to appeal. And by a two-to-one vote, with Judge Smith writing a tepid dissent, the panel declared that Proposition 8 violated the Constitution's equal protection clause.

Writing for the majority, Reinhardt laced his opinion with the narrower arguments that Terry Stewart had made in the separate brief she had filed with the court. As she had urged, he adopted a rationale that limited the impact of the ruling to California, striking down Proposition 8 while leaving intact, for the time being, bans in the other states covered by the Ninth Circuit. It was irrational to deny gays and lesbians the right to call their unions marriage, Reinhardt found, but leave in place laws and policies that make those unions the functional equivalent in all but name, as California had done. He also quoted repeatedly from Justice Kennedy's opinion in the *Romer* case, holding that, like the voter initiative at issue in that case, Proposition 8 had the peculiar property of "withdrawing from homosexuals, but no others" an existing legal right that had been broadly available. Withdrawing a right from a disfavored group is different than declining to extend it in the first place, he wrote. "The Constitution simply does not allow for laws of this sort."

Proposition 8, however, would remain in effect for the time being; until Cooper had exhausted his appeals, gays and lesbians would not be allowed to marry.

In San Francisco, Terry Stewart breathed a sigh of relief. Now they had options. Reinhardt had written an opinion that, just maybe, the Supreme Court would let lie. Spencer and Elliott grabbed Kris, and Paul and Jeff hugged each other.

"All right guys, it's a win!" Chad said.

———

"Yeah, baby!" Rob Reiner rejoiced.

He and Michele had just joined Olson and Chad in Ted Boutrous's office. Kristina, who had gotten word over the internal White House news alert, e-mailed Chad: "OMG!!!!" "Congratulations, AFER Family," wrote Bruce

Cohen, who was home with the baby's first cold. "Following everything from Ilaria's room." "Thank you Sandy, Kris, Paul and Jeff for your commitment and willingness to lead history toward justice," Mehlman wrote in.

Everyone was bumping fists as the television in the corner of Boutrous's office tuned to MSNBC offered instant analysis. The team, Boutrous said, was going to get questions about the narrowness of the opinion, and they needed to be careful not to downplay what was still a landmark ruling: For the first time, a U.S. court of appeals had found a law banning gays and lesbians from marrying unconstitutional.

"It's no small thing," Boutrous said.

"Absolutely," Olson said. "Take that hard line. It's true, and we will take it."

"Here's a good line," Boutrous said, reading from the part of the opinion in which Judge Reinhardt outlined the social significance of marriage, quoting everyone from the legendary crooner Frank Sinatra to Shakespeare. "'A rose by any other name may smell as sweet, but to the couple desiring to enter into a committed lifelong relationship, a marriage by the name of "registered domestic partnership" does not.'"

"That's great," Olson said.

"I'm liking the tone of this a lot," Boutrous replied.

While it was true that Reinhardt had skirted the question of whether Proposition 8 targeted a suspect class or infringed upon a fundamental right and instead decided the case using the rational basis standard, the language was actually fairly sweeping in its rejection of the justifications put forth by the proponents of Proposition 8 and bans like it.

The opinion rejected as "implausible" the notion that denying two men or two women the right to marry could somehow bolster the stability of families headed by one man and one woman. It found Cooper's claim that Proposition 8 expressed the voters' reasonable desire to proceed with caution unconnected to reality, given that it was enacted after eighteen thousand couples had already married and that it imposed a permanent ban on same-sex marriage rather than a time-specific one. It rejected the notion that the initiative was designed to promote responsible procreation, or child rearing by biological parents, or ensure that parents controlled what their children learned in school.

"Proposition 8 is so far removed from these particular justifications that we find it impossible to credit them," the panel's majority found. "All that

Proposition 8 accomplished was to take away from same-sex couples the right to be granted marriage licenses and thus legally to use the designation of 'marriage,' which symbolizes state legitimization and societal recognition of their committed relationships. Proposition 8 serves no purpose, and has no effect, other than to lessen the status and dignity of gays and lesbians in California, and to officially reclassify their relationships and families as inferior to those of opposite-sex couples."

"Boy, this is, this is grist for Justice Kennedy," Olson said. "Feeding right into it."

Boutrous lit up. "We're liking that."

"There's no 'fuck you to Ted and Chad' on behalf of the ACLU?" Chad interjected, a joking reference to that long-ago lunch with Judge Reinhardt's wife, who had since stepped down as the organization's Northern California executive director, and other advocates.

"Not as of page 41," Olson said, and everyone dissolved in laughter.

"All right, we'll be upstairs," Chad said, taking the Reiners with him to find the plaintiffs. "Everyone is so excited."

"It's really strong," Boutrous told Olson, now that they were alone.

"Yeah, but I don't like the 'we don't decide whether they have a fundamental right to marry,'" Olson said. "I wish they did."

―――

That evening, the decision led the news on all three national networks. At the press conference in San Francisco, Spencer said that the ruling meant that "in the eyes of the government, my family is finally normal."

Listening, Enrique Monagas became emotional, thinking about his own family. Jason had been watching some of the news reports about the case with their daughter, Elisa, now four. When Enrique had explained that he'd been working so hard to make sure that everyone could get married, just like he and Jason, her reply had stunned him. "But you can't be married," she had said. "Men can't be married to men."

"So she'd been listening to news reports but not the ones I wanted her to hear. We had to explain. She grew up in a family where we are telling her the other story, but it's amazing how she'd been indoctrinated."

Judge Reinhardt, he would later say, obviously wanted to try to stop the case from going to the Supreme Court. He understood the judge's logic, just as he understood that it was odd to urge the Supreme Court, as Olson had done during a call with national reporters immediately following the Ninth Circuit's ruling, to review a decision they had just won. (Terry Stewart, listening, said that "the idea that the Supreme Court would now rule more broadly in our favor is crazy. Ted's been smoking something—they are not going to shove marriage equality down the throats of 44 states.")

But for Monagas, that one moment with his little girl had reminded him why it was so important that the justices put their stamp of approval on families like his.

"I want an opinion now," he said. "Are we equal, or not?"

At the White House, spokesman Jay Carney refused to comment. Out on the campaign trail, Mitt Romney, the front-runner in a four-way Republican presidential primary, declared that "unelected judges cast aside the will of the people of California." On CNN, Jeff issued an invitation to Romney and the rest of the Republican candidates running for president: "Come to my house. Sit down with me. Sit down and have dinner with me. Let's have a conversation. Look at my loving home."

And when Chad arrived home to his, he found Jerome had decorated the outside with red, white, and blue balloons and AFER's never-ending supply of American flags. Inside, he was waiting with cupcakes and champagne.

TWENTY-NINE

8

Rob Reiner stood before a bank of camera monitors as his all-star cast filed into the Wilshire Ebell Theatre in Los Angeles. It was Saturday morning, March 3, and later that night, *8*, the play about the trial, would have its West Coast premiere.

Brad Pitt, who was playing Judge Walker, chatted with pal George Clooney, cast as David Boies. The actor Martin Sheen, who Rob joked had been "arrested more times than a crack dealer" for his environmental activism, quizzed the movie director about where the case stood as he prepared for his role as Olson.

The excitement that their case finally seemed to be headed for the Supreme Court had been short-lived. Rather than filing a certiorari, or "cert," petition asking the justices to review the decision, Cooper instead had asked that the case first be reheard by a different, and larger, panel of Ninth Circuit judges, in what is known as an *en banc*—French for a "full bench"—review. The court was under no obligation to grant his request that it sit en banc to decide whether the three-judge panel led by Reinhardt had erred. And given the ideological makeup of the court, success was unlikely; it would take thirteen of the Ninth Circuit's twenty-five active judges to grant his request.

But Cooper had once again succeeded in stopping the case in its tracks. The Ninth Circuit judges could take as long as they liked in responding to his request for an en banc review, meaning that it was now all but certain that there was no way Proposition 8 could reach the Supreme Court before the November presidential election.

Kevin Bacon, playing Chuck Cooper, and Jamie Lee Curtis, cast as Sandy, studied the binder on their laps as Jesse Tyler Ferguson, of ABC's Emmy Award–winning sitcom *Modern Family*, and three members of the cast of Fox's hit musical comedy *Glee* took their seats onstage.

Most big-budget thrillers could not boast this kind of star power, and all the actors were volunteering their time. Rob thanked them profusely. It took a long time for the *Brown v. Board of Education* case to fully integrate the schools, he said, and it would take some time before gays and lesbians throughout the country would be free to marry. "But we are fortunate enough to be in the world of what George Bush called the 'Internets,'" he said. "We are hitting critical mass. . . . You all are part of doing something that will move the ball down the field and win this game."

The performance was a staged reading, meaning that the actors did not have to memorize their lines, but Rob wanted to make sure it came off without a hitch. The play had debuted on Broadway to a sold-out audience that included media elites like *The View*'s Barbara Walters and NBC anchor Brian Williams, and even the National Organization for Marriage's Maggie Gallagher had bought a ticket; her character makes a cameo appearance. But tonight's performance would be live-streamed by YouTube, which had been slotted to broadcast the actual trial before the Supreme Court killed that plan. With the potential to reach a worldwide audience, Rob had ceded his Broadway role as Cooper's star witness to direct.

"When Brad comes in," he instructed, "everyone stand, everyone stand."

Pitt looked down from his stage bench with mock judicial imperiousness, leading Clooney to wisecrack, "Man, oh man." Everyone laughed, before settling in to go over their lines.

Pitt could not manage to keep Walker's straight face as Clooney cross-examined a bumbling Blankenhorn, now played by John C. Reilly, who had starred in Academy Award–winning films like Martin Scorsese's *Gangs of New York* and Stephen Daldry's *The Hours*. *Glee*'s Jane Lynch played Maggie Gallagher as a gay-marriage-hating Sue Sylvester, the fictional high school cheerleading coach and comic villainess she portrays on the show who terrorizes the misfits of the William McKinley High glee club.

Chad quietly slipped in to watch the rehearsal, after an overwhelming forty-eight hours that had resulted in huge news: He had just been named the next president of the Human Rights Campaign, the gay civil rights equivalent of the NAACP.

Chad's unique ability to leverage the legal proceedings into front-page headlines and sustain the often episodic attention span of the mainstream national media, coupled with the twin victories in Judge Walker's courtroom and the Ninth Circuit, had gone a long way toward bringing the establishment gay rights community around. A number of groups were starting to borrow from Chad's bipartisan playbook. Evan Wolfson's group, Freedom to Marry, had recently hired a Republican lobbyist, and Wolfson had been magnanimous in congratulating Chad on a call of gay rights leaders after the Ninth Circuit win. Lambda Legal was about to file its own federal lawsuit, challenging Nevada's ban on same-sex marriage and citing the Ninth Circuit's decision in the Proposition 8 case. "Prop 8" was the most searched term on Google the day following the appeals court ruling.

"They turned that trial into a truth commission," said Mary Bonauto, the lawyer who filed the initial DOMA challenge.

Still, the out-of-the-box offer had come as a shock. Its genesis had been a Washington cocktail party conversation between Kristina and Hilary Rosen, who had served on the board of the Human Rights Campaign and remained a large donor. Rosen felt that that the organization needed a media-savvy tactician to lead it, someone with a bold vision who could take advantage of the moment. The current president was about to step down. Would Chad be interested? Kristina called him that night.

"No way," he'd exclaimed, giving her a litany of reasons why. But the more he thought about it, the more excited he became. No longer would he have to juggle paying clients with his work on behalf of the gay community. He could devote himself to it full-time. After talking it over with Rosen—"Mark my words: this is your path," she recalled telling him—he had thrown his hat in the ring.

The final interview with the board had taken place the previous day. He was asked to step outside the room, and when he returned, everyone had started applauding.

It represented a full-circle moment, a validation by the very community that had once rejected what it considered his rash call to action. He was not due to start until June, and once he did, he would stay on the board of AFER and continue to be involved in strategic decisions. But now he would be able to guide the movement from the inside, with an annual budget of more than $40 million and a full-time staff of more than 150 people.

"He just got the most important job," Rob gushed to the cast. "He's got huge balls, huge balls! He's going to light a fire under those old people there."

Next to Reiner, Lance Black was furiously doing one last read-through of the script, looking for cuts in the hope of getting the run time down to ninety minutes.

The gay rights movement had long suffered because of its invisibility; people did not know that their homophobia was hurting people they actually knew. The movement had come as far as it had in large part because people were willing to come out and make their stories known. So when their opponents had gone all the way to the Supreme Court to keep the plaintiffs' tale from the public, Black had taken it personally. He had written the play to make the invisible visible, and he wanted to be sure that people stuck with it to the end.

"Kevin," Rob said, interrupting Black's reverie. Bacon had just delivered Cooper's infamous "I don't know" line a little too matter-of-factly. "That was, like, the most incredible moment in the whole story, in the whole thing of the trial."

What was happening on that stage was not just art imitating life. It was a refraction of the history of a once cloaked movement now blossoming out in the open, and the catalyzing role that Hollywood and social media had played in that metamorphosis. Studios still did not green light many films about strong gay characters; *Brokeback Mountain* and *Milk* were the exceptions, not the rule, and both took years to get made. But television, with its eye on the younger demographic demanded by advertisers, had long led the way.

In the early 1990s, MTV's *The Real World* became the first reality show with gay story lines. A few years later, NBC's *Will & Grace* brought adorable, funny gay characters into people's homes, albeit in somewhat stereotypical and sexless fashion. These days, television catered to the millennials, a hyperconnected generation who had grown up with openly gay friends, anthems like Lady Gaga's "Born This Way," and a deeper embrace of diversity and difference than any that came before it.

Modern Family, featuring a divorced patriarch who marries a bombshell

Colombian, a realtor and his stay-at-home-wife, and two gay dads all hilari-
ously struggling to raise their kids, became the most watched comedy on television not in spite of those story lines, but in large part because of them. Enough
Americans had taken on board and metabolized the idea that today's families
come in many different forms to make the show not just a critical but a commercial success.

Glee's multicultural, well-off and poor, gay, bisexual, and straight cast of
show-tune-singing misfits averaged close to nine million viewers per episode.
The show, with its nuanced story lines about everything from first love, teen
pregnancy, and a father coming to terms with his gay son, was influential with
teens because it offered an authentically hip window into their lives; songs performed on the show often instantaneously became among the most down-
loaded on iTunes.

Onstage, actor Chris Colfer was playing Ryan Kendall, the young trial witness from Colorado whose mother forced him to attend "conversion therapy"
after she found out he was gay. If he had not stopped attending, "I probably
would have killed myself," Colfer, reading from the testimony, said. On *Glee*,
Colfer played Kurt Hummel, whose gay fictional character is temporarily
forced to leave school because of a bullying episode that creator Ryan Murphy
deliberately wrote into the show after the rash of gay teen suicides. And in real
life, Colfer kept a book on his coffee table of all the letters he had received from
teens telling him he had helped them come out.

"The one I remember the most was wrinkled, because you could tell that it
had been held so tightly," Colfer, himself gay, said during a break. "Up on that
stage, I feel like we are living a chapter in a history book."

Adam Umhoefer, who would take over the leadership of AFER once Chad
left, sat alone in one of the theater seats, watching the tableau. Growing up in
Wisconsin, and later attending the Jesuit Boston College, being gay was not
something that was discussed. How, he had often wondered, would his life
have been different, easier, if a show like *Glee* had been around?

His older brother had a hard time accepting Adam after he came out. A
former military intelligence officer who now worked as a civilian for the Defense Department, he had once told Adam that military unit cohesion would
suffer if gays were allowed to serve openly. Military guys aren't going to accept
someone like that living and working among them, he'd said.

"Like what, someone like me?" Adam had asked.

But even his brother watched *Glee* on occasion with his wife, and Adam credited the show with helping to bring him around. On a recent visit to see his new nephew, Adam had been struck by just how far his brother had moved, and how much he wanted Adam to be part of his son's life. It was nice to feel close again, to see how the work he had been doing to move the country was playing out in his own life.

Not so long ago, Adam had been that high school theater kid. Now he was one of the coproducers of a show starring some of the biggest names in the business. It had been his idea to live-stream the sold-out production. The play was the hottest ticket in town, with seats snapped up by the likes of Barbra Streisand; director Steven Spielberg and his wife; media executive Barry Diller; film producer Jeffrey Katzenberg; A-list actresses like Olivia Wilde; and the town's top talent agents and casting directors. Camera crews and paparazzi from mass market gossip outlets like *Access Hollywood*, *Us* magazine, and *Extra* would be lined up to shoot the plaintiffs and the stars as they walked the red carpet.

When the curtain rose, with Brad Pitt playing a bemused Judge Walker, a gospel choir would not be playing "God Bless America." But otherwise, it would be pretty close to Adam's dream, the one that had prefaced their huge trial win.

THIRTY

OBAMA "COMES OUT"

C had almost didn't ask the question. A little over a month had passed since the West Coast premier of *8*, and he was cohosting a small gathering for Vice President Joe Biden at the Los Angeles home of HBO executive Michael Lombardo and his husband, architect Sonny Ward. Chad was working hard to reelect President Obama—he was one of his top fundraisers—but he had given up hope that the president would embrace marriage equality before the November election.

The previous year, Chad had attended a high-dollar fund-raiser for the president at the St. Regis Hotel. "How can we help you evolve more quickly?" he had asked the president. Obama's answer—that Chad ought to be able to tell from the actions he had taken on DOMA and Don't Ask, Don't Tell the direction he was headed—was heartening in substance but noncommittal in terms of timing.

"The sense I got from him was, 'Give me credit—look what I already have done,'" Chad said afterward.

Three events had cemented that impression. The first was a private conversation Chad had with First Lady Michelle Obama during a Los Angeles fundraiser he cohosted for the campaign in June 2011. Reporting back to the AFER team afterward, he said the first lady's message was clear: "Hang in there with us, and we'll be with you after the election." Days later, White House communications director Dan Pfeiffer, Chad's close friend, was asked about the president's stated support for same-sex marriage on that old 1996 questionnaire from back in the days when Obama was just an unknown state senate candidate. Pfeiffer first claimed it had been filled out by someone else, then, after it was pointed out that Obama had signed it, claimed Obama was "really referring to civil unions." And then there was the president's tepid states' rights response to the passage of same-sex marriage in New York that same month.

More recently, as incoming president of the largest gay rights organization in the country, Chad had been invited to a White House State Dinner. He and Jerome had been seated at the president's table, along with the guest of honor, British prime minister David Cameron, a conservative leading the push to legalize same-sex marriage in Britain. There were still places in the world where being gay was a crime, punishable by up to life in prison or even death by public stoning. Still, nine countries, including deeply Catholic nations like Argentina and Portugal, now recognized same-sex marriages, as did parts of Brazil and Mexico City, and Chad had talked to both leaders about the growing trend. But there was little to indicate that Obama was ready to take such a bold step here at home.

Why ask the vice president about the administration's position on marriage equality, Chad thought as he sat waiting for Biden to address the group he had gathered together at Lombardo and Ward's home in Los Angeles, when he already knew the answer? Instead, he planned to press Biden on why the administration was refusing to take a far less controversial step: Just days before the event, the White House had infuriated gay rights activists with an announcement that while the president continued to support stalled legislation that would prohibit employment discrimination based on sexual orientation, he would not be signing an executive order banning federal contractors from engaging in it.

But as Chad watched the hosts' two children, ages four and seven, press flowers and a note into Biden's hand, he changed his mind. They were sitting in the home of two married men, with their children. The vice president should have to answer to them. When it was Chad's turn to speak, he decided to make it personal.

"When you came in tonight, you met Michael and Sonny, and their two beautiful kids that they're the married parents of. And I wonder if you can just sort of talk in a frank, honest way about your own personal views as it relates to equality, but specifically as it relates to marriage equality."

It was clear from Biden's body language that the question made him uncomfortable. His public position was no different than the president's. As a senator, he had voted for DOMA. As a presidential candidate, he said he supported civil unions. And as vice president, he had studiously towed the administration's evolving line, except to note that that there was a growing national consensus that made same-sex marriage inevitable.

The vice president stood up and flipped his barstool around, so that the back was between him and the rest of the guests, then straddled it. He looked almost pained, Chad would later remark to Lance Black, who was standing next to him.

"I look at those two beautiful kids—as a matter of fact, your daughter said, 'Can we go out and play? Can you come outside with me?' They're the only good thing in the whole world," Biden began. "I wish everybody could see this. All you got to do is look in the eyes of those kids. And no one can wonder, no one can wonder whether or not they are cared for and nurtured and loved and reinforced. And folks, what's happening is, everybody is beginning to see it.

"Think about how much has changed. And think about what you guys—and one of you in particular—did," Biden continued, referencing Chad and the case. "Things are changing so rapidly, it's going to become a political liability in the near term for an individual to say, 'I oppose gay marriage.' Mark my words."

Having started down this road, he seemed incapable of stopping. People his kids' age could not understand why gays and lesbians should not be allowed to marry, he said. "'I mean, what's the problem, Dad?'

"And my job—our job—is to keep this momentum rolling to the inevitable."

The answer stunned everyone in the room, even top aides who were used to the gaffe-prone vice president's habit of going off script.

"He'd been answering that question the same way for years," said one. "But being in that house, seeing that couple with their kids, the switch flipped. It was like his hard drive got erased."

===

Sitting in his West Wing office more than a year and a half later, the vice president said he could still picture that moment "like it was ten minutes ago."

"It was one of the most poignant questions I had ever been asked in my life," Biden said. "The only other time—it ranks up there when this little girl in Afghanistan was looking at me about two weeks after the Taliban fell, and I was in Kabul, and she looked at me with those beautiful hazel eyes. And she said—I said, 'Well, I have to leave now,' and she said, 'You can't. You can't. America can't leave. I want to be a doctor.'

"He was standing against the wall behind the couch after I had answered all these questions with the gay leaders from the Los Angeles area, and he just looked at me and, like my mom would say, out of the mouths of babes comes gems of wisdom—it was the most innocent. He said, 'Well, let me just ask you, Mr. Vice President. What do you think of us?' And that comes—'What do you think of us?' And it was like wow, whoa."

Biden thought back to a summer afternoon when he was in his twenties. He was sitting on the beach with his dad and some friends when an older gay couple walked over to say hello. His father, a realtor, had sold them their penthouse apartment. The elder Biden got up, gave them both a hug, and said, "Let me introduce you to my family." One of his buddies made a derogatory remark about the couple, and his father's reaction to it had stayed with him always.

"He says, 'As soon as they get in the apartment, you go up to the ninth floor. You walk up and knock on the door, and you apologize to them,'" the vice president recalled. When his friend refused, his father said, "Well, goddamn it, you're not welcome in my house anymore."

And he thought about another day, years later, when his own son had looked up at him quizzically after seeing two men headed off to work kiss each other goodbye on a busy street corner. "I said, 'They love each other, honey,' and that was it. So it was never anything that was a struggle in my mind."

The truth was that, other than being concerned as a Catholic that churches not be forced to perform ceremonies for same-sex couples, "I didn't see a problem with it," and never had: "It wasn't like I had an epiphany, as we Catholics say, one day, 'Oh my God, I guess there should be gay marriage.'" So when Chad asked the question the way he did, in the privacy of that home in Los Angeles, Biden decided to go ahead and say what he actually thought.

The encounter was still fresh in the vice president's mind when David Gregory, the host of the Sunday talk show *Meet the Press,* asked him during a pretaped interview fifteen days later on Friday, May 4, whether his own views on gay marriage had evolved. Biden talked about the couple he had just met in Los Angeles and, without mentioning Chad's name, the question he had been asked, and then he gave pretty much the same answer.

"What this is all about is a simple proposition," he told Gregory. "Who do you love? Who do you love, and will you be loyal to the person you love? And that's what people are finding out is what all marriages at their root are about. Whether they're marriage is of lesbians or gay men or heterosexuals."

"Are you comfortable with same-sex marriage now?" Gregory pressed.

"I, I—look. I am vice president of the United States. The president sets the policy. I am absolutely comfortable with the fact that men marrying men, women marrying women, and heterosexual men and women marrying one another are entitled to the same exact rights, all the civil rights, all the civil liberties."

Only this time, Biden was not speaking at a private event, closed to the press. The interview, which took place on a Friday, was embargoed, but that Sunday it would be broadcast to the nation.

"I think you may have just gotten in front of the president on gay marriage," his communications director, Shailagh Murray, told him on the limo ride back from the studio.

━━━

Several months before his vice president spoke his mind, the president had gathered together his senior advisers. With a push by progressives to add marriage equality to the Democratic Party platform, the issue was not going away. If asked again for his position, the president said, he wanted to answer honestly.

"For as long as I've known him, he has never been comfortable with his position on this," said David Axelrod, one of Obama's closest and longest-serving aides and a senior campaign strategist for the reelection campaign. "The politics of authenticity, not just the politics, but his own sense of authenticity, required that he finally step forward. And the president understood that."

Obama's opposition to same-sex marriage had always stretched credulity, and Pfeiffer's acrobatics over that old 1996 questionnaire the previous June had caused eye rolling even inside the White House. Since then, it had become increasingly clear to the president and his team that maintaining the "evolving," "grappling," "struggling" status quo had a real downside as he headed into the final lap of the presidential election.

Internal campaign polling showed that same-sex marriage was a touchstone issue for likely Obama voters under the age of thirty, right up there with climate change. The campaign needed those voters to turn out in the record numbers they had four years earlier, a difficult enough task in an economy where many were having difficulty finding jobs, and Obama's refusal to say he favored allowing gays and lesbians to wed was one of the biggest impediments.

But Obama's aides did not want the president answering a random question off the cuff. If he was going to endorse same-sex marriage before the election, it needed to be done right, at a time of his choosing, using language designed to minimize any political fallout.

David Plouffe, a senior adviser to the president and the manager of his 2008 campaign, reached out to AFER's Ken Mehlman for some across-the-aisle advice. Mehlman had offered his assistance earlier in the year, when Obama had invited him to lunch after the repeal of Don't Ask, Don't Tell. Obama and Mehlman had attended Harvard Law School together, and over salmon and a salad in the dining room just off the Oval Office, they had talked at length about the politics of same-sex marriage.

Mehlman strongly believed that the way voters perceive a candidate's character is more important than where a candidate stands on issues. In 2004, he told Obama, President Bush ran a simple, character-based campaign: You may not agree with me on everything, but you know where I stand. In 2008, Obama had been elected because people viewed him as an idealist who would put politics aside and do what was right. Coming out in favor of allowing gays and lesbians to wed, Mehlman told the president, would remind people why they had elected him by reinforcing those attributes. "The notion that politically this is going to kill you—I don't buy it," Mehlman recalled saying.

He believed that even more deeply now. Mehlman was launching a new venture called Project Right Side, aimed at showing Republicans that supporting same-sex marriage was not just good policy, but good politics. Mehlman had hired George W. Bush's former pollster and the microtargeting consulting firm he had used in the 2004 reelection to document a tectonic shift in public opinion that threatened to leave the GOP behind. It was not just that young people's overwhelming support for same-sex marriage made it inevitable. A

massive survey of five thousand Republican and Republican-leaning independent voters found that a majority actually supported some form of legal
recognition of gay relationships. Those in favor of calling that recognition
marriage, while still a minority, felt more strongly about the issue than those
opposed. Social issues like gay marriage simply were not a top priority for the
vast majority of Repbulicans heading into the 2012 elections, the data showed,
and the base was amenable to a conservative case for same-sex marriage that
did not require an abandonment of core conservative principles. An impressive
74 percent of those surveyed, for instance, believed government should stay out
of people's private lives, including the lives of gays and lesbians, while 53 percent agreed that "freedom means freedom for everybody, including gays and
lesbians, who should have the freedom to enter into relationships with each
other."

Mehlman's takeaway: "Republicans are ambivalent about this issue. They
may be for marriage amendments but they now have gay friends and relatives
and this is difficult for them. And I've not talked to a single Republican who
doesn't understand the long-term demographic issue."

Simultaneously, Mehlman was working with Chad and the rest of the
AFER war room team on tweaking the communication strategy around the
case. They had hired Democratic pollster Lisa Grove to help them incorporate
the core "dignity, liberty, and freedom" phrases the lawyers had pulled from
Justice Kennedy's opinions into a more multitasking message that would simultaneously appeal to the Supreme Court's swing voter and Americans still
on the fence.

AFER had done a good job, in Grove's view, of explaining why the plaintiffs
wanted to marry. Gay rights advocates used to talk about benefits like tax
write-offs and hospital visitation rights, but her polling showed that voters
were far more likely to support same-sex marriage when they understood that
gays and lesbians wanted to marry for the same reason straight couples did: to
commit to one another.

But she found the legal arguments AFER was making resonated more with
everyday voters when wrapped around a message that framed same-sex marriage as consistent with core American values. Saying that denying gays and
lesbians the right to marry "violates their constitutional rights" was not nearly
as effective as saying that singling out "one class of citizens because of a trait

that is fundamental to who they are is unfair, unlawful, and violates the basic principles of equality that are so important to who we are as a nation." One principle that Americans took to heart was the golden rule—treating others the way they wanted to be treated themselves. Referencing that, with its Judeo-Christian overtones, helped move people who felt torn between their desire to see people treated equally and their religious beliefs. Messaging built around what Mehlman liked to call "everyday heroes," like members of the military, was particularly effective, especially when it tapped into voters' antipathy toward government intrusion: "Are we really going to say to Americans who risk their lives for us that we are going to deny them something as fundamental as the right to marry the person they love?"

On November 10, 2011, Mehlman sent Plouffe an e-mail that drew upon everything they had learned so far, with detailed talking points for both the president (POTUS) and the first lady (FLOTUS):

> Suggested venue: Should come up as a question in a larger interview with both POTUS and FLOTUS together. Interviewer should be a woman.
>
> All 3 should be sitting. Soft lighting
>
> Overall messages:
>
> 1. Our family, like a lot of others, have talked about this and concluded it is wrong for the government to treat some of its citizens differently because of who they love.
>
> 2. We should be encouraging more people to make lifelong commitments to each other, particularly in challenging times like these.
>
> Possible language:
>
> I've said before that my position has been evolving, and Michelle and I have been having a similar conversation in our family that lots of American families have been having on marriage equality.
>
> I fully understand that some will agree, while others will disagree, with where our family has come down on this. Thankfully in America we can talk about these complex issues with civility, decency and respect.

I've been a proponent of civil unions. But as Michelle and I have been think-ing through what we teach Sasha and Malia about America's greatness and how we've constantly enlarged the circle and expanded freedom, we know [*sic*] longer feel we can make an exception that treats our gay friends differ-ently just because of who they love.

I've been told that being public about this might hurt me politically.

But one of the things I've really come to appreciate in the past 3 years is that, when you're President, you're President of all Americans. And all includes gays and lesbians—men and women who are serving across this country—firefighters, doctors, teachers, courageous soldiers who serve and protect the rest of us.

Many of them have made life-long commitments to people they love, just like Michelle and I have. And they should be treated the same by their gov-ernment. Michelle and I believe this doesn't threaten or change our mar-riage. It strengthens it.

We can do this while protecting religious liberty, because what we're talking about is civil marriage. It's really important that this doesn't change how any faith defines marriage in a religious way.

These tough economic times remind all Americans—regardless of their po-sition on this issue—that we should encourage life-long committed adults to look after each other, allow them to visit each other if they're in the hospital, care for each other when sick, and after a lifetime of hard work, share the fruits of their labor.

Happy to discuss

Ken

"Thanks for this," Plouffe immediately e-mailed back.

———

One of the cardinal rules of politics is that if an issue has the potential to cause problems for a candidate, it is best to deal with it well before the election so that the dust has time to settle. But weeks, and then months, went by with no presidential announcement.

"This was so past the sell-by date, yet there was still no real plan in place," said one senior administration official. "It just shows you how scared everyone was of this issue."

Inside the White House, the first lady and Valerie Jarrett urged the president to go with his gut. The Obamas had a number of gay friends, and though the White House had kept it quiet, the first lady had attended a wedding celebration for her hairdresser when he married his husband. The first lady felt strongly that her husband had the power to help change the conversation on marriage equality. And it was not lost on the president that his failure so far to do that was "a source of disappointment to people who otherwise appreciated him," Axelrod said.

This is consistent with who you are, Jarrett told Obama.

Mehlman and Lisa Grove, the Democratic pollster, continued to pass data along to the White House. By this time, national polls consistently showed that support for same-sex marriage exceeded opposition to it. A clear majority of Democrats favored allowing gays and lesbians to wed, putting the president at odds with his own base. Forty-eight companies, including Nike, Time Warner Cable, Aetna, and Xerox, had signed on to a legal brief arguing that DOMA negatively affected their businesses, and much of corporate America, from the CEO of Starbucks to the chairman of Goldman Sachs, had come down on the side of marriage equality.

In addition to all the Republican megadonors Mehlman had brought to the cause, the list of Republicans publicly supporting same-sex marriage now included former first lady Laura Bush, Steve Schmidt, who helped run Senator John McCain's race against Obama in 2008, McCain's wife and daughter, and Grover Norquist, an influential conservative activist best known for his ability to browbeat GOP candidates across the country into signing his no-new-taxes pledge, to name a few. Billionaire industrialist David Koch, whose bankrolling of conservative causes had made him one of the most influential men in the Republican Party, had privately told Olson that he too supported same-sex marriage, a position he would soon make public. Meanwhile, on the Democratic side, former president Clinton had publicly said that he had been "wrong" to oppose same-sex marriage. Clinton had then pushed for passage of the New York law legalizing it, saying that allowing gays and lesbians to wed was part of the nation's permanent mission "to form a more perfect union."

But Obama's campaign team remained wary. They feared that embracing same-sex marriage could splinter the coalition he needed to win a second term, depressing turnout among socially conservative African American and Latino voters and working-class Catholic whites. North Carolina, a battleground state Obama had won in 2008, appeared poised to pass a constitutional amendment banning both same-sex marriage and civil unions by wide margins in a special election in May.

"We understood that this would be galvanizing to some voters and be difficult with other voters," Jim Messina, who had left the White House to manage Obama's 2012 campaign, recalled. "My thing was, let's do it in a way that makes sense."

Mehlman talked to Plouffe again when he ran into him in April 2012 at OutGiving, the annual gathering of gay donors where Black had tested the waters for AFER three years earlier. In addition to the May special election in North Carolina, same-sex marriage was on the ballot in four states in November: Lawmakers in Washington and Maryland had voted to allow gays and lesbians to wed, twin legislative victories that voters were now being asked to ratify, voters in Maine would decide whether to reverse the ban there, and voters in Minnesota, where same-sex marriage was already prohibited by statute, would be asked whether to write a Prop 8–like ban into their constitution. Mehlman was working with groups in all four states to build Republican support, but he told Plouffe he worried that the president's silence would be used against them.

"Good point," he said Plouffe told him. "We need to deal with this."

And that was where things stood when Biden, Chad's question still ringing in his ears, gave the answer he did on *Meet the Press* on May 4, sending everyone into panic mode and forcing the president's hand.

———

In the immediate aftermath, media commentators would speculate that Biden's comments either constituted a trial balloon or were cleared by the

White House as a way to mollify the gay community without the president having to take a position. They were not privy to the chaos that erupted inside the West Wing after an e-mailed transcript of the interview landed in the in-box of the White House press team.

Jarrett, who had been hoping and pressing for a big presidential moment, was so furious she accused Biden through an intermediary of downright dis-loyalty. The president was often accused of "leading from behind," and this would play into that meme. Biden had launched his 2016 campaign—at the president's expense, other aides bitterly complained. Campaign officials were also agitated. As one White House official with direct knowledge put it, "They felt they already were vulnerable, and they had not fully resolved yet what they wanted to do."

The White House's early attempts at spin reflected that lack of resolution. Biden, in the interview from his West Wing office eighteen months later, said he fully meant to endorse marriage equality. As vice president, "I didn't go out volunteering a position, but when asked a question, I had to say, because I think it's the ultimate civil right of our day. I had to respond to it," he said.

But his comments were just elliptical enough that the White House's first response was to try to walk them back. "What VP said—that all married cou-ples should have exactly the same legal rights—is precisely POTUS's position," Axelrod tweeted on Sunday, May 6, the day Biden's interview aired. The vice president's office was told to put out a "clarification" echoing that sentiment: "The Vice President was expressing that he too is evolving on the issue," it said.

Though the statements were greeted with outright disbelief within the gay community, the entire episode nevertheless seemed "headed into the category of Joe Biden-isms, where the vice president accidently speaks the truth," said one top official, "but then [Education Secretary] Arne Duncan was asked on Monday for his position, and had to answer that he supported same-sex mar-riage. And then it was like, 'Oh, shit—they are going to ask every single cabinet member.'"

The president had to act, sooner rather than later. On Tuesday, the White House hastily offered *Good Morning America*'s Robin Roberts an exclusive sit-down the following day. She was a woman, as Mehlman had suggested, but as important she was African American, a community that the political team was particularly worried about, and the White House liked her conversational style.

Then everyone scrambled to get the president ready. Axelrod drafted the White House's in-house expert: Kristina, who was flourishing in her job as Michelle Obama's communications director. "Focus on the golden rule," she advised.

In explaining how his "evolution" had come full circle, Obama brought up Malia and Sasha, and how "it doesn't make sense to them" that the law treats same-sex parents of their friends differently than their own. As Mehlman had advised, Obama stressed the need to respect religious liberty—"What we're talking about are civil marriages"—but said that as a practicing Christian, his faith was rooted "not only [in] Christ sacrificing himself on our behalf, but it's also the golden rule." The president spoke about the "soldiers or airmen or marines or sailors who are out there fighting on my behalf, and yet feel constrained, even now that Don't Ask, Don't Tell is gone, because they're not able to commit themselves in a marriage." And he said that while he respected the views of those who disagreed with him, "I think it's important to say that in this country we've always been about fairness, and treating everybody as equals.

"I actually think that, you know, it's consistent with our best and in some cases our most conservative values, sort of the foundation of what made this country great."

"He was very much at peace once he did that interview," Axelrod said. "It was cathartic."

Some of the president's top advisers had urged him to take Biden to the woodshed, but he had refused to do it. One of the things the president liked best about Biden, according to Axelrod, was his "exuberant honesty." In his interview with Roberts, Obama said he was "probably" going to endorse same-sex marriage before the election. The vice president, he said, just "got out a little bit over his skis."

The first lady, relaying her conversation with her husband to several other White House officials, saw it as a blessing in disguise. You don't have to dance around this issue anymore, she told him over breakfast, before he left the residence that morning. Now you can speak from your heart.

"Enjoy this day," she said. "You are free."

ABC kept a tight lid on its exclusive, which the network planned to begin air-
ing in a special report Wednesday afternoon. But by the time Chad and Adam
woke up in California, rumors were already flying that the president was going
to make a major announcement that day. We need to be ready, Chad told Adam
before heading into the office.

The day before, the initiative to amend North Carolina's constitution had
passed. Frank Schubert, the consultant who had engineered Proposition 8's
passage, had run a campaign that pitted much of the state's religious establishment against gays and lesbians. One pastor sermonizing in favor of the ban had
even urged congregants to beat their effeminate children.

"Dads, the second you see your son dropping that limp wrist, you walk over
and crack that wrist," Sean Harris, senior pastor of Berean Baptist Church, said
in a sermon caught on videotape. "Man up. Give him a good punch. Okay? 'You
are not going to act like that. You were made by God to be a male and you are
going to be a male.'"

The video had gone viral, forcing the pastor to say he wished he had chosen
his words differently, but its exposure did little to alter the political landscape:
The amendment passed by a 22-point margin. Chad, who served as a media
adviser in the race and had enlisted former president Clinton to record a call
urging voters to reject the initiative, was demoralized. Once again, despite rising popular support for same-sex marriage and legislative success stories like
New York's, gays and lesbians had been crushed at the ballot box.

Now, North Carolina all but forgotten, he texted Kristina. Are the rumors
true?

Her reply electrified him. Confirmed, she wrote. But embargoed until 3 P.M.

Chad's next call was to Mehlman. The presidential endorsement would be
a watershed moment, one that would show just how far gays and lesbians had
come in their fight for equality. "How can we ring the bipartisan bell on this?"
Chad asked.

When Mehlman first came out, Mitt Romney had sent him a note. Romney,
now the presumptive Republican nominee, had praised his character, saying
that his love life was irrelevant. It had meant a lot to Mehlman, arriving at a

time when he was still uncertain how his Republican colleagues would react. Since then, he had shared his Project Right Side data with the all the leading Republican presidential campaigns, including Romney's, as well as the Republican congressional leadership. As he put it, "I'm not going to persuade all Republicans to come around, but if I can make them ambivalent, that's my goal."

With their candidate about to make the pivot into the general election, the party's leaders understand that it is not in their political interest to make a lot of noise about this, he assured Chad.

Chad next reached out to Olson. We need to get this into our next court filing, he said.

The rest of the day was a blur of press calls and appearances.

"If you are one of those who care about this issue you will not forget where you were when you saw the president deliver those remarks," Chad told the *New York Times* after the interview aired. "Regardless of how old you are, it's the first time you have ever seen a president of the United States look into a camera and say that a gay person should be treated equally under the law."

By the time Chad had wrapped up the day with an appearance on CNN's *Piers Morgan,* both he and Adam were exhausted. Arriving home, Adam sat down at his desk and began reading the coverage. Romney had declined to attack Obama, instead merely reiterating his own position: "My view is that marriage itself is a relationship between a man and a woman, and that's my own preference, I know other people have different views," he said. It was a far cry from the kind of red-meat rhetoric he had thrown out on the subject in the heat of the primaries.

"Today Obama did more than make a logical step. He let go of fear," wrote Andrew Sullivan, a prominent gay blogger. "That's the change we believed in."

Adam looked up at his bulletin board. Next to an OBAMA 08 pin in the shape of Montana, where Adam had worked as a field organizer, was a photograph of him standing next to the president. For months, he had been talking about how important it was to reelect Obama, even though he was totally wrong on the issue Adam cared most about. He had rationalized it by telling himself that as wrong as Obama was, Romney was worse. But in that moment, it hit him just what a bitter pill that had been to swallow. The president's symbolic step changed nothing, and yet, at a personal level, it changed everything.

"I realized I'd been totally lying to myself about how much it meant to me,"

Adam said. "It reminded me of being in the closet, when you are trying to reconcile things in your head that don't quite make sense. It's mostly the pretense, knowing there's this thing that's really important to you that you are shutting out or denying. Here we are, this supposedly rebel organization that people were saying had jumped the gun or moved too fast, and if I'm honest with myself, I was being too conservative. I thought, 'This is a smart campaign team,' and I thought, 'We just can't cost him the election.'"

He thought back to the 2011 White House Christmas party he had attended with Chad, and how the president had thanked him for the work he was doing. When Adam told the president he was looking forward to the next step in his evolution, the president had replied, "You just keep doing what you're doing."

Would Obama have done what he did if the polls still showed that the majority of the country opposed same-sex marriage, as they had at the outset of the case? Adam couldn't say, but he did know that it was a hell of a lot easier to embrace it now.

Sitting there in his pajamas, he began to get emotional. "Not teary," he later explained. "I was smiling. I felt proud. I was reminded that this is how you make things happen."

Chad, back at his own home, was feeling it too. He sent a text to Adam and Lance Black: "Shouldn't we be out celebrating?"

Adam changed into a pair of jeans and dug through his closet until he found his old OBAMA 08 T-shirt. He hesitated—too dorky?—then put it on.

"Let's go toast Barry!" he texted back.

Across the country, Chuck Cooper was feeling nearly as good. Because for all the hoopla surrounding the announcement, Obama had added a few important caveats that may have assuaged the concerns of his political team, but that would be featured prominently in briefs and decisions still to come.

THIRTY-ONE

CHAD AND THE CASE ENTER A NEW PHASE

Over the years, Chad had been to hundreds of events at the Reiners' home in Brentwood. He'd organized fund-raisers there for Bill and Hillary Clinton, Howard Dean, and Al Gore. But he had never before been the guest of honor, and as he mingled with the guests who had gathered in the candlelit courtyard on June 4 for his going-away party, he kept having to remind himself that he wasn't a staffer, responsible for everything from the temperature of the outdoor heaters to the care and feeding of donors.

The guest list was a mix of people old and new. Longtime supporters of the case like Norman Lear mingled with old friends of the Reiners: "Jerry and Janet Zucker, how are you?" Rob boomed in his New York accent, introducing the director and his wife to some of the young lawyers on the team. They had just gotten word that the Ninth Circuit would issue its decision on whether to rehear the case en banc, or leave the three-judge panel's ruling in place and allow the case to proceed to the Supreme Court.

Elsewhere, befitting Chad's new status, Human Rights Campaign board members socialized with supporters of the organization like talk show host Ellen DeGeneres's mom. Everyone was talking about Obama's endorsement of same-sex marriage a few weeks earlier. Since then, marriage equality for gays and lesbians had been endorsed by both the NAACP and the National Council of La Raza, the largest civil rights advocacy groups representing African Americans and Hispanics respectively, the two communities the president's advisers had most worried about. A *Washington Post*/ABC News poll found that 59 percent of African Americans now supported same-sex marriage, compared with 41 percent before Obama's announcement. It was proof that nothing leads like leading.

But the initial jubilation had worn off as people began to focus on a few lines in the president's interview that, while offering him political cover, presented a legal danger to the case. Once again, even as Obama personally endorsed the right of gays and lesbians to marry, he had hedged by framing it as a matter for the states to decide.

"What you're seeing is, I think, states working through this issue in fits and starts, all across the country," Obama had said. "And I think that's a healthy process and a healthy debate. And I continue to believe that this is an issue that is going to be worked out at the local level, because historically, this has not been a federal issue, what's recognized as a marriage."

Yeardley Smith, an actress best known as the voice of Lisa Simpson on Fox's animated sitcom *The Simpsons,* chatted with Kris and Sandy about how the cover of *Newsweek,* featuring an image of Obama with a rainbow halo over his head, had made her want to throw up. Smith was one of AFER's most generous straight allies—she had donated $1 million and had played one of the expert witnesses in the play *8.* She liked to joke that her donation to the marriage equality cause had cost her less than her two divorces and brought her more joy. Smith couldn't figure out why many of her gay friends weren't equally exercised.

How, she seethed, could the president have said such a thing? "I was so mad."

Kris tried to explain why she personally wasn't all that bothered. There was still something profoundly important about the president telling gay and lesbian kids, growing up in places like Bakersfield, California, where she had, that their love was equal. She had cried, sitting in her office, listening to the interview.

"He's a politician, himself controversial," she said, excusing him, "and he has to be careful navigating the divisions in this country."

"You have to give him kudos," Chad said, "but I thought, okay, if you're going to do it, go all the way."

The magnitude of Chad's new job had truly begun to sink in. He would be responsible for a portfolio that went well beyond the Proposition 8 case and marriage equality, representing the entire LGBT community. His role would entail taking on the Boy Scouts' ban on gay scouts and leaders, working in the corporate world to expand the number of companies that provided benefits to the partners of their gay and lesbian employees, and standing up for the transgendered community. He would oversee the funneling of millions of dollars into state and federal campaigns, and work with the White House, Congress, and state lawmakers on issues ranging from HIV/AIDS treatment to employment discrimination.

He was leaving AFER in safe hands with Adam. The two fund-raising productions of 8 had raised close to $3 million, and AFER now had nearly enough money on hand to fund its operations through 2014 and pay its mounting legal bills. Though Boies had quietly donated back everything he had been paid and then some, Olson had negotiated a more than 50 percent increase in Gibson Dunn's fees, to $5.6 million, citing the unexpected twists and turns in the case. That was still deeply discounted, but with donors increasingly directing that their money be used for purposes other than to pay for legal work that other attorneys would have done pro bono, the hike had caused some consternation on the board. The ticket sales from 8 could be used to pay off that debt.

More important, the plaintiffs' stories had been heard. Close to a quarter million people had viewed the day-of YouTube live stream of 8, and three-quarters of a million more had watched the taped version since. Three million had listened to an audio version of 8 on National Public Radio stations. It had been performed by community, university, and high school theater groups 186 times and counting. There were even plans for readings abroad, but at the urging of Mehlman, the team was currently focused on organizing productions in the four states where marriage would be on the ballot in November. The war room, thanks to a foundation grant, now had eight full-time staffers and consultants, and a fully realized social media machine, with 125,292 Facebook and nearly 14,890 Twitter followers, and celebrities like Hilary Duff retweeting case-related news to huge audiences. By contrast, ProtectMarriage.com's social media presence was virtually nonexistent, and the group's supporters had recently sent out a plea to donors for more money, saying legal costs had topped $12 million.

"When the Southern Poverty Law Center sued the KKK, the goal wasn't to win—it was to bankrupt them," Chad happily told his team after reading about the opposition's financial woes. "They're losing the case, spending money, and more states are coming into our column. In politics and in war, when you are on the defensive, you are losing."

That is not to say that there weren't huge challenges ahead at the Human Rights Campaign. Richard Socarides, President Clinton's former adviser on gay and lesbian issues and a friend of Chad's, summed them up this way: "Hiring Chad was like hiring the general of an opposing army. This was someone who refused to go along just because things had always been done in a certain way, who wasn't afraid to upend the status quo and take on powerful interests. But he still has a lot of enemies who are praising him now, but looking for an excuse to take him down."

Mehlman had plenty of advice, telling Chad that he needed to avoid becoming the master of a feckless bureaucracy, instead of its "kickass strategist." The organization needed to be more bipartisan, with less focus on influencing Washington and more on influencing society and changing the reality on the ground, he counseled. It needed to be more welcoming to people who changed their mind on same-sex marriage or other gay rights issues. But most of all, Mehlman advised, the organization needed to learn how to wield power. To that end, he had arranged for Chad to visit with Howard Kohr, the chief executive director of what he considered to be one of the most powerful and effective groups in Washington: AIPAC, the American Israel Public Affairs Committee.

"Obama did what politicians do, which is he followed the electorate," Mehlman said. "So don't say, 'It's brave that Obama came out in favor of marriage equality.' That's counterproductive. The point is it's good policy and good politics. The pro-Israel lobby and the National Rifle Association do not go around saying, 'Thank you, you're brave.' They say, 'Damn right—what you did is in your best interest.'"

Chad was excited, but it was hard to say goodbye to his old life. The Human Rights Campaign was headquartered in Washington, D.C. "Wait a minute— you're moving? This is sad," Michele Reiner had said when she learned the news. Now her husband grabbed a microphone. He was not about to let Chad move across the country without a proper send-off. Chad was standing next to Jerome, who had agreed to give up his job and move with him; he'd find another one, he said, with a serenity Chad marveled at. "Would you just stress out more?" Chad sometimes joked.

"I love Chad to death," Rob began. "I'm gonna say this now, and he's hearing it for the first time. If there ever is going to be—and there will be at some point—the first gay president, you're looking at him."

Chad grabbed Jerome's arm so hard that he looked down at him. "Stop pinching me," Jerome whispered.

"I don't know what else to do with all my emotions," Chad whispered back.

———

Chad arrived for his last day at the AFER office the following morning, wearing a hoodie over a pressed blue button-down. His office on Sunset Boulevard overlooking the famed Hollywood sign was bare. The photos of a far younger version of himself, sitting on Air Force One with President Clinton and looking very 1990s with more hair than he had now, had been packed away. So had his vintage "Fight Briggs" political poster; it came from a 1978 campaign in California, the first to beat back a proposed initiative to ban gays and lesbians from teaching in the state's public schools since Anita Bryant had started the national effort with her "Save the Children" campaign in Florida. His consulting business would be taken over by Felix Schein, a former journalist turned political consultant who had taken over for Kristina when she left.

Jerome was home, supervising the movers.

"I love you," Chad texted.

"Stay away!" Jerome wrote back.

Kris and Sandy were in the conference room, waiting for the Ninth Circuit's ruling on whether it would rehear the case en banc with Michele Reiner, Adam, and the expanded war room team. Jeff and Paul had to work, but Jeff was keeping in touch via Facebook. "Tick, tick, tick, tick," he wrote.

Rob was thinking about making a movie about the case, but if asked, Michele told Kris and Sandy, "Just say, 'who knows, blah-blah.'" It was exciting, and both could see the public education potential, but the prospect also made them a little nervous.

Things had been going well in the Perry-Stier household, with even Sandy's mom beginning to accept her relationship. When Sandy's dad had died, following a long bout with dementia, her mother had surprised her by listing Kris, along with the spouses of his other children, in the obit. And on a trip home to Iowa the previous Thanksgiving, her mother had opened up during a quiet moment in the kitchen.

"She said, 'I was listening to a talk show about gay marriage, and I think civil unions, that kind of makes sense because marriage is something that belongs in the church,'" Sandy recalled. "I said, 'But Mom, that's not the same. Anything that treats people differently is discrimination. Marriage doesn't have anything to do with religion. Think about water fountains in Georgia.' And she said, 'That makes sense.'"

But 8 had opened up some old wounds. Both women had been with other people before they were with each other. Kris's ex, Spencer and Elliott's other mom, Adria-Ann McMurray, had watched the play on YouTube. To keep it simple, she had been written out of the script, and both boys had been worried about how "AA," as they called her, would react. "I'd go into my own head and say, 'I wonder what AA would feel about this, how she'd feel watching this scene,'" Elliott recalled afterward. And she had been upset, especially when Sandy's character read her lines about bringing the twins to their first day in kindergarten, when in fact it had been her and Kris.

"She probably thought she did," Elliott told her, "but that's not really fair to you." "Well, that's okay," she'd said, but Elliott could tell it wasn't, not really.

Tom, Sandy's oldest boy, had gone to both the Broadway and Los Angeles productions of 8. He was twenty-three, handsome with an unruly surfer's mop of sun-bleached hair, and hoping to go to film school. Sandy thought he would enjoy mingling with the celebrities and watching how the play came together. And he had. But in New York, when the woman playing Sandy, reading her testimony during the dress rehearsal, said she had never loved anyone else before Kris, he had fled outside to the sidewalk.

"It just crushed me," he said afterward. "I was like, 'Fuck.' I started crying. That's a lie. That's a lie. And if it isn't a lie, it's even worse."

He and his younger brother, Frank, had never gotten along well with Kris. It wasn't because of the whole lesbian thing. Both had friends who were gay and believed that Cooper's arguments against allowing them to marry were, as Tom put it, "bogus." Theirs was the more mundane heartache of divorce. They were several years older than Spencer and Elliott, and had been going to Catholic school in Alameda when Kris and Sandy got together. Their dad, in a losing battle with his alcohol demons, had moved in with his parents, and they moved to Berkeley with their mom for high school.

"It was this dreamy family thing that was forced on us," Tom said. "So at the time that my brother and I most needed her attention, it was cut short. It was messed up."

Both had since moved past blaming their dad's death on the relationship. "Emotionally, he was totally abusive—he was drunk all the time," said Frank, his soft blue eyes a mirror of Sandy's. "I don't blame her for leaving."

But at the time, they had both been angry, sad, and deeply resentful of Kris's attempts to curb the rebellion that followed. Frank had hated the way that the *People* magazine made them all out to be some kind of modern-day Brady Bunch, when the reality was he spent much of his teen years in sullen escape, listening to punk music and hardcore metal and lifting weights.

"I said some awful things," he said. "If Kris makes my mom happy, that makes me happy, but . . ."

He trailed off.

"My mom was mine, and now she's Kris's."

"There's just a pile of human detritus," Sandy had said sadly, as they drove over to the Reiners' the night before.

―――――

Now, around the AFER conference table, everyone kept their eyes glued to their laptops, waiting to see if they would have to endure yet another round at the Ninth Circuit.

"Denial," Eric Kay, a newcomer to the team who handled research, suddenly announced.

Everyone started clapping. "Cool," Kris said, the relief evident in her voice. "Yes!"

"Wow," Chad said. "That's—that's amazing. Nice parting gift."

The vote denying the rehearing that Cooper had requested was 21–4. Diarmuid O'Scannlain, a deeply Catholic, conservative judge on the Ninth Circuit, had written the dissent. Kay began reading aloud. Obama's political hedge was featured front and center.

"A few weeks ago, subsequent to oral argument in this case, the President of the United States ignited a media firestorm by announcing that he supports same-sex marriage as a policy matter," O'Scannlain had written. "Drawing less attention, however, were his comments that the Constitution left this matter to the States and that 'one of the things that [he]'d like to see is that [the] conversation continue in a respectful way.' Today our court has silenced any such respectful conversation."

Kay asked if he should read on.

"No," Adam said firmly. "All we need to know is it's denied."

PROP 8 HEADED TO SUPREME COURT, read a sample headline. But Reinhardt and Hawkins had taken the unusual step of writing an opinion that concurred in the decision to deny Cooper's request for a rehearing, but practically begged the justices not to take the case. Kay, unable to help himself, began reading what Olson would later call Reinhardt's fit of "pique" aloud:

"We did not resolve the fundamental question that both sides asked us to; whether the Constitution prohibits the states from banning same-sex marriage. That question may be decided in the near future, but if so, it should be in some other case, at some other time."

Chad put his chin in his hand. Sandy frowned. Kris, who had been smiling just a moment before, hunched her shoulders forward and looked down at the table. No one said anything.

"Fuck Judge Reinhardt," one of the younger AFER staffers finally muttered, summing up what everyone was thinking.

———

Judge Walker would not have put it so colorfully. But he too was disappointed. He had known throughout the trial that it was only a matter of time before his sexual orientation became the subject of headlines. It had crossed his mind that it might have been better if the case had been assigned to a straight judge, because as he listened to the weight of the evidence, "it seemed pretty clear where this was headed."

"I thought, 'Your personal life is going to get in the way and that's not going to be helpful,'" he said.

In the end, he had wound up thinking that it was not such a bad idea to have a gay man try the case, for the same reason that it was not a bad idea for a woman to hear a sex discrimination case. But it had not been easy to sit silent during the multiple attacks on his impartiality. He had just returned to private practice as a mediator when Cooper filed his motion arguing that Walker's ruling that Proposition 8 was unconstitutional should be thrown out, or vacated, in legal terms, because he should have recused himself from the case or disclosed that he was in a long-term relationship. "Dirty pool" is how Walker characterized the move.

"You wonder what people are going to say at work. Not only is there a gay man in our midst, but one whose sexuality is being litigated. I was at the gym one day and a friend was reading the story about the motion to vacate my order. As I walked by, I thought, 'I wonder what's going through his mind?'"

He had stepped up and done what he though the law and the facts required. The Ninth Circuit's opinion was, to his way of thinking, "too clever by half," an assessment shared by not a few legal analysts. By holding that the many benefits California granted gays and lesbians made Proposition 8 particularly irrational, Reinhardt had created a perverse incentive: States currently contemplating extending domestic partnerships or other protections to their gay and lesbian citizens might now think twice.

It was also, Walker said, a stretch to read *Romer* the way Reinhardt had. Circuit judge O'Scannlain, whom Walker considered a friend, had written that the panel's interpretation of the landmark Supreme Court case was a "gross misapplication" that "would be unrecognizable to the Justices that joined it, to those who dissented from it, and to the judges from sister circuits that have since interpreted it." Just because a court says that a right exists, as the California Supreme Court did when it cleared the way for gays and lesbians to marry, does not in and of itself make it unconstitutional for voters to amend their constitution, Walker thought. "It really doesn't hang together."

When he ran into Reinhardt weeks after the en banc decision at the Ninth Circuit judicial conference in Hawaii, he told him as much, saying he wished he had decided the case on broader, and in his view, more defensible grounds. Reinhardt's response made it clear to Walker that the decision had been written in the way it had because Reinhardt was worried that if the justices of the Supreme Court took up the case, they might vote to uphold bans like California's.

"I told him he shouldn't have given up so easily," Walker said. "And he said, 'You have more faith in those people than I do.'"

Section IV

THIRTY-TWO

A STAR WITNESS'S
MEA CULPA

The way that Chuck Cooper found out that his star witness at trial had switched sides was by e-mail. At 12:52 P.M. on June 22, 2012, a lawyer on his team, alerted by ProtectMarriage.com, forwarded him a link to an op-ed on the *New York Times* Web site. It was headlined, "How My View on Gay Marriage Changed," and it was written by David Blankenhorn.

"I thought it was pretty lousy," Cooper said, recalling that moment. "I sure did."

The timing was terrible. Cooper was in the midst of preparing his cert petition, asking the Supreme Court to hear the case and reverse Judge Reinhardt's holding that Proposition 8 was unconstitutional. The Court grants review in only about a hundred of the approximately ten thousand petitions it gets each term, and it takes a vote of at least four of the nine justices. But it was hard for Cooper to fathom that the votes weren't there, given the makeup of the Court, the sheer size of California, and the importance of the constitutional principles at stake.

The Ninth Circuit panel's 2–1 decision against his clients had not come as a surprise, though he had been prepared for and even expected a much broader ruling. Judge Reinhardt had been smart and savvy to avoid taking the fifty-state step that Olson had urged, Cooper thought, but in the end he did not believe the panel's reading of the *Romer* case would hold up.

He had also fully expected to lose his bid for en banc review, but the maneuver had produced the result he had desired. Judge O'Scannlain, in dissent, had laid out a more fiery case for Supreme Court review than had Judge Smith, whose understated conclusion—"I am not convinced that Proposition 8 lacks a rational relationship to legitimate state interests"—was not exactly a legal call to battle.

The months-long delay had also given the various DOMA challenges time to catch up to the Proposition 8 case, setting the stage for both to be considered by the Supreme Court sometime the following spring. In recent weeks, district court Judge Barbara S. Jones had ruled that the provision of DOMA that denied federal benefits to legally married gay and lesbian couples failed to meet the rational basis test in Edie Windsor's case. And in a separate challenge, a unanimous panel of the U.S. Court of Appeals for the First Circuit in Boston had struck down the DOMA provision using what law professors call a rational basis "with teeth" analysis.

Circuit judge Michael Boudin, one of two Republican appointees on the panel and a jurist who was highly regarded in conservative Federalist Society circles, wrote the opinion. He declined to consider gays and lesbians a suspect class, citing circuit precedent, meaning that heightened scrutiny did not apply. And under a strict rational review test, he found that DOMA could survive a constitutional challenge. But because DOMA targeted an unpopular group and intruded on an area of regulation traditionally reserved to the states, Boudin wrote, Supreme Court precedent required "a closer than usual," case-specific inquiry that lies somewhere in between the two standards. In other words, it should be subject to a rational basis "with teeth" test.

Among the Supreme Court precedents Boudin cited: A 1973 decision in a case called *Department of Agriculture v. Moreno*, striking down a congressional statute aimed at preventing hippies living in communal housing from taking advantage of the food stamp program, and a 1985 decision case called *City of Cleburne v. Cleburne Living Center*, overturning a local zoning ordinance that discriminated against homes for the disabled.

Justice John Paul Stevens famously wrote that "there is only one Equal Protection Clause," and it did not require that the Court apply different standards to different cases, but only that the state govern impartially. In his concurrence in *Cleburne*, he wrote that the rational basis test, properly understood, is adequate to decide whether laws that single out classes of citizens for special treatment are constitutional, and he provided a framework for deciding cases that offered an alternative to the old multitiered scrutiny system:

"I have always asked myself whether I could find a 'rational basis' for the classification at issue. The term 'rational,' of course includes a requirement that an impartial lawmaker could logically believe that the classification would serve a legitimate public purpose that transcends the harm to the members of the disadvantaged class," he wrote. "In every equal protection case, we have to ask certain basic questions. What class is harmed by the legislation, and has it been subjected to a 'tradition of disfavor' by our laws? What is the public purpose that is being served by the law? What is the characteristic of the disadvantaged class that justifies the disparate treatment?"

Boudin, in his DOMA decision, appeared to apply the kind of rationality test that Stevens had laid out, with a federalist twist. In weighing the purported governmental purpose of DOMA against the burden imposed by the law, Boudin found no "demonstrated connection between DOMA's treatment of same-sex couples and its asserted goal of strengthening the bonds and benefit to society of heterosexual marriage." Instead, he said, the statute constituted an effort by Congress to "put a thumb on the scales and influence a state's decision as to how to shape its own marriage laws.

"To conclude, many Americans believe that marriage is the union of a man and a woman, and most Americans live in states where that is the law today. One virtue of federalism is that it permits this diversity of governance based on local choice, but this applies as well to the states that have chosen to legalize same-sex marriage."

The Justice Department was appealing both decisions in order to avoid the kind of standing questions that had been raised in California when the state refused to defend Proposition 8. But the actual defense of the law had been taken over by a standing body of the House of Representatives led by Speaker John Boehner, who had been elected Speaker after Republicans took over leadership of the chamber. Paul Clement, a protégé of Olson's who had succeeded him as President Bush's solicitor general, was the group's lawyer.

The Supreme Court bar was an elite bunch, but even by those standards, Clement shone. Since 2000, he had argued more cases before the Court than any other lawyer, and had an easygoing rapport with the justices. He was known for his ability to argue polarizing legal causes—most recently he had challenged the president's health care overhaul and defended an Arizona law aimed at rooting out illegal immigrants—in eminently reasonable fashion.

Cooper knew and liked Clement, but he hoped the two cases could be played off one another to the advantage of his clients, the proponents of Proposition 8. Kennedy, in his *Romer* decision, had written of the "sheer breadth" of the Colorado amendment depriving gays and lesbians of the protection of antidiscrimination laws, declaring it "at once too narrow and too broad. It identifies persons by a single trait and then denies them protection across the board."

In deciding whether Proposition 8 was passed out of animus toward gays and lesbians, Cooper wanted the Court to compare what the federal government had done, in denying them a huge array of federal marital benefits, against what California had done, in granting them all the benefits of marriage but the name. And to the extent that the justices bought into the federalism argument that the definition of marriage should be left to the states, that could also be helpful.

Then there was a purely practical consideration. The justices look to the Constitution in deciding how to apply the law, but they must look to one another in deciding any given case. Building a majority of at least five can involve a fair amount of horse-trading.

"Practically and strategically, I thought that having these cases argued and decided concurrently favored us," Cooper said. "Because it always seemed to me that if the justices were looking for a Solomonic way to resolve these cases, that favored Proposition 8 being upheld and DOMA struck down."

The only real downside to all the delay was that it had allowed for political victories like the passage of same-sex marriage in New York and, as Cooper put it, for public opinion to shift "with a velocity unlike anything I have ever seen." Olson believed momentum only helped his side of the case, but Cooper saw it differently. "It's not at all clear that cuts in Ted's favor more than mine," he said. "It's a Mexican standoff."

To the extent the Court does not like to get out ahead of public opinion, public opinion was giving the justices "the green light," he said. But "the other side of that sword," in his view, was that the growing acceptance of same-sex marriage weakened Olson's position that gays and lesbians needed the Court to intervene in the democratic process because they lacked sufficient political power. He planned to "jujitsu that" into an argument designed to keep the Court from applying heightened scrutiny.

All in all, he was feeling pretty good about the way things were lining up. Then he clicked on the link to Blankenhorn's mea culpa.

Over the course of the year and a half that had passed since the trial, Blankenhorn had given much thought to the position he had taken on the stand.

His high school– and college-aged kids disagreed with him, though they mostly expressed that to their mother. And debate sparring partners like Jonathan Rauch, the author of *Gay Marriage: Why It Is Good for Gays, Good for Straights, and Good for America*, and Dale Carpenter, a constitutional law professor, had forced him to challenge his assumptions.

"Getting to know them personally affected me," he said, sitting in his office in New York a few months after his op-ed appeared. "I was ignorant about gay people. I'm not excusing myself from that charge of bigotry, because bigotry can be omission. You can have a wall of thought that prohibits you from asking interesting questions."

When he was researching his book on same-sex marriage, he had read everything he could get his hands on. The elite debate, he found, was dominated by extremes. "A lot of people involved were hostile to the institution of marriage itself, and my fear was that gay marriage was a way to make marriage dead as a dodo," he said. "But then, as I talked about it with people I knew, it slowly dawned on me. Most gay couples aren't like that. They aren't interested in destroying the institution of marriage. They are just trying to live their lives. I used to think that personal relationships shouldn't affect your thinking. But I now know that it can be really helpful, because you realize that some of the things you thought are just not true."

He was not alone in coming to that conclusion. A month earlier, a pioneering psychiatrist at Columbia University had retracted a controversial study he had published in 2003 concluding that reparative therapy could "cure" homosexuality in motivated patients. The study had been entered into evidence by Cooper during the trial to buttress the idea that homosexuality was not an immutable trait. But since then, the therapy had been denounced as a "serious

threat to the health and well-being—even the lives—of affected people" by the
World Health Organization. The study's author, Dr. Robert Spitzer, had acknowledged in a letter to the *Archives of Sexual Behavior,* the journal that originally published his study, that it lacked scientific rigor and had been deeply
flawed. "I believe I owe the gay community an apology," Spitzer wrote.

Blankenhorn's evolution came about over a period of months. Professor
Carpenter talked to him about how when he was a lawyer in Texas, people from
his firm would take down the licenses of cars parked outside gay bars and
cross-reference them with the names of the firm's employees. "This is our history," Blankenhorn recalled Carpenter telling him. "This is what we are fighting about."

That hit a nerve with Blankenhorn, whose formative moral experience was
growing up in Mississippi during the civil rights movement. He had not gotten
into this battle to hurt gay people, or to stop them from getting what they
wanted.

He still believed that society should do all that it could do ensure that children do not grow up in broken, one-parent families. But in private conversations, Rauch would ask him probing questions: If you admit that there is some
benefit to gays and lesbians being able marry, wouldn't there have to be significant harm to the institution to justify banning them from doing so? Is fighting
gay marriage really going to increase the likelihood that children will grow up
with their own married mother and father?

The answer, he had come to realize, was no, because the trends on that front
were getting worse every year. All the fight over same-sex marriage was doing,
he concluded, was miring the country down in a culture war.

"I didn't want to spend the rest of my life fighting this battle, which by the
way, is over. It's over. People have made up their minds. It's just a huge mopping
up at this point. The people who disagree are no longer willing to say they disagree. And that too, that should be one consideration, that there isn't a way to
stop this from happening."

His Institute for American Values had lost half its funding—"It happened
like this," Blankenhorn said, snapping his finger—but he did not regret writing
the op-ed.

He had thought about calling Cooper and David Thompson to tell them what he was about to do, knew, really, that he should have done. But he had not been able to force himself to do it. "I didn't want for them to be mad at me," he said. "I feel really bad about that. I like those guys."

═══════

There had been moments when Cooper thought that if he had to do it all over again, he never would have agreed to take on this fight. "Any case has its trying elements and its challenges," as he put it, "and this one had more of them and at different kind of levels than any case, honestly, that I've been involved in."

Terry Stewart, for instance, had really gotten under his skin when she told the Ninth Circuit panel that his motion to disqualify Judge Walker showed that he and his clients thought "gay people were inferior" and could not seem to understand that "different rules don't apply to gay people." Olson had told members of his team that he thought Cooper was going to have a seizure when, voice shaking, Cooper had glared and jabbed his finger at him in rebuttal.

And it had been upsetting to Cooper, "very upsetting," he said. He might have lost, but he believed Walker's relationship was at least worthy of the court's attention, and was certainly not the act of bigotry that Stewart portrayed it to be.

"I still think that we were entitled to know, did he have any desire to marry? Our point was simply that if a judge potentially stands in the same shoes as a party in the case, it isn't crazy to argue that he should at least disclose that, if not recuse himself."

But in terms of trying moments, reading Blankenhorn's op-ed, in the *New York Times* of all places, ranked up there. "If fighting gay marriage was going to help marriage over all, I think we'd have seen some sign of it by now. So my intention is to try something new," Blankenhorn had written. "Instead of fighting gay marriage, I'd like to help build new coalitions bringing together gays who want to strengthen marriage with straight people who want to do the same."

Cooper could have lived with that, just like he could live with President Obama's endorsement. People of goodwill had changed their minds. But what was truly harmful, and legally consequential, was this passage:

"In the mind of today's public, gay marriage is almost entirely about accepting lesbians and gay men as equal citizens. And to my deep regret, much of the opposition to gay marriage seems to stem, at least in part, from an underlying anti-gay animus."

"Of course that was not helpful," Cooper said. "I realize that if the dominant thrust of some political decision is seen to be motivated by hatred, then it's not going to stand. It doesn't matter how sound my legal proposition is."

THIRTY-THREE

CHAD'S BIG TEST

In a large meeting room on the first floor of the Human Rights Campaign's headquarters in Washington, D.C., dozens of staffers sat at long tables, typing furiously on laptop computers and taking calls from the some of the seventy-five field organizers the organization had deployed around the country. Over big-screen televisions, political analysts for all the major cable networks were filling the airtime with babble as the country waited for the polls to begin closing and the results of election night 2012 to begin trickling in.

Since taking the job more than four months earlier, Chad had been traveling the country nonstop, raising money and urging the Human Rights Campaign's 1.6 million members to get out and vote. All told, more than $20 million had been raised and contributed in Election 2012, making it the largest mobilization in the organization's history. A whiteboard listed all the races, from Massachusetts to Hawaii, in which the gay rights behemoth had a stake.

Would President Obama win a second term, or would his endorsement of same-sex marriage sink him in the swing states, as some aides had feared? Would Tammy Baldwin, a congresswoman from Wisconsin, defeat the state's former Republican governor to become the first openly gay candidate to be elected to the U.S. Senate? What about the more than two hundred other candidates the organization had endorsed? Chad obsessively checked the exit poll data, hoping to get a read.

But the races he was following most closely were in Washington, Maine, Maryland, and Minnesota, where same-sex marriage was on the ballot. Gays and lesbians may have been on a winning streak in the courts and in state legislatures, but they had yet to win a popular vote at the ballot box. Tonight he would learn whether the 0-for-32 losing streak had come to an end.

It was Chad's first big test as president, and it came as the old doubts about the Proposition 8 case had resurfaced, fanned by Judge Reinhardt's opinion. If the "liberal lion" of the Ninth Circuit did not think the Supreme Court was ready, the thinking went, maybe the Olson-Boies legal team wasn't smarter than everyone else after all. William Eskridge, a prominent gay Yale law professor, had filed a brief urging the Supreme Court to let the marriage debate percolate longer before taking action. When members of the legal team, at Olson's request, had asked him to reconsider or tone it down, taking into account how much the climate had changed as a result of the Prop 8 litigation, resentment had bubbled over into outright anger. "Ellen DeGeneres has done more for the movement than Ted Olson," Eskridge had snapped. At a recent meeting of some of the movement's leading legal rights groups, to which Chad was not invited, the consensus was that the Proposition 8 case should go no further.

Shortly before 6 P.M. Jerome popped into Chad's office. Chad had a sore throat and a bad case of the sniffles. He was talking to a reporter. Jerome kissed him on the top of his head, put the jacket and red tie that he had brought for him from home on a chair, then headed back to their apartment to change out of his sweatshirt into something more suitable. "Back soon," he whispered.

Several press releases, prepared by his staff for all possible outcomes, awaited Chad's approval. One read, "2012: The Year LGBT People Won at the Polls." After reading the other, which would be released in the event of one or more losses, he instructed his director of media relations, Michael Cole-Schwartz, to make a change.

"It's the word 'heartbreaking' I didn't like," Chad said.

"I wanted to make sure it was emotive, that we feel people's pain."

"Yes, but what people are going to be looking for is hope. What's next."

Four years earlier, Chad and Kristina had sat in that suite in San Francisco and made their pact. Out of one of the worst days of Chad's professional life had come something good. Proposition 8, like the police raids that sparked the Stonewall riots, had become a catalyst for change. The trial had forced opponents into open court, where they were required to defend their views, and the country was having a national conversation on the nature of equality.

Polling showed that support for same-sex marriage was growing across every demographic, albeit at different rates, a remarkable transformation in public attitudes that had accelerated since 2010 and the filing of the case. The Pew Research Center would soon release data showing that 14 percent of Americans who supported same-sex marriage used to hold the opposite view, comprising more than a quarter of those who now believed that gays and lesbians should be able to wed. Republicans continued to oppose same-sex marriage, but by smaller margins. The nation had come to a clear consensus that sexual orientation was a trait, not a choice, and more and more Americans, regardless of age, race, political ideology or religion, were coming to embrace the idea that who you were, and who you loved, should not dictate who you could marry.

"This is the most significant, fastest shift in public opinion that we've seen in modern American politics," said Alex Lundry, a Republican political consultant who served as director of data science for Mitt Romney's presidential campaign and was analyzing the same-sex marriage data for Mehlman's Project Right Side. "And what is remarkable about it is that no demographic has been immune. You name it, and it has shifted in favor of gay marriage."

In three of the four states where marriage was on the ballot, gays and lesbians were on the offensive. In Washington and Maryland, voters would decide whether to approve same-sex marriage laws already blessed by their state legislatures, and in Maine they would decide whether to reverse themselves and allow gay couples to wed. In Minnesota, where gays and lesbians were playing defense against a proposed constitutional ban, the National Organization for Marriage had been reduced to pleading with companies to stay on the sidelines, as major employers like Target and General Mills declared the ban bad for business.

The marriage debate, which once largely divided Americans along secular and religious lines, was increasingly dividing religious Americans. The Episcopal Church and the conservative branch of American Judaism had recently blessed gay wedding ceremonies, and faith leaders from the denominations that favored allowing their gay and lesbian congregants to wed had been providing testimony and political cover in the state-by-state political battles.

Institutions like the Catholic Church and the Conference of Southern Baptist Evangelists remained staunch opponents. But young evangelical voters were increasingly supportive of the right of gays and lesbians to marry, causing some church leaders to rethink how best to talk about the issue, and it remained an open question as to how Catholics would divide on the question when it came time to vote. Quiet discussions with the Mormon Church, which had provided the bulk of the funding for Proposition 8, were beginning to bear fruit: It was not playing a funding role this cycle. And while the church's position had not changed, it was moving toward what it called a more "Christlike" approach, working to address high rates of gay Mormon youth homelessness and suicide, for instance, by calling on parents not to reject their gay children.

Back in California, the legislature had recently voted to outlaw conversion therapy as junk science. More prominent Republicans were stepping forward to endorse same-sex marriage, most recently former secretary of state Colin Powell. Straight allies from what had long been considered a bastion of homophobia—the professional sports locker room—were also joining the cause.

In Maryland, Baltimore Raven Brendon Ayanbadejo was so outspoken that Emmett C. Burns Jr., an African American state delegate opposed to same-sex marriage, pressured the football team's owner to order his linebacker to cease and desist. That so angered Minnesota Vikings punter Chris Kluwe that he published a profanity-laced response, then jumped into the marriage campaign in his state.

"Your vitriolic hatred and bigotry make me ashamed and disgusted to think that you are in any way responsible for shaping policy at any level," Kluwe wrote in an open letter to Burns that went viral. "I can assure you that gay people getting married will have zero effect on your life. They won't come into your house and steal your children. They won't magically turn you into a lust-ful cockmonster. They won't even overthrow the government in an orgy of hedonistic debauchery because all of a sudden they have the same legal rights as the other 90 percent of our population—rights like Social Security benefits, child care tax credits, Family and Medical Leave to take care of loved ones, and COBRA healthcare for spouses and children. You know what having these rights will make gays? Full-fledged American citizens just like everyone else, with the freedom to pursue happiness and all that entails. Do the civil-rights struggles of the past 200 years mean absolutely nothing to you?"

In one sign of just how much the times were changing, rising hip-hop artist Frank Ocean came out about falling in love with a guy on his blog, and rather than having it derail his career in an industry known for intolerant lyrics filled with references to "faggots," he was met with an outpouring of support. "Thank you," hip-hop megastar Jay-Z wrote on his Life+Times Web site. "We are all made better by your decision to share publicly." The album Ocean released shortly afterward debuted at number two on the U.S. *Billboard* 200 chart and earned six Grammy nominations.

Olson's legal briefs would not take note of what happened that evening, win or lose, in part because it would be unseemly to suggest that the justices decide cases with a finger to the political wind, and also because the entire point of the case was that the rights of a minority should not be put up for a vote. The Con-stitution, with its guarantee of equal protection under the law and substantive due process embrace of fundamental rights that the Court sees as "implicit to the concept of ordered liberty," trumps elections.

But earlier in the year, Justice Ginsburg had reiterated her concern that the Court had moved too fast in issuing its milestone *Roe v. Wade* decision. In what was reported as a possible window into her thinking on the Proposition 8 case, she told a symposium at Columbia Law School that it might have been better to decide the case more incrementally or delay hearing it altogether in order to allow the political debate over abortion that was under way more time to play out.

In Olson's estimation, "atmospherically," winning mattered, quite a bit.

Chad had invested $5.3 million into the four states where marriage was on the ballot, plus $145,000 to keep Iowa Supreme Court justice David Wiggins from becoming the fourth justice to be ousted in a retention vote over that court's unanimous 2009 decision, which made the Hawkeye State the third in the nation to allow gays and lesbians to marry.

Maine looked solid. Ken Mehlman had been working closely there with Marc Solomon, the national campaign director for Evan Wolfson's group, Freedom to Marry. Solomon felt an affinity for Mehlman; he too had been a closeted gay Republican, as an undergraduate student at Yale working to elect Bob Dole president and later as a staffer on the Hill. They had met to talk about how they might advance the cause together, and Solomon had come away thinking that Mehlman was a huge asset. "He was like, 'You're the expert, I'm just a foot soldier,'" Solomon recalled. "I took that with a grain of salt, because he's a mastermind."

Mehlman, as he had in New York, called Republican state lawmakers in all four states. He helped raise money. He also drafted the Republican microtargeting firm, TargetPoint, the one he had used to help reelect President Bush, to identify and persuade likely same-sex marriage supporters. Consumer data, such as the kinds of books or music a person buys, and public records containing information such as whether a person owns a pickup truck or a Volvo, were used to slice and dice the electorate. In Maine, TargetPoint created thirty-three different groups and, using predictive modeling, ranked them according to their likely support for same-sex marriage. Voters who might lean their way but were judged to be susceptible to the message of opponents were visited by door knockers, who were armed with particularized, focus-group-tested talking points designed to assuage their concerns. By election day, Solomon said they had knocked on the doors of "more than half of the movable middle."

Maryland had started off looking unwinnable. It had the highest percentage of black voters of any state outside the South, and early polls showed a majority opposed to same-sex marriage. Freedom to Marry had urged donors to send their money elsewhere, where there was a bigger chance of success. But following President Obama's endorsement, those numbers had flipped virtually overnight. There had been slippage since, as opponents worked the black churches. But prominent African American ministers like the Reverend Delman Coates of the Mt. Ennon Baptist Church in Prince George's County were offering black voters a countervailing theological narrative, one that evoked the spirit of Martin Luther King Jr. to argue that standing up for gays' and lesbians' right to marry was in keeping with the social justice traditions of evangelical black Christianity.

Chad, seeing promise, had funneled money to the NAACP, which was headquartered in Baltimore, to run a grassroots campaign. The civil rights group's chairman emeritus, AFER advisory board member Julian Bond, had cut a radio ad as part of the effort. "I know a little something about fighting for what's right and just," Bond said in the ad. "I believe that people of faith understand this isn't about any one religious belief—it's about protecting the civil right to make a lifelong commitment to the person you love."

With the strong leadership of the state's governor, Martin O'Malley, and Ben Jealous, the current president of the NAACP, it just might be enough. "It was an honor to fight by your side in this noble battle," O'Malley e-mailed Chad after voting himself. "Whatever happens, we have made progress here and the future is bright."

Minnesota and Washington could go either way. David Blankenhorn had been enlisted to cut a Minnesota campaign video. In it, he played off his famous Prop 8 trial admission that "we would be more American on the day we permit same-sex marriage than the day before."

"There are powerful reasons to believe that we will be a better society if we include gay and lesbian people and their relationships as full and equal parts of society," Blankenhorn said in the campaign video. "The good people of Minnesota should not do this."

And a game-changing $2.5 million donation from Jeff Bezos, the founder of Seattle-based Amazon.com, had allowed for a state-of-the-art media blitz in Washington. The advertising campaign by Hilary Rosen and her firm SKD-Knickerbocker, which had run the New York campaign, drew upon all the available polling data and lessons learned to date.

Mehlman liked to say that "a great Ford dealer does not say, 'You were wrong to buy a GM.' A great Ford dealer says, 'GM is a lot like Ford, only Ford is better.'" That applied equally to same-sex marriage. Nobody wants to feel bad about themselves. Rather than tell voters why they were wrong to believe gays and lesbians should not marry, the key was to give them permission to change their minds. Straight people describing their own evolution, sharing why they had come to believe that family members and friends should be able to marry the person they love, just as they could, was one of the most effective ways to do that. Rosen's campaign had emphasized that "journey" message, as had the campaigns in the three other states.

But over lunch earlier that day, Rosen told Chad that the internal overnight polling numbers had been trending down in recent days. "I'm worried," she confided.

═══

Maggie Gallagher was too. As Chad and Rosen were finishing up their lunch, the cofounder of NOM—the National Organization for Marriage—was sitting down to hers, at a restaurant nearby called D.C. Coast.

A heavyset woman with a dark, fringed bob, Gallagher was gay marriage's most ardent foe, and she came to it from a deeply personal place. As a young woman at Yale University in the 1970s, she had accidentally gotten pregnant. She was already deeply conservative, eschewing the counterculture to join Yale's conservative debating society, the Party of the Right, and she did not want an abortion. The father, though, wound up wanting little to do with her or her baby, and she had raised her boy on her own.

Listening to her small son's make-believe stories about some imaginary millionaire father, and answering his questions about why he was not a part of their lives, had been heartbreaking, she said. "It was very challenging. Most days I'd come home and weep for ten minutes from the stress."

The experience had led her to the view that children have a right to be raised by a married mother and father, and nothing her good friend and former employer David Blankenhorn was now saying about the disconnect between fighting same-sex marriage and achieving that goal could convince her otherwise.

What about the fact that her own son had grown up, gone to college, and done just fine?

"I was advantaged," she said. "I had a lot of help. But when I ask myself, was I able to give my son as much as I was given? The answer is no."

What about the children of gay parents? Don't they have a right to grow up with married parents?

Gallagher paused and put down her fork before answering. She had gone to see *8*, the play, because she liked the theater, and said it was amusing at some level to see herself portrayed as a zealot. She had once called same-sex marriage one of "the most destructive ideas of the sexual revolution" and compared losing the same-sex marriage battle to "losing American civilization." But now she chose her words carefully.

If it could be definitively proven that children of gay couples do better when their parents are able to marry, she said slowly, that would pose a "morally troubling" question, because "you have to care for all children. I'd have to re-think my position.

"What I'd really want is two generations of a society which adopts gay marriage as the norm, and manages to sustain a reasonably functional marriage institution. Then I'd say I was wrong."

Of course, if she and NOM had their way, no such data would exist, because gay marriage would be banned everywhere, a tension she glided over as she made her election night predictions. She was hopeful, she said, that when the votes were all counted later that evening, Minnesota would enact the constitutional prohibition on the ballot there. Maryland and Washington, though less likely, could also tilt her way. But she acknowledged that Blankenhorn was right about one thing: Opponents of same-sex marriage were losing the war of ideas.

Most of the National Organization for Marriage's budget these days came from just a few megadonors. Onetime supporters were abandoning the cause. Thanks in part to the efforts of Ken Mehlman, fewer GOP elected officials were willing to appear on news programs to speak out against same-sex marriage, while prominent Republican commentators like former Bush White House communications director Nicole Wallace were out making the case for it. And it was getting harder and harder to find platforms that could be used to persuade this new generation of voters that, as Gallagher put it, "this vision of marriage that I have is a good thing."

Conservative outlets like the *Drudge Report,* so influential on the right in other areas, covered developments on the same-sex marriage front matter-of-factly, with none of the lathered outrage they worked up for, say, the president's health care overhaul.

"You don't even get on Fox News if you are opposed to gay marriage," she complained. "Basically we don't get a message out anymore unless we are willing to pay for it."

———

"How are you doing," Jerome asked, patting Chad's knee. "Is your throat okay?"

"I'm good," Chad said.

It was a little after 7 P.M., and they were in Chad's Ford Escape driving over to pump up the crowd that had gathered at the restaurant where Chad was holding an election night party for supporters. Checking his e-mail, Chad saw that Maryland governor O'Malley had sent in an update from the field.

"It's happening," Chad said as they pulled up to the restaurant. "The governor has exit polls showing us two points up."

Inside, the noise was deafening. Hundreds of people—donors, supporters, and staffers—many of whom Chad was still getting to know, had come to watch the results now beginning to flash across a huge television screen. Chad stuffed his hands in his pockets and stood still, just watching for a few moments. Election day was the one day over which he had no control. Then, shedding his shyness, he climbed up on a riser and grabbed a microphone.

"Hi," he said. "I'm feeling good. How 'bout you?"

The crowd cheered.

"We have an opportunity to finally win marriage equality at the ballot box, and we will take that talking point away from our opponents," he said. "All the breaking news is it's too close to call, but I feel optimistic. I feel optimistic, because of you!"

Back at headquarters a half hour later, Chad grabbed a seat at one of the long tables in the conference room. Around him, staffers updated the whiteboard as states were called in the presidential race. Chad absently clicked and unclicked the pen he was holding. Open. Shut. Open, shut. The back of his chair tipped back and forth as his right foot did a tap dance of its own, the way it always did when he was nervous.

Kristina, from the president and first lady's suite in Chicago, sent him a text. Ohio now looked like a lock, according to the president's campaign team. Though the race had yet to be called, they were all just waiting for Mitt Romney to concede. Tammy Baldwin was declared the winner in Wisconsin, making history, and as more Senate races were called, it seemed clear that the chamber would remain in Democratic control.

Chad conferred by phone with Mehlman, who was in New York watching the returns come in with friends. Olson had already gone to bed. He had played Joe Biden in debate prep with Romney's running mate Paul Ryan, and had even packed a bag in the event that Romney needed his services in a recount. He was hoping for the best when it came to the marriage initiatives, but he was a Republican, and he had not felt like staying up to watch his party get routed.

"Wake me up if anything changes," he told his wife, Lady, somewhat grumpily.

Chad texted Richard Carlbom, the manager of the campaign to defeat the constitutional amendment in Minnesota. "Richard says it's going to be close," he announced.

In Maryland, with more than half the vote counted, they were winning 51 percent to 49 percent, a staffer announced. Heavily black Baltimore County was in, and more than half of liberal Montgomery County was still out. O'Malley e-mailed that they should hold off making a announcement, but it was looking good.

"Jesus," Chad said.

Then, at 10:12 P.M., NBC projected that President Barack Obama had won a second term in office, with just over 50 percent of the vote.

"The world is not a crazy place," Jerome said to Chad.

Obama had swept most of the battleground states, riding a diverse wave of support to overcome a still foundering economy and crises at home and abroad, from a disastrous oil spill in the Gulf of Mexico to the Arab Spring roiling the Middle East.

And while he had lost North Carolina, fears that his support for same-sex marriage would hurt him had proven unfounded. Black voters had turned out in force, and an Edison Research exit poll found that 51 percent supported same-sex marriage. Obama won the Catholic vote and crushed Romney among Hispanic voters; exit polls showed that both groups favored same-sex marriage by sizable margins.

"It was the bomb that did not go off," Dan Pfeiffer, Chad's friend and a top adviser to the president, said afterward. Obama's decision to come out in favor of same-sex marriage so close to the election had, Pfeiffer admitted, given him "a bit of a heart attack," but in the end, "the fact that it was a nonissue is maybe the most gratifying thing of all.

"Society has just changed."

Indeed, it was a net positive. It did little to motivate Romney's base; in exit polling of religious conservatives done by Republican operative Ralph Reed, the founder of the Faith and Freedom Coalition, abortion showed up among their top five concerns, but same-sex marriage did not.

Obama's endorsement did, however, motivate the president's base. Exit polling done on behalf of the media found that three out of four Obama voters said his embrace of same-sex marriage made them "much more" likely to support him. Postelection analysis would credit large youth turnout in four crucial swing states with helping secure the president's reelection. In Florida, for instance, Obama won 66 percent of voters under the age of thirty. Across the country, LGBT voters also turned out in numbers, comprising 5 percent of the electorate, up from under 4 percent in 2008, and they broke even more decisively for Obama this time around, giving him 77 percent of their vote.

"AP is reporting that Maine makes history for marriage equality," a staffer announced.

"*Woohoo*," Chad cheered. "That's state number one."

"The *Washington Post* is reporting that Maryland passes same-sex marriage," said another staffer.

"The Iowa judge looks like he's going to hold on," someone else said.

On Twitter, real estate mogul and television personality Donald Trump was seething over Obama's reelection, calling for a revolution.

"We just had it," Chad said. "A gay revolution!"

Someone went to fetch champagne.

"So much better than 2008," said Fred Sainz, the organization's vice president for communications and marketing.

"Two thousand eight was the most depressing election," Chad agreed. "It was like Obama wins, gays lose everything. This year, it's Obama wins, gays win everything!"

"There are still some states left," one of the political staffers said.

"I know, I know."

But Chad could not summon his usual pessimism as he read over a press release, entitled "Landslide Victory for LGBT Equality Up and Down the Ballot," that had been prepared for release later that night.

The National Organization for Marriage had just sent out an e-mail of its own, a plea for money. "Help us spoil gay activists' election night celebration parties," it read.

"Fuck you, NOM," Cole-Schwartz said.

On the television, Romney was conceding. Cleve Jones had posted a photo to his Facebook page of people celebrating in the streets in San Francisco.

"Look at the Castro right now," Chad said, showing it around.

And then Obama was on television, talking about the "promise of our founding."

"It doesn't matter whether you're black or white or Hispanic or Asian or Native American or young or old or rich or poor, abled, disabled, gay or straight. You can make it here in America if you are willing to try."

The promise of Obama's presidency, to end the petty grievances that had, as he put it in his first inauguration speech, "strangled our politics" and turned the nation into a polarized quilt of red and blue states, was now threadbare. The "fierce urgency of now" had given way to expedient incrementalism, in the face of implacable opponents.

But for Chad, the astonishing sense of promise that had swept the country four years earlier, the promise of an America where anything could happen, where a black man with a name like Barack Obama could be elected president of the United States of America, had finally been fulfilled. Four years ago, before that crowd in Grant Park, with Chad watching from a hotel room in San Francisco, Obama had declared his victory an answer, an answer to cynicism, an answer to those who believed that "this time must be different, that their voice could be that difference," an answer that had "led those who have been told for so long, by so many, to be cynical, and fearful, and doubtful of what we can achieve, to put their hands on the arc of history and bend it once more toward the hope of a better day."

Tonight, unlike last time around, those words rang true to Chad.

Shortly before 3 A.M., reports from the field in Washington and Minnesota made it official. By a vote of 53.7 percent to 46.3 percent, voters in Washington had approved the law legalizing same-sex marriage there, and 51 percent of voters in Minnesota had voted to reject the proposed constitutional ban.

Four for four, plus they had saved the judge in Iowa.

"Talk about a great atmosphere going up to the Supreme Court," Chad said, deep bags under his eyes but a smile on his face. "Wow."

THIRTY-FOUR

"DON'T THEY HAVE A RESPONSIBILITY TO ACT?"

At 9:30 A.M. on the morning of December 7, 2012, the nine justices of the Supreme Court gathered in a tasteful conference room just off Chief Justice Roberts's office. They ranged in age from fifty-two to seventy-nine. There were six men and, for the first time in history, three women. Six were Catholic, and three were Jewish. One was black, another Latina, and two were Italian American. All but one had graduated from Harvard or Yale law schools; the holdout had graduated from Columbia University law school. Two of the three women were unmarried, the third a widow.

Chief Justice Roberts, along with Justices Antonin Scalia, Samuel Alito, and Clarence Thomas made up the Court's conservative wing. Justices Ruth Bader Ginsburg, Stephen Breyer, Sonia Sotomayor, and Elena Kagan made up the court's liberal wing. And then there was Justice Kennedy, who more often than not determined which wing won in controversial cases.

The question they faced was momentous.

In addition to the DOMA challenges, should they grant cert and agree to hear the Proposition 8 case, since renamed *Hollingsworth v. Perry*? In other words, had the time come for the Court to step in and decide the question of same-sex marriage for the country?

The justices vote yay or nay; they do not discuss the merits of a case until after oral argument. Per tradition, the newest justice, Elena Kagan, kept track of what was decided; clerks were strictly banned from these deliberations.

The history of the Supreme Court is replete with moments of great courage.

What is less widely appreciated is that those moments often followed years of half-measures or outright ducking. In the name of preserving the credibility of an institution that can claim no democratic mandate when it countermands the will of the majority in the name of the Constitution, the justices at times have made a virtue of not deciding, or at least not deciding all at once.

The Court, for instance, did not desegregate the South in one fell swoop. In a 1950 case called *Sweatt v. Painter,* the Court held that a black student must be admitted to a whites-only law school in Texas because the separate law school for blacks set up by the state was not, in fact, substantively equal. It would take another four years for the Court to issue its *Brown v. Board of Education* ruling striking down the separate but equal doctrine as unconstitutional in all instances.

In the wake of the *Brown* decision, faced with massive resistance in the South to the Court's integration decrees, the Court refused to hear a constitutional challenge to Virginia's interracial marriage ban in a 1955 case called *Naim v. Naim.* Though private papers make clear that a number of the justices believed the ban to be unconstitutional, Justice Felix Frankfurter's argument for inaction ultimately prevailed: "To throw a decision of this court, other than [one] validating this legislation, into the present disquietude," would, he worried, thwart and "very seriously embarrass the carrying out" of its school desegregation orders. It would take another twelve years for the Court to take up and strike down antimiscegenation statutes in the *Loving v. Virginia* case.

The country, as evidenced most recently by November election results, was in a very different place on same-sex marriage than it had been when the Proposition 8 case was first filed. Nine states plus the District of Columbia now recognized same-sex marriage, versus just two when the Proposition 8 case was filed, with the result that nearly fifty million Americans now lived in states where gays and lesbians could marry.

Still, the issue was judicial nitroglycerin, hurtling right at the fault lines of a deeply divided Supreme Court, at a time when the percentage of Americans who viewed the institution favorably had sunk to a quarter-century low. While the Court was still the most popular of the three branches of government, only 52 percent viewed it favorably, down from a peak of 80 percent in 1994.

Before he stepped down from the bench, Justice David Souter had written a dissent that was viewed by some Court observers as a warning on same-sex marriage, though he never explicitly mentioned the subject and the case was wholly unrelated. When deciding whether to recognize a right "unsanctioned by tradition," Souter counseled in 2009, a few months after the Proposition 8 case was filed to front-page fanfare, "the beginning of wisdom is to go slow."

"We can change our own inherited views just so fast, and a person is not labeled a stick-in-the-mud for refusing to endorse a new moral claim without having some time to work through it intellectually and emotionally," Souter wrote. "The broader society needs the chance to take part in the dialectic of public and political back and forth about a new liberty claim before it makes sense to declare unsympathetic state or national laws arbitrary."

In New York, Edie Windsor waited for the justices to render their cert verdict with her lawyer, Robbie Kaplan. The assumption was that the Court would grant cert in one of the DOMA cases, given that a failure to do so would mean that a federal law was constitutional in some circuits but not in others. There were four to choose from, but both Edie and Kaplan had a feeling theirs would be the one.

Less than two months earlier, the U.S. Court of Appeals for the Second Circuit had ruled in Windsor's favor, becoming the first federal appellate court in the country to agree with Judge Walker that laws that targeted gays and lesbians deserved heightened scrutiny. Kaplan, who was at home when she heard, called Edie.

"We just won!"

The first thing Edie had thought to do was to tell Thea. There were days, fewer now but still frequent, when Edie would be sitting at her computer and turn around to tell Thea something, only to realize that she was gone. She had hung up the phone, and then, rummaging through a drawer for something, had come across a handwritten note. It must have been written long before Thea died—at the end she could not hold a pen—maybe when Edie had quit smoking.

> *Congratulations Darling*
> *You DID It!!*
> *PS I AM good for you.*

It was like she knew, Edie said, when she phoned Kaplan back to tell her. "This is why I believe in God," Kaplan, a practicing Jew, said she thought.

———

Across the country in California, Adam, the plaintiffs, and the AFER team maintained a similar vigil, obsessively checking SCOTUSblog.com, a Web site devoted to Supreme Court news. The justices meet weekly to discuss cases in "conference." The justices had been distributing the marriage cases for conference since before the election, only to emerge with no decision on which, if any, they would take.

Chad, who had traveled out west to be on hand for the decision, was "more nervous than a bride at the altar whose husband is late," said Fred Sainz, his vice president and right-hand man at the Human Rights Campaign.

Chad had accepted that the Supreme Court was unlikely to rule more broadly than the Ninth Circuit had already done—meaning that the most likely outcome was a ruling that would apply only to California—but Olson still thought a fifty-state ruling was a possibility, and that prospect remained tantalizing to both Chad and the plaintiffs. The justices had it within their power to turn a patchwork of licensing laws into a national civil right, but would they?

"Can't someone knock on the door and ask them what is going on?" Chad said to Adam, only half joking.

"If they recognize that there's discrimination," Jeff asked earnestly, if somewhat naïvely, "then don't they have a responsibility to act?"

The waiting game was made all the more excruciating by the fact that if the Supreme Court declined to review the Ninth Circuit's decision, then the stay that the Ninth Circuit imposed would be lifted, the state would cease enforcing

Proposition 8, and same-sex marriages in California would resume. Elaborate plans had been put in place to capitalize on that media opportunity by having at least one of the two couples get married immediately. Jeff and Paul had gone back and forth about whether they wanted to join Kris and Sandy by tying the knot immediately. It might be nice, twenty years from now, to celebrate their anniversary on what would also be a historically important day. But Adam had urged them to wait. The wedding would be as much for the cameras as it was for the couple, and unlike the two women, they had never had a proper ceremony. Kris and Sandy had nixed an AFER-hatched plan to hold a celebrity-studded reception in Los Angeles; San Francisco City Hall would do just fine. But it was still stressful to be on standby for a wedding that had to happen at the drop of a hat, especially since Kris had recently taken on a big new job as the executive director of a Washington, D.C.–based early childhood education foundation that had her traveling between the two coasts.

Every time the Supreme Court pushed off the decision to the next conference, Kris and Sandy had to resend "save the date" e-mails to all their friends, and figure out all over again how to corral the twins, Tom and Frank, for a ceremony that no one really wanted to take place: They would all rather that the Supreme Court take the case, even though that would delay their own weddings, so that millions across the country could potentially share in the right to marry.

"I'm anxious and miserable," Kris told Jeff after one stakeout resulted in no orders yet again. "It's like—just do your job. Every time we think we know what could happen there is some new wrinkle."

"Good," Sandy said, trying to relieve the tension after another episode. "My hair looks like shit."

Then she set about canceling the plane reservations she had made to fly in her boys, and contemplated aloud what she should tell the thirty-plus people who were on standby to attend a quickie wedding that day.

"Dear Family," she said. "You won't have to come see us get married."

Thanksgiving had offered everyone a brief respite. In Burbank, Paul took all of his frustration out by baking for two straight days: a lemon icebox pie from the lemon tree in their yard, a heaven/hell peanut butter and chocolate angel food cake, and, in honor of the holiday, a pumpkin pie. Jeff ate way too much of it, out of nerves.

In San Francisco, all four boys watched football with Kris's extended family, devouring the turkey, ham, scalloped potatoes, and fixings that Sandy had laid out on the dining room table. Kris's mom commented on the recent landscaping work they had done. Her stepbrother, a born-again Christian who in his younger years had traveled the world evangelizing, distributing Bibles in China and putting on religious plays in Africa, asked her how the case was going. He had once opposed same-sex marriage, even knowing that Kris was a lesbian, but had come to believe he was wrong to think it was his religious duty to "protect marriage" from people like his stepsister. Spencer and Elliott showed off new, matching Swedish flag tattoos they had gotten in honor of their heritage, causing Kris to just shake her head. Sandy showed a friend who had stopped by the dove gray St. John knit dress she had picked out to wear to the wedding that might, or might not, soon be taking place. Hair up? she asked. Or down?

Hopefully the Supreme Court would just take the case, she said. Not only would that get them all to where they wanted to go, but, she joked, "It will give me more time to drop a few pounds before the wedding."

———

Cooper's cert petition and Olson's response had been filed months earlier. Cooper, in asking the justices to overturn Judge Reinhardt's decision, had cited a 1982 Supreme Court precedent called *Crawford v. Los Angeles Board of Education*. In that case, which involved a busing desegregation plan, the justices held that just because a state chooses to do "more than" the Constitution requires, does not mean it may never recede. Reinhardt's decision to skirt the question of whether the U.S. Constitution contained a right to marry allowed Cooper to argue that Californians could withdraw from gays and lesbians the ability to marry, so long as they had some legitimate reason for doing so.

Olson disputed that he was asking the Court for more than the Constitution required. Cooper's argument that California's generous domestic partnership law meant that the state's "gay-friendly" voters could not have acted out of animus had been dismissed in a biting footnote: "There is no 'Mostly Equal Protection Clause' or 'Separate but Equal Protection Clause.'"

But Olson had tried to walk a fine line, opposing Cooper's request for Supreme Court review, but not too strenuously. The case did offer an "attractive vehicle" for the justices to consider the issue, he allowed, coming before the Court with the "most comprehensive record ever developed in a case challenging a restriction on the right to marry."

Whenever Olson had an argument before the Supreme Court, he asked a single lawyer on his team to put together a binder on each of the nine justices, with everything from relevant case decisions to items about their personal lives that might make them more or less sympathetic to a particular line of argument. This time, he planned to assign the task to nine lawyers, one for each justice. Already delivered was a twenty-one-page list of every clerk who had ever worked for any of them.

Olson told Boies that he thought the odds were good that the Court would take the case. But he had been at this game long enough to know better than to bet on it, or to waste a lot of time speculating. As he put it, "I don't open the oven door too much to see how the bread is baking. They'll tell us what they want, when they are ready."

"I don't have the faintest idea what they are going to do," he said, sitting in his office one day. "Do the liberals want to take the case? Do they think they are going to win? I don't know. Do the conservatives? It all could depend on things we can't control. How much vote counting are they doing in their own heads, subliminally or not, or are they just looking at it on the merits?"

It could all come down to how the other justices read Kennedy, or the "sphinx of Sacramento," as the California-born, Reagan-appointed justice was sometimes called. It might be known as the Roberts Court, but Kennedy was still the must-get vote in controversial cases.

He was a man of many contradictions. He was formal in dress and speech, wearing pocket squares and addressing one audience as "my fellow citizens," and inhabiting gilded red-and-gold chambers that could have been decorated by Versace. He was a voracious reader, fiction generally, and loved to talk about the books he was reading. One former clerk recalled a lengthy discussion about Russian novelist Fyodor Dostoyevsky and the nature of the human soul. But unlike Justices Ginsburg and Scalia, who regularly attended the opera together, he was not a fixture in highfalutin Washington circles, preferring to cook out over his Weber grill with his wife and family.

Entire treatises have been written about Kennedy's jurisprudence. Chief

Justice Roberts liked to see himself as a pragmatic umpire, calling constitutional "balls and strikes," Scalia and Thomas as judicial mediums, channeling original intent. But Kennedy, according to former clerks, was less mechanical, more empathetic.

He had a "romantic and optimistic view of the Court," said one, viewing it as a "shining light on a hill, a place where enlightened judges help to shape a civil society," said another. While generally conservative, he had no trouble breaking with his conservative brethren when it suited him. He was less concerned than some of the other justices with what he called the "temper of the times."

"You have to remember that we live in a constitutional democracy, not a democracy where the voice of the people each week, each year, has complete effect," he said in an interview on PBS's *Frontline*. "There are certain enduring human rights that must be protected."

He looked not just to the law, but at what was "right and wrong, fair and just," said a third former clerk, using a prism that took into account evolving societal mores. Justice Scalia searched the Constitution's text before reaching a decision; Kennedy had spoken of also searching his conscience. "We must never lose sight of the fact that the law has a moral foundation," he once said, "and we must never fail to ask ourselves not only what the law is, but what the law should be."

When brooding over a ruling, Kennedy tried to put himself in the shoes of the people who would be impacted, as he did in a 1991 case called *Edmonson v. Leesville Concrete Company* that struck down race-based jury selection in civil trials. Thaddeus Donald Edmonson, an African American construction worker, had sued the company for injuries he suffered while on the job. The company had used preemptory challenges to dismiss two black jurors from the jury without asking any questions that would determine whether they could serve impartially. The case pitted two private parties against one another, but it was the request of Edmonson's lawyer to consider the feelings of the jurors that most swayed Kennedy.

"It was a very beautiful statement, to the effect that, 'may it please the Court this case is not just about my client . . . it's about two jurors who are not in this court room and not a party to this suit," Kennedy later recounted in an interview recorded for a Web site called LawProse.org. "Those jurors, when they went into a United States District courthouse that day knew, or thought, that the right of service on a jury was as important as the right to vote, and for them, service on a jury was especially important because their fathers and their grandmothers and their mothers and their grandfathers could not have served."

He was known to dramatically switch his vote, as he did in a 1992 abortion case. Privately, he was critical of the Court's reasoning in the *Roe v. Wade* decision, which predated his tenure, viewing it as "an institutional disaster," according to one former clerk. But he infuriated the Right by upholding the right to abortion in a case called *Casey v. Planned Parenthood*, in a ruling that referenced the Court's hesitancy to overturn prior decisions: "Liberty finds no refuge in a jurisprudence of doubt."

Years later, when the late justice Harry Blackmun's papers were released, it would become clear that Kennedy had abandoned what would have been a conservative majority to overturn *Roe* at the last minute. But he hinted at it at the time when, looking out at the protesters gathered outside the Court just before the decision was announced, he suggested to a reporter that he had reached a point of no return. "Sometimes you don't know if you're Caesar about to cross the Rubicon, or Captain Queeg cutting your own tow line."

He might say one thing on the bench, or at conference when the justices took their preliminary vote, but his opinions sometimes came out altogether differently. He had a habit of breaking out an easel and jotting down potential rationales. "Let's talk about this, what's your view?" he would ask his own clerks, and sometimes, especially if he was trying to bring a colleague around to his side, clerks from other justices' chambers as well. It helped him to think aloud, and his opinions often became more expansive as he talked them through. As one former clerk put it, "When he swings, he swings hard." He spoke often about the arc of history, and he viewed the Court's role as a force for good, "confirming the movement of society toward a place of more perfect union, equality and liberty," according to a fourth clerk.

He saw the promise of the Constitution's due process clause, that no person may be deprived of "life, liberty, or property, without due process of law," as transcendent, the "right to define one's own concept of existence, of meaning, of the universe, and of the mystery of human life," as the *Casey* opinion put it.

In blazing the Court's path on gay rights in the *Romer* and *Lawrence* cases, Kennedy had elevated the concept of human dignity into constitutional principle. According to one former clerk who remained close to him, his views on sexual orientation were unambiguous. "He thinks that you are born that way, and that it has no relevance to your capacity to be a productive member of society."

He was offended by what he viewed as petty meanness. A state may not, as he wrote in the *Romer* case, single out a class of citizens and make them a "stranger to its laws." But Kennedy was also a staunch federalist, who viewed the states' power to regulate certain aspects of public life as a necessary check against tyranny. And those familiar with his thinking said that his *Lawrence* opinion, striking down antisodomy laws, was driven less by the law's discriminatory impact and more by a libertarian antipathy toward government intrusion into constitutionally protected, private sexual conduct that in his view hurt no one.

Early on, Olson had asked Paul Cappuccio, the general counsel of Time Warner Inc. and a friend who had clerked for both Scalia and Kennedy, for his view on how Kennedy would come down. With public opinion shifting as rapidly as it was, Olson had tried to frame the Proposition 8 case so as to present the justices with the starkest of choices:

Did this Court want to be viewed by history as the *Plessy v. Ferguson* of its day, condemning another generation of gays and lesbians to separate but unequal marriage status, just as that 1896 decision upholding segregation condemned African Americans to second-class citizenship for another half century? Or did it want to be viewed as a modern-day *Brown v. Board of Education*, sweeping away the last vestige of government-sponsored discrimination?

Cappuccio's best guess at the time was that Kennedy would care about being on the right side of history, and that his expansive views on liberty and equality would trump any federalist reluctance to stick it to the states that wanted to keep the status quo. But that was before the convergence of the DOMA cases and Prop 8.

That changed the calculus, he told Olson and Ted Boutrous. Kennedy also liked to view himself as measured, he said, and Olson was asking for an aggressive read of the Constitution. If both cases were heard in the same term, Kennedy might decide to split the baby. He could strike down the DOMA provision denying same-sex couples federal benefits on the grounds that the federal government had no legitimate interest in denying recognition to marriages that had been blessed by the states, burnishing his legacy as the Court's chief advocate for gays and lesbians and nudging the country in the direction of equality, but uphold Proposition 8 on federalism grounds by finding that the definition of marriage was the realm of the states.

Be careful what you wish for, Cappuccio warned.

"The only person who should want this case to go up is Chuck Cooper," he said.

Finally, at 3:13 P.M. eastern time, SCOTUSblog lit up. The justices had emerged from their December 7 conference.

"We have the orders now. Prop 8 is granted. So is *Windsor*. Those are the only two marriage cases granted."

In a conference room at Robbie Kaplan's firm in New York, everyone started jumping up and down and screaming. At AFER's office in Los Angeles, Chad, Adam, and the rest of the crew did the same. Enrique Monagas was in his office at Gibson Dunn, unable to get anything done, when the news flashed across his screen.

"Yes!" he thought.

At his firm in San Francisco, Judge Walker was taking a break from a lengthy mediation he had been overseeing. Like Olson and Chad, he was hoping that the Court would "bite the bullet," as he put it, and deal head-on with the questions raised by the passage of Prop 8. But he had forgotten that today could be the day the Supreme Court announced its cert decision until he saw it flash across the *New York Times* Web site and his e-mail pinged. Walker had bet a friend dinner that the Court would take the case.

You won, the friend e-mailed. Pick your favorite restaurant.

Bruce Cohen was driving along Santa Monica Boulevard when he got a text from AFER. He pulled over to the side of the road as CBS national news broke into his local radio station's report. He had talked himself into the idea that if the Supreme Court declined to hear the case it would be good for gay Californians, if not the rest of the country. Only now did he realize just how much he had been hoping for this outcome.

"There's only one Supreme Court of the United States," he recalled thinking, "and our case is going there!"

Nearby, the Reiners were in a theater, watching Cohen's latest hit movie, *Silver Linings Playbook*. Soon enough, a measure of trepidation would set in. Which justices voted to grant cert? Was it the four conservatives, and if so, did that mean that they believed they could win Kennedy's vote to uphold bans like Prop 8? If it was the four liberals, would they be hesitant to decide the issue broadly? But for now, they just looked at each other, high-fived, and ran out to the car to call Chad and the rest of the AFER gang.

In Florida, though, a less euphoric scene was unfolding. David Boies had just stepped off a private jet when he heard the news via a four-word e-mail from Olson: "Cert has been granted." He had flown in from Rhode Island, where he had taken on a massive new case: defending the state's attempt to overhaul its pension system against a challenge by the unions.

The night before, he and Dawn Schneider, who handled press for Boies, had been talking about the case. He had set the odds of the Supreme Court taking the case at between 30 and 35 percent, so the decision came as a surprise.

"David," she said, hugging him, "congratulations on getting the attention of the highest court in the land."

He looked at her, subdued. "But I didn't want them to grant cert," he said, before climbing into the gray Chevy Suburban waiting for him on the tarmac.

He had mostly kept quiet about his growing unease, but he had stunned Adam several weeks earlier by telling him that he put the team's chances of winning the case at the Supreme Court at only fifty-fifty. "Where was that three years ago?" Adam recalled thinking.

Boies was less trusting of the justices than Olson. A Court that had done to him what it did in *Bush v. Gore* could do anything, and, as his wife, Mary, and taken to warning of late, "Nothing good has come out of this court recently." She worried aloud that some members of the team were getting drunk on their own whiskey, and when Schneider e-mailed her a copy of the cert order to keep for posterity that afternoon, she wrote back darkly, "Don't frame it yet."

But Boies did not share his fears when he joined Olson and Boutrous, who were at the Peninsula Hotel in Los Angeles for a partner meeting, on a conference call. The Supreme Court, in its orders, had made clear that in addition to the equal protection claims raised in both cases, the lawyers should be prepared to argue whether standing questions prevented the Court from reaching the merits and deciding the constitutionality of Proposition 8 or DOMA. In the Prop 8 case, those questions arose from the state's failure to defend the initiative on appeal. In the DOMA case, they arose because the federal government was appealing a ruling finding DOMA unconstitutional, even though the government agreed that was the correct outcome, in order to enable members of Congress, who arguably might not be able to invoke the Court's jurisdiction to challenge that decision.

By including those questions in both cases, the Court gave itself the option of dismissing them on procedural grounds, without confronting the important constitutional claims raised by Kris, Sandy, Jeff, Paul, and Edie Windsor. That would leave intact the decisions of the trial courts that had heard the two cases. So in California, the state would stop enforcing Proposition 8 based on Judge Walker's order, but the question of whether bans like it were unconstitutional would go unaddressed. And while Edie Windsor would get her money back, per the New York district court's order in her case, DOMA would remain the law of the land.

"It's almost like they are leaving themselves an out," said Josh Lipshutz, a former Scalia clerk had recently joined the Gibson Dunn Prop 8 team.

When the call was opened up to reporters, Boies acknowledged some "mixed feelings" about the Court's decision to review the Ninth Circuit ruling, even as he pronounced himself "encouraged and excited." But Olson made no pretense at being disappointed. He felt as strongly as ever that this was the right case at the right time, and, as he once put it, any good poker player knows that is the moment to "go all in."

"I think it's going to be so important for the Supreme Court to address the merits here," he said, ostensibly to the reporters, but in reality to the justices. "We all felt all along, that this case was—and we said it in our briefs filed in the Supreme Court—that this case was a perfect vehicle to decide the fundamental rights of all Americans with respect to the right to marry."

"As much as we want to get married," said Kris, who was also on the call, "what we have ultimately wanted was the, the very biggest and broadest, boldest outcome possible. And that can only happen if the Supreme Court listened to our case."

Hanging up, Boutrous turned to Olson. The adrenaline was still pumping, but the enormity of what the case meant to so many people suddenly hit them both at once.

"Now," Boutrous said, "all we have to do is win."

THIRTY-FIVE

SELMA TO STONEWALL

On January 18, 2013, Ted Olson returned to the U.S. Department of Justice, David Boies and Terry Stewart in tow, and made his way up to an ornate conference room on whose walls a photo of Olson still hung, where he was greeted by a man whose job he once held: Donald Verrilli, the solicitor general of the United States of America.

Verrilli, a mild-mannered man with a salt-and-pepper mustache, had taken over the office in 2011, after the Justice Department's internal deliberations led it to take the position that DOMA's denial of federal benefits to same-sex couples was unconstitutional. Olson was a man on a mission, there to convince Verrilli that the time had come for the administration to get off the fence and do the same in the Prop 8 case, by filing a brief with the U.S. Supreme Court that embraced a constitutional right to marry for gays and lesbians.

Part of the strategy in any major Supreme Court case involves marshaling outsiders to file amicus curiae, or "friend of the court," briefs that augment the primary arguments. All parties in the marriage case had been hard at it since cert was granted in December.

Cooper, for instance, had been working with Nelson Lund, a professor at George Mason University School of Law, on a brief arguing that the case should be decided solely on the basis of the law, not social and behavioral science "with a long history of being shaped and driven by politics and ideology." A number of state attorneys general from parts of the country where same-sex marriage was outlawed had filed another arguing that it was within the states' purview to define marriage. Officials from different religious denominations had weighed in on both sides of the debate. And dozens of briefs, with the guidance of both Olson's and Robbie Kaplan's teams, had been filed in support of the four Prop 8 plaintiffs and Edie Windsor.

One played to Kennedy's interest in international law by outlining the increasing number of countries that had legalized same-sex marriage. Another, dubbed the "red state brief," made the case for Court intervention by arguing that millions of gays and lesbians live in deeply conservative states where they are powerless to dismantle systems of "de jure denigration" that deprive gay and lesbian citizens of legal equality "from cradle to grave." In an episode that "echoed an era when municipalities closed swimming pools rather than integrate them," the brief noted by way of example, "the Salt Lake City School district shuttered all non-curricular school clubs rather than allow a Gay-Straight Alliance to meet." A third, signed by 214 members of Congress, urged the Court to find DOMA's denial of benefits to married same-sex couples unconstitutional.

Ken Mehlman was working with Reginald Brown, who served in the White House Counsel's Office under President George W. Bush, on a brief in the Proposition 8 case that would soon make front-page news. Quoting liberally from conservative tomes like Barry Goldwater's *The Conscience of a Conservative* and Alexis de Tocqueville's *Democracy in America,* the brief argued that Proposition 8 failed the rational basis test because there was no legitimate, fact-based reason to keep gays and lesbians from entering into an institution that "promotes the conservative values of stability, mutual support and mutual obligation." Marriage, the brief concluded, provides a "protective shelter and reduces the need for reliance on the state," and would greatly benefit the children of gay and lesbian couples.

It was signed by 131 Republican officials, many of them brand names and newcomers to the cause of same-sex marriage, including senior members of the Reagan administration like former White House chief of staff Ken Duberstein, Bush cabinet members like former Homeland Security chief Tom Ridge and former commerce secretary Carlos Gutierrez, Bush Justice Department veterans like Deputy Attorney General Jim Comey, Bush's undersecretary of the Treasury, Bush's godson, the former general counsel of Romney's campaign, four former Republican governors, and former Proposition 8 defender Meg Whitman, who had once vowed to appeal Judge Walker's decision but had changed her position after losing the California gubernatorial race to Jerry Brown.

All of those voices were important, but the one Olson strongly felt was most crucial was still missing: Verrilli's. Justices leaning their way might feel more comfortable striking down bans like Proposition 8 if that position had the stamp of approval of another branch of government. "It adds institutional impetus and imprimatur," explained Amir Tayrani. Conversely, if the administration failed to take the position that Proposition 8 was unconstitutional, it would give "everybody on the Court who wanted to come out against us a fig leaf, and a pretty big fig leaf at that," Boies said.

The solicitor general is often called the "tenth justice." Unlike other "friends of the Court," the justices afford the solicitor general argument time. Because the office argues cases on behalf of the U.S. government and appears so often before them, the justices tend to afford its views great weight. With that in mind, it picks its battles carefully, mindful of the need to articulate a federal interest.

The office had to take a position in DOMA; Edie Windsor had sued the federal government to get her money back, and it was a federal law involving federal benefits that the federal government was still enforcing. But it was not a party to the Proposition 8 litigation, and it had declined weigh in on some notable past challenges to state laws. It took no position in the *Loving v. Virginia* case striking down state interracial marriage bans, for instance, or in the two landmark gay rights cases, *Romer v. Evans* and *Lawrence v. Texas*.

What interest, asked one of the lawyers whom Verrilli had brought to the meeting, did the U.S. government have in a California voter–approved ban?

Terry Stewart had prepared for this question. She and Olson had made their peace with the idea that neither could completely control what the other did. Their strategic disagreement had evaporated once the justices decided to take the case. With multiple choices now before the Court, Stewart saw no reason why Olson shouldn't make the broadest possible argument: In her view, "It's going to shame them out of doing nothing for us." She still thought that Olson and Chad, in their desire to be the saviors of the gay community, had set expectations too high. But when she shared her worry about the Court with Olson, he had been empathetic. He understood why she, of all people, would feel that way, he had said. It was her victory in the California Supreme Court, after all, that the voters had snatched away when they passed Prop 8.

Now she rallied to Olson's side with a list of precedents supporting the solicitor general's involvement. In the 1960s, the solicitor general had argued to strike down a California voter initiative and an Akron, Ohio, city ordinance in two landmark housing discrimination cases called *Reitman v. Mulkey* and *Hunter v. Erickson.* The first was argued by then solicitor general Thurgood Marshall, whose portrait hung in Verrilli's office and who would go on to become the nation's first African American justice. And citing the "federal government's special responsibility for assuring vindication of the fundamental rights guaranteed by the Constitution," the solicitor general had argued to strike down state segregation laws in *Brown v. Board of Education.*

Olson, never one to mince words, was impassioned as he argued that it was no less a moral imperative that Verrilli take a position in the Prop 8 case. "This," participants recall him saying, "is one of those 'what did Daddy do in the war' moments."

———

Three days later, after taking the oath of office on a Bible once owned by Martin Luther King Jr., President Obama stood before a crowd of close to one million people and gave an inaugural address that drew a straight line between the iconic civil rights fights for racial and gender equality and the current struggle being waged by gays and lesbians.

"We, the people, declare today that the most evident of truths—that all of us are created equal—is the star that guides us still; just as it guided our forebears through Seneca Falls and Selma and Stonewall; just as it guided all those men and women, sung and unsung, who left footprints along this great mall, to hear a preacher say that we cannot walk alone; to hear a King proclaim that our individual freedom is inextricably bound to the freedom of every soul on Earth. It is now our generation's task to carry on what these pioneers began."

When he was sworn in to office in 2009, Obama had infuriated gay rights advocates by inviting Rick Warren, an evangelical pastor of a megachurch in California and an outspoken supporter of Proposition 8, to give the invocation.

But four years later, on a sunny, brisk afternoon, Obama delivered his clearest and boldest declaration yet that in a country whose march through the centuries had been defined by an ever-expanding ideal of freedom, the disparate treatment of gays and lesbians could no longer be tolerated.

"Our journey is not complete until our gay brothers and sisters are treated like anyone else under the law," he said, "for if we are truly created equal, then surely the love we commit to one another must be equal, as well."

Boies, who was sitting with his wife, Mary, in prime seats in the stands, felt a shiver go up his spine. Surely a man who had just given an address like that could no longer stand on the sidelines.

───

Chad and Boies were not yet in full panic mode when they walked up the driveway of the White House nine days later on January 30, but they were close. The day after the president delivered his stirring inaugural speech, two things had happened, neither of them good.

Cooper had filed an opening brief with the U.S. Supreme Court that quoted the president three times, drawing liberally from the preelection interview in which Obama disclaimed any desire to "nationalize" the "healthy debate" taking place in states around the country on marriage and declared that supporters of marriage bans "are not coming at it from a mean-spirited perspective," thus undercutting the legal argument that Proposition 8 was motivated by animus. And White House spokesman Jay Carney, asked whether the president's speech indicated a shift from his previous position that the states should be left to chart their own course on marriage, said it did not, adding that "we're not involved" in the Proposition 8 case.

Since the election, Chad and Mehlman had been talking about the need for the gay rights movement to become more assertive in general, and on this issue in particular. Asking the Supreme Court to overturn Proposition 8 would require the president to evolve yet again, and Mehlman had already e-mailed senior adviser David Plouffe some suggested talking points for the president to use to publicly explain why he now believed it was a matter for the Supreme Court, rather than the states, to decide:

- On 14 different occasions, the US Supreme Court has held the right to marry the person you love to be one of the most important relationships in the human condition.

- This right is particularly personal to me as the child of parents who, prior to the Supreme Court's landmark decision in *Loving v. Virginia* in 1967, would not have been recognized as married in at least 16 states.

- My parents were married in Hawaii, but if they had moved to a state like Virginia or Maryland at this time, their marriage would not have been recognized. Today, it seems inconceivable that such discrimination was tolerated and widespread.

- My parents' situation is not unlike the one faced by loving gay and lesbian couples legally married in states like New York or Maryland, or here in the District of Columbia.

In the wake of Carney's unhelpful comments, Mehlman offered Chad some typically blunt advice. "This is not about friendship," Mehlman recalled saying. "It's about interests. The gay community raised a lot of money for Obama, and now they want something in return. No more beaten down, begging for scraps at the table."

Chad had fired off a press statement, then privately asked for the meeting at the White House. "In the contemporary challenge to the Defense of Marriage Act, the law barring federal recognition of lawful same-sex marriages, the Justice Department has made clear its belief that that odious law defies our Constitution's promise of equality," his public statement read. "As the Justices deliberate in a building that bears the chiseled words 'equal justice under law,' we hope the White House will ensure that its thinking in the *Perry* case—and the voice of a decisive majority of Americans—is heard loud and clear."

But time was running out when Chad and Boies sat down in the West Wing with Valerie Jarrett, the president's friend and adviser, and White House counsel Kathryn Ruemmler. The Supreme Court was set to hear arguments in the two marriage cases on March 26 and March 27, and the solicitor general had only a month left to make a decision.

Olson, in e-mail exchanges with Chad prior to the White House meeting, had advised him to stress the moral argument, the president's legacy. Chad had forwarded the exchanges to Kristina, asking for her thoughts. Absolutely not, she said. The president and his people were perfectly capable of assessing his legacy on their own. Stress the law, and why bringing in the solicitor general would legally make a difference.

Boies, following that advice, began by laying out those reasons, at one point becoming teary-eyed. He spoke about the inaugural speech in the context of the case. Now that the president had said what he said, Boies argued, "silence would not be considered neutral." It would, in fact, be deeply harmful, sending a signal to the Court that even the Obama administration believed that the position that gays and lesbians have a fundamental right to marry was a bridge too far. It could cost them the case.

"It's already being used against us," Boies said, citing Cooper's briefs.

It had already been decided that Olson alone would be arguing before the Supreme Court. To have a conservative make the case for same-sex marriage to the justices had been the point from the outset, and Chad was insistent. But Boies did not know that. On press calls, Olson had said it was up in the air. ("It's awkward," he explained in a private aside.)

If the solicitor general jumped in, Boies now told the two women, Olson would have to give him ten minutes of his time, which meant that he, Boies, would not have a chance to argue.

"And there's no case in my entire life I'd rather argue than this one."

Both White House officials seemed impressed by their pleas. But further lobbying via the press, Boies recalled Jarrett saying before they took their leave, would not be helpful. This was a legal decision, not a political one.

The easiest course for Solicitor General Verrilli to take would have been to give the Proposition 8 case a pass. Arguing that state bans like California's were unconstitutional complicated the administration's case against DOMA.

It was possible to make a logical argument that Congress had intruded on an area traditionally left to the states in passing DOMA, while simultaneously arguing in the Proposition 8 case that states cannot do whatever they want in the marriage arena: The Supreme Court had demonstrated that there was a constitutional floor when it struck down state laws banning interracial marriage in *Loving v. Virginia*.

The bigger hurdle was a strategic one. Verrilli's view, expressed during robust internal debates, was that the department could not just go gliding down this path in order to reach a happy place without first understanding the risks.

DOMA was by far the easier lift of the two cases. The justices did not have to declare a nationwide right for same-sex couples to marry; they simply had to find that the law unconstitutionally undermined a democratic process that had led some states to recognize the marriages of same-sex couples by treating those marriages differently for no good reason. The remedy was relatively uncontroversial: Already married couples would simply start receiving benefits.

What happens, Verrilli had pressed Olson during their meeting, if you prevail on your broader argument? What is the remedy?

"We said it wouldn't be like *Brown v. Board of Education*, where you had to redesign entire school systems," Terry Stewart recalled. "It would just be a matter of county clerks issuing licenses. And then Don said, 'Yeah, but I'm thinking about county clerks in Mississippi.'"

It was clear he was concerned that a fifty-state ruling finding a constitutional right for same-sex couples to marry had the potential to create the kind of backlash that could give some justices pause. If Justice Kennedy became convinced that the only way he could strike down DOMA was to adopt a rule of law that would require striking down same-sex marriage bans across the country, the worry was that he might get cold feet. He might also see the administration's entry into the case as political. Either way, as Attorney General Eric Holder later put it, "we potentially run the risk of losing him."

On the other hand, the justices were smart people. They understood that the position the Justice Department had already taken in the DOMA case, that laws targeting gays and lesbians deserved heightened scrutiny, made it difficult for bans like Proposition 8 to survive a constitutional challenge. There were ways for Verrilli to dance around that—deflecting questions as hypothetical and best left for another day—but the real question was, should he?

Olson had sent over a memo, prepared by Terry Stewart at Verrilli's request, outlining the parallels between the arguments used to defend interracial marriage and same-sex marriage bans. They were, Verrilli told colleagues, striking.

The proponents of Proposition 8 argued that allowing gays and lesbians to marry could deinstitutionalize traditional marriages. The Alabama Supreme Court, in an 1877 case, opined that the state must "guard" against the "disturbances" interracial marriage would produce. The proponents of Proposition 8's argument that the impact of allowing gays and lesbians to marry was unknown was also echoed in some of the interracial marriage ban cases: In *Loving v. Virginia*, for instance, the Commonwealth argued that the Court should defer to the wisdom of the states in determining the "desirability of a policy of permitting or preventing such alliances," given the "conflicting scientific opinion upon the effects of interracial marriage." It also referenced the state's interest in promoting an optimal child-rearing environment, noting the burden "half-breed" children faced in being accepted by society.

Verrilli read Martin Luther King Jr.'s "Letter from Birmingham Jail," responding to criticisms by fellow black clergymen that his demands were premature and ill timed. The oppression of African Americans was beyond compare, but the civil rights leader's words, about how one can only fight a "degenerating sense of 'nobodiness'" for so long before "the cup of endurance runs over," resonated. He lingered over the lopsided suicide statistics that charted the despair felt by many gay, lesbian, bisexual, and transgender teens. He followed his own heightened scrutiny argument to its logical conclusion. And then he shared his recommendation with Holder: The government should take a stand.

Holder and Chad went way back; Holder had served on the board of Rob Reiner's foundation. He, like Verrilli, believed that there were "collateral consequences" to the department's decision that could not be ignored. "I mean, Chad is right. The way a gay boy or young gay girl view themselves is similar, again, to the way African Americans in 1953, '52, saw themselves when they had to deal with this notion of 'separate but equal.'"

"Staying out was just not consistent," Holder said, "with where we wanted to be tactically, legally, or morally."

Verrilli, he believed, had made the right decision.

President Eisenhower famously read and edited the solicitor general's amicus brief in the *Brown v. Board of Education* case. That did not happen in *Hollingsworth v. Perry*. But at a meeting in the Oval Office to go over the Justice Department's recommendation, President Obama did play an instrumental role in shaping the final product.

In addition to Holder and Verrilli, Ruemmler, his White House counsel, and Denis McDonough, his chief of staff, were also in attendance. The meeting lasted close to an hour, an extraordinary block of presidential time that spoke to the importance of what they were discussing. "This was not a briefing," Holder recalled. "This was an interaction. This wasn't where we were getting him up to speed for a decision. This was a meeting of equals in terms of knowledge of the facts, knowledge of the law. This was four lawyers and then Denis getting together to talk about what the appropriate position was."

Anticipating what the justices might do, "the president was asking Don very hard questions," Ruemmler recalled, including how the court should reconcile Obama's own prior comments that definition of marriage was a matter that should be decided by the states.

"He was almost using us to question himself, to check his own—where he may have been himself," Holder said.

At Chad's request, Ben Jealous, the head of the NAACP, had joined him in coauthoring a private letter to the president, pleading the case for intervention. Chad had also lobbied Vice President Biden's chief of staff. But the president did not need to be persuaded on the larger moral question; he too saw the marriage debate through the prism of civil rights, according to both Ruemmler and Holder.

Obama had seen firsthand just how much his endorsement of marriage equality meant when one of the first lady's good friends told him afterward that it took the president's words for his mother to finally really accept him.

With everyone in agreement on the threshold question of whether the government should take a position, much of the rest of the meeting was dedicated to what position it should take. The president had in the past spoken to Holder about the fragility of the Court's power. Now, he talked about Justice Kennedy's devotion to federalism and states' rights. He made it clear that he wanted to offer the justices an incremental way to decide the Proposition 8 case that would not force them to overturn bans across the country.

"By the time we leave," Holder said, "we know what position we're taking, what our strategy is, and it's all decided at that point."

On the afternoon of February 28, Ruemmler called Chad with a heads-up: When the plaintiffs stood before the justices, they would not be standing alone. Standing with them would be the U.S. government. "The next time I see you will be at the Supreme Court," she said.

Jarrett called him next, excitedly talking about what a historic moment it would be when the solicitor general argued the case alongside Olson in just a few short weeks.

The administration's brief, filed at 6:30 P.M. that evening, argued that Proposition 8 violated the Constitution's equal protection clause. And, as the president directed, it offered the Court a path to rule in favor of the Proposition 8 plaintiffs without going the full distance. In what became known as the "eight-state solution," the solicitor general said that while heightened scrutiny should be applied to all same-sex marriage bans, those bans were particularly hard to justify in the states with domestic partnership laws that offered all the benefits of marriage but the name. Besides California, that argument would cover Delaware, Hawaii, Illinois, Nevada, New Jersey, Oregon, and Rhode Island.

Chad instantly sent out a press release: "The President has turned the inspirational words of his second inaugural address into concrete action."

Then he and Adam, who had relocated to Washington, D.C., in advance of the arguments, headed off for a celebratory frozen custard at a nearby Shake Shack.

THIRTY-SIX

FRAMING THE ARGUMENTS

Robbie Kaplan did not want to be arguing her case alongside Olson, any more than he wanted to be arguing his alongside hers. But the Court had not given either of them any choice in the matter, which was why the two legal teams converged in a conference room at Gibson Dunn on March 15.

In less than two weeks, the Court would first hear arguments on the constitutionality of Prop 8 in the *Hollingsworth v. Perry* case on March 26, followed by the DOMA arguments in *United States v. Windsor* on March 27. Each side would have just thirty minutes to make its case, and ten minutes of Olson's and Kaplan's time would go to the solicitor general.

Preparing for a Supreme Court argument is a little like running a marathon: It is important to train hard and do some shorter practice runs in the lead-up, but not so many as to risk exhaustion. The way appellate advocates do that is through practice sessions known as moot courts. The mock arguments are mentally draining, as lawyers playing the justices poke holes in the advocates' arguments, trying to goad them into making mistakes, and afterward offer strategic, and sometime contradictory, advice on how to avoid traps.

"I think of it as spring-loading yourself," said Ted Boutrous, who was helping to coordinate the prep sessions. "You have to consume all this information and have it at your fingertips, and it involves screening out everything else. You really are trying to get into this space."

Both Olson and Kaplan had already done several moots, but this was their first and only together, and it was especially critical given the built-in federalism tensions between the cases. Care needed to be taken to ensure that an answer by one could not be used against the other.

The teams were as different as could be. The Proposition 8 team was led by two straight men; Kaplan's was predominantly female, and led by three lesbians; Kaplan had recruited Pam Karlan, the codirector of Stanford Law School's Supreme Court Litigation Clinic, and Mary Bonauto, the gay-rights lawyer who had filed the two DOMA challenges the Court failed to take, to help her.

Olson, as a veteran advocate, was used to multitasking, and up until a few weeks before had been juggling several other major cases as well as several joint projects with Boies; the two had filmed a pilot legal talk show for Bloomberg TV and had announced a book deal. Kaplan, who had never before argued before the Supreme Court, had in recent months devoted more than half her time to Edie's case alone, at one point barely leaving her apartment for sixteen straight days while writing the umpteenth version of her brief.

Terry Stewart, who knew everyone on the DOMA team and had been helping to coordinate the amicus briefs that supported both cases, greeted Kaplan warmly. Coffee and snacks had been laid out, and the lawyers who had not yet met introduced themselves. Chad, whose role as president of the Human Rights Campaign meant he had to speak for both cases in the media, came in and took a seat.

———

While Olson had been hunkered down in his windowless, binder-strewn inner sanctum at Gibson Dunn, jotting down points and counterpoints on yellow legal pads with the meticulously sharpened number 2 pencils he insisted on using, and putting himself though his paces in the moot court sessions, Chad had been overseeing a small army that was hard at work on a final media push aimed just as squarely at the justices.

Housed in one conference room on the first floor of the Human Rights Campaign headquarters was the AFER war room operation, headed by Adam. Nearly a dozen staffers were there to handle all the press around the Prop 8 case, from reporter inquiries to live tweets to putting together video clips of the plaintiffs for the Web.

"I don't think it is an overstatement to say that Tuesday, March 26, is going to be the most high-profile day the gay rights movement has ever had," Adam had told his AFER team. "I want to make sure we have thought about everything."

Next door to AFER was the Respect for Marriage Coalition, an umbrella organization comprised of all the groups involved in the legal battles as well as Evan Wolfson's Freedom to Marry political operation. Chad had brought them together to try to ensure that the gay rights movement spoke with one voice in a moment when the justices, and the nation, would all be listening. Hilary Rosen, whose PR firm SKDKnickerbocker was fresh off the New York and Washington State victories, had been hired to coordinate the $2 million effort.

The goals of the media campaign were straightforward, though the execution required a tricky balancing act. First, do no harm to the cases. Kaplan wanted to make her case to the Court, not the public, and the media blitz made her nervous. Even Olson, whose case had always been a public education vehicle, was starting to get the jitters, worried that someone might say or do something that could offend the justices. Adam, in an attempt to reassure the lawyers, had put it this way during a conversation with Boutrous: "Everyone's going to be talking about it, so we damn well better be the ones shaping the message."

The second, and most delicate goal: Create an echo chamber, and infuse it with a message of inevitability, with the aim of convincing the justices that ruling in their favor would put them on the right side of history without creating a backlash. To that end, the coalition had released a poll showing that even people who disagreed with same-sex marriage had accepted it was coming; 77 percent of Americans believed that same-sex marriage would be the law of the land in "a couple of years." An ad featuring Republican supporters had gone up. "Marriage: The Country Is Ready" pamphlets tracking the sharp uptick in support across demographic groups had been mailed to five thousand journalists. The trick was to create what Rosen called a "permission structure" that would allow the Court to rule their way, without ever appearing to be lobbying the Court directly or suggesting that anything other than the facts and the law would play a role in their decision. "What we are focused on is not that marriage is a good thing, but that the country has already decided it's a good thing. And then tying that to the Court's place in history on this issue," she said. "That's the most subtle thing."

The third and final goal of the campaign was to showcase the impact that laws like Proposition 8 and DOMA had on real families. The idea was both to demonstrate the "real harm, right now" legal imperative for the justices to act and, as Rosen described it, to continue to move public opinion in the event that the justices left gays and lesbians to the whims of the democratic process by either upholding Prop 8 and DOMA or failing to reach the merits in one or both of the two cases.

A study by the Pew Research Center of the news coverage in the week leading up to the arguments would find that the coverage of the same-sex marriage debate had been overwhelmingly positive, and it was thanks in large part to the presidential-level political operation that was working behind the scenes to make it all happen. Olivia Alair, who had been the first lady's campaign press secretary before joining Rosen's firm, was overseeing an operation that pitched stories and op-eds and booked handpicked, bipartisan surrogates armed with coalition talking points on the news shows. She was working closely with some of the Republican operatives whom Mehlman had recruited to the cause. "It feels strangely good," she said of sharing trade secrets that they would normally have deployed against one another.

One day, the pitch might be about how while gays and lesbians could now openly serve in the military, when they were posted overseas their spouses were not entitled to benefits like on-post housing. Another day might focus on children, like the eleven-year-old girl who had sent each of the justices a three-paragraph letter, letting them know that in case they had any concerns about the children of gay parents, "I can tell you I am doing great," and asking them to look at the photos she sent of her moms' wedding and "think of us when you make decisions."

The message of inevitability was balanced with a "hard stop" message, with surrogates making the case that only so much legislative progress could be made before it came to a grinding halt in the thirty states that had enacted constitutional bans that prevented lawmakers from voting to give gays and lesbians the right to marry.

The big news of the day involved Senator Rob Portman, a prominent conservative from Ohio who had been on Romney's vice presidential short list. With behind-the-scenes help from Mehlman, he had announced his support for same-sex marriage in an op-ed for the *Columbus Dispatch*, becoming the first sitting Republican U.S. senator to do so. He had once voted to ban gay couples in Washington, D.C., from adopting, and had supported the failed effort to amend the U.S. Constitution to ensure that they could never marry, but said he had changed his mind after learning his son, Will, was gay.

"I wrestled with how to reconcile my Christian faith with my desire for Will to have the same opportunities to pursue happiness and fulfillment as his brother and sister," he wrote. "Ultimately, it came down to the Bible's overarching themes of love and compassion and my belief that we are all children of God."

Chad had more than a thousand Human Rights Campaign members in Ohio write letters of thanks. He and Mehlman often talked about the need to meet and talk to people where they were at, not where they might wish them to be, and his press statement glossed over the fact that Portman had also said that he opposed judicial intervention.

"Like countless dads across the country, Senator Portman has made the basic and courageous choice to put parenting before politics," Chad's statement read. "When it comes to marriage equality, all Americans are on the same journey toward recognizing our common humanity. But while 8 in 10 Americans know a gay or lesbian person, it still takes unique courage to speak out publicly for equality. We are very grateful to Senator Portman for his virtuous stand in support of this civil rights cause."

"I've spent the morning trying to avoid the fact that he is actually advocating a state-by-state strategy," Rosen told Chad, as the two waited for the moot to start.

"No one's picked up on that?"

"Not yet," she said. "The only bad thing is that it knocked Eastman off the front page."

John Eastman, the chairman of the National Organization for Marriage, had made their day by calling Chief Justice John Roberts's family "second best" in an interview with the Associated Press. Eastman was explaining his view that laws like Proposition 8 were justified because they promoted an "optimal" environment in which children are raised by biological parents. But in doing so, he managed to insult not one but two of the sitting justices: Roberts was the father of two adopted children, Josie and Jack, and Justice Clarence Thomas and his wife had taken in and raised Thomas's grandnephew.

"The [network and cable news] producers are all saying that Chuck won't respond to interview requests," Rosen said. "This is definitely the latest 'I don't know.'"

Adam laughed. "'I don't know,' 'more American,' 'second best'—*Perry*'s greatest hits."

Just then, Matt McGill wandered over to join them. He was playing one of the justices in the moot that day.

"What do you think that Chuck did when someone sent him the Eastman link?" Chad asked him.

"He probably lost his fucking mind," McGill said. "I know Chuck pretty well, and he can get pretty salty."

=====

It is often said that it is difficult to win a case based solely on the force of one's oral argument. That is because the justices generally form their views on how a case should be resolved before a single word is uttered, based on briefs that the parties must file in accordance with persnickety Court rules that dictate everything from the typeface (Century only, please), to the number of copies (forty), to the paper stock (not less than sixty pounds in weight).

The briefs, laying out the facts, relevant case law, and arguments, must be bound into 8.5-by-11-inch color-coded booklets. The opening brief of the "petitioner"—the party that sought Supreme Court review—is light blue. The respondent's reply brief is light red, and the solicitor general's is gray. The briefs must condense voluminous trial and appellate records into fifteen thousand words or less. The petitioner then gets the last word in the form of a yellow brief no longer than six thousand words.

"Of the two components of the presentation of the case, the brief is ever so much more important," Justice Ruth Bader Ginsburg once said. "It's what we start with; it's what we go back to."

Good briefs are fast-paced and conversational; Justice Clarence Thomas once said the best ones read like an episode of the TV show *24*. They avoid the linguistic pet peeves of the justices; Justice Kennedy did not appreciate adverbs, for instance, while Justice Scalia was a self-described snoot, a fastidious nit-picker "for the mot juste, for using a word precisely the way it should be used." They are direct; Justice Roberts did not want to be made to hack "through a jungle with a machete to try to get to the point."

The briefs in both the DOMA and Prop 8 cases reflected the caliber of the lawyers involved. Kaplan's brief was a legal love story. It opened with a detailed description of the four decades that Edie and Thea had spent together, in an effort to persuade the justices that there was no real difference between Edie's marriage and their own. In "sickness and in health," Kaplan wrote, they bought a home, supported one another's careers, coped with Thea's progressive multiple sclerosis as "she moved from a cane, to crutches, to a wheelchair," and ultimately married, in a legal ceremony in Canada that was subsequently recognized by the state of New York.

The brief filed by Paul Clement, Kaplan's opponent, reflected his view that DOMA was probably dead on arrival if he could not prevent the Court from applying heightened scrutiny. It played up the recent political victories with a declaration that "the democratic process is at work," and played on the justices' institutional concerns with a warning that "constitutionalizing an issue yields a one-size-fits-all solution that tends to harden the views of those who lose out at the courthouse."

Cooper's offered a sharper version of the arguments he had been making all along, branding "plaintiffs' genderless, adult-centered understanding of marriage" an "academic invention." Borrowing Olson's line at the press conference announcing the case, it declared that the citizens of California bore gays and lesbians no ill will: "They are our family members, our friends, our colleagues and co-workers, our community and business leaders, and our public officials."

Olson's brief stood out for two reasons. The Supreme Court's guidelines warn lawyers in no uncertain terms to "focus only on the question or questions presented in the petition that was granted. Do not deviate." And generally, lawyers in Olson's position defend the grounds upon which a lower court decided in their favor.

Because of the narrow way the Ninth Circuit had decided the case, only one question regarding the merits of Proposition 8 was presented to the Court: "Whether the Equal Protection Clause of the Fourteenth Amendment prohibits the State of California from defining marriage as the union of a man and a woman."

But the question that Olson set out to answer first, before any other, was a different one: whether the Constitution's due process clause prohibited states across the country from denying the fundamental right to marry to gays and lesbians—the very question that the Ninth Circuit had said should not be decided in the Proposition 8 case.

"This case is about marriage, 'the most important relation in life,'" Olson's brief opened, "a relationship and intimate decision that this Court has variously described at least 14 times as a right protected by the Due Process Clause that is central for *all* individuals' liberty, privacy, spirituality, personal autonomy, sexuality, and dignity; a matter fundamental to one's place in society; and an expression of love, emotional support, public commitment, and social status."

An earlier version, drafted by some of the younger appellate lawyers on the team and approved by Boutrous, had emphasized the discriminatory nature of Proposition 8, both because that was the equal protection argument the Court had instructed them to make and because it offered the Court an easier, more incremental way to decide the case; if the justices were so inclined, they could find that Proposition 8 was motivated by prejudice while leaving open the possibility that bans in other states in fact did serve some legitimate governmental purpose.

Olson fully understood the power of the equal protection argument. The final version of the brief quoted the Court's most famous equal protection decision, *Brown v. Board of Education,* on its very first page, declaring that Proposition 8 "'generates a feeling of inferiority' among gay men and lesbians—and especially their children—'that may affect their hearts and minds in a way unlikely ever to be undone.'"

"But he felt strongly, in his gut, that he wanted to lead with due process," Boutrous recalled.

Due process was the basis of Justice Kennedy's decision in the landmark *Lawrence* case striking down laws criminalizing sodomy. Resolving the Proposition 8 case on due process grounds also obviated the need for the Court to declare a new suspect class, something it had not done since 1972; when the government infringed on a fundamental right, the Court applies a strict scrutiny test regardless of the nature of the group involved. Most important, it allowed Olson to talk about the importance of marriage, the right at stake, to his clients and people like them, and deciding the case on that basis would require the justices to issue the nationwide decision that he wanted.

The case was certainly about the right to be treated equally, to not be singled out and relegated to a lower rung in some voter-imposed caste system. But fundamentally what their clients wanted, in Olson's view, was to be freed from government intrusion into their lives so they could marry one another. "Ted wasn't going to shy away from that argument just because it was a fifty-state decision," Boutrous said, "because his view was that it ought to be."

The fundamental right to marry was a theme the brief returned to repeatedly. "Proponents accuse Plaintiffs (repeatedly) of 'redefining marriage.' . . . But it is Proponents who have imagined (not from *any* of this Court's decisions) a cramped definition of marriage as a utilitarian incentive devised by and put into service by the State—society's way of channeling heterosexual potential parents into 'responsible procreation.' In their 65-page brief about marriage in California, Proponents do not even mention the word 'love.' They seem to have no understanding of the privacy, liberty, and associational values that underlie this Court's recognition of marriage as a fundamental, personal right."

As the moot got under way, however, his inquisitors quickly zeroed in on the potential problem with Olson's framing. If the fundamental right to marry was the right to marry the person you love, what was the limiting principle?

Olson had asked Lisa Blatt, an attorney for Arnold & Porter who had argued more than thirty cases before the Supreme Court and won all but one of them, to play the role of devil's advocate, which she did now with zeal.

"Could I marry my sister?" she asked.

The government might well have a good and constitutionally justifiable reason to prohibit incest, he parried. Blatt came right back at him: "Okay, we won't have sex. I want to marry my sister. I love her.

"I think under your view," she pressed, "you have a constitutional right to marry anyone."

This slippery slope question had come up at every moot court, usually framed around whether polygamy bans were unconstitutional. Terry Stewart had suggested saying that the right to marry the person one loved was the right to marry one person, not two. Olson had toyed with a number of other responses, including that prohibiting polygamy did not single out a disfavored class and served important enough governmental interests to meet the strict scrutiny test, such as preventing the exploitation of women. But given that spending even a minute on this issue would eat up one-twentieth of his time, his plan was to brush past it as quickly as he could, then look to a friendly justice to redirect the argument. In the end, he just did not feel as though it was going to be dispositive.

"This court isn't going to decide this case on polygamy grounds," he'd said during a previous session. "It could be time-consuming and a little like quicksand, so I don't want to stay there."

Olson swatted away other questions with ease. He had three words for the state's interest in promoting procreative relationships: "*Turner v. Safely*," the holding by the Supreme Court that the fundamental right to marry could not be denied to prisoners, who by virtue of their incarceration were incapable of procreating. Pressed on whether he was simply arguing over a "cocktail conversation—when you introduce someone at a party you can't say, 'This is my wife,'" he shot back that it was not simply a word.

"The institution of marriage is understood and appreciated in this country. It is like the word 'citizen.' You could give every individual the right to vote, the right to travel, the right do all the things that citizens can do, and withhold from them the right to call themselves citizens, and they would know, everyone would know, that's second class. That's not as good as being a citizen."

"So, it feels better to be married," Blatt pressed, trying to be as acerbic as possible.

"And it would feel better to be able to drink out of the same drinking fountain, to go to the same schools, and marry someone of the same race," he retorted.

"I love the way you argue," said Blatt, critiquing him afterward. "I'm not sure that I buy your answers with respect to polygamy and incest. I don't know that it's going to matter, in the end, to Justice Kennedy. I'm very moved by everything you said. It just comes down to—"

She paused. "What he thinks."

———

In Olson's view, the first words in an oral argument are the most likely to be remembered. Kaplan shared that assessment, which was why, when it was her turn, she began with the less than stirring declaration that "this is an as-applied challenge."

Olson had framed his case as a landmark, explicitly asking the Court for a *Brown*-like decision by quoting the case on the opening page of his brief. "He's shooting for the stars," she had thought, reading it. Kaplan had the opposite strategy. She wanted the Court to believe that hers was a run-of-the-mill, easy-to-decide estate tax dispute, nothing historic about it. She had even given the Court the out of declaring the law unconstitutional "as applied" to her client and the estate tax, rather than filing a facial challenge to the law that would require them to find the denial of all benefits to any legally married same-sex couple unconstitutional.

She and the other lawyers on her team privately joked that Edie was "already married, already gay." The only question the Court need decide was whether the federal government was justified in treating Edie and Thea's marriage differently when it taxed her client on property she had inherited from her wife, based on a law that insisted they be treated as legal strangers.

If Olson's challenge was to convince the Court that the fundamental right to marry the person of your choice extended to gays and lesbians, but not, as Blatt had put it, to "my cat," the challenge Kaplan faced was that there was no fundamental right to a tax break. Clement, in his brief, had argued that Congress had plenty of reasons to pass DOMA, including a desire to save money by denying gays and lesbians survivor benefits, that could pass constitutional muster under a strict rational basis test.

"It's a federal benefit," McGill challenged her, "so there is a federal interest in determining who gets a federal benefit."

"We could all agree," she protested, "that the federal government could not say we are only going to give estate tax relief to couples married in the springtime."

What about Clement's argument that the federal government had an interest in promoting relationships that could produce children?

"It's hard to see," she said.

No babies, no tax base, came the rejoinder.

"DOMA had nothing to do with that," she said.

"How do you explain the child tax credit?" McGill pressed.

She answered the questions one by one, which was where the critique began once the session came to an end. She had a good voice, and a good tone that she should seek to maintain, Blatt said. "Don't look even remotely bothered by any question. You look at them and say, 'More, more, more.' The minute they think they have you, you are hosed." But, she added, Kaplan needed to avoid getting bogged down in the weeds. "You gotta get your affirmative case out. You're not there to just answer questions."

At another moot court session, Kathleen Sullivan, one of the appellate lawyers whom Olson had originally approached before teaming up with Boies, advised Kaplan to "de-gay" the case. Sullivan's view was that Kaplan should emphasize the Supreme Court decisions that struck down laws that singled out hippies and the disabled, despite the fact that neither group was considered a suspect class, over the Court's landmark gay rights decisions in *Romer* and *Lawrence*.

Blatt gave Kaplan the exact opposite advice. The DOMA case was about, as Olson put it in his opening, "fencing" gay people off, Blatt said. She needed to be more passionate on that front. "I did not like your opening. If you want to keep it about estate taxes, fine. But I'd use some of Ted's lines."

Kaplan, as the first-timer of the group, took it all in, but she was feeling whipsawed. She would incorporate some of the suggestions, but at the end of the day it was her case, and she wanted to leave a little daylight between DOMA and Prop 8. If Olson won, she would invariably win too. But if he lost, she did not want to go down with him.

The best piece of advice came from Olson himself: You can't listen to everyone, he said. Pick a few people you trust, and tune everyone else out. "You were great—you really got it," he said, giving her a hug. "Enjoy it. It's a big fucking deal."

To everyone else, Olson announced, "All right. I'm going back to my cave."

———

"Look at the camera," instructed Anita Dunn, Hilary Rosen's partner and, for the better part of Obama's first year in office, his White House communications director. "Smile for me."

Chad obliged. Behind him was a realistic-looking backdrop of the Capitol. A camera was rolling in the mock television studio SKDKnickerbocker used for media training.

"Hmmm," she said, looking at the monitor before delivering her pronouncement. "You gotta get new glasses before Sunday."

With what spare time? Chad thought. It was already Thursday, and with the first of the two arguments now just five days away, he had a full plate, and no one at home to help. He and Jerome had split up over the holidays. Jerome, who had left a big job to move across the country with Chad, had struggled to carve out his own identity living in a new town where a person's line to power was what counted, where he was Chad Griffin's boyfriend. And Chad's all-in approach to his job and constant travel had not helped. To live in Chad's world was to live in his vortex, and in the end it had proven too much. They remained friends, but the breakup had been hard on them both, and Chad did not much like to talk about it. After a brief trip home to visit family in Arkansas and regroup, he had come back and buried himself even deeper into work.

For days, Chad had been doing his own version of moot courts, to prepare for the multiple network and cable television appearances on his schedule. As the president of the largest gay rights organization in the country, he was a frequent guest on news programs, and by now was an old pro. But with the first of the two arguments just five days away and the Sunday talk shows just around the corner, the stakes suddenly seemed exponentially higher. What if a justice was listening? What if he said the wrong thing? He'd been waking up most mornings at around 2:30 A.M., mind racing with all the things he still needed to nail down.

As Boutrous had said earlier that afternoon, "We're in a different realm."

The smallest of missteps now took on crisis proportions. That morning, a nonprofit California-based gay rights group had sent over an advance copy of an ad it planned to run in the *Washington Post*, with a picture of Clarence Thomas and his white wife and a reference to the *Loving* decision. "Clarence Thomas and Virginia Thomas could not have married in the state of Virginia where they now reside," it said. Kill it, Olson had urged. The entire team was closely monitoring another situation that threatened to take them off message: A blogger had somehow got his hands on an e-mail that Judge Walker had sent to a Gibson Dunn partner he knew, asking whether Olson thought it would be an unwanted distraction for him to attend the oral argument, along with a response in which the partner had said that he and Olson had reluctantly concluded that it would.

Earlier that afternoon, the four plaintiffs had done a press conference call. They were still in California, due to arrive on Sunday. For years, national reporters had focused largely on the Olson-Boies story line, but now the plaintiffs were fully in the spotlight. Multiple television crews had been to both Kris and Sandy's home and Paul and Jeff's, and some forty reporters had joined that afternoon's call, including representatives from all the major networks.

"There is an opportunity here for the court to send a message that who we love is important and we should be treated equally under the law," Kris told the reporters.

"We would expect the Court to step in and right these wrongs," Jeff added.

All four plaintiffs had said similar things in the past, but as soon as they hung up, Boutrous had turned to Chad, an unhappy look on his face. "Two things I did not like," he said. "We don't want them saying what the Court should do, 'the Court should send a message,' 'we would expect the Court to solve this problem.'"

The previous week Boies had broken the team's cardinal rule, which was to never, ever talk about how individual justices might vote. During a sit-down with *USA Today*'s editorial board, he had predicted that it would not be a "5–4 decision" and made public his private concern about how old the justices were. Most, he had said, had grown up in an environment of "extreme hostility to homosexuals," and while they were supposed to set that aside, "it's not an easy task."

Cooper, who had indeed been less than pleased with Eastman's "second-best" comments about adoptive families like Justice Roberts's, had been happy to see that his side was not the only one with foot-in-mouth disease, while Olson had sent Boutrous to have a word with Boies. Time had been set aside for members of the legal team to prep Boies before he appeared on *Meet the Press* that Sunday. This was not a time for loose lips.

"Talking about the Court is dangerous," Boutrous said, once they got Jeff back on the line. "We don't want to be presumptuous."

Chad had already done his prep session with the lawyers. He had his own balancing act to do. He had to hammer away on the inevitability factor, but, as Boutrous had warned him, "steer clear of suggesting that politics affects the justices." He was sure to be asked about *Roe v. Wade* and the shadow it cast over the case, given that the *New York Times* was working on just such a curtain-raiser piece for the Sunday paper. *Roe*–based fear of potential backlash was, in Mehlman's view, "the most potent message pushed by the other side in the final weeks," and it needed to be addressed. Chad needed to find a way to say that gays and lesbians were not asking for new right and that allowing two people who love one another to marry was unlikely to inflame passions in the same way that the Court's decision to allow women to terminate pregnancies did, but to do so in a way that did not throw the pro-choice community under the bus.

Chad had staff pull up questions about same-sex marriage that his inter-viewers had asked in the past. He had drawn up an elaborate "message box," designed to allow him to pivot to the points he wanted to make no matter what question came his way. If remembering all that wasn't difficult enough, now Rosen and Dunn gave him dozens of stylistic debating pointers.

"Half the game is how you look," Rosen told him, admonishing him to stop fidgeting and waving his hands around. "The other half is what you say. Tele-vision is 55 to 60 percent visual. It's so important not to be all beady-eyed and scrunchy-faced."

He nodded. She continued. "Do not nod. It signals nonverbal agreement." No "ums." Use a bridge like, "What we're really looking at here is." When your opponent is saying something, keep a bemused expression on your face, "like, 'You're not getting to me, but you are just so out there.'" Dunn chimed in. "If there is cross-talk, most people think viewers will listen to them if they speak higher and faster. They are wrong." Speak lowly and slowly, in what Dunn called a "Mommy tone of voice, the one she uses when she wants you to pay attention because she's really serious."

Rosen threw a few more questions his way. "I love the way you talk about committed couples," she said. "But don't call them 'committed couples.' Give 'em names, give 'em faces."

"How's his listening face?" Dunn asked Rosen.

Chad made as though he were listening to an opponent of same-sex marriage answer a question.

"Your listening face is a slightly unhappy face," Dunn said. "I want to work on your smile. It's not hard. It's about lifting the corners of your mouth."

Chad tried out a "listening" smile.

"Try to go bigger," Rosen said.

"Really? Oh my God, it feels like I'm smiling so big."

"Little more, bring it up," she replied.

It took several more attempts until Rosen was satisfied. "That's nice."

"You need to send a nonverbal message that you are a nice guy," Dunn explained. "You are in people's living rooms. What you are saying to people is, you're a guest in their house, and these are serious issues, but I'm a pleasant person. I'm the kind of person you want to have back."

———

"Hey!" Adam said, urging the black SUV they had hired to pull over. "There are the Zarrillos!"

Jeff and Paul were still in the air, due to touch down later that afternoon, But there, standing on the street in front of the White House, were his mom and dad, along with Paul's sister. The AFER team was headed over to the Supreme Court to do a walk-through of the area where Tuesday's rally would be staged. Did they want to come along? Adam asked.

"This was supposed to happen," Jeff's mom said, climbing into the backseat as everyone scooted over to make room.

The war room team was on a high, riding a crush of positive news coverage.

The coalition's surrogates had blanketed the Sunday talk shows that morning. Boies had not been able to resist repeating his prediction that, one way or another, the ruling wouldn't be close, but otherwise had been pitch-perfect.

"David nailed it," Adam said.

The American Academy of Pediatrics had released a report, just in time for the arguments. "Scientific evidence affirms that children have similar developmental and emotional needs and receive similar parenting whether they are raised by parents of the same or different genders," it said. Gays and lesbians were raising nearly two million children in the United States, according to 2010 Census figures. "If a child has 2 living and capable parents who choose to create a permanent bond by way of civil marriage, it is in the best interests of their child(ren) that legal and social institutions allow and support them to do so," the report concluded.

Former federal judge Michael McConnell, a standard-bearer in Federalist Society circles, had written an op-ed in the *Wall Street Journal* urging the Court to strike down DOMA on the grounds that Congress had unconstitutionally trampled on the states' prerogative to define marriage. As to Prop 8, he wrote that the justices should allow marriages to resume in California but deny the decision any precedential value by finding Cooper's clients had no standing, not the outcome the team wanted most but still better than nothing.

Support for same-sex marriage had reached an all-time high, according to the latest polling by ABC and the *Washington Post*, with 58 percent of those surveyed saying it should be legal. An overwhelming 81 percent of adults under thirty were supporters, as were a bare majority of Republicans coupled with Republican-leaning independents. Support among Catholics, an especially critical data point given the Court's makeup and the fact that the U.S. Conference of Catholic Bishops had filed a brief asking the justices to uphold Prop 8, had jumped to 58 percent. And in one of the poll's most important findings, it appeared that a majority of Americans would be comfortable with the Supreme Court deciding the issue once and for all; 64 percent of those polled said that the U.S. Constitution trumps state laws on marriage.

The way to change a business is to change the buying habits of its customers, and politics is not much different. Following the release of the poll and Portman's announcement, a slew of politicians had made a figurative rush to the altar. Every Democratic senator who had been in office long enough to have endorsed DOMA had come out against it. Days before, Hillary Rodham Clinton had become the latest high-profile Democrat to endorse the right of gays and lesbians to wed, recording a videotaped announcement that Chad had arranged after running into her on the Acela train that speeds between New York and Washington. What had once seemed politically toxic was now considered not only safe but, at least for Democrats, necessary: *Politico*, a news Web site for political junkies, had declared that endorsement by Clinton, who had recently stepped down as secretary of state, was a sure sign that she was running for president in 2016. Four years earlier, it likely would have come to the opposite conclusion.

A just-released Republican National Committee "autopsy" on why Romney lost the election to Obama mentioned the party's position on same-sex marriage four times. While it did not explicitly call for a platform change, it noted that "there is a generational difference within the conservative movement about the issues involving the treatment and rights of gays—and for many younger voters these issues are a gateway into whether the party is a place to be." Its authors included Sally Bradshaw, a Florida strategist close to former governor Jeb Bush, and Ari Fleischer, former White House press secretary to George W. Bush. Mehlman had talked to them both. And that morning, top Bush strategist Karl Rove had said that he could imagine a pro–gay marriage 2016 GOP presidential nominee.

The Supreme Court was under renovation, and the façade was draped with a giant screen, a photographic replica of the building. But it was still majestic, and after the SUV that had carried them there dropped them out front, everyone just stood on the Court's steps for several minutes under a gray sky. Flanking the group on either side of the steps were two marble statues atop fifty-ton marble blocks, a woman contemplating a blindfolded figure of Justice she holds in her hand, and a man holding a tablet of laws and a sheathed sword, representing the authority of law.

More than four years of theoretical planning, and here they finally were. In the group photo that they took, with the Court's monumental bronze door in the background and its EQUAL JUSTICE UNDER LAW inscription overhead, everyone was smiling and leaning into one another, one big family.

Adam, Jones, Jeff's parents Dominick and Linda Zarrillo, Paul's sister Maria McGuire, and researcher Eric Kay were in the back row. Elizabeth Riel, who had taken over as AFER's senior communications strategist, stood next to Shumway Marshall, the team's online projects coordinator, and Manny Rivera, who handled press. Fund-raiser Justin Mikita, who was soon to be married to *Modern Family* (and 8) star Jesse Tyler Ferguson, hammed it up with Melissa Gibbs, who handled the team's logistics and advance needs. Videographer Matt Baume and intern Hannah Faust stood on either side of Evan Sippel, the one staffer other than Adam who went all the way back to the trial. He had left in the middle of the case to attend law school, but had returned on a volunteer basis to help the team out.

"Listen up," Adam said, finally breaking the trance. "If you guys could focus!"

Kevin Nix, a member of Chad's staff who was coordinating the rally events, walked them through what would be happening on the opening day of arguments. Nothing about the logistics had been left to chance. The lawyers did not want an out-of-control stampede, so a group called United for Marriage had been set up to channel grassroots energy. Cleve Jones had been enlisted to call on people to march in their hometowns, and more than 175 events had been organized in all fifty states. The Human Rights Campaign was also urging people to change their Facebook profile photos to a new marriage equality logo it had developed: a pink equals sign over a red background, poll-tested as the colors of love.

At the same time, everyone understood they had to give supporters a place to congregate in Washington, D.C.; the National Organization for Marriage was busing in thousands of opponents. Chad had gone over every detail of the rally in the nation's capital in multiple briefings: American flags? Check: Three thousand had been ordered, along with a thousand red IT'S TIME FOR MARRIAGE T-shirts. Volunteers would hand palm cards to supporters, with suggested talking points to use if they were interviewed by reporters, directions to the nearest public bathrooms, and a request that they be respectful to the other side. Others trained in crowd deescalation techniques would be on deck to ensure that nobody got out of hand.

The National Organization for Marriage's base of operations would be blocks away; the organization had obtained a permit for an area near the Natural History Museum. Chad, knowing that the television crews would set up just outside the Court, wanted to be right out front, with a small stage for the coalition's speakers and marriage equality supporters filling the 252-foot wide oval plaza. There was just one problem: That space was first-come, first-served; there was no way to reserve it with a permit. The solution had been to enlist volunteers from Occupy Wall Street to save the area for them. The Occupy Wall Street protest movement had drawn worldwide attention in 2011 when it camped out in a park in lower Manhattan near the New York Stock Exchange to protest income inequality, resisting eviction efforts for nearly two months.

Chad had not been wild about the idea, but, as one staffer put it, "Nobody can hold space like they do." He had acquiesced after being assured that they would not identify themselves. They were camped out in a circle of folding chairs, bundled up against the cold, when the SUV pulled up. Nearby, line standers hired by Adam were first in a line that had already begun to form for the limited number of seats the Court reserves for the public. Only the plaintiffs themselves were guaranteed a seat inside; the Reiners and the rest of the board, along with the plaintiffs' families, all had to nab one of the public tickets that would be handed out on the morning of the argument.

Speakers would keep the crowd entertained before and during the arguments. They included civil rights leaders, prominent Republicans, the NFL football players who had campaigned for marriage equality during the election, and regular families talking about what the ability to marry would mean to them. A thousand signs with slogans like FREEDOM MEANS FREEDOM FOR EVERYONE and MARRIAGE IS LOVE COMMITMENT AND FAMILY had been printed for supporters to hold, visible to any of the justices if they happened to look out their windows.

The pastor of the Westboro Baptist Church, a virulently antigay church out of Kansas with aggressive picketing techniques, would also be holding a protest outside the Court. "Fag Marriage Dooms Nations. WBC to Picket" read a faxed press release announcing his plan and predicting that a pro-gay ruling "will usher in your final doom!" Chad was happy to have the church be the face of their opponents. "Make sure you give reporters a copy of this," he had said, pointing to the fax during one briefing. "I want to help him get his message out."

A light snow blanketed the city overnight, and as the bus passed by the National Mall that stretches from the Lincoln Memorial to the Capitol the following morning, the tour guide whom Adam had hired for the day pointed out the place on the frozen lawn, about the size of a football field, where the AIDS quilt was first laid out in 1987, commemorating the lives of those lost to the pandemic. By now, it had grown to forty-eight thousand panels and weighed fifty-four tons.

"That's Cleve!" Sandy exclaimed, though Jones, the quilt's creator, was back at his hotel resting.

"Keep us calm," Kris had begged on one phone call before they arrived. "Make sure there are moments when we can take a breath."

This tour, of some of Washington's civil rights landmarks, was Adam's answer. Chad, Lance Black, all four plaintiffs, Kris's two boys, Jeff's parents, and Paul's sister had all piled on a bus shortly after 9 A.M. The plan was to go to the National Archives, which housed the Constitution, the Declaration of Independence, and the Bill of Rights, then on to President Abraham Lincoln's cottage, where he developed the Emancipation Proclamation during the Civil War.

Chad, who had an interview later that afternoon on CNN, checked his e-mail for news. In the last twenty-four hours, two swing-state Democrats, Senator Claire McCaskill of Missouri and Senator Mark Warner of Virginia, had jumped on the bandwagon and announced their support for same-sex marriage. Chris Cillizza, a popular blogger for the *Washington Post,* wrote that "no matter how the high court rules . . . one thing is already clear: The political debate over gay marriage is over." The dustup du jour was an *L.A. Times* story reporting that Chief Justice Roberts's lesbian cousin, who lived in California and wanted to marry her partner, would be attending the arguments the following day. Per the lawyers' instructions, talking points had been sent out warning surrogates not to comment on the development, and Jeff had been asked to take the story down from his Facebook page. But, Hilary Rosen had e-mailed, "we are allowed to be secretly thrilled."

Elizabeth Riel gave the plaintiffs a rundown of what to expect when they arrived at the National Archives. Several of the networks and a couple of still photographers had been invited to meet them at the Archives. There would be no Q&A, but everyone needed to hold on the stairs near the front door so the crews could get their shot. They would then be led around to a side door; the front was actually not in use.

For the most part, the plaintiffs had gotten used to such stagecraft, but every once in a while the oddity of it all still struck them. "Don't look," Kris had said with a grimace, emerging one day for an interview with CNN wearing lipstick and mascara. "I have makeup on and they made me take off my glasses." She'd shrugged. "I guess to look girly."

Paul, over dinner one night at the Reiners', put it this way. "It's like, there's your private life, and then there's your private life that's packaged for public view."

"I just keep projecting out to tomorrow," Kris said. "It's kind of like"—she stopped, searching for the right phrase—"like we're all just jumping off. Here. We. Go."

Stepping out into the cold, the two couples hit their mark as the cameras rolled and clicked. PLAINTIFFS INSPECT U.S. CONSTITUTION AHEAD OF GAY MARRIAGE CASE, read one headline. But what started off as a photo op and an opportunity to keep everyone occupied became something deeply meaningful once inside. Forty-eight years earlier to the day, Martin Luther King Jr., after completing his march from Selma to Montgomery, had given one of his most famous speeches. "How long will justice be crucified, and truth bear it? I come to say to you this afternoon, however difficult the moment, however frustrating the hour, it will not be long, because truth crushed to earth will rise again. How long? Not long, because no lie can live forever." The timing of the archives tour was completely coincidental, but it felt like an omen.

The group wandered from room to room, somberly trying to take it all in. The Archives' collection of important governmental records runs to about twelve billion pieces of paper, including all documents associated with Supreme Court cases. In the "Courting Freedom" room, warrants for fugitive slaves were displayed under glass. Chad paused for a long moment at a mural depicting a courtroom scene, under the words WHEN HAVING THE MOST VOTES IS NOT ENOUGH.

"Your records will be here in twenty to twenty-five years," Jesika Jennings, an Archives employee, told the plaintiffs, adding that she was honored to show them around. "It's like having the opportunity to give Rosa Parks a tour of the Declaration and the Constitution."

Later that night, when everyone sat down in a cozy private room at the Jefferson Hotel, Chad gave a toast. The gang was all there: The Reiners and Ken Mehlman had joined them for dinner, as had David and Mary Boies. Olson was still working, polishing, absorbing.

No one was in celebration mode yet, Chad said when he stood. But they had arrived at the place where they had set out to be.

"Folks told us to slow down. But we gave hope to those thousands and thousands of Californians just by standing up for them," he said. "This case—it's gone from being a case of a small group of people to being everyone's case. This case is now America's case, and it was birthed by everyone in this room.

"One more chapter. Tomorrow. And may we all have the best of luck. I love you all."

THIRTY-SEVEN

KENNEDY V. KENNEDY

D id you sleep last night?," Jeff asked his mom.

It was a little after 6 A.M., and the two couples and their families were gathering in the lobby of the Palomar Hotel, where everyone was staying. Outside, a bus was waiting to take them to Chad's apartment.

"No. You know me."

He checked his phone. Facebook was a sea of red; the campaign asking people to replace their profile photos with the red Human Rights Campaign marriage equality logo had gone viral; more than 2.77 million users in the United States alone had joined in, plus tens of thousands more in Canada, the United Kingdom, Germany, and even far-off Australia. On Twitter, celebrities were cheering the plaintiffs on. Beyoncé, a mega R&B star who was married to the rapper Jay-Z, posted a scanned handwritten note on a red sheet of paper to her account on the photo-sharing site Instagram: "If you like it you should be able to put a ring on it," she wrote, a twist on the lyrics to her hit song "Single Ladies," along with the hashtag "#wewillunite4marriageequality."

Paul let out big breath.

"So this is the moment," Jeff's mom said.

"This is it," he said.

"We've all been waiting for," she finished. She smiled. "You both look handsome."

Kris and Sandy were the last to arrive in the lobby. They had both tossed and turned all night. The AFER staffers began herding everyone outside, into the dark and onto the bus.

"Let's go change the world, boys," Paul's sister, Maria, said.

"This isn't weird," Sandy said as the bus pulled away from the curb.

Everyone laughed.

"Good morning, D.C.," she continued, looking out the window. "Sleeping in? Enjoying yourself?"

The bus dropped them in an alley that led to the back door of Chad's apartment, so the television crews stationed out front would not swarm them. Inside, Kristina, who had taken the day off of work at the White House to attend the arguments, was sitting on Chad's couch, going over his press statement, like the old days.

Neither had slept much. Kristina had kept waking up in a panic, afraid that she had overslept. Chad, Adam, and Matt McGill had e-mailed one another well into the early morning hours. "Who's still awake?" went the joke.

Chad had sent Olson an e-mail. "As you know, the world will be watching. [The Court] is already surrounded by media from around the globe. BUT behind all that there is some kid, alone in his room in America . . . who will hear the message that he is equal, and that he too can someday grow up with the same hopes and dreams as his straight brothers and sisters," he wrote. "You are my hero."

The AFER staff had arranged for coffee and breakfast snacks, which were laid out on the kitchen counter. The apartment was lovely, with high ceilings, but it had an unlived-in feel. Chad still hadn't gotten around to unpacking a lot of boxes from the move out from Los Angeles, or even purchased a dresser. The guest room consisted of a mattress on the floor.

Paul peeked into his refrigerator and cracked up. "Yup, it's completely empty," he told Jeff. Turning to Chad, he added, "We had a big joke about that."

"You guys want to watch a movie?" Chad said facetiously. "I've got some sweatpants. Sweatpants and hoodies."

Lance Black sent a photo from outside the Supreme Court. He and Cleve Jones, the Reiners, Bruce Cohen, and Ken Mehlman had taken the place of the paid line standers at around 5:30 A.M. and were now shivering in the cold, waiting outside the Court to go in.

Jerome texted love to the entire group from Boston, where he was now living. "I'm with you in my heart," Chad's mom wrote in from Arkansas. Ben Jealous, the president of the NAACP, could not be in Washington, D.C., that day, but had sent a note to Chad that he would forever treasure. "Sending you prayers and much success this week," it said. "Yours in the struggle."

Chad parted the blinds and looked out at the news crews that were waiting for them to emerge. He had taped a giant American flag to his front door. "It never ends," Kristina said with a laugh, about Chad's patriotic decorating flair. "We can never get enough."

Paul read over the simple statement he planned to give. "We have faith in our country's judicial system."

"It kind of feels like we're all just standing in that town house in San Francisco," Chad said, recalling the opening day of trial. "How far we've all come."

Jeff and Kristina started to cry.

But Chad felt almost eerily calm. He had done everything he possibly could to prepare the political ground for a Supreme Court victory. That morning's *Washington Post* editorial urged "liberty and justice for all," while the *New York Times*'s called for A 50-STATE RULING.

Now all the pressure was on one man: Olson.

———

Olson was ensconced at the counsel table in front of the raised mahogany bench just to the right of where the chief justice would sit when the Court was called into session, reading over notes. Across the way sat Cooper. A white quill had been placed in front of both lawyers, a tradition that went back to the Court's earliest sessions.

Both men had their own traditions. For years, before every oral argument, Olson had been placing a laminated saint card into his pocket that his late wife, Barbara, had given him on the morning that he argued the *Bush v. Gore* case, a prayer to Saint Michael: "Do not forsake me in my time of struggle with the powers of evil." The saint is known as the "the Archangel," but Olson liked to call him "the Avenger." Nestled next to that was a gold ladybug pin that Lady had given him after they married. Cooper, across the way, sat twirling his pen through his fingers. He and his entire team wore their good-luck cuff links, as they always did. They were engraved with a laurel leaf and sword, a visual representation of the firms's motto: victory or death.

Only four seats are available at each counsel table. Boutrous, Boies, and McGill sat with Olson. The Supreme Court also reserves a certain number of seats for lawyers who are members of its bar. When they heard that a line for those seats was starting to form the previous afternoon, Enrique Monagas had dashed down to the Court. He and Josh Lipshutz, the former Scalia clerk and newest member of the team, had spent a snowy, blustery night waiting in temperatures that dropped down to the thirties, but it was worth it to be sitting here now. His husband, Jason, was just outside, at the rally on the steps with their daughter, Elisa.

"Being here right now, I'm really nervous," he had said after one of the moots. "Not over how Ted is going to do but—it's very real right now. Arguments we thought were bullshit, we are looking at with new eyes, thinking, does this argument have legs?"

With the help of the former Supreme Court clerks who worked for them, Terry Stewart and her boss, San Francisco city attorney Dennis Herrera, had snagged seats reserved for guests of the justices. They were seated near Ron Prentice, the ProtectMarriage.com campaign's executive director. Stewart was not without anxiety—"That would take the ability to read Kennedy's mind"—but she was cautiously optimistic. Olson, she thought, had been at the very top of his game at the final moot court: "Fantastic!" she'd gushed.

Paul Cappuccio, Olson's friend, had been one of the grillers. The only question that the former Kennedy/Scalia clerk had managed to trip Olson up on was when he asked whether the Court should decline to reach the merits of the Proposition 8 case and instead dismiss the case on standing grounds. Breaking role for a moment, Olson had asked whether there any way to answer that other than a flat-out yes—potentially yielding a technical, California-only victory that didn't equal Olson's ambitions. "No," Cappuccio had told him. But whatever the Court decided, he recalled telling Olson, the country was in a profoundly different place than it had been when the lawsuit was filed.

"You've already won," Cappuccio said, as they walked to lunch after the moot court session. "The real lasting impact of this case is that it changed the nature of the conversation, which, by the way, had you not done, your case never would have stood a chance at the Supreme Court."

Paul Smith, the lawyer who had argued and won the *Lawrence* case but declined Olson's invitation to join the Proposition 8 case, shared that assessment. He had come to court today to hear the arguments, no longer worried that the justices would deal a blow to the community the way they had in the *Bowers* case, when they upheld laws criminalizing sodomy. The country had moved too far, too fast, for the Court to want to do something so potentially legacy tarnishing, he thought, a shift he credited in large part to Olson and the Proposition 8 case. Olson might have wanted for the case to move more quickly, but he, for one, was glad it had not.

"Look at the difference three years has made," he said. "They weren't solely responsible for the changes, but anyone who says their contribution wasn't hugely significant is wrong. That trial was a remarkable PR event."

———

The bus that had ferried the plaintiffs to the Court had been forced to drop them about a block away; security measures prevented it from stopping out front. An old man had caught sight of Kris and Sandy holding hands as they walked to the Court. "Shame," he had hissed.

"Stay close, stay tight," Chad had said, hustling them along. They approached the building from the side, and when the crowd below spotted them on the steps, they began to cheer. Chad's plan to hold the space in front had worked: It was filled with marriage equality supporters. Sandy's hands flew to either side of her face as she looked down at everyone. Kris clasped hers together, as though in prayer, as a tear slipped below her thick brown-framed eyeglasses. "Good luck!" someone shouted as the line began to move.

The classic Corinthian architecture made the Court chamber feel like a temple. The soaring forty-four-foot-high elaborate coffered ceiling was painted red and pale blue, with an intricately carved ivory flower design, and supported by twenty-four marble columns. The floor was carpeted red and bordered in Italian and African marble.

The Court seats only four hundred people, and spectators are escorted into the room in small groups. The system is a rigid one, and Sandy and Kris wound up split off from the rest of the group. They were seated behind President Obama's adviser, Valerie Jarrett, while everyone else, including the twins, was seated on the other side of the room.

"It was incredibly stressful for Paul and Jeff and Chad," Kristina said. "They've all formed such a unit, they didn't want to be separated. It was good in a way, though, because it was nice to focus on something inconsequential."

Michele Reiner almost did not make it in at all; she had made a stop at the ladies' room while the rest of the board was ushered into the room, and had to beg to take her seat. Lance Black and Adam craned their necks, looking around. The last time Chad and Rob Reiner had come to the Supreme Court, they had been out on the street, on the night that the *Bush v. Gore* decision was handed down. "Both times," Rob joked to Chad, "because of Ted Olson."

Shortly before arguments were due to begin, the man himself wandered over to say hello. Olson hugged both Reiners. He had been up for hours, and was, Boutrous said, in a "great place." At 5:31 that morning, he had returned Chad's e-mail, thanking him for his friendship and partnership. "I'm enormously gratified, and humbled, by our journey and where we are today," he'd said. But now he was at an uncustomary loss for words.

"Well," he said.

Olson and the other lawyers had warned everyone not to read too much into the arguments. It is possible to pick up on a general gestalt, but vote counting is tricky. Sometimes a justice who appears to be giving a lawyer a hard time, for instance, is actually helping to shore up the argument or address what he or she knows to be a colleague's point of concern. But as the minute hand of the clock above the bench ticked toward 10 A.M., it was impossible not to think that they would at least get an inkling of what the only nine people who had ever really mattered to their case actually thought, and to worry about what that might be.

Cleve Jones took out a square cloth and mopped his forehead. Chad fiddled with the pen and pad he had brought with him to take notes. The room was now hushed, and when the marshal called the Court into session, both men startled.

"Oyez! Oyez! Oyez! All persons with business before the Honorable, the Supreme Court of the United States are admonished to draw near and give their attention, for the Court is now sitting. God save the United States, and this Honorable Court!"

———

"It was over," Kristina would say afterward, "in an instant—an instant."

Cooper had gone first, and there were times, preserved in black chicken-scratch on the notes Chad kept passing to Kristina, when it seemed hard to imagine that the justices could deny them. Cooper's answer to one question, about whether, outside the context of marriage, he could envision any other rational basis for the state to use sexual orientation as a factor for denying gays and lesbians benefits or imposing burdens on them, had stunned Chad: "No, Your Honor, I cannot."

"In more than 50% of states it's legal to fire/hire," Chad wrote down on his pad, a reference to the fact that because there were no federal employment pro-tections in place, employers in pockets across America could legally discrimi-nate on the basis of sexual orientation.

"That is an enormous concession," Boies thought, "with implications for both DOMA and our case."

But at other moments, it appeared that everything that Chad had worked so hard to do had been for naught. The country might have undergone a seismic shift in its embrace of same-sex marriage, but if the justices were aware of it, they did not let on. They talked in fusty terms befitting a Court that still had fallout shelter signs painted on its walls. Even liberal justices like Sotomayor, a New Yorker who had lived in the West Village just blocks from the Stonewall Inn, kept referring to gays and lesbians as "homosexuals." "Newer than cell phones or the Internet," was how Justice Alito described same-sex marriage. Chief Justice Roberts dismissed the case Olson, Chad, and the rest of the team had worked so hard to make on why the term "marriage" mattered this way:

"If you tell a child that somebody has to be their friend, I suppose you can force the child to say, 'This is my friend,' but it changes the definition of what it means to be a friend."

"I just felt at times like they hadn't seen anything," Chad said afterward. "It was a little disheartening."

The pivotal Justice Kennedy, meanwhile, seemed to be having a debate with himself. Kristina grabbed Chad's arm when Kennedy spoke of the "legal injury" caused by Proposition 8 to the "forty thousand children" in California who lived with same-sex parents. "The voice of those children is important in this case, don't you think?" he asked Cooper.

At another point, he asked whether "this can be treated as a gender-based classification," an indication that he might be willing to apply heightened scrutiny not by declaring gays and lesbians a new suspect class, but by finding that same-sex marriage bans discriminated on the basis of gender.

But then he tacked in a different direction. "There's substance to the point that sociological information is new," he told Cooper. "We have five years of information to weigh against two thousand years of history or more."

"He's expressing a Burkean concern," Cooper recalled thinking. Maybe all that talk at trial about Edmund Burke, and the political philosopher's warning that "infinite caution" should be used when mucking about with age-old institutions, or the amicus brief on the perils of using sociological studies to decide cases, had penetrated.

"The problem," Kennedy said to Olson, "the problem with the case is what you're really asking, particularly because of the sociological evidence you cite, [is] for us to go into uncharted waters, and you can play with that metaphor— there is a wonderful destination [or] it is a cliff," he said getting a little tangled up. "Whatever that was," he added.

Cite the evidence from trial, Terry Stewart wanted to say to Olson. Tell Justice Kennedy about the expert testimony, the studies they had entered into evidence to prove that heterosexual marriage would not be harmed if gays and lesbians were allowed to wed. Or point to the brand-new ten-page American Society of Pediatrics report, the one that coalition surrogates had been talking about on television all week, declaring that scientific evidence showed no cause-and-effect relationship between parents' sexual orientation and children's well-being.

Ted Boutrous, for his part, wanted hold up a sign: READ OUR BRIEF! it would have instructed Kennedy. LOOK AT FOOTNOTE 6!

The footnote was one of Boutrous's proudest contributions to the brief. He had noticed that Cooper's brief, in an effort to buttress his argument that social scientists were divided on the question of same-sex marriage, repeatedly cited the work of people who had never appeared at the trial. One was a sociologist named Kingsley Davis, who had died in 1997. "Bring me the head of Kingsley Davis!" he'd told members of the team, and the footnote reflected their research.

"Rather than rely on witnesses at trial, who would have been exposed to cross-examination, [Proposition 8's] Proponents now rely on historical writings by dozens of philosophers, sociologists and political scientists—from Locke to Blackstone, Montesquieu to Kingsley Davis (a sociologist who advocated 'zero population growth' while fathering four children with three different women, including a son at age 79)—to support their view that marriage is suited only to opposite sex couples," it read. "None of those authorities, however—not one—expresses an opinion about same-sex marriage or argues that allowing gay men and lesbians to marry would harm the institution."

Olson, however, chose to emphasize broad principles over specific studies or footnotes. "There was a twelve-day trial, the judge insisted on evidence on all of these questions," he replied, without going into detail. "You suggested that this was uncharted waters. It was uncharted waters when this Court, in 1967, in the *Loving* decision, said that interracial—prohibitions on interracial marriages, which still existed in sixteen states, were unconstitutional."

Kennedy seemed unconvinced. At times, leaning back in his chair, he looked visibly pained. He expressed little willingness to go along with the more incremental options before him. Dismissing the case on the basis that Cooper's clients lacked standing to appeal Judge Walker's order, the California-born Kennedy declared, would be tantamount to giving the governor and others "a one-way ratchet" that they could use to "thwart" California's citizens. And relying on the reasoning that Judge Reinhardt had used to limit the impact of the Ninth Circuit's ruling to California seemed to Kennedy "a very odd rationale upon which to sustain this opinion."

But he also, in a comment that made all the lawyers in the room pay attention, indicated that he felt it might be too early for the Court to go all in. He would, in a speech in which he talked about same-sex marriage several months later, tell students at the University of California that "all of us were surprised at the speed of the thing."

Now, all he said was this: "I just wonder if—if the case was properly granted."

It seemed clear, in that moment, to lawyers on both sides, that it had likely been the four conservatives who had voted to grant cert. No one could know for sure, but it sounded like Justice Kennedy had not wanted to hear this case, at least not at this time. That, in turn, could explain why the liberals on the Court all seemed intent on finding a way to avoid deciding the constitutionality of Proposition 8.

On occasion, the Court dismisses a case, effectively deciding that it had been a mistake to grant cert in the first place. In Supreme Court lexicon, it's called a "DIG," for dismiss as improvidently granted. And, like Justice Kennedy, Justice Sotomayor seemed eager to DIG this one.

"If the issue is letting the states experiment and letting the society have more time to figure out its direction, why is taking a case now the answer?" she asked Cooper.

The question might have stemmed from a desire by Sotomayor to protect the Ninth Circuit's ruling from a conservative majority she feared now might be ready to uphold laws like Prop 8 banning same-sex marriage. But there was no way to know as the questions kept flying.

"Because, Your Honor—"

She interrupted. "We let issues perk, and so we let racial segregation perk for fifty years from 1898 to 1954."

"Your Honor, it is hard to—" Cooper managed, before she jumped in again.

"And now we are talking about, at most, four years."

Justice Scalia jumped into the fray.

It takes just four votes to grant cert. A majority of five justices may do whatever they like, including deciding to dismiss a case that four justices had believed should be heard. But as a matter of form and comity, the justices who lose the cert battle generally just decide the case. If that courtesy was followed in this case, one of the justices who voted to hear the case would have to change his or her mind and agree to DIG the case, which Justice Scalia seemed to intimate was unlikely to happen.

"It's too late for that, too late for that now, isn't it?" he said, a note of triumph in his voice. "I mean, we granted cert." Then, in what some saw as a direct slap at Kennedy, he appeared to reference Kennedy's comment, just before voting to uphold *Roe v. Wade,* about feeling like Caesar crossing the Rubicon.

"We have crossed that river," Scalia declared.

Sitting there, Boies could not help but think it was not going as planned.

"We were both surprised about the DIG suggestion," he said afterward. "Justice Kennedy seemed unhappy—on the one hand this, on the other hand that. The general sense, and it wasn't just Kennedy, the general discomfort around this case surprised me a little bit."

At the lectern, Cooper tried his best to protest to both Sotomayor and Kennedy. A DIG, undoing the Court's decision to grant cert, would effectively bless the Ninth Circuit's ruling that, as Cooper put it, "at least in the state of California, the people have no authority to step back, hit the pause button, and allow the experiments taking place in this country to further mature."

Of course, there was another route for the justices to sidestep the case: they could find that Cooper's clients had no standing to appeal Judge Walker's decision, a route that Justice Ginsburg seemed especially eager to embrace. "Have we ever granted standing to proponents of ballot initiative?" she demanded of Cooper. "The concern is, certainly the proponents are interested in getting it on the ballot and seeing that all of the proper procedures are followed, but once it's passed, they have no proprietary interest in it. It's law for them just as it is for everyone else. So how are they distinguishable from the California citizenry in general?"

She was egged on by Roberts, the Court's standing hawk. When Olson tried to open by saying that Proposition 8 was really about "stigmatizing a class of Californians based upon their status and labeling their most cherished relationships as second rate," Roberts cut him off. "Perhaps you could address your jurisdictional argument."

Listening, especially to the Court's liberals, Terry Stewart felt heartsick, as the hope she had started to harbor ran up against the justices' words. "I'm not in a good space," she told her wife, Carole, afterward.

"They didn't seem to like the broad argument, they didn't seem to like the narrow argument, and it just felt painful," she said. "It was like, 'What are you doing bringing us this case?' like a collective stiff-arm: 'Get away from me.' It was like they didn't even want to touch us."

———

"It was rough on both sides," Paul said.

The plaintiffs, along with their families, and Chad and Kristina, were back on the bus. Everyone was trying to analyze what had gone on inside the Court, without the benefit of the lawyers, who had taken a separate car.

The two couples had emerged from the Court with Chad, Olson, and Boies. The scene around them had been a zoo, with the network reporters who had been listening to the arguments racing past to connect with crews and go live, and there was no time to talk before they were standing at a podium, mics pointed at them.

They had not been there to hear Hilary Rosen's comment to Ken Mehlman. "Pete Williams is being super negative right now," she had said, referring to NBC News's justice correspondent. "He said very little eagerness on a broad ruling, and it's been retweeted thousands of times."

Boies had reiterated that they should not try to read too much into what the justices had said, and for the most part they focused on the positive as the bus made its way across town to Morton's Steakhouse for a postargument lunch that Olson had arranged.

"The justices were fascinating, fascinating," Kris said. "It was very rapid-fire. The justices were interrupting each other. Their heads"—she grabbed her own—"there's just so much going on!"

Everyone talked about the moment when Justice Kagan had pounced on Cooper's argument that laws like Prop 8 are justified because marriage is an institution designed to further responsible procreation. "Suppose a state said that, because we think that the focus of marriage really should be on procreation, we are not going to give marriage licenses anymore to any couple where both people are over the age of fifty-five," Kagan had asked. "Would that be constitutional?"

"No, Your Honor," Cooper had said.

But when he tried to suggest that even with respect to couples over the age of fifty-five, it would be rare that both the man and woman would be infertile, Kagan was having none of it.

"No, really," she said, as people in the courtroom began laughing. "I can assure you—if both the woman and the man are over the age of fifty-five, there are not a lot of children coming out of that marriage."

"It's almost like she trapped him," Jeff said.

Sandy thought it was strange that Justice Thomas had swung around in his chair, turning his back to the Court. He had famously not asked a single question during oral arguments in years. Elliott thought that Justice Ginsburg looked old and frail, with the tall back of her chair towering over her, and her whispery voice barely audible.

"I just wanted to help her out," he said chivalrously.

The consensus was that that the solicitor general had done well. He was particularly strong in rebutting Cooper's argument that it was rational for California voters to want to wait a bit and let the marriage debate play out elsewhere. "California did not, through Proposition 8, do what my friend Mr. Cooper said and push a pause button. They pushed a delete button. This is a permanent ban. It's in the [state] constitution." He also hit back on the not-enough-data theme, telling the justices that the same argument was used in the 1967 *Loving v. Virginia* case, when defenders of interracial marriage bans had argued that social science was still uncertain with regard to how biracial children would fare. "And I think the Court recognized that there is a cost to waiting and that that has got to be part of the equal protection clause."

But it seemed clear to everyone on board the bus that the justices weren't buying the narrow argument he was selling. "I thought he got questioned pretty harshly on his eight-state solution," Sandy said.

The liberals had been particularly antagonistic. Justice Breyer quickly picked up on the perverse incentive that would be created if the Court were to agree with Verrilli's argument that it is particularly irrational for states like California, which offer gays and lesbians all the benefits of marriage but the name, to ban them from marrying. "A state that does nothing for gay couples hurts them much more than a state that does something . . . I mean, take a state that really does nothing whatsoever. They have no benefits, no nothing, no nothing. Okay?" Breyer had said. "So—so a state that does nothing hurts them much more, and yet your brief seems to say it's more likely to be justified under the Constitution."

Jeff and Paul talked about the "give me a date moment," when Scalia had asked Olson about when, precisely, it became "unconstitutional to exclude homosexual couples from marriage? Seventeen ninety-one? Eighteen sixty-eight, when the Fourteenth Amendment was adopted?"

Boies would later say he would have liked to tell him that it happened when

Justice Scalia said it did, in 2003, in the *Lawrence* decision that struck down laws criminalizing sodomy, the one that Scalia, in his scathing dissent, said left "on pretty shaky grounds state laws limiting marriage to opposite-sex couples." But Olson, unwilling to spend a lot of time debating the original intent of the framers with a justice unlikely to be in his corner no matter the answer, had shot back with some questions of his own.

"When did it become unconstitutional to prohibit interracial marriages? When did it become unconstitutional to assign children to separate schools?" It happened, Olson finished, "when we—as a culture determined that sexual orientation is a characteristic of individuals that they cannot control, and that that—"

Scalia interrupted him. "I see," he said, voice dripping with sarcasm. "When did that happen? When did that happen?"

During oral arguments before the Supreme Court in the *Bowers v. Hardwick* case, which upheld laws criminalizing sodomy before the *Lawrence* decision struck them down, then–chief justice Warren Burger had blurted out, "Didn't they used to put people to death for this?" This morning's rhetoric had been tame by comparison. "I expected much more vitriol," Chad told Kristina.

Still, at times it had been difficult to just sit there. When Justice Alito started talking about the newness of same-sex marriage and the lack of data, Sandy grew angry. "I'm not an experiment," she thought.

Spencer wondered whether Justice Scalia knew that that he and Elliott were sitting there when, in an effort to help out Cooper, he suggested one reason a state might be justified in banning gays and lesbians from marrying was to keep them from having kids. Cooper had been getting grilled by Justice Kagan, who kept demanding to know what harm would be caused if gays and lesbians were permitted to marry, and Justice Kennedy had picked up on it, asking, "Are you conceding that the point there is no harm or or denigration to traditional opposite-sex marriage couples?"

"It seems to me that you should have to address Justice Kagan's question," Kennedy had said.

"Mr. Cooper, let me—let me give you one—one concrete thing," Scalia had interjected. "If you redefine marriage to include same-sex couples, you must— you must permit adoption by same-sex couples, and there's—there's considerable disagreement among—among sociologists as to what the consequences of raising a child in a—in a single-sex family, whether that is harmful to the child or not. Some states do not—do not permit adoption by same-sex couples for that reason."

"That hit pretty close to home," Spencer said.

Overall, Jeff's mom asked, how did Cooper do? There had only been enough tickets for three family members to watch the arguments, and she and Paul's sister had volunteered to give up their seats and attend the rally instead. When the National Organization for Marriage had marched by, Jeff's mom had been outraged by some of the signs. "How dare they," she'd said.

"He did a good job," Sandy said.

"He brought his A game," Kris agreed.

They had been sitting near Cooper's wife, who had waved and smiled at them before the arguments started. Cooper, spotting Kris afterward as she made her way down the stairs, had made a beeline over to her. He looked her in the eye and warmly shook her hand. They had all been at this for years now, albeit on different sides. The courtesy he showed her felt good, and she had responded in kind. He was just doing his job; he had never made it personal.

"I felt like he respected our struggle and our right to be there, making these arguments, and that there were no hard feelings," Kris said.

———

Cooper and his team were already at the Monocle, a restaurant on Capitol Hill where they always went to relax and recover at oral arguments. The Court had asked penetrating, difficult question of both sides, Cooper thought, and it could go either way.

"For the first time in this case, I don't know how it's going to turn out," he said a few weeks later, after he had time to digest it all. "And that feels pretty damn good."

At the plaintiffs' gathering across town, a good deal of wine had been poured by the time Olson and Boies rose to speak. The lunch at Morton's was in full swing, and everyone was eager to finally hear the blow-by-blow assessment of the two lawyers. In the background, a television was playing the just-released audio of the argument. But neither Boies nor Olson wanted to dwell on what had happened, and they spoke mostly in platitudes.

"I think we took a big step forward today," Boies said, noting that there were plenty of conflicting views as the justices struggled to find a "route for us." But he quickly moved on to a hypothetical world in which he would get to cross-examine Justice Scalia, as he had the witnesses at trial. "He, also, would have no place to hide," he said.

Olson, too, talked about the district court trial, and Boies's withering cross-examination, until finally Michele Reiner finally put her foot down. "You might not want to do this," she said. But everyone else would like to hear Olson's thoughts about how the hour and a half they had just spent before the U.S. Supreme Court had gone.

Earlier, on the steps of the Supreme Court, the Reiners and Ken Mehlman had buttonholed Matt McGill, who tried his best to give them an honest assessment. "I was encouraged by Justice Kennedy's question, recognizing that there's kids on the other side of the equation," he said.

Why did they spend so much time on standing? Michele asked.

"Because I think there are doubts," McGill replied. "I think the chief justice certainly had doubts."

But Olson mostly ducked, talking about the moots, and the process, and how he would read the transcript later to see how it had all shaken out, before returning to the courtroom that had delivered them their greatest victory to date, Judge Walker's.

As the get-together broke up, Kristina tried not to jump to any conclusions. She had known, going in, that "we were all going to feel a little sick to our stomachs after it was all over, because of the tough questions that would be asked," as she put it, and she knew as well as anyone that the Court was hard to predict. After the justices heard arguments on Obama's signature overhaul of the nation's health care laws, it looked to most to be dead on arrival. Instead, the chief justice switched his vote, and when the decision came out, the law was upheld.

But it was odd, she thought, that Olson and Boies spent so much of lunch reliving the glory days of the trial. Everyone was feeling raw and emotional, and they needed to hear the lawyers say that it would all turn out okay. And Olson's half-joking farewell had left her even more unsettled.

"Well," he said as he passed by her near the coat-check room, "if we lose, hopefully people will remember the party."

THIRTY-EIGHT

"SKIM MILK MARRIAGES"

Robbie Kaplan was not known for having a Zen personality. But the typically frenetic lawyer took her seat at the counsel table for her first Supreme Court argument feeling refreshed and unusually relaxed.

Weeks earlier, she had attended an oral argument, just to watch how the justices interacted with each other and the lawyers before them. She'd been sitting behind two women military lawyers, both of them in uniform. When one of them started talking about her wife, Kaplan took it as a sign. "We're going to win," she said to herself.

Nothing that had happened since had changed that view. The argument fell on the week of Passover, commemorating the liberation of the Israelites from slavery in Egypt. That Sunday, at a Seder dinner she had hosted at the Mandarin Oriental Hotel for Edie and her entire legal crew, everyone had agreed that it did not feel coincidental that their case would be heard over a holiday that celebrates freedom.

Watching the justices grill Olson the day before during the Proposition 8 arguments had not intimated her in the slightest. "There's nothing I can't handle, even Scalia," she said she thought. "I've been in front of angry judges before." And while she'd been worried for months about arguing her case alongside Olson's, listening, she had actually decided it was a good thing: Olson's big ask made her request to the Court look like small potatoes.

And so, after heading back to her hotel, she'd ordered in some room service

Thai curry chicken, done a little reading, and gotten a massage, before swallowing two NyQuils to ensure a good night's sleep.

Waking up, she said she had just one thought: "Let me at 'em. I'm ready."

At the counsel's table across the way sat Paul Clement. "Fasten your seat belt," Cooper had told him when he'd agreed to defend DOMA, but Clement had still been caught off guard when his firm, King & Spalding, moved to withdraw from the litigation amid fierce criticism.

The case had seemed a natural to him, different from Prop 8. "To me," he had said one day over coffee, "this is about separation of powers. Congress has the right to a defense of the acts it passes."

Rather than abandon his clients in the House of Representatives, Clement had resigned, a principled move that Cooper, and Olson as well, for that matter, admired. Attorney General Holder had even come to his defense, telling reporters that Clement was doing "what lawyers do when we are at our best."

Olson and Clement approached cases with the same ferociousness, but their argument styles were completely different. Olson had a commanding presence, what Mark Corallo, who worked for them both in the Bush Justice Department, called a "put-the-lights-on-me star quality, like John Wayne or Gary Cooper, while Paul is an aw-shucks Jimmy Stewart."

Now Clement waited quietly to begin, a slight hunch to his back as he peered through his oval wire-rimmed glasses. Some Supreme Court advocates bring reams of paper with them to oral arguments, filled with all the points they want to make and case law they might need to cite. Clement was known for bringing not a single note. Everything he needed was in his head, and the table in front of him was bare but for a pad he would use to jot down points he might want to make during his rebuttal time.

———

Edie was in her element. She was wearing a brilliant fuchsia scarf, the diamond brooch that Thea had given her, and, because she was a little deaf, special earphones to help her hear the argument. Nancy Pelosi, the House minority leader, stopped over to say hello, as did Valerie Jarrett, who was again in the audience. Edie's heart had started acting up again, and she had recently been hospitalized for chest pains, but sitting there she was the picture of health.

Olson and Chad arrived separately. Olson wished Kaplan luck, then took his seat in the bar section, eager to hear more that might give him a better read on where the Court was headed. Chad sat alone farther back, against a wall, near a priest who was wearing his collar. The plaintiffs in Prop 8 were all headed home, but Chad's work was not done.

He and his team at the Human Rights Campaign were working with Attorney General Holder to ensure that federal agencies were ready to move quickly to allow legally married same-sex couples to begin to collect benefits in the event that Edie won her case. As court was called into session, the priest nearby closed his eyes, clasped his hands together, and began praying, lips moving silently.

Kaplan had upped her passion game since the moot, and when she rose, her argument was sharply drawn. "Because of DOMA," she said, "many thousands of people who are legally married under the laws of nine sovereign states and the District of Columbia are being treated as unmarried by the federal government, solely because they are gay."

As had been the case the day before, a significant amount of the argument was taken up with the standing questions in the case. Several of the conservative justices, led by the chief justice, did not like the fact that after determining DOMA was unconstitutional, the administration had nevertheless filed an appeal with the Second Circuit to promote the defense of a statute it wanted to see invalidated. Where was the controversy? they wanted to know. It sounded to them like the government was asking for an advisory opinion. The answer—that because the president was continuing to enforce the law and as such was refusing to give Edie her tax rebate, there was a controversy that needed resolving—incensed Roberts.

If the president believed the law was unconstitutional, Roberts suggested that the best course of action would have been to stop enforcing it, "rather than saying, 'Oh, we'll wait till the Supreme Court tells us we have no choice.'"

"I don't see why he doesn't have the courage of his convictions," the chief justice snapped.

But the liberals who had seemed willing to join Roberts in finding that the Court had no jurisdiction to hear the Proposition 8 case did not appear as willing to go along for this particular ride. The government, Justice Kagan said, had a clear-cut stake in the matter that gave it standing. "There's $300,000 that's going to come out of the government's treasury if this decision is upheld, and it won't if it isn't," she said. Whether the government is "happy to pay that $300,000," she added, was irrelevant.

Justice Ginsburg, during the Proposition 8 argument the previous day, had mentioned a 1964 case called *McLaughlin v. Florida*. It was the predecessor to *Loving v. Virginia,* and involved a Florida statute. Florida, at the time, banned interracial couples from marrying, and the law at issue also made it a crime for them to live together. The Court had struck down the cohabitation law, but waited another three years to deal with the larger question of whether interracial couples had the right to wed. "So first there was the question of no marriage, and then there was marriage," she had said.

Resolving the DOMA case on the merits offered the Court a similarly incremental way to tackle the issue of same-sex marriage, and today she seemed far more comfortable, eager even, digging into the merits of the equal protection case against DOMA.

By denying federal benefits to same-sex but not opposite-sex couples, she declared, in one of the more memorable lines of the day, the law created "two kinds of marriage: the full marriage, and then this sort of skim milk marriage."

Clement responded by asking the justices to take a trip down memory lane, to 1996, when DOMA was passed. At that time, it appeared as though Hawaii might be forced, by judicial fiat, to allow gays and lesbians to wed. Congress made what he said was a rational decision to act to define marriage as the union of a man and a woman for the purpose of eligibility for federal benefits, because the federal government had an interest in "uniform treatment of people across state lines."

"Ms. Windsor wants to point to the unfairness of the differential treatment of treating two New York married couples differently, and of course for purposes of New York law that's exactly the right focus," he said. "But for purposes of federal law it's much more rational for Congress . . . to say, 'We want to treat the same-sex couple in New York the same way as the committed same-sex couple in Oklahoma.'"

"He took a real stinker and made it compelling," Monagas said afterward.

But Justice Kagan was not buying it, pointing out that the uniform rule that the federal government had pursued prior to the passage of DOMA, a law that targeted "a group that is not everybody's favorite group in the world," was one in which it uniformly recognized marriages that were recognized by the states. "Do we really think that Congress was doing this for uniformity reasons, or do we think that Congress's judgment was infected by dislike, by fear, by animus, and so forth?" she asked. She quoted from the House report, which said that DOMA reflected a "collective moral judgment" to express "moral disapproval of homosexuality."

Justice Kennedy, who had been looking up at the ceiling, leaned forward, placing his chin in his hand. Olson leaned forward as well.

"Just because a couple legislators may have had an improper motive," Clement responded, was irrelevant; the question now before the Court was whether, under a rational basis test, the uniform rule defense passed muster.

The solicitor general, when he rose, made the case that heightened scrutiny should be applied. But if the justices had seemed to Chad, during the Proposition 8 argument, somewhat oblivious to the growing acceptance of same-sex marriage around the country, today the conservatives seized on what Justice Scalia called that "sea change" to try to knock down the notion that gays and lesbians represented a suspect class in need of heightened Court protection.

"You don't doubt that the lobby supporting the enactment of same-sex marriage is politically powerful, do you?" Roberts asked Kaplan.

"I would, Your Honor," she said.

"Really?"

"Yes."

"As far as I can tell, political figures are falling over to endorse your side of the case."

Kaplan refused to be cowed. "The fact of the matter is, Mr. Chief Justice, that no other group in recent history has been subjected to popular referenda to take away the rights that have already been given or exclude those rights, the way gay people have. And only two of those referenda have ever lost."

But with the Court as closely divided as it was, it was Justice Kennedy who was once again the center of attention. Kaplan, Clement, and Olson all hung on his every word. Kennedy spoke about the breadth of DOMA, and the fact that in denying some eleven hundred benefits to same-sex couples, it had become "intertwined with citizens' day-to-day life" and was at "real risk of what has always been thought to be the essence of the state police power," the regulation of marriage. That federalist theme was one he returned to repeatedly, which was worrisome not only to Clement, who thought it did not bode well for his clients, but also to the Prop 8 team. If Kennedy decided the case on the grounds that, as he put it at one point, the law passed by Congress was "not consistent" with the states' historic regulation of marriage, then where would that leave them?

Kaplan was careful on that point, sidestepping when Chief Justice Roberts, and then Justice Scalia, repeatedly asked whether the law created a federalism problem. The justices often use lawyers as props to debate one another, and there was a complex dynamic between the two conservatives and Justice Kennedy going on here. Roberts, at least on the surface, was playing a high-stakes game. It seemed to members of both legal teams that rather than trying to get Kennedy to split the baby and strike down DOMA while upholding Proposition 8 on the basis that the definition of marriage should be left to the states, he was effectively trying to paint Kennedy into a corner: You can either stand with us, or stand with the liberals, but you can't hide behind the fig leaf of federalism, and if you want to strike down DOMA, you will have to do so on equal protection grounds, which will have real implications for the ability of your beloved states to define marriage as they might wish.

Kaplan did a careful lawyer's dance, telling the chief that the fact that DOMA intruded upon an area traditionally regulated by the states spoke to the "novelty" of the law, which in turn added to the perception that it was, in fact, motivated by animus toward gays and lesbians.

"So eighty-four senators . . . based their vote on moral disapproval of gay people?" Roberts asked.

Kaplan, answering, drew a line out of Justice Kennedy's opinion in the *Lawrence v. Texas* decision. "No, I think—I think what is true, Mr. Chief Justice, is that times can blind, and that back in 1996 people did not have the understanding that they have today."

———

Walking out the Court's bronze front door, Kaplan thought she had never had so much fun in her life. Her wife, Rachel Lavine, was waiting outside with their seven-year-old son, Jacob, who flew into her arms.

Chad, out on the courthouse steps again, watched as supporters swarmed Edie. "We love you!" people chanted. She tilted her head toward the heavens, stretched out her arms, and, with her pink scarf whipping wild in the wind, looked for all the word as though she might fly away.

The consensus of the network and cable legal correspondents, who were already pontificating live, was that the Court appeared ready to strike down DOMA, a far more bullish take than yesterday's. Hilary Rosen, who was out on the courthouse steps helping the DOMA team navigate the media scrum, felt for Chad. As the president of the nation's largest gay rights organization, he wanted badly to win both cases. But the insta-analysis, comparing day one with day two of the arguments, could not have been easy for him to bear.

Before any reporters could waylay him, he quietly slipped away. This was Edie's day, and, wrung out from lack of sleep, Chad just wanted to go home to his semifurnished apartment and collapse.

"They've operated in this fantastic fantasy land of righteousness," Rosen said after he had gone. "'Everyone else thinks we are crazy, but we just believe!' Well, the people who are most important threw cold water on them. No one else over the last four years could, but they did."

The Court-trained media operation would continue right up through decision day. Justices do occasionally change their minds as opinions are circulated, with the result that a majority opinion becomes the minority's dissent, and Ted Boutrous had told them that every little bit helped. Rosen had heard that Justice Kennedy read the *Catholic Reporter,* and she was hoping to run an ad the following week featuring Catholic families who supported marriage equality.

But the truth was that by then it would probably all be over but the shouting. On Friday, the justices would meet behind closed doors, in the conference room behind the chief's chambers, and a preliminary vote would be taken. Each justice would spell out where they stood on each of the two cases. The justices speak by order of seniority, so the chief would go first, followed by Scalia. Then Kennedy, assuming he did not buy the standing arguments, or pass, would have to say where he was on the merits, meaning that the liberals would presumably have at least some inkling of whether there were five votes to overturn Proposition 8 and DOMA before they cast their lot.

It was, as Boies had said at the previous day's press conference, now in the hands of the Supreme Court.

THIRTY-NINE

"DIGNITY"

Benjamin Franklin, one of the nation's founding fathers, once said, "Three may keep a secret, if two of them are dead." In Washington, a town that leaks like a rickety old dinghy, the Supreme Court is the exception to that rule.

The nine justices and their clerks swap opinions back and forth for months, yet throughout the Court's history only rarely has an opinion spilled ahead of its announcement. Deliberations, with some notable exceptions, usually stay within the justices' chambers until one dies and releases their papers. Even the Court's timing remains frustratingly opaque; parties only learn which opinions will be issued on any given day when the justices begin reading them aloud from the bench.

Because the Supreme Court tends to hold on to blockbuster cases until the very last minute, everyone assumed that the Proposition 8 and *Windsor* decisions would be handed down near the end of the term, in late June. And because the Court divides its term into sittings, with each justice generally writing at least one majority opinion per sitting, it seemed likely based on a numbers game Court watchers call "Supreme Court Bingo" that Chief Justice Roberts was writing one of the opinions, while Justice Kennedy was writing the other, because neither had yet delivered an opinion from the March sitting when both cases were argued.

With no way of knowing when the decisions were coming, Chad and Olson had been filing into the Supreme Court every decision day since the middle of June. It was a measure of the importance Olson placed on the case; he was usually not so religious about needing to hear the outcome in person. Like a sports fan who won't look away from a game for fear of his team losing, it was almost as though Olson believed that just by being there in front of the justices he could will them into ruling his way.

Recently the plaintiffs had begun joining them, bags packed, ready to jump on a plane to California for a rally in West Hollywood the minute they knew their fate. Repeating the same drill over and again was anxiety-producing, to say the least. Every time Chief Justice Roberts would announce, "Justice Kennedy has the next opinion," Olson's head would jerk up and Chad would lurch to the edge of his seat, heart thumping. It made Kris feel out of control, "like a leaf in the wind." Jeff couldn't sleep without taking half of a Xanax: "My mind, just—race, race, race," he'd said after one abortive trip. For Edie Windsor and the DOMA team, convening every decision day at lead attorney Robbie Kaplan's apartment in New York was equally torturous. Edie's doctors, worried that the stress was too much for her weak heart, had forbidden her from traveling to D.C.

But finally the wait was over. The previous day, Justice Roberts had signaled that today, Wednesday June 26, was to be the final day of the Court's term. Tonight, for the first time in years, they would all go to sleep knowing the outcome.

———

"Well, well, well," Chad said, jumping out of a black SUV as it pulled up to the hotel where the plaintiffs were pacing, waiting to be picked up. "How you guys doing?"

He was wearing a dark suit and the same silvery blue tie he had been wearing to court every day for the past several weeks. It was the one he'd worn at the press conference announcing the case in May 2009. Its breadth was out of fashion, but it had taken him this far, so rather than pick a new one he had taken it to a tailor and had it slimmed.

Getting dressed that morning, Sandy had grabbed everything red she owned, in honor of the Human Rights Campaign's red "equal" logo. Peeking out from under her blazer was a red blouse, and in addition to her regular purse, she held up a random red nylon bag, "for luck," for everyone to admire. Kris, always one to try for a little levity during times of stress, had to laugh at that particular accessory. "We're going to the farmers' market before the Supreme Court," she joked. "That is so Sandy."

"I brought Jeff," Paul piped in. "If I have anything lucky, it's him."

They were all feeling a little superstitious, in part because today was the only day that Olson could not be with them. He was due to appear in the Third Circuit Court of Appeals in Philadelphia that morning on behalf of the state of New Jersey, which was challenging a law that limited betting on professional and college sports to Nevada and three other states. Defending the law was none other than Paul Clement, who had argued that DOMA was constitutional.

"Jesus, how could this happen?" Olson had said, crestfallen after Roberts made the announcement. Then, seeing the plaintiffs' long faces, he'd moved to comfort them. "We haven't lost the case, guys," he said, promising to try to join them for a postdecision rally in West Hollywood.

Olson had become their sherpa in this legal expedition, and they felt more than a little lost without him as they climbed into the SUV that would, for the last time, carry them to the nation's highest court. Rob and Michele Reiner, the parent figures of the operation, were also absent; Rob was in Connecticut, filming a movie. "Feel so bad I can't be with you," he texted Chad. "Give big hugs and kisses from me to everyone."

Chad read an e-mail from Kristina, who was on her way with the president and first lady to Andrews Air Force Base and then on to Africa. "This is all surreal," she wrote.

"Do you believe we're going to know in one hour, or one hour and a half?" Sandy said.

"Don't make me throw up back here," Paul replied.

Kris joked that between nerves and the sweltering heat, there was no way they would be able to follow the old "never let 'em see you sweat" adage. "Nothing works on Sandy. Would deodorant work on a hummingbird?"

"I finally have a hankerchief because I know I'm a blubbering mess at these things," Paul said, holding out an old-fashioned white square trimmed in pale blue. "Jeff was like, 'Really? You're my grandfather right now!'"

Since the oral arguments, France, Brazil, Uruguay, and New Zealand had become the latest countries where gays and lesbians could wed, and Britain was about to follow suit. Closer to home, after voters in Minnesota rejected the constitutional ban on same-sex marriage, lawmakers in that state had voted to legalize it. Delaware and Rhode Island had also passed laws allowing gays and lesbians to wed, bringing the total number of states to thirteen, plus the District of Columbia. Two more Republican U.S. senators, Lisa Murkowski of Alaska and Mark Kirk of Illinois, had come out in favor of allowing gays and lesbians to marry.

The Boy Scouts, under pressure from donors who themselves were under pressure from Chad, had dropped their prohibition on gay scouts, if not gay scout leaders. The first active major-league American sports player, NBA center Jason Collins, had come out as gay in a *Sports Illustrated* cover story.

Even the Catholic Church was softening, if not its position, its message. A new pope had recently been elected, and would soon, in a series of headline-making remarks, declare that gays and lesbians should be treated with respect: "If someone is gay and he searches for the Lord and has goodwill," Pope Francis said, "who am I to judge?" But under his leadership, the church's tone was already changing.

Cardinal Timothy Dolan, who during the New York State legislative battle had predicted that allowing gays and lesbians to marry would lead to a "perilous" and "Orwellian" future, had recently declared that "we gotta do better to see that our defense of marriage is not reduced to an attack on gay people. And I admit, we haven't been too good at that."

Predicting with any certainty what the Supreme Court might do in this atmosphere was a fool's errand, but that did not stop either the DOMA or Prop 8 teams from parsing even the smallest of signs for meaning.

Justice Kagan had been spotted out and about over the weekend, shopping at a supermarket and attending a dinner party. Did that mean that she was in the majority, since she wasn't buried in her office writing a dissent? And then there was the scathing speech Justice Scalia had given the previous week in North Carolina. Entitled "Mullahs of the West: Judges as Moral Arbiters," it made for interesting tea-leaf reading. Why would he be decrying judges who believed they, rather than the community, were qualified to decide questions of morality such as same-sex marriage, where, as he put it, there was no "scientifically demonstrable right answer," if he had emerged victorious in the Court's internal debates?

The day before, Olson had told the plaintiffs that the most likely outcome was that they would win on standing. Former justice John Paul Stevens, the man who Olson had hoped would sway Justice Kennedy his way, had made the same prediction in a speech that month, the lawyer noted to Chad.

But there was still a real sense that anything could happen, even an outright loss, particularly now that it appeared Roberts was writing one of the opinions. In recent days, the Supreme Court had gutted the Voting Rights Act and stepped up scrutiny of race-conscious college admissions policies in a high-profile affirmative action case.

"Those decisions have not made me more optimistic," Boies said over lunch one day at a Washington steakhouse.

Mary, his wife, nodded her agreement. "I just hope there aren't any broken hearts."

AFER had prepared seven different press releases to cover every possible outcome. The one they would release if Proposition 8 was upheld had been the last, because everyone kept refusing to write it. "I know we don't want to focus on this," Jeff had said the night before. "But what if we lose?"

"It's going to be rough," Adam had replied. What else could he say?

Kris, checking her iPhone, saw an e-mail from Jim Messina, Obama's 2012 campaign manager. Kris, who in her new job was working with Messina to promote the president's early childhood education initiative, shared his message: "Please know you have already won. 9 old fucking judges can't change that, either way."

Silence. Fiddling with her iPhone again, Kris looked for a song to fill it, to capture the moment. She settled on one by hip-hop artist B.o.B. The lyrics filled the SUV:

Can we pretend that airplanes
In the night sky
Are like shooting stars?
I could really use a wish right now
Wish right now
Wish right now.

Kris, swaying back and forth, leaned over and kissed Sandy's cheek. "No matter what happens, we won," she said, trying to sound convincing. "We did."

As the SUV pulled in front of the U.S. Supreme Court, one by one everyone began softly singing along with the music.

I could really use a wish right now
Wish right now
Wish right now.

———

The noise hit them as soon as they stepped onto the sidewalk. Beyond the crush of cameras and reporters shouting questions, a sizable crowd had gathered, pressing close and chanting two words over and over as Chad, Jeff, Paul, Kris, Sandy, and Adam made their way up the courthouse's marble steps.

"Thank you! Thank you! Thank you!"

Inside, the courtroom was hushed. Boies had already taken his seat in the bar section. Olson had managed to secure seats reserved for guests of Justice Clarence Thomas and retired justice Sandra Day O'Connor for everyone else. Cooper was not there, but a number of his clients were.

As the clock ticked close to 10 A.M., Chad squeezed Kris's arm, who grabbed Sandy's, and on it went down the row.

Suddenly, the justices appeared all at once, stepping like wizards of Oz through invisible openings in the cascading red draperies that backdropped their bench. Justice Alito seemed to be grimacing; the rest were their usual inscrutable selves.

When everyone was seated again, Chief Justice Roberts made the following pronouncement:

"Justice Kennedy has the opinion in—"

Chad felt as though he held his breath for minutes, though scarcely half a second passed before the chief finished:

"—*Windsor.*"

In New York, Edie and her legal team began jumping up and down. Chad, who had been sitting tall, dropped his head. That meant that Roberts was writing the Proposition 8 opinion, which likely meant one of two things: Either they were about to win on standing, or the Court was going to uphold bans like Proposition 8 as a proper exercise of the state power to regulate marriage, the outcome the entire gay legal community had feared when they had announced the case.

—————

Only after the justices verbally summarize their opinions from the bench does the Supreme Court hand out written copies to the public. With no way to flip to the end to see the holding and rationale, the experience of those sitting in the audience is an impressionistic one.

Justice Kennedy, looking straight ahead, delivered his in a regal tone. First, there was the question of standing. He went on for quite a bit about that, before declaring that DOMA was properly before the Court. When he finally turned to the merits, Boies, who said he never lost sleep over a case, was in a state approaching alarm, as his mind tried to process phrases about laws "which for centuries had been deemed necessary," and marriage being the "exclusive province of the state." If Justice Kennedy, joined by the court's four liberals, had decided *Windsor* based solely on federalism grounds, it might be time to hit the panic button.

"That's not good, that's not good," thought Matt McGill, who was standing in a hallway in the Third Circuit Court of Appeals in Philadelphia where Olson was preparing to argue his case, holding his phone up to a window in order to get enough bars to follow what was happening in Washington via SCOTUSBlog.

But then Kennedy started throwing around modifying phrases, making clear that the states' power was "subject to constitutional guarantees" and using terms like "stigma" to describe the federal law's effect. He seemed to be saying that while he could have decided this case based on federalism grounds, he was going to go bigger.

It was going to be okay, Boies thought, then, as Justice Kennedy continued, he recalculated. It was going to be more than okay.

The 5–4 opinion was filled with the kind of flowery rhetoric that had marked the *Lawrence* decision, issued ten years earlier to the day. If Justice

Roberts, in attacking the narrower federalism argument during oral argument, had bet that Justice Kennedy would be unwilling to find DOMA unconstitutional on broader grounds, he had seriously miscalculated.

In explaining the decision by states like New York, where Edie Windsor lived, to allow gays and lesbians to marry, Kennedy wrote of an "evolving understanding of the meaning of equality." The state had acted to "give their lawful conduct a lawful status," in what was "a far-reaching legal acknowledgement of the intimate relationship between two people, a relationship deemed by the State worthy of dignity in the community equal with all other marriages." The "essence" of DOMA, he wrote, was to interfere with that dignity, to "disparage and to injure those whom the State, by its marriage laws, sought to protect in personhood and dignity."

This was more than just a victory. It was a validation, by the highest court in the land, of an entire community. In the bar section, a group of women sitting together began dabbing at their eyes. As Justice Kennedy pronounced DOMA "unconstitutional," based on both due process and equal protection grounds, someone let out a wail. In New York, Edie Windsor, watching from her lawyer's apartment, let out a whoop. "I want to go to Stonewall right now!" she said.

But what, exactly, did it mean for Prop 8 and bans like it?

Justice Scalia, reading a summary of his dissent from the bench, provided part of that answer.

"The penultimate statement of the majority's opinion is a naked declaration that this opinion and its holding are confined to those couples 'joined in same-sex marriages made lawful by the State.' In other words, today's opinion does not say anything about whether same-sex marriages must be made lawful," Justice Scalia said.

"It takes real cheek for today's majority, as it is going out the door, to leave us with that comforting assurance—when what has preceded it is a lengthy lecture on how superior the majority's moral judgment in favor of same-sex marriage is to Congress' hateful moral judgment against it."

To Chad, hanging on each word, it now seemed clear that the majority of the Court would not reach the merits in the Proposition 8 case. But it seemed equally clear that the five justices who had just delivered the *Windsor* opinion weren't going to vote to declare Proposition 8 constitutional either. Instead, they would duck for now, even as the *Windsor* opinion provided a road map for the next challenge.

Justice Scalia, still thundering his dissent from the bench, had reached the same conclusion. "By formally declaring anyone opposed to same-sex marriage an enemy of human decency, the majority arms well every challenger to a state law restricting marriage to its traditional definition."

Winding down, Justice Scalia then proceeded to read the majority opinion in another case, an interminable delay for everyone waiting to hear the Prop 8 opinion that he seemed to recognize. "Sorry, but this is a short one," he quipped, good humor now returned.

And then, finally, Chief Justice Roberts delivered the opinion of the Court in the Proposition 8 case. On a vote of 5–4, the Court cleared the way for same-sex marriages to resume in California, while leaving for another day the question of whether all fifty states must follow suit. Kris, sitting next to Chad, gasped aloud.

Notwithstanding the California Supreme Court's finding that the state constitution gave proponents of Proposition 8 the authority to stand in for the governor and the attorney general for the purpose of defending the initiative, the majority declared that the question of standing was a federal question. Cooper, who was reading the opinion on SCOTUSBlog in his office, couldn't believe the way that Roberts sidestepped the Supreme Court precedents that he had relied upon to reach the conclusion of the Court.

While it was true that the Supreme Court had granted New Jersey state officials standing to defend a school prayer law in the 1987 *Karcher v. May* case, it had limited standing to elected officials still in office, Roberts wrote. Then, in a piece of reasoning that Cooper found breathtakingly disingenuous, Roberts buttressed his opinion by turning to a passage in the Court's 1997 *Arizonans for Official English* opinion.

In that case, the Court had cast doubt on ballot proponents' ability to defend initiatives because there was nothing on Arizona's books or in the state constitution allowing them to act as agents of the state *"in lieu of public offi-cials."* But Roberts turned the passage "on its head," Cooper would later say, in order to conclude that because Proposition 8 proponents were not elected of-ficials, but rather mere private citizens, answerable to no one, they could not by definition be agents of the state as required by *Arizonans.* And as private citizens, Roberts explained from the bench, Prop 8 proponents "must have suffered some injury." That was a test, the majority concluded, that they could not meet, meaning they never should have been granted standing to challenge Judge Walker's decision.

Boies, listening, seized on those words: That was what they had been argu-ing all along, that allowing gays and lesbians to marry harmed no one.

In Philadelphia, McGill ran into the courtroom where Olson, with no ac-cess to the news, was sitting. The court was in session so he had to whisper the news. "You could see the tension drain away," McGill would later recall. Ol-son's shoulders, which had been bunched up around his ears, relaxed. "We won," he said.

———

The Gulfstream IV carrying Chad, Boies, the plaintiffs, and the AFER team took off for California a little after 1 P.M. Boies had paid for another private jet to pick up Olson in Philadelphia so he could meet them at the West Hollywood rally that night, and the stewardess reported that from time to time it could be glimpsed just up ahead.

This was a group that had never let a milestone go by without speeches and toasts, but the whirlwind of the last few hours had left little time to process what had just happened. After only the briefest of huddles in a vestibule near the Supreme Court's front doors—"If you listen to the DOMA decision it's only a matter of time before it goes across the country!" a jubilant Boies had told the plaintiffs—the team had stepped outside and into a media melee, culminating in a call from President Obama.

Everyone was still giggling about how Chad, in the media pit outside the Supreme Court where every major network had set up their cameras, had tried to get producers' attention, saying, as loudly as he could, "Hello, Air Force

One." When that hadn't worked, he had shoved his way into an MSNBC live shot of Kris and Sandy, speakerphone on, as the president praised everyone for their courage and Paul invited him to their wedding in a call heard round the world. "I do know a little about media," Chad said with a laugh.

But overall, the mood on board was subdued. The proponents of Prop 8 had just issued a press release signaling that they intended to try to limit the scope of the day's Supreme Court ruling with yet another round of litigation, arguing that Judge Walker's decision applied only to the four plaintiffs because the case had not been filed as a class action. The idea had gained some traction after Judge Reinhardt, during the Ninth Circuit's arguments, had flummoxed Boies with his question about whether they had sued the right people.

No one on the legal team gave much credence to the argument. But given that Judge Reinhardt had included an aside in his opinion chastising the team for not filing the case in a way that ensured statewide enforcement, the team had been preparing for this eventuality.

In recent weeks, Chad, Adam, and Ted Boutrous had met privately with California attorney general Kamala Harris and Governor Brown's legal staff. Legally and practically, they had argued, as the top legal officers in the state, you are the ultimate arbiters on the matter. The coordination had paid off: Shortly before takeoff, Governor Brown had called Chad directly to tell him he had just ordered California's county clerks and county registrars to begin issuing same-sex couples marriage licenses as soon as the Ninth Circuit, whose decision on the merits had now been vacated, gave the state the go-ahead.

Chad, checking his e-mail, saw that the Associated Press was reporting that marriages would not resume in California for at least twenty-five days. The losing side in a Supreme Court case has that long to ask for a rehearing, and while that request is rarely granted, the wire service was quoting a spokesperson for the Ninth Circuit saying the court would likely wait for that time to run before lifting the stay it had imposed after ruling in the plaintiffs' favor. He called the news back to the plaintiffs and Adam.

With no immediate wedding to plan, Kris and Sandy passed the time by sharing the e-mails flooding their in-box. Paul, looking emotionally exhausted, stared intensely out the window for several minutes, before laying his head on Jeff's shoulder and falling asleep.

Up front, Boies spread copies of both opinions in front of him and began reading carefully for the first time, while Chad called Robbie Kaplan, Edie Windsor's lawyer, from the plane's satellite phone.

"Robbie? Robbie, it's Chad Griffin—congratulations!"

He listened for a second.

"We thank you! Everyone is sending their love to you and Edie."

The front page of the following day's *Washington Post* would feature an iconic photo of Chad, Boies, the plaintiffs, and Adam triumphantly emerging from the Supreme Court with their hands held high in the air under the headline VICTORIES FOR GAY MARRIAGE. The *New York Times*'s double-barreled headline sat over a picture of a joyous Edie Windsor, celebrating in the West Village near her home in New York City. The *Huffington Post* was already up with a headline that said it all: DOUBLE RAINBOW.

And indeed, for all the worry about the tension, perceived and actual, between the two cases, each had benefited from the other.

Practically, *Windsor*'s victory meant that when Paul and Jeff and Kris and Sandy did get married, real tangible benefits would attach to what, up to now, had largely been a symbolic step. It would also make it difficult to argue, as Cooper had done, that domestic partnerships represented an equitable compromise; *Windsor* had "changed the landscape," the New Jersey Supreme Court would soon declare, in a ruling that cleared the way for gays and lesbians to marry in that state, making the harm to couples unable to marry and thus avail themselves of benefits "real, not abstract or speculative."

Shortly before takeoff, Attorney General Eric Holder had called Chad to brief him on the administrative steps the government was already taking to ensure that the *Windsor* opinion applied as broadly as possible. Gay and lesbian couples would now be entitled to file joint tax returns. The Pentagon would immediately begin extending survivor benefits to the spouses of gay and lesbian service members killed in action, who would also now be eligible to be buried alongside them in veterans' cemeteries. The Department of Homeland Security would immediately begin processing spousal citizenship applications for transnational couples who up to now faced the possibility of separation due to deportation. The list went on and on. It would be trickier for legally married couples who resided in a state with no right to marry, given that some programs like Social Security consider where people live rather than where they were married to determine spousal benefit eligibility, but the administration planned to issue regulations to solve that problem.

"Congratulations on all the work you've done, my friend," Holder told Chad.

Legally, Olson had been proven right that the broadest arguments were the key to Justice Kennedy's vote. Kennedy had dissented from the majority's standing opinion—written by Chief Justice Roberts—meaning he had been willing to rule on the constitutionality of Proposition 8. Denied that opportunity, he seemed to have grafted whole passages of the arguments that Olson had put forward in the Prop 8 case onto his opinion in the DOMA case.

Windsor's brief, narrowly tailored to convince the justices that they could find in her favor without deciding the larger question of whether denying gays and lesbians the right to marry was unconstitutional, sought only to convince the Court that there was nothing so fundamentally different about gays and lesbians that could justify DOMA, and therefore, like the Colorado initiative in the *Romer* case, the federal law was motivated by animus.

Kennedy agreed, but he went further. While he left open the question of whether his opinion was based on a belief that gays and lesbians had a fundamental right to marry, and avoided the other crucial question of whether heightened scrutiny ought to apply, it seemed clear from what he did say that this case was, as Olson had maintained, very much about the importance of marriage. Where Olson had argued that denying gays and lesbians the right to marry labels them "second-class and not equal," Kennedy found that DOMA "demeans the couple" and places them in the "unstable position of being in a second-tier marriage." Where Olson argued that a ban like Proposition 8 "generates a feeling of inferiority" among gays and lesbians and "especially their children," Kennedy had this to say about DOMA: It "instructs all federal officials, and indeed all persons with whom same-sex couples interact, including their own children, that their marriage is less worthy than the marriages of others." And as Olson had done, Kennedy repeatedly returned to the concept of human "dignity" in explaining his decision.

By intertwining arguments from both cases, Kennedy gave the *Windsor* opinion a heft and precedential value it might otherwise not have had, providing powerful legal ammunition for a slew of future challenges to state bans on same-sex marriage. Robbie Kaplan would later ruminate that "had the Prop 8 case not been there, maybe they would not have ruled so expansively in the *Windsor* case, because clearly they were trying to send a signal on the larger question."

"I don't know if you've had any time to focus on it," Boies said, finally reaching Olson on his plane, "but I just get happier and happier." He listened for a minute. "Take care, my friend," he said, before signing off and turning to Chad. "It hasn't quite sunk in yet."

And in truth, it was hard not to feel a little ambivalent, when they had wanted so much more. As forward-leaning as Kennedy's opinion was, it was still vintage Kennedy, teasing in its vagaries, designed to be read in multiple ways. Scalia's blistering dissent, by contrast, was far more straightforward, and in its own way heartening to Chad, but reading it he could only shake his head. "It's hard to respond."

"I just cringe," Boies replied.

Among other things, Scalia had accused Justice Kennedy and the majority of a "jaw-dropping" assertion of judicial supremacy, of making only "passing mentions" to the arguments made by DOMA's defendants, of employing "rootless and shifting" justifications in an opinion that, "whatever disappearing trail of its legalistic argle-bargle one chooses to follow," amounted to declaring that DOMA was motivated by a "bare desire to harm couples in same-sex marriages."

"To hurl such accusations so casually demeans *this institution*," Scalia had charged.

"He doesn't sound like an independent jurist," Chad said.

"Duh," Boies interjected.

The dissent was tame compared with the one that Scalia had penned in the *Lawrence* case, when he argued that states should be able to pass laws that promote "majoritarian sexual morality" and accused the Court of buying into the "homosexual agenda," but the distinction was lost on Chad.

"He sounds like a right-wing politician," he said.

Only then did the irony of the odd alliance that had combined to hand them their victory truly hit them. Justice Scalia had joined Chief Justice Roberts and three of the Court's four liberals in denying Cooper's clients standing. Justices Alito, Thomas, and Sotomayor had joined Justice Kennedy in a dissent that accused the majority of undermining the entire purpose of initiatives, which was to check the power of state officials, by handing those same officials a "de facto" veto over those they did not like.

In other words, Kris and Sandy and Jeff and Paul had Justice Scalia to thank for the fact that they would soon be getting married. Or, seen another way, the couples in the thirty-seven states without marriage equality might have Scalia, and three of the court's liberals, to blame for the fact that they would have to wait.

It was possible, of course, that each had simply been following their view of the law. Both Justices Roberts and Scalia were longtime standing hawks, and Justice Ginsburg had authored the opinion in *Arizonans*. But it seemed to many on the legal team that it was equally possible that the two conservatives had joined forces with the liberals to stop Justice Kennedy from reaching the merits in the Proposition 8 case, thus limiting the impact of the decision to California.

With the political winds blowing so strongly in favor of same-sex marriage, the justices seemed to have blinked—too conflicted to hand down a nation-wide decision allowing gays and lesbians to marry, but too aware of their place in history to be seen as moving the country backward by denying a right polls now showed most Americans supported. It was, in a certain sense, a perfect political face-saving maneuver.

The more Olson thought about it, the more it seemed a modern-day *Marbury v. Madison*. In that landmark 1803 case, the Supreme Court managed to reach the result it wanted—establishing the judiciary as coequal to Congress and the executive branch, with the authority to strike down laws they had approved—but it did so in a way that gave a victory to then president Thomas Jefferson, making it harder for him to complain about an outcome that he disliked.

Olson could see the three liberals on today's Court saying, as he put it later, "This is a pretty good outcome. You blow away DOMA in a strong opinion, and you blow away Prop 8 but in a way that people on the other side can't get as exercised about."

In Washington, Cooper analyzed it much the same way: It seemed to him that no justice in the *Windsor* majority, Kennedy included, would be likely to peel off and uphold a ban like Prop 8. "That gives additional force to the suspicion, voiced by many, that the standing ruling was a negotiated outcome to postpone the date when the Court would have to decide the larger constitutional issue," he said.

But if that were the case, why did three of the liberals go along? Boies, mulling that mystery over with Chad, said he could understand Justices Ginsburg and Breyer. Justice Ginsburg would later reject comparisons to *Roe v. Wade*, telling the *New York Times*, "I wouldn't make that connection," but she sure had seemed eager to get rid of the Proposition 8 case rather than decide it. Maybe she simply thought the country was not yet ready for a fifty-state ruling. And Breyer, Boies said, had often spoken about the fragility of the Court's power. In the justice's 2010 book *Making Our Democracy Work*, Breyer cited an 1831 decision in which the Court validated the Cherokee Indians' claim to lands given to them by treaty with the government, a ruling that then president Andrew Jackson promptly countermanded. His concern that the Court's authority derived from people's willingness to comply with its dictates "could lead Breyer to worry about moving too fast," Boies said.

But Kagan? Why did she sign on to the opinion? Was she worried, when the justices first voted, about where Kennedy would come out? If so, why was Sotomayor confident enough to vote the other way? "They would have reached the merits if either Ginsburg, Breyer, or Kagan, any one of those three, had gone the other way," Boies mused.

And what about Roberts? His technocratic dissent to the DOMA decision, on standing grounds, contained none of Justice Scalia's fire eating language. He mildly chastised Kennedy, saying, "I would not tar the political branches with the brush of bigotry." He agreed that DOMA should not have been struck down, but limited his rationale to the notion that when Congress passed the law in 1996, its interest in uniformity was justified given that no states at that point allowed same-sex marriage.

"He even tries to walk Scalia's comments back," Boies told Chad, noting the portion of Roberts's opinion in which he disagreed with Justice Scalia's assessment that the majority's opinion in *Windsor* would inevitably lead to same-sex marriage.

On the ground in San Francisco, Judge Walker, who first heard the news on television while on a treadmill at the gym, would be struck first and foremost at how "savvy an operator" Roberts was in cobbling together a majority to kick the Proposition 8 case on standing and avoid, for the time being, committing himself to a course that history would surely someday judge. By holding a trial that subjected each of the purported justifications for same-sex marriage bans to the crucible of cross-examination, Walker had made Olson's path forward far less risky, creating a record that made it harder for the justices to rule in Cooper's favor, even under the deferential rational basis standard. Walker had hoped that the Supreme Court would find Proposition 8 unconstitutional for the same reasons he had—"It would have taken me off the hook"—but he was "neither surprised nor dissatisfied with the result." Roberts "knew which way the winds were blowing," he said, "and this was an easy out."

"He preserves his position," was the way Boies put it to Chad.

Just then, Adam, who was watching the flight path on a wall-mounted screen, interrupted the what-if legal reverie.

"Hey, we just crossed into California," he called out from the back of the plane, "where we are now full and equal citizens."

It took a moment to process the import of those words. Then, for the first time that day, everyone began to cheer.

FORTY

JUNE IS FOR WEDDINGS

T wo days later, at 10:40 A.M. Pacific time on June 28, the following e-mail went out to AFER staff:

Subject: Go Time

CONFIDENTIAL—DO NOT SHARE WITH ANYONE. Weddings may start today.

No one had planned on this. Olson and the rest of the legal team were still debating whether to file a motion asking the Ninth Circuit to lift its stay, or whether to stick to protocol and wait the twenty-five days Cooper had to file for a rehearing. But when Chris Dusseault and another member of the team, Josh Lipshutz, had called to speak to Molly Dwyer, the clerk of the Ninth Circuit, that morning about logistics, her cryptic answers to their question about the court's procedures put them on high alert.

Have you considered whether the Ninth Circuit could lift the stay on its own? she had asked.

Whoa, Lipshutz thought. What exactly is she telegraphing here?

Hypothetically, if we were to be working on a motion to lift, Dusseault started to ask, carefully wording his question as theoretical so as not to run afoul of rules prohibiting ex parte communications with court officials.

She interrupted him: Betting money would say not to spend your weekend on that motion.

"We'll know more at 3 P.M."

The two lawyers had immediately called Adam, who would later recall the conversation this way: "'Hey Adam. Pause. We just had, pause, this, pause, interesting call with the, pause, clerk of the Ninth Circuit.'

"The pace they were talking, I was like, what, what?"

The team had long hoped to ensure that the four plaintiffs were the first to marry in California, so a fair amount of planning had already been done. Now they would just have to improvise on the fly.

The two couples wanted separate ceremonies, and so Adam decided that Kris and Sandy, who had already flown back to San Francisco, would marry there, while Jeff and Paul would stay in Los Angeles. A car was dispatched to take Paul and Jeff to Norwalk, a predominately Latino enclave of southeast Los Angeles and the only place the team could find in the county that would be open and issuing licenses after 3 P.M. Enrique Monagas, the lawyer who filed the case more than four years earlier, happened to be in town for an argument. He and Dusseault, who lived in Los Angeles, would meet Paul and Jeff there.

Sandy was at work when Kris reached her with the news. She dropped everything and picked up Kris's son Elliott at the science camp where he was working as a counselor; the other three boys were scattered throughout the country, too far to make it on time. Racing home, Sandy threw a silvery knit dress, shoes, and makeup into a bag, and twenty minutes later the three of them were heading to Gibson Dunn's San Francisco office, where Sandy got dressed for her wedding in the bathroom. Kris, who had already put on a gray pantsuit at home, texted her mom, who had driven into the city to pick up a visa for an upcoming trip to Brazil. Taking the team's confidentiality warning seriously, Kris told her only that she might want to drive her car to City Hall and stay put.

Chad and Lance Black had been incommunicado, doing an interview with the *Hollywood Reporter*. When he finished up, Chad called Fred Sainz, his vice president of communications and marketing at the Human Rights Campaign, to talk about some unrelated business. "Dude, I have something soooo much more important to talk to you about," Sainz said, and filled him in.

"Cancel your shrink appointment," Chad told Black, who was scheduled to see his therapist that day. "We're leaving now."

Charging through the lobby of the Sunset Tower Hotel, Chad made the decision to head to the Los Angeles airport and on to San Francisco, the city where this had all begun, and where three years earlier Judge Walker had issued the sweeping opinion that was now, as the only one left standing, controlling. "June is, after all, the month for weddings," Walker had said all those years ago during closing arguments. Chad hoped so.

Grabbing his bag, he ran back downstairs to meet the car he had ordered. "I'll double your fee if you can get me to the airport in record time," he told the driver. Just then, Sainz called him back. The lawyers, seeing AFER's massive planning machinery kick into high gear, were now trying to talk everyone off the ledge.

"Let's just be clear, we don't know what this means," Sainz said, relaying the lawyers' message. "It could be that at 3 P.M. they just announce that it will start next week."

"What's the fucking headline here?" Chad interrupted. "I don't need to know the details."

He decided to keep going. He wasn't about to chance missing Kris and Sandy's wedding. The next available flight was at 1 P.M. on Virgin America, in less than an hour. Chad's bag was massive, with clothes spilling out of it because he'd packed so fast, and he was worried that the airline would make him check it. That would mean precious minutes lost on the San Francisco end of the trip. Rummaging through it, he grabbed his Human Rights Campaign pin.

"Virgin has tons of gay employees," he said to Black, "so if they try to make me check it, we will look for a gay guy to save us!"

Arriving at the airport, they ran through the terminal. At the gate, there was bad news: The flight was delayed by forty-five minutes. The trip itself took just over an hour. It was going to be very, very tight if weddings started precisely at 3 P.M. By the time the flight was called, Chad was going out of his mind. "It's the perfect continuation of the four-year drama," he said to Black, laughing. "If you tried to write this into a script, people would be like, 'Come on.'"

The handsome young attendant taking Chad's ticket glanced down at his name, looked back up at him, and did a double take. "Thank you," the attendant said, smiling warmly. Then, remembering his job, he added, "Oh, and thank you for flying Virgin America."

The plane landed at San Francisco airport at 2:53 P.M. Adam, who had flown in from Burbank, was ahead of them. "Get off fast," Chad texted Black, who was seated a dozen rows back. "I think it's happening."

Another mad dash through another airport terminal ensued. Gasping for air, dragging his bursting bag, Chad climbed into a waiting black SUV that had been sent to meet them, while frenetically checking his e-mail and texts.

"And we're off," he said as the driver pulled away from the curb. "Phew. Fuck!"

Seconds later, Chad's phone rang. It was Bruce Cohen, down at City Hall. Cohen was in San Francisco producing a musical called *I Am Harvey Milk*, featuring the San Francisco Gay Men's Chorus. Kris and Sandy had seen it the night before, and had asked whether it would be possible for the chorus to sing at their wedding. Little did anyone know that it might take place less than twenty-four hours later.

Cohen had called Adam to say that since the chorus was in rehearsal that afternoon, he could still make that happen. Okay, Adam had said, but for God's sake don't say a word about what is going on: "You can't tell three hundred gay men that this is going to happen and expect it to stay a secret!" So Cohen had kept them at the ready, in the theater where the musical was showing down the street from City Hall, with no explanation.

A leak could give the proponents of Prop 8 a chance to file for an emergency injunction so they could litigate just how broadly Judge Walker's ruling should apply. But once the marriages began, as Judge Walker himself later put it, it would be "very hard to stuff that genie back in the bottle."

So Kris and Sandy were on ice, in a car parked outside City Hall, so as not to attract any media attention. Someone had even thought to call a makeup artist, who was applying foundation and blush in the backseat. A photographer, hired at the last minute to shoot the wedding, had almost blown everything by tweeting about the job with a #Prop8 hashtag. The team caught the tweet within minutes and it was quickly deleted.

"Do we know anything more?" Chad asked Cohen, who was standing by with Terry Stewart.

Negative, Cohen replied, promising to call back the moment that he did.

Willing the driver to go faster, Chad spoke with an assistant about the press release that would be issued the moment they knew for sure what the Ninth Circuit was going to do.

"I just want it to be"—he paused—"super powerful. What's the headline today?"

"To be in a state that has twice had marriage taken away?" Black mulled it over, before suggesting, "This is permanent. I think that's meaningful, because marriage is supposed to be permanent."

They settled on, "In California, a time of struggle and indignity are over, and love, justice, and freedom begin anew. And now, no election, no judge—no one—can take this basic right away."

"Going to the chapel," Black began to sing. "Gonna get married!" Chad chimed in.

Chad's phone rang again. It was Cohen. Chad put him on speakerphone.

"The order has been issued, but we don't yet know what it says," Cohen said. "It's just upstairs."

Seconds ticked by. Everyone was silent.

"Okay, we have it!"

Another pause, then: "We're a go!"

Hanging up, Chad looked at Black. The day before, Chad had gotten up at 4:30 A.M. to fly to Salt Lake City, Utah, in many ways the Montgomery, Alabama, of the gay rights movement, to give a speech at the Utah Pride Center. It was an important symbolic stop, his first since the decisions. At the press conference that took place just after the rulings on the U.S. Supreme Court steps, Chad had made a promise. "It took less than five years to strike down Proposition 8," he'd said. "Within five years, we will bring marriage equality to all fifty states in this vast country."

Utah was still ground zero in that battle. Though the Mormon Church was no longer in the business of funding initiatives like Prop 8, public school teachers in Utah could still be fired just for speaking about homosexuality in a positive manner. This was not a place where marriage equality could be won anytime soon at the ballot box, or through legislative action. It would likely take another case, and a Supreme Court willing to go the distance.

Tomorrow, there would be time to contemplate next steps. Tomorrow, Chad would have to figure out where and when to bring the next case.

But right now, sitting in the SUV as it careened toward City Hall, jerking from one lane to the next in an effort to steer around traffic, to Chad the victory he had already achieved finally felt as momentous as it was. For the first time in American history, a federal district and appellate court had found a constitutional right for gays and lesbians to marry. And if Justice Scalia was right, it would not be long before the Supreme Court did too. He had bucked the oddsmakers in the gay rights establishment, and he had won. Even Judge Smith, who had ruled against them on the merits in the Ninth Circuit, had signed on to the order lifting the stay, allowing same-sex couples in California to resume marrying "effective immediately."

"It's happening now," Chad told Black. "Weddings can start now!"

Then he typed a text to his mom: "Hurry, turn on your tv."

"Holy crap!" Black exclaimed. "We did it. Like, it's gonna happen!"

As the SUV pulled up to City Hall, Chad's eyes welled. "Uh-oh," he said, waving his right hand in front of his face. Then he and Black jumped out and ran up the stairs.

———

Stepping inside the doors, they spotted Adam, Kris and Sandy, Elliott, and Kris's mom. Then the entire entourage began moving as one through the spectacular Beaux-Arts rotunda toward the county clerk's office, where the plaintiffs would be issued their license. City employees came out of their offices, lining the balconies that ringed the rotunda, and cheered. Camera crews, now alerted, began pressing in on all sides.

"Wait for me!" yelled Cleve Jones.

He had been scheduled to give a speech when Cohen reached him with the news. "Pretend to be me," he'd ordered a friend, then ducked out and dashed to City Hall. Running to join the group, he wheezed, "I ain't never run so fast!"

"I can't believe we pulled this shit off, and everyone is here," Adam said, shaking his head.

Jones's hand shook as he took a photo inside the county clerk's office of Black, Adam, and Chad. "Try not to look so smug." He laughed, tears running down his face.

Just then, California's attorney general, Kamala Harris, rushed in. She had agreed to marry Kris and Sandy in lieu of Olson, who had flown back east the day before and was stuck in West Virginia attending a judicial conference with Boies.

Her presence was fortunate. The clerk in Los Angeles, confused about what the Ninth Circuit had done, was hesitant about giving Jeff and Paul a license. Someone from the AFER team in San Francisco was on an open line with the couple, and now handed Harris the phone.

"This is Kamala Harris," she said sternly. "You, you must start marriages immediately."

She loudly repeated her directive, ensuring the camera crews filmed her every word, then listened to the response.

"Okay. That's wonderful. Have a good day," she said. "And enjoy it—it's gonna be fun."

At 3:58 P.M. the San Francisco county clerk, with dramatic flair, called out. "Can we help the next customer, please?"

As Kris and Sandy stepped to the desk, Jones looked over at Chad. "Oh, Chad, the places you take us."

"It's real," Chad replied, his voice quavering. "Do you see that?"

Jones nodded. "It's real."

Across the country, Cooper watched it all unfold in shock. It was inconceivable to him that the Ninth Circuit had given him no notice of what it was about to do, "one of the most questionable events in a case that was rife with questionable events," he would later say. His view of the law had not changed. Still, seeing the plaintiffs' faces, he couldn't help but wish them the best.

"At a personal, human level, I rejoiced in their happiness."

Over the years, Cooper had often thought about what would happen if his argument prevailed at the Supreme Court, playing it out like a movie in his mind. He had followed the polls in California carefully, and it seemed likely to him that Proposition 8 would go back on the ballot, and be repealed. "At that time, Kris and Sandy and Jeff and Paul would have gotten married," he said, of his imaginary scenario. "And I often thought, that would be a ceremony I would like to attend."

And he now understood, in a way that he could not possibly have when the two couples testified at trial, what this moment meant to them, because he now understood what it meant to his own daughter.

They had been sipping iced teas and eating sandwiches outside, during a family vacation at their home on the beach in Bonita Springs, Florida, when Cooper finally broached the subject with Ashley, a vibrant young woman in her twenties with long brown hair, a freckled nose, and an impish grin.

"So," he said, "when am I going to meet Casey?"

"I hope soon," Ashley replied. "Because she's really special to me."

It had been midway through the case, during the interminable Ninth Circuit phase, when his wife confirmed what he had suspected for months. Debbie Cooper had known, even before her husband agreed to take the Proposition 8 case, that her daughter was a lesbian.

Listening to the trial testimony by day and talking to Ashley on the phone at night had been like living in two parallel universes. Debbie Cooper had been deeply moved by Jerry Sanders, the mayor of San Diego with the lesbian daughter who had testified about his own unthinking prejudice. She worried for her daughter, because "it's a hard life, and you can't help but realize that there are places in this country where she could be harmed." But listening to the testimony of Kris and Sandy had given her comfort.

"Here were two women who were much older than Ash, and they were so okay, in every emotional way, in their lives, in their heads, and in their family. And I remember Chuck coming back from court that day and talking about their strength of character, their integrity."

Still, she had held off sharing Ashley's secret with him, out of respect for her daughter's wishes that she be allowed to come out to him in her own way. But if he asks, Ashley told her, you can tell him. And he had, which is what led to the conversation in June of 2012 in Florida. Chuck had married her mother when Ashley was just seven, and he was as much her dad as her biological father. She was nervous about telling him, but he had made it so much easier by bringing it up himself.

"I said, 'You know, it's not easy to talk about,'" Ashley recalled.

"It's not easy for anyone," he replied, "but I love you, and you love me, and that's all that matters."

Her mother initially asked her if she was sure she was a lesbian, but Cooper accepted it without question.

"I sometimes wonder if what made him so amazing to come out to was the experience of being part of that trial," she said.

Cooper would like to think he would have reacted the same way regardless. But he said the trial, and especially the wrenching testimony of Ryan Kendall—the Denver Police Department employee who testified about how his parents forced him to attend sexual orientation "conversion therapy"—did teach him one thing: "It certainly acquainted me with ways that are not the right way for a parent to react," he said.

He spent hours talking to her about the case, to make sure it did not come between them. She disagreed with him about the constitutionality of bans like Proposition 8, and it was hard not to be hurt by some of his arguments. "I think the most upset I got was being called an 'experiment' that people deserved to see the outcome of before accepting. It just made me feel—alien, I guess."

But she could tell how important it was to him that she understood that he was not trying to take anything away from her personally. Some of her friends found Ashley's family situation hard to fathom, but they didn't know Chuck the way she did, couldn't see him for the father he was, the man who danced and sang along to the Rolling Stones at family get-togethers, and who cared more for her than to use her for his own benefit.

Shortly after the Supreme Court granted cert in the Proposition 8 case, in December of 2012, Ashley had proposed to Casey, with the blessing of both her parents. She and Casey lived in Massachusetts, where Ashley worked on Cape Cod as a chef—and where it was legal to marry. Cooper told Ashley that if she wanted to tell the world, she could. If she wanted to tell no one until after the Supreme Court had decided the case, that was fine with him too. In the end, she decided that she did not want to subject herself, her fiancée, or her family to a media frenzy, a decision that relieved Cooper, despite the fact that the publicity might have helped his case.

"I didn't want, and I didn't think she wanted, for her and Casey to suddenly become the most famous lesbians in America," he said. "But can you imagine how riveting it would have been if at the oral argument I disclosed this? I kind of personified what I was arguing."

Now, with the case behind him, he and Debbie had their own wedding to throw.

"I consider my life to be a storybook life—I had this Prince Charming come and scoop up me and my children, and you can't help but want that for your children," Debbie Cooper said. "And the thing is, except for one thing, my storybook life for Ashley looked a lot like hers does now—happy, healthy, and in love with someone that I do think is a wonderful person."

"We love all our children and we respect them, and we know our script isn't necessarily their lives," her husband added. Cooper still did not feel it was appropriate to say how he might vote on same-sex marriage. But "what I will say only is that my views evolve on issues of this kind the same way as other people's do, and how I view this down the road may not be the way I view it now, or how I viewed it ten years ago."

———

Back in San Francisco, with the paperwork done, Kris and Sandy and the rest of the group headed back to the rotunda.

In a small holding room just off the mayor's suite, with a connecting door to the office where Harvey Milk had been shot, someone handed Kris and Sandy matching bouquets of white flowers. Picking one of them up, Sandy held it strategically in front of her, suddenly every bit a blushing bride who had only been given twenty minutes to deliberate over her outfit. "See, then all the attention is drawn to the flowers, away from the hip."

Kris, doing the same, laughed. "Slenderizing!"

Chad reached Jeff and Paul, using an app on his iPhone called FaceTime, which allowed for videoconferencing. He put the state's attorney general on the line first.

"Thanks for making the call," Paul said to Harris, marriage license now firmly in hand. "You should have seen the registrar's hand shaking. It was awesome!"

Chad panned his phone toward Kris and Sandy, who could see that Paul and Jeff were in a car, on their way from Norwalk to Los Angeles City Hall, where the mayor of Los Angeles had been enlisted to perform their wedding ceremony. The team had arranged for Rachel Maddow to broadcast it live on MSNBC.

Kris laughed. "Are you in L.A. traffic on your wedding day?"

"For about an hour or so," Paul replied.

Boutrous, who had been arguing a case on behalf of Walmart in the federal district courthouse where the Prop 8 trial had taken place, burst into the room, just in time. Cohen just kept shifting his weight from one foot to another, repeating, "Oh my God, oh my God, oh my God."

"Don't leave without the license," Harris called as the group moved out the door, camera crews in tow, toward the balcony off the mayor's office where the actual ceremony would take place.

As Kris and Sandy walked through the halls, the crowd following them grew larger. Everyone began clapping, a rhythmic ovation that grew louder and louder. Chad was banging his hands together so hard that his watch fell off.

"This is fun," Boutrous whispered, as Harris, Kris, and Sandy took their positions. "Don't cry," Terry Stewart admonished herself. After all these years of tamping down expectations, if she started now she might never stop.

Harris, introducing the couple, said, "They have waited and hoped and fought for this moment. Their wait is finally over."

Elliott held up his iPhone so that his brother, Spencer, who was in North Carolina at a leadership camp, could see the proceedings via FaceTime. Sandy's boys, one in New York and the other in San Diego, had sent their love via text. Directly across the way, the bust of Harvey Milk watched over the nuptials.

"Do you Kris, take Sandy to be your lawfully wedded wife, to love and cherish, from this day forward?"

"I do."

"And do you Sandy, take Kris to be your lawfully wedded wife, to love and cherish, from this day forward?"

"I do."

Kris slipped a ring onto Sandy's finger, the fourth of a set. She had given her the first when they got engaged, the second when they were married in the ceremony that was later invalidated, the third on the day that Judge Walker had issued his decision, and now this one, first presented on the Supreme Court steps.

"May your love never falter," Harris said. "By the power vested in me by the state of California, I now pronounce you spouses for life."

On the grand staircase leading up to the balcony, the San Francisco Gay

Men's Chorus waited for the newlyweds to make their way downstairs. Already, other couples had begun to gather, some pushing wheelchairs, others strollers. One woman, sobbing with happiness and dressed in white, thrust her flowers into Sandy's hand. They had come to join the ranks of the married, a status Justice Kennedy had said would confer upon them "a dignity and status of immense import."

Then the chorus began belting out a song based on Milk's most famous speech.

"The young gay people in the Altoona, Pennsylvanias, and the Richmond, Minnesotas, who are coming out," Milk had said in 1978. "The only thing they have to look forward to is hope. And you have to give them hope. Hope for a better world, hope for a better tomorrow, hope for a better place to come to if the pressures at home are too great. Hope that all will be all right."

Forty-four years after Stonewall, and thirty-five years after Milk's speech, that dream, at long last, seemed within reach. "Equal feels different," Jeff said, directly after he and Paul were married. Kris, contemplating the last four-plus years, put it this way: "It's like, you're good, you're not good, you're trying to get it all regulated." She'd looked skyward, and then over at Sandy. "It's all good now. From here on out, it's all good."

As for Chad, he just stood on the steps of City Hall, chin lifted, grinning like an idiot, listening to that chorus sing:

"You gotta give 'em hope, you gotta give 'em hope," the words rang out, a clarion call. "Oh, you gotta give 'em hope."

AFTERWORD

The Supreme Court's June 2013 twin marriage rulings and the events that have transpired since have produced a profound, and astonishingly rapid, transformation of the legal landscape for gay and lesbian couples in America.

Fear that there might not be five justices willing to declare that same-sex couples have a constitutional right to marry all but evaporated, replaced with a near certainty that it was only a matter of time. All the major LGBT legal rights groups began litigating marriage-equality cases in the federal courts, guiding a new group of plaintiffs down the path cleared by Edie Windsor, Kris Perry and Sandy Stier, and Jeff Zarrillo and Paul Katami.

So far, nearly every federal district court and four of the five circuit courts of appeals to take up the issue have come to the same conclusion that Judge Walker first reached: that the bans violate the Constitution's guarantees of equal protection, due process, or both. As of this writing, a year and a half after the justices struck down the Defense of Marriage Act and allowed same-sex marriages to resume in California, the number of states where gays and lesbians are free to marry has grown from thirteen plus the District of Columbia to thirty-five. Every remaining state ban is under challenge, with decisions coming down so fast it can be hard to keep track.

"We are a better people than what these laws represent, and it is time to discard them into the ash heap of history," federal district court Judge John E. Jones III, a Republican George W. Bush appointee, wrote in an opinion that cleared the way for same-sex couples to marry in Pennsylvania.

"Totally implausible" and "so full of holes that it cannot be taken seriously," wrote Judge Richard Posner, the conservative Reagan appointee, dismissing the gays-can't-procreate argument put forth to justify same-sex marriage bans in Indiana and Wisconsin, and striking them down in a unanimous Seventh Circuit Court of Appeals panel decision.

Judge Reinhardt, who only a few years earlier had defended his narrow, California-specific decision in the Proposition 8 case by referencing the Supreme Court and telling Judge Walker that "you have more faith in those people than I do," showed no such reticence in a 2014 ruling that struck down bans in Nevada and Idaho and cleared the way for same-sex couples to marry across the Ninth Circuit.

"The question before us is not whether lesbians and gays have a fundamental right to marry a person of the same-sex; it is whether a person has a fundamental right to marry, to enter into 'the most important relation in life' . . . with the one he or she loves," Judge Reinhardt wrote. "Once the question is properly defined, the answer follows ineluctably: yes."

Just as Justice Scalia predicted in his dissent, the decisions striking down state same-sex marriage bans all rely on the majority opinion in the *Windsor* case as binding legal precedent. But given that all but one of the subsequent rulings was reached without the benefit of a trial, many also cite Judge Walker's opinion and factual findings to underpin their own.

Laurence Tribe, a renowned constitutional law professor at Harvard Law School, said that when the history of this era is written, he believes that both cases will be seen as pivotal, each bookending the other. It is the *Windsor* opinion that has compelled the recent wave of victories. But even though the Supreme Court declined to reach the merits in the Proposition 8 case, he said it acted as a legal and political accelerant, one that both "humanized and factualized this issue" and "moved the ball forward in a dramatic way that would not have happened otherwise."

"In my opinion, if the Prop 8 case hadn't been argued alongside the *Windsor* case, the odds that Justice Kennedy would have struck down DOMA entirely on federalism grounds would have been much higher," he said. "By its very presence, the Proposition 8 case made a huge difference because it made the sweeping nature of the Windsor opinion seem moderate."

Of course, none of the remarkable advances that gays and lesbians have achieved in recent years on the legal front would have been possible without the collective courage of generations of leaders and foot soldiers. This book tells a specific narrative, one of inarguable consequence, about the group of people who dared to bring the cause of marriage equality to the highest court in the land. The teams that challenged Proposition 8 and the Defense of Marriage Act recognized a moment, and, when others hesitated, seized it. That is how history is made.

But this is a movement filled with civil rights heroes, too many to be contained in any one volume. The men and women who said "enough" and fought injustice when the police raided the Stonewall Inn. The activists who overcame ignorance and indifference and demanded better treatment for HIV/AIDS, even as they nursed dying friends and lovers. Richard John Baker and James Michael McConnell, the couple who had the temerity to ask for a marriage license in Minnesota all the way back in 1970; after it was denied, the Supreme Court summarily dismissed their appeal in what became the *Baker v. Nelson* case. The lawyers and plaintiffs who subsequently brought the *Romer v. Evans* and *Lawrence v. Texas* cases, key legal cornerstones for the current crop of marriage cases.

If you enjoyed *Forcing the Spring*, I hope you will be inspired to read about other aspects of this struggle. A book called *Winning Marriage* by Marc Solomon focuses on the years of pioneering work done in the states by leaders like Freedom to Marry's Evan Wolfson and Tim Gill of the Gill Foundation. I am personally looking forward to reading the memoir that Edie Windsor's lawyer, Robbie Kaplan, is writing, called *Then Comes Marriage: United States v. Windsor and the Defeat of DOMA*. And an entire book could and should be written about the critical work done by Mary Bonauto, the attorney for Gay & Lesbian Advocates & Defenders whose DOMA challenges the Supreme Court declined to hear. Without the landmark victory she won in state court, making Massachusetts the first in the country to allow gays and lesbians to marry, Olson and Boies would not have had the statistics that Judge Walker found so persuasive, showing that allowing gays and lesbians to wed there had not harmed the institution of heterosexual marriage.

And then there are the anonymous contributions and acts of bravery and solidarity and tenacity that no history will record. Each and every person who has come out and told his or her story has contributed to the tipping point at which the country finds itself today. I stand in awe of that rich history, which of course endures and gets written to this day, every day.

The ending to the marriage equality struggle has yet to be written. There have been groundbreaking moments since the Supreme Court's rulings, as when Justices Ginsburg and Kagan, along with retired justice Sandra Day O'Connor, became the first members of the high court to officiate at the weddings of gay and lesbian friends. There have been personal milestones, such as Terry Stewart's appointment to the California Court of Appeal, making her the first open lesbian justice to serve on that court. And there has been some brilliant legal work, along with the kind of jockeying that one might expect now that victory appears within sight.

Robbie Kaplan, after securing the landmark *Windsor* win, was briefly sidelined when the ACLU opposed her motion to join its case challenging Ohio's ban; ultimately she found new clients in Mississippi and filed a successful federal challenge there, which is currently on appeal. After winning the Proposition 8 case, Olson and Boies teamed up with a private Norfolk law firm to challenge Virginia's ban on same-sex marriage, but soon found themselves sparring with the ACLU and Lambda Legal, which had filed a competing Virginia challenge; in the end they all joined forces, and forty-four years after the Supreme Court affirmed the right of interracial couples to marry in the landmark *Loving v. Virginia* case, the Fourth Circuit Court of Appeals did the same for gays and lesbians.

To date, events have conspired to deny all the lawyers involved the distinction of crossing the finish line. On October 6, 2014, the justices let stand without comment rulings out of the Fourth, Seventh, and Tenth Circuit courts of appeals that immediately paved the way for same-sex couples to marry in Virginia, Utah, Wisconsin, Oklahoma, and Indiana, and imperiled bans in six additional states. The extraordinary nondecision decision to deny cert was a major surprise, but perhaps it should not have been; Justice Ginsburg had been signaling for weeks that the high court was in no hurry to dive back into the fray, and might not need to wade back into the marriage debate at all.

"As of now, all the Courts of Appeal agree," she explained afterward, "so there is no crying need for us to step in."

That changed on November 6, when a divided panel of the Sixth Circuit Court of Appeals broke with the pack. The 2–1 decision overturned lower court rulings and upheld bans in Michigan, Ohio, Tennessee, and Kentucky. The justices will hear arguments in those cases in April, making it all but certain that they will soon be forced to settle, once and for all, the question of whether gays and lesbians have a constitutional right to marry the person they love.

Jo Becker
March 9, 2015

Most journalists believe they have a book in them, and I was no exception. But writing is a solitary, neurosis-inducing endeavor, and I kept waiting for the story that would compel me to embark on such journey, the book I could not *not* write. I found it in the spring of 2009, when I began reporting for the *New York Times* what would become the first in-depth look at how Ted Olson came to embrace the cause of same-sex marriage.

The story ran on the front page. Afterward, I found I could not let it go. I knew both Ted Olson and David Boies from covering the Florida recount in the deadlocked 2000 presidential election, and had come to know Olson even better over the course of my reporting on the Bush administration. I met Olson in Washington and Chad Griffin in New York to talk about the idea of doing a fly-on-the-wall account of this chapter in the nation's civil rights history.

After talking it over with the four plaintiffs, they agreed. For more than four years, leading up to and throughout the trial and subsequent legal proceedings, I had complete and unfettered access to the plaintiffs and their team. I wandered freely in and out of rooms where the lawyers prepared witnesses and debated legal strategy. I sat in the war room as Chad and his team pitched reporters on stories, crafted messaging strategies, and mounted a campaign aimed at winning over the country. When the lawyers and the plaintiffs and the AFER war room team arranged conference calls, I was often on the line. Kris and Sandy and Jeff and Paul allowed me into their homes and into their lives. I rode with them to court, sat next to them as they digested every opinion handed down in the case, flew back with them to California after the Supreme Court ruling, and was there, eventually, when Kris and Sandy married.

The thoughts and feelings of the main characters are as described to me, often contemporaneously, or to each other, in the moment. The dialogue described in this book was personally observed by me, unless otherwise noted. In some instances, particularly at the beginning of this narrative before the trial began and I was fully embedded with the team, and in describing the Obama administration's internal deliberations, I had to rely on the accounts of others. Endnotes provide readers with the sourcing in those cases, and where snippets of conversation are quoted in those instances, it is based on the verbatim recall of participants and, often, their notes. Similarly, the vast majority of the e-mails, texts, and documents quoted in this book were seen by me personally. If they were described by others, then that is noted. I have also delineated quotations that were the result of my interviews with participants, versus dialogue that I was there to witness, by providing endnotes to make that clear.

It was agreed from the beginning that my access to the legal and war room team came with no prepublication review or veto rights. The only restriction was that I promised to keep everything I learned confidential until after the legal proceedings were concluded, and I was not given access to materials produced in the case that were sealed by the court or otherwise subject to court-ordered confidentiality.

It was an enormous act of faith on everyone's part, especially for lawyers trained to guard such privileged discussions, and I will be forever grateful to everyone involved for their trust.

I also owe a debt of gratitude to Chuck Cooper, whom I also approached at the outset of the Proposition 8 case. He did not agree to give me contemporaneous access to his team or clients, with the result that much of this book is told from the vantage point of the plaintiffs. But we occasionally talked during the legal proceedings, and he promised to sit down with me once the last argument had been made. He was a man of his word, and he spent many hours, first patiently explaining his thinking and decision making in a series of lengthy interviews following the Supreme Court arguments, then, many months later, trusting me to tell the story of his family.

Judge Walker deserves my heartfelt thanks for the hours he spent with me after the trial had concluded, as do the dozens of people in the Obama administration who shared their knowledge of events with me.

I am also thankful to the lawyers on both sides of the DOMA case. Paul Clement, who defended the law, agreed to explain his strategy over several interviews. And Robbie Kaplan and Edie Windsor sat with me on multiple occasions as their case headed to the Supreme Court and afterward. The courage shown by all the plaintiffs in this book will inspire me always, and it was my great honor to bear witness to their journey.

This book, which took close to five years to report and complete, would never have happened but for the support of my agent, Sloan Harris, who believed in me when I doubted myself, the guidance of my brilliant editor, Ann Godoff, who believed in this book back when no one knew where the litigation or the country was headed, and finally her deputy editor, Benjamin Platt, who played the role of therapist during occasional panic attacks.

This project also would not have been possible without a generous grant from the Ford Foundation, which allowed me to take leave from the *New York Times* to write this opus, and without the support of Jill Abramson and Matthew Purdy at the *New York Times*, who agreed to give me the time off. A big shout-out to Julie Tate, whose sharp fact-checking eye saved me from many a mistake.

I am also grateful to the many people from within the LGBT community who offered kind words for *Forcing the Spring*, and wise counsel to its author. I especially want to thank Elizabeth Birch, the former executive director of the Human Rights Campaign; Torie Osborn, the former executive director of the Gay and Lesbian Task Force; David Mixner, an activist who was fighting anti-gay initiatives in California long before Proposition 8 came along; Richard Socarides, President Clinton's principle adviser on gay and lesbian civil rights issues; the journalists Rex Wockner, Karen Ocamb, and Jonathan Capehart; John Becker of the Bilerico Project; and Arthur S. Leonard, a professor at New York Law School and the editor of *Lesbian/Gay Law Notes*.

On a personal note, I want to thank my father, Bob Becker, for instilling in me a love of books in general, and *To Kill a Mockingbird* in particular. He is my Atticus Finch. Many thanks to my brother, Scott, for putting me up during reporting jaunts to Washington, D.C., to my friend Carleen Hawn for lending me her apartment during the many weeks I spent in San Francisco as this project got off the ground, and to all the friends who offered their advice along the way.

Anyone who knows me knows I would be remiss if I also did not thank my trusty canine companion, Humphrey, who spent hours staring at me as I stared at a computer screen. And finally, as I wrote I thought often of my wonderful aunt, Ellen "Curly" DeLeyer, who was an inspiration to me in too many ways to count.

NOTES

SECTION I

1   **Section I:** Some of the scenes and information in section I of this book first appeared in a story written by the author. Jo Becker, "A Conservative's Road to Same Sex Marriage," *New York Times*, August 18, 2009.

CHAPTER 1: THE "PACT"

5   **"Look around the room":** Author interviews with Kristina Schake and Chad Griffin, August 6, 2010.

5   **"It feels," he told Kristina:** Author interviews with Chad Griffin and Kristina Schake, summer 2009, January 2013.

5   **"That night, we made a pact":** Author interview with Kristina Schake, summer 2009.

7   **A staggering $44.1 million:** "Proposition 8: Who Gave in the Gay Marriage Battle," *Los Angeles Times*, June 30, 2012.

7   **"Every single time":** Author interviews with Kristina Schake, summer 2009; Rob and Michele Reiner, 2010; and Chad Griffin, January 2013.

7   **Just then, an acquaintance of the Reiners:** This section is based on author interviews with Kate Moulene, Chad Griffin, Kristina Schake, and Rob and Michele Reiner, spring and summer 2009.

7   **It was a brief conversation:** Author interview with Michele Reiner, January 24, 2013.

7   **"My ex-brother-in-law is a constitutional lawyer":** Author interviews with Michele Reiner and Kate Moulene, August 2009.

8   **"I've watched for twenty years how he treats people":** Author interview with Kate Moulene, August 19, 2009.

8   **"This sounds crazy":** Author interview with Kristina Schake, summer 2009.

9   **"The whole issue has been too much":** Dean E. Murphy, "Some Democrats Blame One of Their Own," *New York Times*, November 5, 2004.

9   **A grassroots uprising:** Torie Osborn, "In Defense of Forcing the Spring: A Longtime Activist's Appraisal," *Huffington Post*, April 30, 2013.

10   **It was not, as Clinton claimed:** Author interview with Richard Socarides, December 19, 2012.

10   **"If someone as conservative"** . . . **"It could be a game-changer":** Author interviews with Chad Griffin and Rob Reiner, summer 2009.

CHAPTER 2: A CONSERVATIVE ICON JOINS THE CAUSE

11   **"I'm going to Washington to meet *this* guy?":** Author interview with Chad Griffin, summer 2009.

12   **"Too often in the debate over same-sex marriage":** Ibid.

12   **"One-third of gay, lesbian, bisexual, and transgender teens":** Author interviews with Chad Griffin and Ted Olson, summer 2009.

12   **"This is not about me":** Ibid.

12   **"God, it's hard enough being a teenager":** Author interview with Ted Olson, summer 2009.

12   **Unbeknownst to Chad:** Author interview with Ted Olson, spring 2009.
13   **When that owner threatened to call the police:** Author interview with Paul Winters, summer 2009.
13   **When a federal prosecutor was fired for being gay:** OLC, Termination of an Assistant United States Attorney on Grounds Related to His Acknowledged Homosexuality, 3 (Mar. 11, 1983) (7 op. OLC 46).
13   **Not only was it bad policy:** Author interview with Ted Olson, summer 2009.
14   **"You have to make peace with this":** Author interview with David Frum, summer 2009.
14   **Yet even as he publicly defended the administration's prerogatives:** Barton Gellman and Jo Becker, "Pushing the Envelope on Presidential Power," *Washington Post,* June 25, 2007.
14   **"Why shouldn't I take this case?":** Author interview with Ted Olson, summer 2009.
14   **Then, leaning forward in his chair:** Author interview with Chad Griffin, summer 2009.
17   **Sexual orientation, Olson believed:** Author interviews with Chad Griffin, summer 2009, January 2013.
17   **"You will not believe this":** This section relies on author interviews with Chad Griffin, summer 2009.
17   **Walking up the circular brick driveway:** Author interview with Ted Olson, summer 2009.
18   **"The time for playing it safe":** Author interview with Bruce Cohen, summer 2009.
18   **Every major gay rights legal group in the country:** Press release issued by the ACLU, Lambda Legal, the National Center for Lesbian Rights, Equality Federation, Freedom to Marry, the Gay and Lesbian Advocates & Defenders, the Human Rights Campaign, and the National Gay & Lesbian Task Force.
19   **Now, walking across the room:** Author interviews with Bruce Cohen, 2009, 2010, and 2012.
19   **"Don't bring DOMA into this":** Author interview with Kristina Schake, summer 2009.
20   **Its passage created what Olson would later refer to:** Author interviews with Kristina Schake, summer 2009, and Chad Griffin, January 27, 2009.
21   **"This isn't about winning five to four":** Author interviews with Kristina Schake and Chad Griffin, summer 2009.
21   **"I will not just be some hired gun":** Author interviews with Kristina Schake, Rob and Michele Reiner, and Chad Griffin, summer 2009.
21   **Olson was willing to take the case:** Contract signed in May 2009 between the American Foundation for Equal Rights and Ted Olson.
22   **"I want a teacher, a police officer":** Author interview with Kristina Schake, summer 2009.
22   **"We are going to the Supreme Court!":** Author interviews with Kristina Schake and Chad Griffin, summer 2009.

CHAPTER 3: "JUST WAIT"
24   **But one day a friend had phoned him:** Author interview with Chad Griffin, August 16, 2010.
25   **"I can't come out":** Ibid.
25   **"Life is too short":** Ibid.
26   **"I think that sometimes we think":** Author interview with Dustin Lance Black, July 13, 2010.
26   **"King," he told Chad:** Ibid.
26   **Jones had agreed to the meeting:** Author interview with Cleve Jones, June 17, 2010.
27   **Midway through breakfast:** Author interviews with Dustin Lance Black, July 13, 2010, and January 19, 2013.
27   **Come with me:** Author interview with Dustin Lance Black, July 13, 2010.
27   **Wolfson had berated:** Ibid.
28   **"This just means we are doing the right thing":** Ibid.
28   **Still, it was with some trepidation:** Copy of Dustin Lance Black's March 21, 2009, speech at OutGiving.
29   **"Harvey Milk didn't start":** Author interview with Evan Wolfson, May 30, 2013.
30   **But he hadn't gotten far:** Author interview with Kristina Schake, January 4, 2013.
30   **"It just felt like there was a lot of disrespect":** Author interview with Jon Davidson, national legal director, Lambda Legal, December 23, 2013
30   **It was not that the movement lawyers disagreed:** Author interview with Ramona Ripston, former executive director of the ACLU's Southern California office, June 27, 2013.
31   **"Really?" said Boutrous:** Author interview with Ted Boutrous, December 24, 2012.

31 **Davidson threw a multipage dossier:** Author interviews with Ted Boutrous, December 24, 2012, and Kristina Schake, January 4, 2013.

32 **"It has to have the word 'American' in it":** Author interview with Kristina Schake, January 4, 2013.

32 **"I think we should all join hands":** Author interviews with Ted Olson and Chad Griffin, summer 2010, and Ted Boutrous, January 10, 2013.

32 **But the biggest breakthrough:** Author interviews with Rob and Michele Reiner, August 6, 2010, and Adam Umhoefer, January 10, 2013.

33 **"Whatever you need":** Author interview with Rob Reiner, August 6, 2010.

33 **"Are we making the wrong choice?":** Author interview with Kristina Schake, January 4, 2013.

33 **The lawyers then produced:** Undated copy of "The Time Is Now" memo.

34 **"Then if our reasons are sound":** Ibid.

CHAPTER 4: A MAD DASH

35 **So the two political consultants:** Author interviews with Kristina Schake, January 2010, and January 2013.

36 **He wanted their lawsuit:** Undated copy of "The Time Is Now" memo.

36 **They could talk all they wanted:** 2008 exit poll data.

37 **"What about Kris?":** Author interview with Kristina Schake, January 4, 2013.

37 **Olson had wanted to avoid:** Author interview with Kristina Schake, January 2010, and Ted Boutrous, March 12, 2013.

37 **But Kris was so excited:** Author interviews with Kris Perry and Sandy Stier, summer 2009.

38 **"This is literally making me nauseous":** Author interviews with Paul Katami and Jeff Zarillo, January 8, 2010.

39 **Afterward, at the diner:** Ibid.

39 **The first person Olson approached:** Author interviews with John August, March 3, 2012, and Adam Umhoefer.

39 **Smith, who had recently been asked:** The following conversation was recounted in an interview by the author with Paul Smith, November 6, 2012.

40 **Olson disagreed:** Author interview with Paul Smith, November 6, 2012.

40 **"We've got the right district":** Author interview with Ted Olson, summer 2010.

40 **Another potential co-counsel:** Author interviews with Dennis Herrera, San Francisco city attorney, January 19, 2010; John August, AFER donor, March 3, 2012; Paul Smith, May 2013; and Chad Griffin, April 16, 2012.

41 **Bringing her on board:** Author interviews with John August, March 3, 2012, and Adam Umhoefer, undated.

42 **After securing Chad's:** Author interview with Rob Reiner, August 6, 2010.

42 **Olson called Boies's firm:** November 29, 2012, e-mail from Alison Preece, communications coordinator, Boies, Schiller & Flexner, LLP.

42 **"Let's do it":** Author interview with David Boies, summer 2009.

42 **represented a fraction:** Contract signed in May 2009 between the American Foundation for Equal Rights and David Boies.

CHAPTER 5: GOING PUBLIC

43 **Enrique Monagas, an associate:** The following section draws upon author interviews with Enrique Monagas, January 6, 2009, and June 19, 2010.

46 **"Unfortunately, gentlemen":** Author interview with Paul Katami and Jeff Zarillo, conducted on January 8, 2010

46 **"We are going to plan your wedding":** Author interview with Paul Katami and Jeff Zarillo, summer 2009.

46 **"These are our neighbors":** Transcript of the May 27, 2009, AFER press conference.

47 **"Oh shit":** Author interview with Judge Vaughn R. Walker, November 21, 2012.

47 **The sixty-five-year-old judge:** Author interview with Judge Vaughn R. Walker, December 4, 2012.

48 **And so he had stayed mum:** Author interview with Judge Vaughn R. Walker, November 21, 2012.

48 **Judges are required to disqualify:** 28 U.S.C. § 455(a), 455(b)(4).

48 **He would later tell friends:** Author interviews with retired San Francisco superior court judge James Warren, December 9, 2011, and Judge Vaughn R. Walker, November 21, 2012.

48 Given DOMA, it made no financial: Author interview with Judge Vaughn R. Walker, December 23, 2012.
49 African American judges hear: Author interview with Judge Vaughn R. Walker, December 23, 2012.
49 "I don't want to get into an argument": Author interview with Robert Bork, summer 2009.
50 To many adherents of this school: Michael J. Klarman, *"Brown* and *Lawrence* (and *Goodridge*): Historic Rulings and How Judicial Decisionmaking Influences Social Reform Movements," *Michigan Law Review* 104, no. 3 (December 1, 2005).
51 Seated at Olson's table: Author interview with Robert McConnell, summer 2009.
51 "When we filed": Author interview with Mary Bonauto, October 31, 2014.
51 "It is a badge I will wear": Author interviews with Ted Olson and Kate Kendall, summer 2009.

CHAPTER 6: "PROVE IT"

54 Kristina had back-channeled: Author interview with Kristina Schake, January 2010.
54 Unbeknownst to the public: Author interview with Daniel Zingale, 2011.
55 "Prove it": Author interview with Judge Vaughn R. Walker, November 21, 2012.
55 The landmark *Romer* case: *Evans v. Romer*, 882 P.2d 1335, 1347 (Colo. 1994).
56 But Olson, unlike Boies, was not: Author interviews with Ted Olson and Ted Boutrous, January 2010 and January 2014.
56 Olson had pulled Cooper aside: Author interview with Chuck Cooper, May 8, 2013.
57 "They need our help": Author interview with Terry Stewart, January 19, 2013.
58 "We think it will be very helpful": Lisa Leff, "Gay Legal Groups Want In on California Case," Associated Press, July 9, 2009.
58 It was also the last thing: Author interview with Kristina Schake, September 8, 2013.
58 "I can help give you cover": Author interview with Dennis Herrera, January 19, 2010.
59 Watching that victory be snatched: Author interviews with Terry Stewart and Carole Scagnetti, December 1, 2010.
61 Gay marriage opponents: Author interviews with Chuck Cooper, May, 8, 2013, June 1, 2013, and June 19, 2013.
61 But a group called the Campaign for California Families: Transcript of August 19, 2009, hearing in U.S. District Court.
64 Walker was stunned: Author interview with Judge Vaughn R. Walker, November 21, 2012.
64 Judges are not supposed: Ibid.
64 "I'm going to hang him": Author interview with Chad Griffin, August 21, 2009.

CHAPTER 7: WHERE'S DAVID?

65 Nationally, polls put public support: Gallup and Pew Research Center polling data.
68 There was also some concern: Author interviews with Matt McGill and Chris Dusseault, May and June 2013.
68 Stewart, of the San Francisco Attorney's Office: August 2009 e-mails between Terry Stewart's office and Gibson Dunn.
68 When citizens, such as Tam: Author interview with Terry Stewart, June 13, 2010.
69 Olson, however, was initially reluctant: Author interviews with Terry Stewart, June 13, 2010, Matt McGill, January, 2010, and Ted Boutrous, March 12, 2013.
69 Portraying the proponents: Author interview with Ted Boutrous, March 12, 2013.
71 Olson knew that Boies: Author interview with David Boies, June 25, 2010.
71 "Not everyone is a genius": Author interviews with Ted Olson, January 2010, and David Boies, June 15, 2010.

CHAPTER 8: AN UNEXPECTED DEVELOPMENT

74 "You need to move fast": Author interview with Rick Jacobs, August 6, 2010.
78 Olson understood, but he worried: Author interview with Ted Olson, January 9, 2010.

CHAPTER 9: "ALL RISE!"

85 One of the first questions she had asked: Author interview with Sandy Stier, December 5, 2010.
88 Olson was just hitting his stride: Author interview with Matt McGill, January 11, 2013.
90 Olson's own mother: Author interview with Lady Olson, summer 2010.

91   Cooper's theory of the case: Author interview with Chuck Cooper, June 1, 2013.

92   *"Loving* is by far [Olson's] best case": Ibid.

94   It had been difficult for Cooper: Author interview with Chuck Cooper, June 1, 2013.

94   Though he believed that the burden: Ibid.

95   "The media focus on this case": Ibid.

95   An Oxford University philosophy professor: Videotaped deposition of Daniel N. Robinson, Washington, D.C., December 18, 2009.

95   Loren Marks, a professor: Videotaped deposition of Loren Marks, Washington, D.C., October 30, 2009.

95   "I wouldn't have wished fifteen minutes": Author interview with Loren Marks, May 7, 2013.

96   Katherine Young was to have testified: Videotaped deposition of Katherine Young, Montreal, Canada, November 13, 2009.

96   Forced to acknowledge: Videotaped deposition of Paul Nathanson, Montreal, Canada, November 12, 2009.

97   It was, Nathanson would later say: Author interview with Paul Nathanson, May 6, 2013.

CHAPTER 10: "A HIGHER ARC"

102   Pulling up to the courthouse: Author interview with Elliott Perry, August 25, 2012.

102   But Jones's optimism: Author interviews with Elliott and Spencer Perry, August 25, 2012.

103   Elliott seemed surprised: Author interview with Elliott Perry, August 25, 2012.

103   In the weeks leading up to the trial: Author interview with Chuck Cooper, June 1, 2013.

103   And atmospherically, it would: Ibid.

104   And that was the problem Cooper: Ibid.

104   Spencer, sitting behind his mother: Author interview with Spencer Perry, August 25, 2012.

106   "Oh my God, that's Chad": Author interview with Kristina Schake, January 25, 2010.

106   Kris's boys had never seen: Author interview with Elliott Perry, August 25, 2012.

106   Olson, oblivious to the effect: Author interview with Ted Olson, January 11, 2010.

109   "When you get hit like that": Author interview with David Boies, January 11, 2010.

109   Olson got closer to the truth: Author interview with Ted Olson, January 11, 2010.

CHAPTER 11: HISTORY LESSONS

114   Over the course of the trial: Author interview with Vaughn Walker, November 21, 2012.

114   Cooper's researchers had compiled: Author interview with Chuck Cooper, June 19, 2013.

116   Burke . . . the father of American conservatism: Edmund Burke, *Reflections on the Revolution in France* (New York: Penguin Classics, 1986 [1790]).

116   The point Thompson was making: Author interview and e-mail exchanges with Chuck Cooper, June 19–20, 2013.

116   "That was, if not the most important concession": Author interview with Chuck Cooper, December 10, 2013.

CHAPTER 12: A DAY OF SURPRISES

122   Cooper had never disputed: Author interviews with Chuck Cooper May 8, 2013, and June 1 2013.

122   Boies had even taken to publicly: Maureen Dowd, "An Odd Couple Defends Couples That Some (Oddly) Find Odd, *New York Times*, January 16, 2010.

123   The first Cooper heard of Tam's views: Author interview with Chuck Cooper, June 1, 2013.

123   Cooper had refused to continue: "An Interview with Terry L. Thompson," *Lifeline* 15, no. 2 (Summer 2006): 4.

124   Cooper would later say: Author interview with Chuck Cooper, June 1, 2013.

124   "Trial is a young man's game": Author interview with Lady and Ted Olson, January 13, 2010.

125   "This was a smackdown of Judge Walker": Author interview with Matt McGill, January 13, 2010.

126   "I haven't had many gay and lesbian friends": Author interview with Amir Tayrani, January 23, 2010.

CHAPTER 13: STIGMA

129   Now, listening to Meyer talk: Author interviews with Sarah Piepmeier, January 18, 2010, and Ted Boutrous, July 20, 2013.

131   Chad and the plaintiffs wove: Author interview with Elizabeth Riel, communications consultant
      for the American Foundation for Equal Rights, June 2012.
132   But surrogates like Los Angeles mayor Antonio Villaraigosa: "The Public and Prop 8," editorial,
      Los Angeles Times, January 11, 2010, and "Discrimination on Trial, but Not on TV," editorial, *New
      York Times,* January 14, 2010.

CHAPTER 14: ON PARENTS AND FAMILIES
134   For a law to pass the rational basis test: *Heller v. Doe,* 509 U.S. 312, 320 (1993), *Vance,* 440 U.S. at
      111.
137   Another of the article's assertions: S. Golombok and F. Tasker, "Do Parents Influence the Sexual
      Orientation of Their Children?" *Developmental Psychology* 32 (1996).
142   He was unquestionably self-promoting: Author interview with Terry Stewart, January 15, 2010.
142   Zia was a former executive editor: Author interview with Rosanne Baxter, January 15, 2010.
143   Back at the Gibson Dunn offices: Author interview with Dawn Schneider, director of communica-
      tions for Boies, Schiller & Flexner, January 12, 2010.

CHAPTER 15: WHO'S A BIGOT?
146   Herrera understood the concern: Author interviews with Dennis Herrera, January 19, 2010, and
      Chris Dusseault, January 20, 2010.
146   By showing that it was possible: Ibid

CHAPTER 16: A COURTROOM JOURNEY TO THE NETHERLANDS, VIA MASSACHUSETTS
151   Cooper, like Olson, had for the most part: Author interview with Chuck Cooper, July 26, 2013.
152   Cooper knew going in: Ibid.

CHAPTER 17: A JUDGE'S MEMORIES
157   Listening to the evidence day after day: Author interview with Judge Vaughn Walker, November
      21, 2012.
159   "I decided to see a psychiatrist": Author interview with Judge Vaughn Walker, December 2, 2012.
160   Walker glanced at Boies: Author interview with Judge Vaughn Walker, November 21, 2012.

CHAPTER 18: GOD, GAYS, AND POLITICAL POWER
164   But as much as Olson wanted to be sensitive: Author interview with Ted Boutrous, July 28, 2013.
164   One of the chief architects of the campaign: Author interview with Maggie Gallagher, November 6,
      2012.
165   There was even a "Pastors' Rapid Response Team": Plaintiffs' Exhibit No. PX2554, *Perry v.
      Schwarzenegger,* 704 F.Supp.2d 921 (N.D. Cal. 2010) (No. C 09-2292 VRW).
165   Even if he could have convinced: Author interview with Chuck Cooper, June 1, 2013.
167   Afterward, Boies said he found Thompson's style: Author interview with David Boies, January 20,
      2010.
169   Chad, reading it out loud: Author interview with Chad Griffin, December 3, 2012.
169   Chad had made something of a study: Author interview with Chad Griffin, August 6, 2010.

CHAPTER 20: THE SCIENCE OF SEXUALITY
179   "Gotta give Nielson credit": Author interview with Ethan Dettmer, the Gibson Dunn attorney who
      handled Dr. Herek's direct exam, January 22, 2010.
179   To stay awake at the counsel's table: Author interview with Ted Boutrous, January 22, 2010.
180   But Cooper's point was more nuanced: Author interviews with Chuck Cooper, May 8, 2013, and
      June 1, 2013.
181   Sandy was just grateful: Author interviews with Sandy Stier and Kris Perry, December 5, 2010.
181   But Posner's writings: Richard Posner, "Gay Marriage—Posner's Response to Comments," *The
      Becker-Posner Blog,* July 24 2005, http://www.becker-posner-blog.com/2005/07/gay-marriage
      --posners-response-to-comments.html.
182   It is, "if not genetic, certainly innate": Author interview with Richard Posner, September 30,
      2013.
182   Posner had also rejected: Richard Posner, "The Economics of Gay Marriage—Posner," *The*

Becker-Posner Blog, August 10, 2008, http://www.becker-posner-blog.com/2008/08/the-economics
-of-gay-marriage--posner.html.
184 **Though Stewart knew the judge meant well:** Author interview with Terry Stewart, December 1,
2010.

CHAPTER 21: THE PLAINTIFFS REST
186 **Incendiary political messaging:** Author interview with Ted Uno, January 24, 2010.
188 **Other excerpts featured prominent:** Plaintiffs' Exhibit No. PX2554, *Perry v. Schwarzenegger,* 704
F.Supp.2d 921 (N.D. Cal. 2010) (No. C 09-2292 VRW).
188 **In a confidential memo:** National Organization for Marriage and American Principles in *Action v.
Walter F. McKee, et al.,* NOM Deposition Exhibit 12: "National Strategy for Winning the Marriage
Battle dated December 15, 2009," United States District Court for the District of Maine, unsealed
March 26, 2012, http://www.scribd.com/doc/86834855/20100716-Doc-128b-NOM-Depo-Exhibit
-2-NOM-Depo-Exhibit-12-Nat-l-Strategy-for-Winning-12-15-09.
189 **"All it took when we asked someone":** Plaintiffs' Exhibit No. PX0390, *Perry v. Schwarzenegger.*
189 **"We bet the campaign on education":** Jesse McKinley and Kirk Johnson, "Mormons Tipped Scale
in Ban on Gay Marriage," *New York Times,* November 14, 2008.

CHAPTER 22: COOPER'S TURN
193 **First, he did not want to take a position:** Author interview with Chuck Cooper, June 1, 2013.
194 **"Whatever good we could get":** Ibid.
195 **Walker, though, was understandably reluctant:** Daubert v. Merrell Dow Pharmaceuticals, Inc., 509
U.S. 579 (1993).
196 **One measure of political powerlessness:** *City of Cleburne v. Cleburne Living Center,* 473 U.S. 432,
445 (1985).
196 **The law, which provided for additional federal penalties:** James Brooke, "Witnesses Trace Brutal
Killing of Gay Student," *New York Times,* November 21, 1998.
197 **Boies once told Terry Stewart:** Author interview with Terry Stewart, undated.
198 **A willingness to deviate:** Author interview with David Boies, January 25, 2010.
199 **Finally, Miller handed the marked-up report:** Plaintiffs Exhibit No. PX0794A, *Perry v. Schwarzenegger,* 704 F.Supp.2d 921 (N.D. Cal. 2010) (No. C 09-2292 VRW), https://ecf.cand.uscourts.gov/
cand/09cv2292/evidence/PX0794A.pdf.
199 **Even Cooper had to admit:** Author interview with Chuck Cooper, June 1, 2013.
202 **"You make me sick":** Author interview with Kris Perry and Sandy Stier, December 5, 2010.
202 **One day while they were in court:** Author interview with Elliott Perry, August 25, 2012.
203 **What was not okay with Spencer:** Author interview with Spencer and Elliott Perry, August 25, 2012.
203 **Kris called the Berkeley police:** Author interview with Kris Perry and Sandy Stier, December 5,
2010.
203 **Kris had tried to adopt:** Author interview with Kris Perry, August 24, 2013.

CHAPTER 23: "A HIGH OL' TIME OF IT"
204 **"You know what I enjoyed?":** Author interview with David Blankenhorn, October 4, 2012.
205 **"Boies made a big thing":** Ibid.
206 **the "issue just hunts you down":** Ibid.
207 **"I wasn't going to be bullied":** Ibid.
209 **"So, Exhibit A was Barack Obama":** Author interview with Chuck Cooper, June 1, 2013.
209 **"The impression he conveyed":** Author interview with David Blankenhorn, October 4, 2012.
209 **"Olson and Boies want to make":** Author interview with David Blankenhorn, November 26, 2012.
210 **"You're a helluva good witness":** Author interview with David Blankenhorn, October 4, 2012.
210 **Years later, Cooper had no regrets:** Author interview with Chuck Cooper, June 1, 2013.
211 **"I guess I'll see you later":** Author interview with Kristina Schake, February 10, 2010.

CHAPTER 24: VICTORY
215 **Remember, she recalled telling her friend:** Author interview with Kristina Schake, June 15, 2010.
216 **And in the nation's capital:** http://www.washingtonpost.com/wp-dyn/content/article/2010/02/09/
AR2010020903739.html.

217 On the legal front, a new study: http://pediatrics.aappublications.org/content/early/2010/06/07/
peds.2009-3153.abstract?maxtoshow=&hits=10&RESULTFORMAT=&fulltext=Bos&searchid
=1&FIRSTINDEX=0&sortspec=relevance&resourcetype=HWCIT.
221 Celebrities have huge online followings: Author interview with Jeremy Braud, AFER social media
consultant, June 22, 2010.
222 "Her position is her position": Author interview with Mike Murphy, December 11, 2013.
223 In San Francisco, David Boies and Ted Boutrous: Author interview with Lady Olson, August 4,
2010.
224 "We did that three or four times": Author interview with Judge Vaughn Walker, November 21,
2012.
227 "I yelled, I screamed": Author interview with Enrique Monagas, August 5, 2010.
228 He started whooping: Author interview with Rob Reiner, August 6, 2010.
228 "It's like a love letter": Author interview with Gabriel Catone, August 7, 2010.
228 Cohen realized just how big: Author interview with Bruce Cohen, August 7, 2010.
229 "Oh my God—Prop 8 is unconstitutional": Author interview with Chad Griffin, August 6, 2010.

CHAPTER 25: A TRUMP CARD, RELUCTANTLY PLAYED
235 "If the governor and the attorney general": Author interview with Matt McGill, July 9, 2013.
236 Both were assured: Author interviews with David Boies, Chad Griffin, and Adam Umhoefer, May
2013.
243 Boutrous had responded: Author interview with Terry Stewart, December 1, 2010.
243 When that failed to produce the desired result: Author interview with David Boies, December 4,
2010.
246 But in what now appeared a serious misstep: Author interview with Chuck Cooper, June 1, 2013.

CHAPTER 27: WHEN A NIGHTINGALE SINGS
264 "I didn't think I had earned that right": Author interview with Ken Mehlman, October 22, 2013.
265 "I call Ted the nightingale": Author interview with Ken Mehlman, November 17, 2010.
265 "Anyone who can get George Bush elected": Author interview with Chad Griffin, December 3, 2010.
266 "Ken's all in on everything he does": Author interview with Mark Wallace, October 22, 2013.
267 "Coming out is hard": Author interview with Kristina Schake, October 22, 2013.
267 "Ken spent a lot of time talking to them": Author interview with Jim Messina, October 7, 2013.
268 "Over a million dollars": Author interview with Bill Smith, August 12, 2013.
268 Mehlman also arranged a confidential meeting: Author interview with Ken Mehlman, October 19,
2011.
269 "You get to the point where": Kenneth Lovett, "Gay Marriage Is Just One Vote Shy of Becoming Law
in New York Despite Archbishop Dolan's Objections," New York Daily News, June 15, 2011.
269 "The vote is going to happen tonight": Author interview with Ken Mehlman, October 19, 2011.

CHAPTER 28: SOME "GRIST FOR JUSTICE KENNEDY"
273 Cooper had been under pressure: Author interview with Chuck Cooper, January 18, 2012.
274 Living with the extended uncertainty: Author interview with Jeff Zarrillo and Paul Katami, December 8, 2011.
279 Judge Reinhardt, he would later say: Author interview with Enrique Monagas, June 4, 2012.
279 Terry Stewart, listening: Author interview with Terry Stewart, February 12, 2012.

CHAPTER 29: 8
282 "They turned that trial": Author interview with Mary Bonauto, November 11, 2012.
282 "No way," he'd exclaimed: Author interview with Kristina Schake, July 2012.
282 After talking it over with Rosen: Author interview with Hilary Rosen, November 8, 2012.
285 But even his brother watched Glee: Author interviews with Adam Umhoefer, December 2010 and
June 13, 2011.

CHAPTER 30: OBAMA "COMES OUT"
286 "The sense I got from him": Author interview with Chad Griffin, April 19, 2011.
286 Reporting back to the AFER team: Author interviews with Adam Umhoefer and Amanda Crumley.

287 But as Chad watched the hosts' two children: Author interview with Chad Griffin, May 14, 2012.
288 Sitting in his West Wing office: Author interview with Vice President Joseph Biden, October 9, 2013.
290 Several months before his vice president: The descriptions of internal White House deliberations contained in this section are based on author interviews with a half dozen senior White House officials, some of whom asked for anonymity in order to speak candidly.
290 "For as long as I've known him": Author interview with David Axelrod, August 9, 2013.
291 "The notion that politically this is going to kill you": Author interviews with Ken Mehlman, September 21, 2011, and May 18, 2012.
292 A massive survey of five thousand Republican: This is a survey by TargetPoint Consulting, on behalf of Project RightSide, conducted in October 2011. http://www.projectrightside.com/contentimages/PRS_ShiftingElec_infographic_21.pdf.
292 Mehlman's takeaway: Author interview with Ken Mehlman, undated.
292 But she found the legal arguments: Author interviews with Elizabeth Riel, communications consultant for the American Foundation for Equal Rights, and Lisa Grove, June 2012, and documents summarizing Grove's analysis.
295 Inside the White House: Author interview with David Axelrod, August 8, 2013.
295 This is consistent with who you are: Jo Becker, "Valerie Jarrett Is the Other Power in the West Wing," *New York Times*, September 12, 2012, A1.
296 "Good point," he said Plouffe told him: Author interview with Ken Mehlman, May 18, 2012.
298 Then everyone scrambled: Author interview with Kristina Schake, October 10, 2013.
298 "He was very much at peace": Author interview with David Axelrod, August 9, 2013.
299 "How can we ring the bipartisan bell": Author interview with Chad Griffin, May 14, 2012.
299 When Mehlman first came out: Author interview with Ken Mehlman, September 9, 2012.
300 "If you are one of those who care": Adam Nagourney, "A Watershed Move, Both Risky and Inevitable," *New York Times*, May 10, 2012, A1.

CHAPTER 31: CHAD AND THE CASE ENTER A NEW PHASE
304 Olson had negotiated: AFER contract with Gibson Dunn.
304 That was still deeply discounted: Author interview with Bruce Cohen, March 2012.
305 "Hiring Chad was like": Author interview with Richard Socarides, December 19, 2012.
307 "She said, 'I was listening to a talk show'": Author interview with Sandy Stier, December 8, 2011.
307 "Well, that's okay": Author interview with Elliott Perry, August 25, 2012.
307 "It just crushed me": Author interview with Tom Stier, August 26, 2013.
308 "My mom was mine": Author interview with Frank Stier, January 20, 2013.
310 "You wonder what people are going to say": Author interview with Vaughn Walker, November 21, 2012.
311 "I told him he shouldn't have given up": Author interview with Vaughn Walker, November 21, 2012.

CHAPTER 32: A STAR WITNESS'S MEA CULPA
315 "I thought it was pretty lousy": Author interview with Chuck Cooper, June 1, 2013.
318 "Practically and strategically": Author interviews with Chuck Cooper, June 1, 2013, and November 22, 2013.
318 "It's not at all clear": Author interview with Chuck Cooper, June 19, 2013.
319 "Getting to know them personally": Author interview with David Blankenhorn, October 4, 2012.
320 "I believe I owe": Benedict Carey, "Psychiatry Giant Sorry for Backing Gay 'Cure,'" *New York Times*, May 18, 2012, A1.
321 "Any case has its trying elements": Author interview with Chuck Cooper, May 8, 2013.
321 "I still think that we were entitled to know": Author interview with Chuck Cooper, December 10, 2013.

CHAPTER 33: CHAD'S BIG TEST
324 "Ellen DeGeneres has done more": Author interviews with Terry Stewart and other lawyers on the call.
324 At a recent meeting: Author interviews with participants.

325   **Polling showed that support:** May 11, 2012, memo from Jan R. van Lohuizen, pollster for President Bush, to Project Right Side, http://www.projectrightside.com/contentimages/Same_Sex_Marriage _Memo_5.11.20121.pdf.

325   **The Pew Research Center would soon release data:** Pew Research Center poll, March 13–17, 2013.

325   **"This is the most significant":** Author interview with Alex Lundry, December 2013.

326   **causing some church leaders:** Author interview with Barrett Duke, director of the Southern Baptist Convention's Ethics and Religious Liberty Commission, December 11, 2013.

327   **Olson's legal briefs:** Author interview with Ted Olson, November 7, 2012.

328   **Maine looked solid:** Author interview with Marc Solomon, January 24, 2012.

328   **By election day:** Author interview with Marc Solomon, January 24, 2012.

330   **But over lunch earlier that day:** Author interview with Hilary Rosen, November 8, 2012.

330   **"It was very challenging":** Author interview with Maggie Gallagher, November 6, 2012.

331   **Most of the National Organization for Marriage's budget:** National Organization for Marriage Form 990 tax returns.

333   **"Wake me up if anything changes":** Author interview with Ted Olson, November 7, 2012.

334   **"Society has just changed":** Author interview with Dan Pfeiffer, November 14, 2012.

334   **Indeed, it was a net positive:** Author interview with Ralph Reed, November 22, 2012.

CHAPTER 34: "DON'T THEY HAVE A RESPONSIBILITY TO ACT?"

337   **At 9:30 A.M. on the morning of December 7, 2012:** Author interview with Patricia McCabe Estrada, spokeswoman for the U.S. Supreme Court.

338   **In the wake of the Brown decision:** Peter Wallenstein, *Tell the Court I Love My Wife: Race, Marriage, and Law —an American History* (New York: Palgrave Macmillan, 2002), 182.

338   **Still, the issue was judicial nitroglycerin:** Pew Research Center, May 1, 2012, poll on Supreme Court Favorability.

339   **Before he stepped down from the bench:** Walter Dellinger, "Souter: A Last Lecture on Gay Marriage," *Slate,* June 29, 2009, http://www.slate.com/articles/life/the_breakfast_table/features/2009/ the_supreme_court_breakfast_table/souter_a_last_lecture_on_gay_marriage.html.

340   **"This is why I believe in God":** Author interview with Edie Windsor and Robbie Kaplan, February 21, 2013.

342   **In San Francisco, all four boys:** Author interview with Tim McGinnis, November 22, 2012.

343   **Whenever Olson had an argument:** Author interview with Ted Olson, December 21, 2012.

343   **Olson told Boies:** Author interview with David Boies, October 5, 2012.

343   **"I don't have the faintest idea":** Author interview with Ted Olson, November 7, 2012.

343   **Entire treatises have been written:** Author interviews with more than a half dozen former Kennedy clerks, all of whom asked for anonymity in order to speak candidly.

344   **"We must never lose sight":** Richard C. Reuben, "Man in the Middle," *California Lawyer,* October 1992, 35.

344   **"It was a very beautiful statement":** Justice Anthony Kennedy, interview by Bryan A. Garner, 2006–7, *LawProse,* http://www.lawprose.org/interviews/supreme-court.php?vid=kennedy_part_1&vidtitle =Associate_Justice_Anthony_Kennedy_Part_1.

345   **"Sometimes you don't know if you're Caesar":** Richard C. Reuben, "Man in the Middle," *California Lawyer,* October 1992 issue.

347   **"The only person who should want this case":** Author interview with Paul Cappuccio, November 8, 2012.

347   **In a conference room at Robbie Kaplan's firm:** Author interview with Edie Windsor and Robbie Kaplan, February 21, 2013.

347   **"Yes!" he thought:** Author interview with Enrique Monagas, December 7, 2012.

347   **You won, the friend e-mailed:** Author interviews with Vaughn R. Walker, November 21, 2012, and December 23, 2012.

348   **"There's only one Supreme Court":** Author interview with Bruce Cohen, December 17, 2012.

348   **Nearby, the Reiners were in a theater:** Author interview with Rob and Michele Reiner, December 8, 2012.

348   **"David," she said, hugging him:** Author interview with Dawn Schneider, December 11, 2012, based on her notes.

348   **Boies was less trusting:** Author interview with Mary Boies, October 14, 2012.

348 **She worried aloud:** Author interviews with Dawn Schneider, December 11, 2012, and David Boies, March 2, 2013.

349 **When the call was opened:** Author interview with Ted Olson, December 21, 2012.

350 **"Now," Boutrous said:** Author interviews with Ted Boutrous, December 17, 2012, and Ted Olson, December 21, 2012.

CHAPTER 35: SELMA TO STONEWALL

353 **All of those voices were important:** Author interview with Ted Olson, January 31, 2013.

353 **"It adds institutional impetus and imprimatur":** Author interview with Amir Tayrani, February 8, 2013.

353 **Conversely, if the administration failed:** Author interview with David Boies, March 23, 2013.

353 **What interest, asked one of the lawyers:** The account of the January 18, 2013, meeting with the solicitor general is based on author interviews with Justice Department officials, Ted Olson, Terry Stewart, and David Boies.

354 **"This," participants recall:** Author interview with Justice Department participants, confirmed by Terry Stewart.

355 **Boies, who was sitting with his wife:** Author interview with David Boies, March 2, 2013.

356 **"On 14 different occasions":** Excerpt from an e-mail sent by Ken Mehlman to David Plouffe on January 17, 2013.

356 **"In the contemporary challenge":** Author interview with Ken Mehlman, April 16, 2013.

357 **Stress the law:** Author interview with Kristina Schake, March 26, 2013.

357 **"It's already being used against us":** Author interviews with David Boies, March 2, 2013, and Chad Griffin, February 6, 2013.

357 **"It's awkward":** Author interview with Ted Olson, January 31, 2013.

357 **"And there's no case":** Author interview with David Boies, March 2, 2012, and Chad Griffin, February 6, 2013.

358 **"We said it wouldn't be like** *Brown v. Board of Education*"**:** Author interview with Terry Stewart, January 19, 2013, based on her notes of the meetings.

358 **Either way, as Attorney General Eric Holder later put it:** Author interview with Eric Holder, August 7, 2013.

359 **Verrilli read Martin Luther King Jr.'s:** Author interviews with Justice Department officials familiar with Verrilli's deliberation.

360 **President Eisenhower famously read:** Philip Elman and Norman Silber, "The Solicitor General's Office, Justice Frankfurter, and Civil Rights Litigation, 1946–1960: An Oral History," *Harvard Law Review* 100, no. 4 (1987): 817–52.

360 **Anticipating what the justices might do:** Author interview with Kathryn Ruemmler, December 23, 2013.

360 **Obama had seen firsthand:** Author interview with Kristina Schake, July 30, 2013.

361 **Jarrett called him next:** Author interview with Chad Griffin, March 7, 2013.

CHAPTER 36: FRAMING THE ARGUMENTS

365 **"What we are focused on":** Author interview with Hilary Rosen, March 14, 2013.

365 **"It feels strangely good":** Author interview with Olivia Alair, March 24, 2013.

368 **"Of the two components":** Justice Ruth Bader Ginsburg, interview by Bryan A. Garner, 2006–2007, *LawProse*, http://www.lawprose.org/interviews/supreme-court.php?vid=ginsburg_part_1&vidtitle=Associate_Justice_Ruth_Bader_Ginsburg_Part_1.

368 **Good briefs are fast-paced and conversational:** Chief Justice John Roberts, Justice Anthony Kennedy, and Justice Antonin Scalia, interviews by Bryan A. Garner, 2006–2007, *LawProse*, http://lawprose.org/interviews/supreme-court.php?vid=roberts_part_1&vidtitle=Chief_Justice_John_Roberts_Part_1.

368 **The brief filed by Paul Clement:** Author interview with Paul Clement, January 4, 2013.

369 **"But he felt strongly":** Author interview with Ted Boutrous, February 21, 2013.

370 **"Ted wasn't going to shy away":** Author interview with Ted Boutrous, March 21, 2013.

372 **In Olson's view:** Author interview with Ted Olson, December 8, 2011.

372 **Olson had framed his case:** Author interview with Robbie Kaplan, February 27, 2013.

373 **The best piece of advice:** Author interview with Robbie Kaplan, April 4, 2013.

376   Cooper, who had indeed been less than pleased: Author interview with Chuck Cooper, June 1, 2013.
376   while Olson had sent Boutrous: Author interview with Ted Boutrous, March 21, 2013.
379   What had once seemed politically toxic: Maggie Haberman, "Clinton Stays in the Game with Gay Marriage Move," Politico.com, March 18, 2013.

CHAPTER 37: KENNEDY V. KENNEDY
385   He checked his phone: Facebook Data Science.
388   "Being here right now": Author interview with Enrique Monagas, March 19, 2013.
388   "You've already won": Author interviews with Paul Cappuccio, June and November 2013.
389   "Look at the difference": Author interview with Paul Smith, May 17, 2013.
390   "Both times," Rob joked: Author interview with Chad Griffin, March 2013.
391   "That is an enormous concession": Author interview with David Boies, May 23, 2013.
392   Cite the evidence from trial: Author interviews with Terry Stewart, March 26, 2013, and December 3, 2013.
392   Ted Boutrous, for his part: Author interview with Ted Boutrous, December 13, 2013.
393   "Bring me the head": Author interview with Ted Boutrous, February 21, 2013.
394   But as a matter of form and comity: Adam Liptak, "Who Wanted to Take the Case on Gay Marriage? Ask Scalia," New York Times, March 29, 2013.
395   "We were both surprised": Author interview with David Boies, May 23, 2013.
397   Boies would later say: Ibid.
399   "I felt like he respected our struggle": Author interview with Kris Perry, March 30, 2013.

CHAPTER 38: "SKIM MILK MARRIAGES"
401   Weeks earlier, she had attended: Author interview with Robbie Kaplan, February 20, 2013.
402   Waking up, she said she had just one thought: Author interview with Robbie Kaplan, April 4, 2013.
406   Walking out the Court's bronze front door: Author interview with Robbie Kaplan, April 14, 2013.

CHAPTER 39: "DIGNITY"
408   Because the Supreme Court tends: Robert Barnes, "Conservatives Likely to Write Most Remaining Decisions in Supreme Court's Term," Washington Post, June 16, 2013.
409   Edie's doctors, worried that the stress: Author interview with Robbie Kaplan, July 9, 2013.
412   The day before, Olson had told the plaintiffs: Author interview with Chad Griffin, undated.
413   In New York, Edie and her legal team: Author interview with Robbie Kaplan, July 9, 2013.
414   "That's not good, that's not good": Author interview with Matt McGill, June 26, 2013.
414   It was going to be okay: Author interview with David Boies, June 26, 2013.
415   "I want to go to Stonewall right now!": Ariel Levy, "How Edith Windsor Learned She Won," New Yorker, June 26, 2013.
416   Kris, sitting next to Chad: Author interviews with Kris Perry and Chad Griffin, June 26, 2013.
417   But Roberts turned the passage "on its head": Author interview with Chuck Cooper, undated.
418   In recent weeks, Chad, Adam, and Ted: Author interviews with Chad Griffin, Adam Umhoefer, and Ted Boutrous.
420   By intertwining arguments: Author interviews with former clerks to Justice Kennedy, Paul Clement, and Laurence Tribe, professor of constitutional law at Harvard University.
422   It was possible, of course: Author interviews with David Boies, Theane Kapur, and Josh Lipshutz, June 26, 2013.
422   In Washington, Cooper analyzed: Author interview with Chuck Cooper, July 18, 2013.
423   Justice Ginsburg would later reject: Adam Liptak, "Court Is 'One of Most Activist,' Ginsburg Says, Vowing to Stay," New York Times, August 24, 2013.
423   On the ground in San Francisco: Author interview with Vaughn Walker, June 29, 2013.

CHAPTER 40: JUNE IS FOR WEDDINGS
426   "We'll know more at 3 P.M.": Author interviews with Josh Lipshutz, June 28, 2013, and Chris Dusseault, July 3, 2013.
426   "The pace they were talking": Author interview with Adam Umhoefer, June 28, 2013.
426   Sandy was at work: Author interviews with Kris Perry and Sandy Stier, June 28, 2013.

427 **"Cancel your shrink appointment":** Author interviews with Chad Griffin and Dustin Lance Black, June 28, 2013.
428 **Cohen had called Adam:** Author interviews with Adam Umhoefer and Bruce Cohen, June 28, 2013.
428 **A leak could give the proponents:** Author interview with Vaughn Walker, June 29, 2010.
431 **"At a personal, human level":** Author interview with Chuck Cooper, July 18, 2013.
431 **Over the years, Cooper had:** This entire section is based on author interviews with Chuck Cooper on December 10, 2013, and January 3, 2014; Debbie Cooper on December 26, 2013; and Ashley Lininger on December 26, 2013 and January 20, 2014.

AFTERWORD

438 **But given that all:** *Bishop v. Smith,* 962 F. Supp. 2d 1252 (N.D. Okla. 2014); *Bostic v. Rainey,* 970 F. Supp.2d 456 (E.D. Va. 2014); *Campaign for Southern Equality v. Bryant,* 2014 WL 6680570 (No. 3:14-cv-818-CWRLRA); *DeLeon v. Perry,* 975 F. Supp. 2d 632 (W.D. Tex. 2014); *DeBoer v. Snyder,* 973 F.Supp.2d 757 (E.D. Mich. 2014); *Geiger v. Kitzhaber,* 994 F.Supp.2d 1128 (D. Or. 2014); *Kitchen v. Herbert,* 961 F: Supp. 2d 1182 (D. Utah 2013); *Latta v. Otter,* 2014 WL 1909999 (1:13-CV-00482-CWD) (D. Idaho 2014); *Wolf v. Walker,* 986 F. Supp. 2d 982 (W.D. Wis. 2014); *Obergefell v. Wymyslo,* 962 F. Supp. 2d 968 (S.D. Ohio 2013).
438–39 **"By its very presence":** Author interview with Laurence H. Tribe, Carl M. Loeb University Professor and Professor of Constitutional Law, Harvard Law School, July 2014.
439 **That is how:** http://www.politico.com/magazine/politico50/2014/roberta-kaplan-05.html#.VFgHGhZ0aII.
440 **Robbie Kaplan:** Author interview with Robbie Kaplan, November 2014.
441 **"As of now":** Justice Ruth Bader Ginsburg, interview by National Public Radio's Nina Totenberg, October 19, 2014, http://92yondemand.org/ruth-bader-ginsburg-dorit-beinisch-nina-totenberg/.

PHOTO CREDITS

INDEX